SHAPERS

— OF THE —

GREAT DEBATE

— ON —

IMMIGRATION

SHAPERS
—— OF THE ——
GREAT DEBATE
—— ON ——
IMMIGRATION

A BIOGRAPHICAL DICTIONARY

Mary Elizabeth Brown

Shapers of the Great American Debates, Number 1
Peter B. Levy, Series Editor

Greenwood Press
Westport, Connecticut • London

Library of Congress Cataloging-in-Publication Data

Brown, Mary Elizabeth.
    Shapers of the great debate on immigration : a biographical
dictionary / Mary Elizabeth Brown.
        p.   cm.—(Shapers of the great American debates, ISSN 1099–2693 ;
    no. 1)
    Includes bibliographical references and index.
    ISBN 0–313–30339–8 (alk. paper)
    1. Immigration advocates—United States—Biography.
2. Immigration opponents—United States—Biography.   3. United
States—Emigration and immigration—Government policy—History.
I. Title.   II. Series.
JV6483.B77   1999
325.73—dc21   98–21664

British Library Cataloguing in Publication Data is available.

Library of Congress Catalog Card Number: 98–21664
ISBN: 0–313–30339–8
ISSN: 1099–2693

First published in 1999

Greenwood Press, 88 Post Road West, Westport, CT 06881
An imprint of Greenwood Publishing Group, Inc.

Printed in the United States of America

The paper used in this book complies with the
Permanent Paper Standard issued by the National
Information Standards Organization (Z39.48–1984).

10 9 8 7 6 5 4 3 2 1

CONTENTS

SERIES FOREWORD

American history has been shaped by numerous debates over issues far ranging in content and time. Debates over the right, or lack thereof, to take the land of the Native Americans, and the proper place and role of women, sparked by Roger Williams and Anne Hutchinson, respectively, marked the earliest years of the Massachusetts Bay Colony. Debates over slavery, the nature and size of the federal government, the emergence of big business, the rights of labor and immigrants, were central to the Republic in the nineteenth century and, in some cases, remain alive today. World War I, World War II, and the Vietnam War sparked debates that tore at the body politic. Even the Revolution involved a debate over whether America should be America or remain part of Great Britain. And the Civil War, considered by many the central event in American history, was the outgrowth of a long debate that found no peaceful resolution.

This series, *Shapers of the Great American Debates*, will examine many of these debates—from those between Native Americans and European settlers to those between "natives" and "newcomers." Each volume will focus on a particular issue, concentrating on those men and women who *shaped* the debates. The authors will pay special attention to fleshing out the life histories of the shapers, considering the relationship between biography or personal history and policy or philosophy. Each volume will begin with an introductory overview, include approximately twenty biographies of ten to fifteen pages, an appendix that briefly describes other key figures, a bibliographical essay, and a subject index. Unlike works that emphasize end results, the books in this series will devote equal attention to both sides, to the "winners" and the "losers." This will lead to a more complete understanding of the richness and complexity of America's past than is afforded by works that examine only the victors.

Taken together, the books in this series remind us of the many ways that class, race, ethnicity, gender, and region have divided rather than united the inhabitants of the United States of America. Each study reminds us of the frequency and variety of debates in America, a reflection of the diversity of the nation and its democratic credo. One even wonders if a similar series could be developed for many other nations or if the diversity of America and its tradition of free expression have given rise to more debates than elsewhere.

Although many Americans have sought to crush the expression of opposing views by invoking the imperative of patriotism, more often than not Americans have respected the rights of others to voice their opinions. Every four years, Americans have voted for president and peacefully respected the results, demonstrating their faith in the process that institutionalizes political debate. More recently, candidates for the presidency have faced off in televised debates that often mark the climax of their campaigns. Americans not only look forward to these debates, but they would probably punish anyone who sought to avoid them. Put another way, debates are central to America's political culture, especially those that deal with key issues and involve the most prominent members of society.

Each volume in the series is written by an expert. While I offered my share of editorial suggestions, overall I relied on the author's expertise when it came to determining the most sensible way to organize and present each work. As a result, some of the volumes follow a chronological structure; others clump their material thematically; still others are separated into two sections, one pro and one con. All of the works are written with the needs of college and advanced high school students in mind. They should prove valuable both as sources for research papers and as supplemental texts in both general and specialized courses. The general public should also find the works an attractive means of learning more about many of the most important figures and equally as many seminal issues in American history.

Peter B. Levy
Associate Professor
Department of History
York College

INTRODUCTION: BEHIND U.S. IMMIGRATION LAW

The United States is often called a nation of immigrants, but what does this mean? There is a debate over the definition of *immigration* itself. The first people to come to the Americas weren't called immigrants. They were nomads who lived by hunting and gathering and farming, activities that led them to spread from the Bering Strait to Cape Horn. The first Europeans weren't called immigrants either. The earliest were explorers. They were followed by fishing crews who, when the fish were in season, lived in what are now the maritime provinces of Canada and by colonists, people who moved from one area claimed by a government to another area claimed (however illegal or immoral that claim may seem to modern people) by the same government, as from Spain to New Spain. The slaves they imported weren't immigrants, for they were considered property, not people who moved of their own free will. U.S. citizens heading out from the thirteen original states weren't immigrants; they were settlers who moved into new areas still claimed (again, however illegally or immorally) by the same government. The exception that proves the rule is U.S. migration into Texas while that territory was still part of Mexico. Those people were immigrants. Immigrants are persons who leave the territory of one government and enter the territory of another government. This definition may not work for everyone, but it is the definition the U.S. government uses, and it does work for the purposes of this book, which focuses on the debate over people who come to the United States.

Similarly, there is a debate over what is the most basic question regarding immigration. One school of thought places the focus on the immigrants themselves. Migration is a basic human right, and the subject of any debate is how to bring the U.S. law into accord with the universal natural laws. A more common school of thought shifts the focus from the common humanity immigrants and natives share to the differences between them created by the fact that one group is native and one is not, and the most basic question has been: is immigration good for the United States or not? People who oppose immigration generally start with the premise that immigration may indeed be good for immigrants, bringing them to a country with more economic opportunity or greater personal freedom. One of the ironies of the immigration debate is that even people who support immigration tend to use these sorts of arguments, not quite realizing the slippery slope they are on. They argue that immigrants are good for the nation, that the United States benefits from their presence. The problem is that the argument makes people dependent on the abstract idea of the "national good" and thus makes immigration a sometime thing: If the United States benefits, the people can come, if not, they have to stay home. This book tries to stay faithful to the historic debate. Thomas Jefferson was a member of the human rights school of immigration, but most of the other people in this book take up the question of immigrants and the national good.

However, that raises another question: How does one define *the national good*? There are a number of elements that make up the definition. Culture and national security are both important. There are numerous economic considerations: capital investment, labor opportunities, the ability to consume goods, and the avoidance of excess environmental degradation. The next section looks at these different components of the national good in more detail.

REASONS FOR AND AGAINST IMMIGRATION

The first possibility to be raised was that the national good was defined in terms of cultural cohesiveness. This had political implications; Thomas Jefferson worried that immigrants coming from countries ruled by despots would not have the same skills in self-government that he observed among native Americans. It could have even more important consequences. Lyman Beecher, who believed that his faith was the true one and the only one that would get a body into heaven, worried that the immigration of Catholics would give the whole country a bad record on Judgment Day. It also had implications for everyday life, as John Tanton noted in the debate over whether to make English an official language.

Jane Addams was a pioneer in pointing out two reasons why immigration might be good for U.S. culture. First, immigrants strengthened U.S. culture by reinforcing its strong points. One could find lovers of liberty in

Poland in the 1790s, in Greece in the 1820s, in Hungary in the 1830s, in Germany in the 1840s, in Italy in the 1860s, and in the People's Republic of China in the 1990s. In this instance, Addams's position has found some unintentional reinforcement in the sociological research of Mary C. Waters. Waters designed a survey that she administered to individuals with various ethnic affiliations ranging from the descendants of Irish, Italian, German, and Polish immigrants to contemporary immigrants from Spanish-speaking countries. She found that each ethnic group placed a high priority on the same values, including family unity and education. Unfortunately for the cause of cultural unity, Waters' research also found that each group tended to trace these values to their own ethnic background—that is, Italians, Puerto Ricans, and others said that their ethnic group was uniquely family oriented and differed from other groups in the value it placed on education—rather than seeing these as common values that transcended ethnic difference.[1]

Addams's second point was that immigrants diversified U.S. culture, bringing new cultural institutions that had not been there before. There is some evidence that immigrants may have brought in cultural traits of more substance. Historian Virginia Anne Metaxes Quiroga did a study of the origins of asylums for unwed mothers and abandoned babies in antebellum New York City. She pointed out that one reason these institutions developed was that there was a demand for them, and one reason there was a demand for them was that there was a large body of Irish immigrant women who had known such institutions back in Ireland.[2] However, Quiroga's finding is so rare as to be noteworthy. More often, attention has focused on cultural contributions such as cuisine and folklore.

Closely related to the issue of culture is the issue of race. The close relationship comes about for two reasons. First, since the Americans in a position to guide the country when it was founded were white, they tended to equate their culture with their whiteness. Second, in the late nineteenth and early twentieth centuries, scientists thought that much culture was passed on genetically, rather than by educating the next generation, and thus that immigration would result in a population that couldn't be assimilated to U.S. standards because it didn't have the proper genes for U.S. culture. Race has come into play in the debate over immigration in a number of ways. The most obvious was difficulties whites imposed on other races' efforts to migrate or to become citizens. Blacks could not become immigrants or citizens until the constitutional amendments that followed the Civil War. The different countries of Asia were barred from migration or citizenship until after World War II. Less obvious, but still important, is the impact of immigration on nonwhites. At the end of the nineteenth century, black leader Booker T. Washington was faced with a dilemma: To discourage immigration in his day was to encourage the racism that hurt blacks more than it hurt immigrants, but he feared that increased immigration would limit black economic advancement. In the middle of the twentieth century, Hispanic leader Cesar Chavez was faced with the same problem. To discourage Mexican immigrants was to play into the hands of those who thought all Mexican ethnics were born in Mexico, but to permit them was to permit labor competition that hurt his developing union, the United Farm Workers.

Another definition of the national good placed a high premium on national security. What happens if a person immigrates and then the United States goes to war with the country from which that person came? Would that person's loyalty be to the country of birth or to the United States? Throughout U.S. history the tendency has been to think of immigration as problematic. The first controversial immigration laws, the Alien and Sedition Acts of 1798, regulated the behavior of immigrants in times of war and peace in the name of national security. As late as the middle of the twentieth century, the United States passed a law, the McCarran-Walter Immigration and Nationality Act of 1952, that included regulations prohibiting the immigration of members of the Communist Party, because of the fear that communists might enter the country and become spies and saboteurs. Ironically, though, immigration may have boosted U.S. national security at one critical time. The United States was the only country to develop an atomic bomb during World War II, and because many scientists left or were expelled from fascist and communist countries and came to the United States for safety, they were available for the Manhattan Project.

A third definition of the national good emphasizes national economic strength. In order to ask whether immigrants have been good for the economy, one has to ask other questions. What part of the economy? Some immigrants, such as Andrew Carnegie, became mighty capitalists, doing the investing that keeps the economy going. Immigrants opened up new industries in the United States, as Germans opened beer brewing, which provided jobs for many people. On the other hand, Denis Kearney thought he was hurt by immigration, especially Chinese immigration, for inexpensive Chinese labor increased competition for jobs and lowered wages for unskilled workers in California in the 1870s. Immigrant consumers played a mixed role. Immigration itself generally enriched the shipping companies of Europe, such as the Cunard Line, founded by Samuel Cunard of Nova Scotia but headquartered in London. Some of the money immigrants earned enriched their home countries as well, for Irish domestic servants and Italian transient laborers sent remittances back to Ireland or Italy for the rest of the family to use. However, even impoverished immigrants could be consumers. Historian Andrew Heinze has demonstrated how Procter & Gamble sought to increase the sale of Crisco by marketing it specifically to Jews as a kosher product that could be used as a substitute for the lard that Americans generally used as a baking fat but that violated Jewish prohibitions against mixing meat and dairy products when it was combined with milk and eggs to make cakes and cookies.[3] In the nineteenth century, frontier states considered immigration such a boon that they had state boards to encourage it. Immigrants helped to settle the prairies and to boost population to the levels required to move from territorial status to statehood. At the same time, seacoast cities and states considered immigrants a serious drain on their budgets, diverting tax dollars to the building of hospitals, almshouses, and other social services. In the late twentieth century, when social services such as Aid to Families with Dependent Children, Social Security supplements, food stamps, Medicare, and Medicaid were funded in part or in whole by the federal government, the question of whether immigrants took more in services than they paid in taxes went to the national level.

As the debate on whether immigrants are good for the national economy shows, one difficulty in answering the question is that the same facts could be used to support either side. Low wages are fine if one is seeking to employ people; they are not so fine if one is competing for work. Remittances are fine if one wants the immigrants' relatives to stay at home and not add to the total number of immigrants; they are not so fine if one wants the immigrants to spend their wages in their own neighborhoods and boost the U.S. economy. Facts used to support or to deny the benefits of immigration to other aspects of U.S. life work the same way. What one thinks of immigrant contributions to U.S. cuisine might depend on what one thinks of pizza, beer, tacos, or stir fry. The interplay between immigrants and foreign policy raises similar paradoxes. On the one hand, the United States prohibited the immigration of communists. On the other hand, it welcomed refugees of communism, because in terms of attracting Cold War allies it made sense to picture the Soviet Union as the place people wanted to leave and the United States as the one that welcomed people with open arms.

So considering the complexity of the immigration issue, it would be impossible to draw a two-column chart, label one column "Reasons for Immigration" and the other "Reasons Against," draw up two lists to determine which was longer, and reach the conclusion that immigration is good or bad for the country.

SCOPE AND OUTLINE OF THE PRESENT WORK

This book, then, is not organized around reasons for and against immigration. Instead, it is organized around twenty biographical vignettes. Some of the people profiled supported immigration; indeed, Thomas Jefferson thought it was a human right. Others, including Madison Grant, Henry Cabot Lodge, and John Tanton, opposed immigration. Between these two extremes are two other sets of people. Some opposed specific kinds of immigration: Lyman Beecher didn't want Catholics; Denis Kearney didn't want Chinese; A. Mitchell Palmer didn't want foreign-born radicals; and Joseph Petrosino didn't want foreign-born criminals. Another group, exemplified by Laura Fermi and her work on refugees from twentieth-century European dictators, supported a specific kind of immigrants. Some people didn't work directly in the field of immigration, but their work was relevant to it: Jacob Riis's agitation for housing reform, Theodore Roosevelt's speech on race suicide, and Henry Ford's writings on anti-Semitism come to mind. Some ended up on both sides at once, as Patrick McCarran sponsored laws admitting immigrant shepherds and also laws limiting immigration. Others ended up caught in strange twists of fate, as Edward Kennedy sponsored one law in 1965 to make immigration fairer for all concerned and then in 1990 supported a second law to relieve those adversely affected by the 1965 law.

This introduction includes sections giving broad time lines for immigration and for immigration law, thus helping students to put the biographies in their proper historical context. An appendix lists other characters who have participated in the immigration debate. The book is organized to facilitate further research. The introduction, the biographical vignettes, and the short biographies in the appendix are drawn primarily from published sources that students can readily access. Student who are interested in anything encountered in the text can start with the index to find how a particular subject is treated in different historical periods, then move on to the selected bibliography to see a starter list of books and articles. There is also a cross-reference system. The names of persons who have biographies in the main text or in the appendix appear in **boldface** when they are first mentioned in this book in sections other than their own biographies.

Why biography? The various arguments for and against immigration—culture, all the different aspects of economics, foreign policy, race, and others—recur repeatedly throughout U.S. history. It is individuals who assign them specific priorities at specific times. Some people's interest in immigration stems from their own experience. The refugee Laura Fermi is the most obvious example, but there are other, more subtle ones: Jacob Riis once had to take shelter in a police lodging of the type he later denounced in *How the Other Half Lives*. In other instances, the personal element is less obvious. Jane Addams, for example, was not an immigrant, but the immigrant experience mirrored the transition that took place in the lives of U.S. women of her generation. Some people, such as African-American leader Booker T. Washington, may not seem to be interested in immigration at all until one digs beneath the surface. There is always, somewhere, a personal element in the voice of participants in the debate over immigration.

Biography shows the interplay of various levels of the human personality. For example, why was A. Mitchell Palmer opposed to immigrant radicals? Because of his background and upbringing? Because one of those immigrant radicals set a bundle of dynamite at his doorstep while he and his wife were inside the house? Or because Congress was demanding the attorney general take action?

Biography has a certain appeal, as Jacob Riis realized when he used photographs, anecdotes, and large doses of his own personality to put a human face on the immigration questions of his day. For open-minded students forming their own opinions, it is a rare privilege to watch other people from theirs. It is moving to watch Theodore Roosevelt react to arguments that Americans were committing "race suicide," not on the basis of what experts in demographics said about the relative birthrates of natives and immigrants but on the basis of his own experience; or to watch Thomas Jefferson extend the debate between his heart and his head to immigration, fearing immigration but holding fast to his commitment to human rights.

Finally, biography is an antidote to simplistic divisions of the population into groups that favor or oppose immigration. It's not even possible to make a correlation between place of birth and opinion. Foreigner Denis Kearney could throw around stereotypes like a native. Native Cesar Chavez could be mistaken for a foreigner. Native Henry Ford's anti-Semitism was matched by that of Canadian-born Reverend Charles Coughlin. Italian-born Carlo Tresca's radicalism had its counterpart in that of Eugene V. Debs of Terre Haute, Indiana. When one gets down to the level of biography, there are few stereotypes, and that might be a good lesson to apply to the discussion of immigration generally.

AN INTRODUCTION TO IMMIGRATION HISTORY AND THE HISTORY OF IMMIGRATION LAW

When studying U.S. immigration history, it is common to divide that history into periods called *waves*. The dividers between the waves are usually either wars or depressions; it does not make sense to migrate to a country experiencing either one (although Samuel Gompers, later founder of the American Federation of Labor, arrived in New York City with his family the week before the Battle of Gettysburg). Migration waves have also been shaped by legislation. For example, historians suspect there was no wave before 1820 because at least until 1815 the Revolutionary War and the Napoleonic Wars would have discouraged it; but they do not know for sure, because the federal law requiring ports to count incoming travelers was passed only on March 2, 1819.

Thereafter, historians have counted three waves. The first runs from 1820, the first year statistics were kept, to 1860, the last year of peace before the Civil War. It was characterized by migration from the United Kingdom (England, Wales, Scotland, and until 1922, all of Ireland) and from German-speaking areas outside of what was until 1867 the Austrian Empire. These were the places shifting from agriculture to industry. They were affected by the major events of the time, such as the Irish potato famine and the liberal revolutions of 1848. They were also the places with the best transportation connections to the United States.

A second wave commenced about 1880, when the United States emerged from the depression that followed the Civil War, and ended in 1914 with the start of World War I. Although people continued to come from the United Kingdom and from Germany, which became an empire in 1871, this wave is characterized by the migration of people from Italy and eastern Europe, meaning Russia and the non-German-speaking parts of the Austro-Hungarian Empire. In some cases, these people were feeling the effects of the Industrial Revolution. More often, they were feeling the effects of their countries' leaders' efforts to become or to remain Great Powers in Europe, which included armed forces maintained by taxes and the conscription of young men. Russian Jews were driven by threats to their physical safety in the form of government-sponsored pogroms. Also, the railroads and the extension of steamship lines made it possible to migrate from more distance places.

Before migration could fully recover from World War I, the federal government passed legislation drastically reducing the number of people who could enter the United States. As dictatorships came into power in Europe, they limited the number of people, especially men of military-service age, who could leave. After the 1929 stock market crash, the Great Depression made the United States an unappealing destination for migrants. From 1939, when Hitler and Stalin invaded Poland, until 1945, World War II made migration impossible. The end of World War II did not bring an end to restrictive U.S. law. There was a small burst of refugees from World War II and the Cold War but hardly a wave.

Historians date the third wave of migration with the switch to a new federal immigration policy in 1965; they have not yet determined an ending date. The post-1965 migration was characterized by the inclusion of migrants from Asia and from the Western Hemisphere. Previously, the former had been forbidden to enter under U.S. law. The latter actually had fewer restrictions prior to 1965 but had less opportunity in terms of transportation and less incentive.

In contrast to historians of immigration with their three waves, historians of immigration policy identify four periods to their story. The first technically begins in 1776, when the United States became independent and thus able to pass its own immigration law.[4] The first actual federal immigration law was passed on March 26, 1790. It required a two-year residency in the United States before immigrants applied for citizenship and made this requirement standard for all states. This period was characterized by two features. The first was the scarcity of legislation under either the Articles of Confederation (1777–1787) or the Constitution (since 1787). Even the Alien and Sedition Acts, famous as the first expression of opposition to immigrants to have the force of federal law, actually affected those seeking citizenship and those already in the country, not those applying for admission. Most federal laws had to do with how to acquire citizenship. One, on March 3, 1855, fine-tuned the process of counting immigrants by requiring separate totals for temporary and permanent immigrants. There was also some consumer protection legislation for ocean travelers. For example, the same 1819 law that required the counting of persons entering the United States also set limits to the numbers of people who could travel on ships entering or leaving the United States. On February 22, 1847, on March 2, 1847, and in the aforementioned 1855 act, Congress established that each passenger was entitled to a certain amount of space on the ship. This was an attempt to protect passengers from exploitation at the hands of those who would pack them into the hold in compartments where freight was normally carried (where the ship's steering mechanism was, or "steerage").

The second feature of this first phase of immigration policy was that the states more than made up for federal inactivity. State action was of two sorts. There were states, especially along the frontier, that wanted to increase the white population vis-à-vis the Indians, to develop a local economy, and to build up sufficient population to justify a larger delegation to the House of Representatives. These states created government offices charged with attracting immigrants. Conversely, states on the Atlantic Coast reeled from the impact of so many migrants, especially refugees of the Irish famine, at their ports. New York created a state board to provide for an orderly admission process. This state board had use of an old fort-turned-entertainment-center, Castle Garden, in Manhattan's Battery Park. Incoming steerage passengers were brought there by barge from the ship docks on the East River. Commissioners collected statistical information on them and tried to help them make postvoyage plans. New York's activities eventually brought this period of immigration policy to a close. In 1875, in the case of *Henderson v. Mayor of New York*, the Supreme Court ruled that immigrants crossed state lines in the course of their voyages and thus were a form of interstate commerce and so subject to federal, not state, regulation.

Still involved with post–Civil War Reconstruction, the federal government did not immediately start to pass laws. The year 1882 introduced two new types of immigration policy. The first type, exemplified by the Chinese Exclusion Act of May 6, was restriction, in which the U.S. government simply forbade certain kinds of people to enter the United States or to become citizens. On February 20, 1907, the principle of restriction was extended to Japanese, with a new law containing a clause that permitted the president to refuse to admit persons deemed detrimental to labor conditions in the United States. Later the principle would be extended even further.

The principle that gave the second phase of immigration policy its name, though, was the second principle the federal government established in 1882, that of regulation. In the regulation phase, people were permitted to enter the United States, provided they met certain requirements. (The terminology is inexact, but in general, regulation requires more checking than restriction. It was relatively easy to establish whether people were Chinese and to restrict them. One could seldom tell just by looking that a potential immigrant didn't meet the regulations; these laws were enforced by examining the immigrants individually.) The first set of requirements became law on August 3, 1882. Persons who were deemed likely to become public charges, that is, to require welfare, were not permitted to enter the United States. After February 26, 1885, contract laborers—those who had already agreed to take particular jobs—were forbidden entry. A law of March 3, 1891, denied admission to persons suffering from certain contagious diseases, persons convicted of felonies and also persons convicted of some misdemeanors, and polygamists. A March 3, 1903, law excluded those advocating certain political opinions, including the overthrowing by violence of the rule of law, governments and the U.S. government in particular. A February 20, 1907, law excluded persons with certain mental disabilities, persons with tuberculosis, minors unaccompanied by their parents, persons with criminal records involving moral crimes, and women coming or being brought to the United States for prostitution. (This last regulation was reinforced by the Mann Act of June 25, 1910.) Of all these regulations, the one involving contagious diseases was most significant. Most of the people excluded from the United States under these regulations had trachoma, an eye disease that was easy to detect, impossible to cure, and very contagious.

On the surface, the February 5, 1917, law excluding illiterates seems just another regulation. After all, another clause of the law added to the list of mental ailments that could get a person excluded. However, there was an ulterior purpose to the literacy law. The thinking of the time was that illiteracy predominated among ethnic groups who were undesirable, and so illiteracy was a way of excluding these people without appearing to be prejudiced against classes of white persons. In this interpretation, it becomes important to know that another clause of the same law added to the category of restricted persons, forbidding anyone whose ancestors came from a "barred zone" in the Asian Pacific from immigrating or from becoming citizens.

The 1917 law started a third phase in U.S. immigration policy, one that was more exclusively and openly restrictionist. In U.S. history, the important word was *quota*, the idea that only a certain number of people in a certain category could enter the United States. Although people who specialized in identifying superior and inferior ethnic groups pointed out that this was insufficiently precise, the most common category was the nation-state. It was easier to tell which government one was a subject or citizen of than it was to tell what ethnic group one belonged to. The first law openly embodying the restrictionist principle to Europeans was passed on May 19, 1921. It limited the number of immigrants from any one country to a number equal to 3 percent of that country's representation in the United States in the 1910 census. In other words, if the 1910 census showed 300,000 persons born in the mythical country of Utopia resident in the United States, then Utopia would get a quota of 9,000, that is, 3 percent of 300,000. The law passed on May 26, 1924, attempted to redo the calculations in favor of the preferred ethnic groups. From 1924 to 1927, each country received a quota based on 2 percent of the number of persons of that country in the 1890 census. Assuming there were also 300,000 Utopian-born persons in the 1890 U.S. census, Utopia's new quota would be 2 percent of 300,000, or 6,000; the thinking was that the least desirable immigrants were also the most recent and the least likely to show up in the earlier censuses. After 1927, each country got a third and final quota. This time, the federal government set a cap of 150,000 on the total number of admissions to the United States in any year. Each country received a quota the number of which bore the same relation to 150,000 that people born in that country and living in the United States bore to the total U.S. population in the 1920 census. To return to the dwindling Utopian quota, assume there were 300,000 Utopian-born persons in the 1920 U.S. census, too. The total U.S. population was 105,710,620; 300,000 is 2.8 percent of 105,710,620. Thus, Utopia would get 2.8 percent of 150,000, or 4,200. Asian migration continued to be forbidden. Colonies (British India, French Indochina, the Dutch East Indies, Portuguese Angola) had subquotas within the quotas assigned their imperial owners.

At the same time, the federal government set precedents for a later phase of immigration policy. Applicants from any one country were ranked according to a series of family preferences so that, within their own rules, officials tried to help families keep together. Unmarried children under twenty-one born to female U.S. citizens got high preference, then the parents of U.S. citizens, then the husbands of U.S. citizens over age twenty-one. Some people did not have to line up under the quota laws. Male U.S. citizens could have their spouses and their children under twenty-one join them without waiting for the quota to favor them.

The concept of the barred zone began to crumble during World War II. American exclusion of Chinese immigrants seemed incompatible with the U.S. alliance with China during that war. On December 17, 1943, a little over two years after the United States entered the war, it assigned the Chinese a quota of 105. The McCarran-Walter Immigration and Nationality Act of 1952 eliminated sex discrimination in immigration and made clear that Asians were eligible for naturalization on the same basis as whites had been since 1790 and blacks since the Fourteenth Amendment of 1868, and there was some hope that Congress would abolish the differential national quotas that governed immigration. However, the real start of the fourth phase of U.S. immigration policy came in 1965 and continued through 1990.

The fourth phase was characterized by emphases on the equality of nations and on the reunification of the family. As passed in 1965, the law divided the world into two halves, with Africa, Asia, Australia, and Europe in the Eastern Hemisphere, and North and South America in the Western Hemisphere. The Western Hemisphere got a ceiling of 120,000 immigrants per year. The Eastern Hemisphere got a ceiling of 170,000, with no one country to get more than 20,000 visas. The applicants for these 20,000 visas per country could be ranked, with preference going to those rejoining their families, then to people who met certain U.S. economic needs, and then to refugees. Some family members of U.S. citizens and legal residents were admitted outside the limits. On October 20, 1976, the federal government modified the law to give each country in the Western Hemisphere the same 20,000-visa limit the Eastern Hemisphere had. On October 5, 1978, the government abolished the distinction between hemispheres and established a global cap of 290,000 quota immigrants per year.

The major change from restrictive quotas to egalitarian ones sometimes overshadows the fact that the 1965 immigration law was not the last. Since then, the law has changed, although whether it has changed enough to justify saying that one era has ended and another has begun is a subject for debate. The current basic immigrant law was passed in 1990. That law provided that after fiscal 1995 (following the federal calendar, fiscal 1995 would begin not on January 1 but on October 1 of that year), the total number of immigrants permitted would be 675,000. This total is divided into three categories. Immigrant visas are to be issued to 480,000 persons for family reunification, to 140,000 persons to meet economic needs, and to 55,000 to increase ethnic diversity among the immigrant pool; the thinking behind this last category is that the 480,000 persons receiving visas for family reunification purposes would probably be in the same ethnic group as the families with which they were reuniting, and thus certain ethnic groups would be favored and others shut out. As always, some people do not come under the overall limit. Certain family members and all refugees are admitted outside the various ceilings. People who come to the United States to study or travel are not considered immigrants and must readjust their legal status if they wish to remain in the country longer than specified in their visas or if they wish to do things, such as take jobs, not specified in their visas. The law was last modified on September 30, 1996, in order to strengthen provisions against illegal immigrants but without modifying this basic framework.

A PERSONAL NOTE

Because this is a book about how personal experience contributes to personal opinion, a few words of biography may be in order. I have immigrants among my ancestors, in-laws, acquaintances, and students, but I was born in Boston and raised in Virginia and have never been far from the landmarks of my national history, a rootedness that contrasts with the immigrant experience. I live in New York City, where immigration is a fact of life. Study and experience lead me to approach immigration as an issue that affects the whole world and that may require international cooperation to secure the welfare of the individual human beings most directly affected. After this burst of biography, I'd like to concentrate on the people in the text, how they were shaped by their study and experience, and how they came to the opinions they held.

Research for this volume in the "Shapers of the Great Debates" series was conducted at Butler Library of Columbia University, the Thomas J. Shanahan Library of Marymount Manhattan College, and the Main Branch, Mid-Manhattan Branch, and New Dorp Regional Branch of the New York Public Library. Particular thanks are due the Center for Migration Studies (CMS), its executive director Lydio F. Tomasi, C.S., Ph.D., who provided photographs of Edward M. Kennedy, Cesar Chavez, and Alan K. Simpson and permission to use them, and Diana J. Zimmerman, who directs the CMS library and archives. Tom Baione, Senior Special Collections Librarian of the Department of Library Services of the American Museum of Natural History, provided material on Madison Grant; and Barbara Mathe supplied a photograph of Madison Grant and permission to use it. Professor Oscar Handlin, emeritus, of Harvard University, Senator Edward M. Kennedy, and John Tanton, M.D., answered inquiries about themselves, and Dr. Tanton kindly supplied his own photograph and permission to use it.

I always look for the pictures in a book first and so was pleased that the publisher included them here. Besides the aforementioned, a number of individuals and institutions supplied photographs. The New-York Historical Society's fine Rembrandt Peale portrait of Thomas Jefferson is included owing to the courtesy of John Kuss of that museum. Peter J. Bahra of the Cincinnati Museum Center provided the print image of Lyman Beecher. Sister Marguerita Smith, Archivist of the Archdiocese of New York, provided the photograph of John Joseph Hughes. The photography staff of the New York Public Library provided the print image of Denis Kearney, and Wayne Furman of the Office of Special Collections took care of the permission. The photograph of Henry Ford and permission to use it were obtained by going through the website of the Henry Ford Museum and Greenfield Village. The Library of Congress furnished photographs of Booker T. Washington, A. Mitchell Palmer, and Patrick Anthony Mc-

Carran. Wendy Rogers of the Museum of the City of New York provided the photograph of Jacob A. Riis and permission to use it. Wendy E. Chmielewski, Curator of the Swarthmore College Peace Collection, provided the photograph of Jane Addams and permission to use it. John Singer Sargent's fascinating oil portrait of Henry Cabot Lodge is included with the permission of the National Portrait Gallery of the Smithsonian Institution. Wallace Dailey at the Theodore Roosevelt Collection of the Harvard College Library provided the photograph of Theodore Roosevelt and permission to use it. Both the University of Chicago and Fermilab provided photographs of Laura and Enrico Fermi. The portrait of Oscar Handlin and permission to use it were obtained through the courtesy of Patrice Donoghue, Assistant Archivist of Harvard University Archives.

Other individuals provided other sorts of help. John E. Brock contributed an unusual combination of assistance, checking the physics in the chapter on Laura Fermi and assisting in gathering information on contemporary anti-immigration leaders. Biographer Kevin Brown made suggestions regarding taking a biographical approach to the subject of immigration. Heather Clarke, the Student Assistant for the Social Science Division of Marymount Manhattan College at the time I was working on this book, assisted with fact-checking and proofreading. Students at Marymount Manhattan College have listened to and read research in progress on John Joseph Hughes, Jacob A. Riis, and Madison Grant. Professor Peter Levy of York College in Pennsylvania, Series Editor, and Cynthia Harris, Executive Editor, Reference Books, Greenwood Publishing Group, oversaw the editing and the final production.

For the assistance of each and every one of these individuals, I would like to express my gratitude. It is my hope that this help has been given in a worthy cause.

NOTES

1. Mary C. Waters, *Ethnic Options: Choosing Identities in America* (Berkeley: University of California Press, 1990).

2. Virginia Anne Metaxes Quiroga, "Poor Mothers and Babies: A Social History of Childbirth and Child Care Institutions in Nineteenth Century New York City" (Ph.D. diss., State University of New York at Stony Brook, 1984).

3. Andrew R. Heinze, *Adapting to Abundance: Jewish Immigrants, Mass Consumption, and the Search for the American Identity* (New York: Columbia University Press, 1990), pp. 176–177.

4. William S. Bernard, "Immigration: History of U.S. Policy," in *The Harvard Encyclopedia of American Ethnic Groups*, ed. Stephen Thernstrom, Ann Orlov, and Oscar Handlin (Cambridge, MA: Belknap Press of Harvard University Press, 1980), pp. 486–495, starts with a colonial period of legislation.

BIBLIOGRAPHY

Regarding immigration policy, see David M. Reimers, *Still the Golden Door: The Third World Comes to America*, 2nd ed. (New York: Columbia University Press, 1992); John Higham, *Strangers in the Land: Patterns of American Nativism, 1860–1925*, corrected and with a new preface (New York: Atheneum, 1969); E. P. Hutchinson, *Legislative History of American Immigration Policy, 1798–1965* (Philadelphia: University of Pennsylvania Press [for the Balch Institute for Ethnic Studies], 1981); and William S. Bernard, "Immigration: History of US Policy," and Reed Ueda, "Naturalization and Citizenship," both in *The Harvard Encyclopedia of American Ethnic Groups*, ed. Stephan Thernstrom, Ann Orlov, and Oscar Handlin (Cambridge, MA: Belknap Press of Harvard University Press, 1980), pp. 486–495, 736–748, respectively. A list of laws affecting migration to the United States, from the first to the most recent, appears in every *Statistical Yearbook of the Immigration and Naturalization Service* (Washington, D.C.: U.S. Government Printing Office; the one used here was published in 1997). Periodic updates can be obtained in the "Legislative Developments" column of *Migration World*.

THOMAS JEFFERSON
(1743–1826)

"A Right Which Nature Has Given to All Men"

Born in the British colony of Virginia on April 13, 1743, Thomas Jefferson played a role in Virginia's, and the American nation's, fight for independence and then remained politically active until his death on July 4, 1826. During his life he held many honors: governor of Virginia, minister plenipotentiary to France, first secretary of state of the United States, and second vice president of the United States. As a candidate for office, he helped to found both the two-party system and an ancestor of the modern Democratic Party. As president, he approved the Louisiana Purchase and the subsequent Lewis and Clark expedition. In private life, he was known for his interest in just about everything, and the home he designed, Monticello, is a tourist attraction. He remains a popular and controversial biographical subject.

Jefferson wanted to be remembered for other achievements. He designed his own gravestone, an obelisk mounted on a rectangular base. He asked that the base be engraved with his three favorite accomplishments: author of the Declaration of Independence, author of the Virginia Statute of Religious Liberty, and founder of the University of Virginia. These pointed not so much to deeds as to ideas and values: self-government, freedom of conscience, and liberal education.

How are those values reflected in Jefferson's stance on immigration? Jef-

Thomas Jefferson, portrait painted by Rembrandt Peale in 1805.
© Collection of the New-York Historical Society.

ferson's writings on immigration show his intellectual side, his interest in trying to think a problem through. They also show his emotional side, his ability to shrink from his own conclusions. Finally, they show where his loyalties lay in the conflict between how he felt and what he thought, between what he termed, in another context, his heart and his head.

Jefferson began writing on immigration late in 1774. In 1773, Bostonians had staged a protest against a tax Parliament said the colonists were supposed to pay for tea, dumping several chests of tea leaves into Boston harbor. Parliament reacted to this destruction of property, and to the attitude of disobedience underlying it, with a series of laws that it called the Coercive Acts and that Massachusetts labeled the Intolerable Acts. Massachusetts appealed to the other colonies for support, and a Continental Congress was called to determine a course of action. Virginia held a convention at Williamsburg to elect and instruct delegates to the Continental Congress. Jefferson was supposed to participate, but when he left his home at Monticello, he found the winter roads impassable, and he also took sick. All of this may have confirmed his sense of how best to participate in the Williamsburg meeting. Jefferson was never good at public speaking. He couldn't speak loudly, and any time he spoke for a long period, he developed a hoarse, raspy voice. He also got flustered easily; he wasn't very good at thinking on his feet and answering objections on the spot. He preferred to write. In this case, he wrote what he intended to say at the meeting and entrusted copies to two other delegates, Patrick Henry and Peyton Randolph. Randolph had a house in Williamsburg and read Jefferson's writing to delegates assembled informally there. Shortly thereafter, Jefferson's thoughts were published in a pamphlet titled *A Summary View of the Rights of British America*.

The first right Jefferson covered was the right to leave one country for another: The Saxons had abandoned northern Europe, taken over the sparsely inhabited island of Britain, and established a government there. Whatever government they had left behind in northern Europe never claimed them for a colony. In the American case:

[O]ur ancestors, before their emigration to America, were the free inhabitants of the British dominions in Europe, and possessed a right which nature has given to all men, of departing from the country in which chance, not choice, has placed them, of going in quest of new habitations, and of there establishing new societies, under such laws and regulations as to them shall seem most likely to promote public happiness.[1]

It is most likely that Jefferson got this idea from an earlier pamphlet, Richard Bland's 1766 *Inquiry into the Rights of the British Colonies*.[2] Readers may notice that Jefferson, characteristically, was skipping some problems. The Saxons in Britain and the British in America encountered natives to whom they denied the rights of life, liberty, and the pursuit of happiness. Another notable point is that Jefferson used some ideas here that he used again later. The first was the idea of natural rights. It is not clear here whether a "right" is a "liberty" (the freedom to do something) or a "power" (the ability to do it), but whichever it is, it is, a priori, as if there were already a person present before any of the accidents of birth were added. Persons were free. Once those persons were born as girls, there were limitations put upon them. Once society cast some into slavery, there were some limitations put on those people. Once persons organized governments, they put limits on themselves, for the sake of the community. But all men were *created* equal.

Sex, and probably race, put limits on individuals that, as far as Jefferson was concerned, no human effort could remove. Governments, which came after people and were created by them, were supposed to be less powerful. Historical accidents had given some governments, notably despotic crowned heads, powers they were not really supposed to have. History, though, had been kind to the Saxons on the island of Britain. They were able to hew closely to natural law in erecting their government. When those born in Great Britain left for North America, they erected their own governments, based on their understanding of the natural law that was preserved and exemplified in British history. And, Jefferson claimed, unlike the Saxons leaving Europe, these emigrants "thought proper" to continue their union with the crown, who became "the central link connecting the several points of the empire thus newly multiplied." Here, again, Jefferson overlooked some historical facts. Contrary to claims Jefferson made in his pamphlet, the colonies would not have been founded without a certain minimum of royal assistance, such as a charter. Although colonies, notably Massachusetts, tried to distance themselves from the royal government, the royal government was involved in colonial administration. These historical inaccuracies may have been deliberate distortions, written to win over delegates in Williamsburg. They do not undermine the fact that Jefferson saw expatriation as a natural right.

Within the newly established governments, participation was to be as broad as possible, as demonstrated by one of the wilder passages in *A Summary View of the Rights of British America*. Having established to his satisfaction the colonists' right to form their own governments and to obey only their own laws, Jefferson launched into a lengthy indictment of how Parliament and the crown tried to force their laws on colonies. Specifically, he claimed:

The abolition of domestic slavery is the great object of desire in these colonies, where it was unhappily introduced in their infant state. But previous to the enfranchisement of the slaves we have, it is necessary to exclude all further importations from Africa; yet our repeated attempts to effect this by prohibitions, and by imposing duties which might amount to a prohibition have been hitherto defeated by his majesty's negative.[3]

Again, Jefferson is ignoring historical fact. It was not just that the British wanted to sell slaves; it was that traders based in the colonies wanted to trade them and that colonists wanted to use their cheap labor. What is important here is that Jefferson used *abolition* and *enfranchisement of the slaves* as synonyms. He had no halfway status between slavery and full citizenship, no free blacks languishing without the vote or civil rights.

As it happened, *A Summary View of the Rights of British America* served only to enhance Jefferson's reputation as a political writer. By the time the delegates chosen at the Williamsburg convention arrived in Philadelphia, matters in Massachusetts had run far ahead of their instructions. On April 18, 1775, a battle broke out between British troops stationed in Boston and militia in Boston and surrounding towns. The Continental Congress had already dissolved, so a Second Continental Congress was called in order to determine how to meet the crisis. Jefferson was chosen a delegate from Virginia to the Second Continental Congress. Arriving at the Philadelphia meeting place of the new Congress in the spring of 1776, he was put on a committee to draft what became known as the Declaration of Independence.

Although the Declaration is shorter, it is set up along the same outline as *A Summary View of the Rights of British America*. It has a short preamble, then the statement of principles that begins with "We hold these truths to be self-evident." It then lists specific examples of how crown and Parliament had violated these principles. In his draft, Jefferson again introduced his charge that King George III had prevented colonists from abolishing slavery. His fellow delegates did not find the accusation sufficiently convincing, and besides, they were writing a justification of their reasons for opposing the crown; it was no time to be accusing themselves of similar bad behavior. Out went the clause regarding slavery. However, Congress did permit another of Jefferson's charges to remain, one that took the same issue of the colonists' efforts to extend the privileges of citizenship but used immigrants as the example: "He has endeavoured to prevent the population of these States; for that purpose obstructing the Laws of Naturalization of Foreigners; refusing to pass others to encourage their migration hither, and raising the conditions of new Appropriations of Lands."[4]

After the Second Continental Congress adopted the Declaration of Independence on July 4, 1776, Jefferson resigned his position as a delegate and returned to Virginia. Once the Declaration was signed, Virginia was no longer a colony. It was a state, a self-governing entity. Specifically, it was a commonwealth, whose people chose their rulers rather than acquiescing to a hereditary aristocracy or a royal line. Its laws needed an overhauling befitting its new status. Jefferson was already involved in this project. In June of 1776, besides the draft of the Declaration of Independence, he had produced a draft of a constitution for Virginia. Between 1776 and 1779, he gathered copies of all the laws passed under the colonial government, no easy task given that, before easy means of making copies, there was only one copy of some of these laws in the entire colony. He studied the laws and made recommendations for new ones. Among these recommendations were several regarding immigration to Virginia, acquiring citizenship there and expatriating from the commonwealth.

Consistent with his belief that migration was a human right, Jefferson made immigration, citizenship, and expatriation easy. Insofar as citizenship for the native-born was concerned, he adopted the tradition of English common law, known as jus soli, or the law of the soil, which ruled that anyone born in Virginia was a citizen of the commonwealth. Because Virginia had slavery, there was an exception to jus soli: Those born of slave mothers inherited their mothers' slavery and were neither free nor citizens of the commonwealth. There were no restrictions on who could enter Virginia. All immigrants could take oaths or make affirmations (some religions forbade the taking of oaths, and Jefferson, respecting freedom of conscience, made provisions for variations in religious practice) that they intended to reside in Virginia for two years (later increased to seven by the legislature) and that they intended to subscribe to Virginia's fundamental laws. With that oath or affirmation, they had the same rights as free native Virginians. All sane men aged twenty-one or more and possessing a certain amount of land (the legislature later set the amounts at one quarter of an acre in a town or twenty-five acres of rural territory) could vote. Citizens could divest themselves of citizenship by declaring, using means admissible in court, that they intended to expatriate.[5] Citizens of the other twelve states in the new United States were extended the same rights, privileges, and immunities of Virginia citizens.[6] This was during a time when few other countries had provisions for accepting immigrants, for making them citizens, or for letting native-born citizens leave.[7]

There was evidence Jefferson understood that his proposals were generous and that he considered them an inducement to migration. He was heard to suggest that Virginia might offer money and land to those willing to migrate to it.[8] Encouraging migration, though, was never one of Jefferson's main themes. During the early years of the United States, he was decidedly ambiguous about it.

After completing the revision of the laws for the newly independent Virginia, Jefferson was elected to a one-year term as governor of the commonwealth. His term was made difficult by the fact that the Revolutionary War had moved south. Traitor Benedict Arnold, now commanding British troops, was in advance of a British force heading north from Savannah, Georgia. During Jefferson's administration, Arnold invaded Virginia itself, ultimately unsuccessfully. Arnold's failure was not due to Jefferson's astute wartime leadership. Jefferson did ride and shoot, but unlike his Virginia colleague George Washington, he had no intellectual interest in military affairs. Instead, while the invasion was going on, his term of office ended, and he did not even stay in Richmond (the capital he had chosen when revamping the laws for its central location in the state) to hand over the reins of government to his successor. He headed back to Monticello and to a new project, a book that he eventually titled *Notes on the State of Virginia*.

The *Notes* are organized as if Jefferson was responding to an interested student's or visitor's questions about his state. It has twenty-three chapters, each titled "Query," because each asked about a different aspect of the commonwealth. Query VIII concerns Virginia's population. Jefferson explained that he considered Virginia underpopulated. The two usual ways of augmenting population are by natural increase—by people having babies—and by immigration. With the attention to detail typical of him when he was engaged in such problems, Jefferson gave the population of all Virginians, slave and free, men and women. In 1782, the latest date available to him, the total was 567,614. He then calculated how many people Virginia could hold; he put the figure at 4.5 million. He determined it would take Virginia until three quarters of the way through 1862 to reach its maximum population if it relied solely on natural increase, and until midway through 1835 if a number of people equal to the number of births immigrated each year. Then Jefferson subtracted 1782 from October 1862 and also from June 1835 to get the relative difference between using natural increase and using natural increase plus immigration to attain his population goals. His conclusion: It would take 81.75 years for Virginia to reach 4.5 million people if it relied on natural increase alone, and 54.5 years if it relied on both natural increase and immigration. Finally, Jefferson subtracted 54.5 from 81.75, to reach 27.25.[9]

Was immigration worth the savings of twenty-seven years and three months to achieve Virginia's population goals? Jefferson thought not.

It is for the happiness of those united in society to harmonize as much as possible in matters which they must of necessity transact together. Civil government being the sole object of forming societies, its administration must be conducted by common consent. Every species of government has its specific principles. Ours perhaps are more peculiar than those of any other in the universe. It is a composition of the freest principles of the English constitution, with others derived from natural right and natural reason. To these nothing can be more opposed than the maxims of absolute monarchies. Yet, from such, we are to expect the greatest number of emigrants. They will bring with them, the principles of the governments they leave, imbibed in their early youth; or, if able to throw them off, it will be in exchange for an unbounded licentiousness, passing, as is usual, from one extreme to another. It would be a miracle were they to stop precisely at the point of temperate liberty. These principles, with their language, they will transmit to their children. In proportion to their members, they will share with us the legislation. They will infuse into it their spirit, warp and bias its direction, and render it a heterogeneous, incoherent, distracted mass.[10]

This is hardly a flattering portrait of immigrants. Buried in it, however, is an interesting statement: "In proportion to their members, they will share with us the legislation." As with the example from his writings on slavery, cited above, Jefferson had no halfway status. He would not admit that a government could protect itself by preventing people with dubious backgrounds and opinions from voting. (He argued, though, that it should protect itself from immigrants, and from its own people's worst tendencies, with a system of free public education from the elementary to the university level.) Even if their previous experience under European monarchies had left immigrants improperly prepared to exercise their natural rights, they still retained these rights.

Shortly after completing the work that led to the *Notes on the State of Virginia*, Jefferson was called to service by the new national government operating under the Articles of Confederation. He was sent to Paris as minister plenipotentiary. While there, he was asked to review an article on the new *Etats Unis* for a French publication, the *Encyclopedie Methodique*. The article criticized the United States for permitting indentured labor, in which individuals contracted to provide several years of labor, free of charge except for their living expenses, in exchange for passage to the United States. Jefferson observed that this was hardly the Americans' fault:

So desirous are the poor of Europe to get to America, where they may better their condition, that being unable to pay their passage, they will agree to serve two or three years on their arrival here, rather than not go. During the time of that service, they are better fed, better clothed, and have lighter labor, than while in Europe. Continuing to work here a few years longer, they buy a farm, marry, and enjoy all the sweets of a domestic society of their own. The American governments are censured for permitting this species of servitude, which lays the foundation of the happiness of these people. But what should the governments do? Pay the passage of all who choose to go into their country? They are not able; nor, were they able, do they think the purchase worth the price? Should they exclude those people from their shore? Those who know their situations in Europe and America, would not say that this is the alternative which humanity dictates.[11]

Jefferson's capacity to fudge the facts shines through here. There is some debate as to the relative difficulty of indentured servitude in the United States and labor in Europe. There was no doubt he was correct in asserting that socioeconomic mobility was more likely in the United States than in Europe. What is interesting is Jefferson's comments about a possible alternative to indentured servitude, that the U.S., or a state, government pay the passage of potential immigrants. He wondered if the federal or state governments would really consider these people a bargain. Yet although he wasn't willing to pay for these people to migrate, he ruled out excluding them. Their natural right to migrate outweighed the governments' interest in selecting immigrants.

One final bit of evidence as to Jefferson's thoughts on immigration comes from a suggestion he made to **John Adams** during 1785. He proposed to make citizenship between contracting nations reciprocal. U.S. citizens living abroad would have all the rights, immunities, and privileges of their host countries, and immigrants would automatically have all those of the United States. For all practical purposes, there would be no immigration; the crossing of national borders would pose no problem. Even Jefferson admitted this was far outside the accepted way of doing things, but it is an example of his commitment to the idea that movement, even international movement, was a basic human right.[12]

The Alien and Sedition Acts of 1798 moved Jefferson from a philosopher debating the proper laws for immigration to participation in a debate. The Alien and Sedition Acts were four in number. The Sedition Act had to do with the right to criticize, in print or in speech, elected officials and their policies. The Alien Enemies Act permitted the federal government to detain noncitizen immigrants in cases in which the United States went to war against their home countries. The Alien Act permitted the president to order out of the country any noncitizen immigrant, to detain those who refused to leave, and to deport those whose detention proved difficult, for whatever reason the president chose. The Naturalization Act superceded a previous act of 1795, which required five years' residence in the United States before an immigrant applied for citizenship. The new law required fourteen years' residence.

There were two motives behind the Alien and Sedition Acts that are significant here. The first was a military motive. The Alien and Sedition Acts were passed because there was a chance the United States would be caught in a war between France and England—specifically, that the United States might declare war on France to protect the rights of neutral ships on the high seas. This was the first time the United States was faced with this situation, and the new country needed legislation to regulate immigrants during the war. In fact, the Alien Enemies Act is still on the books and could be activated in time of war.

The second motive was partisan politics. The Alien and Sedition Acts were passed shortly after the first two political parties, the Federalists and Jefferson's Democratic Republicans, were formed. The Federalists controlled the presidency. The Jeffersonians interpreted the Alien and Sedition Acts as directed against themselves. For example, the Alien Act was set to expire on June 25, 1800, and the Sedition Act on March 3, 1801. These expiration dates gave the Federalists the power to suppress opposition to their rule during the presidential campaign of 1800. The best evidence of a Federalist plot to suppress Jeffersonians was the Naturalization Act, with its lengthy waiting period for citizenship. It was thought that recent immigrants voted for the Jeffersonians, and the Naturalization Act made it look as though the Federalists were determined to deny immigrants citizenship, and voting rights, until they got over their Jeffersonian leanings.[13]

It was Jefferson's private opinion that the Alien and Sedition Acts were unconstitutional extensions of executive power. A personal protest, though, would not be very effective. Someone with authority had to rule the laws were unconstitutional. This was before John Marshall, in *Marbury* v. *Madison*, set the precedent on which the Supreme Court ruled as to the constitutionality of laws. At that point, the only precedent had been set by George Washington. When he was president, Washington would receive bills passed by Congress. If he was uncertain as to their constitutionality, as he was when Congress authorized a national bank, he would ask for advice from his cabinet and then make a ruling. According to this precedent, John Adams was now charged with responsibility for ruling on the constitutionality of the law. However, it was unlikely that Adams would rule as Jefferson desired; Adams was more sympathetic toward the Federalists. Anyway, Jefferson had his own candidate for the proper authority for ruling on the constitutionality of laws. The states, which until the Fourteenth Amendment stood outside the Constitution, could judge it.

Jefferson drafted a document laying out this theory and applying it specifically to the Alien and Sedition Acts. Introduced into the Kentucky legislature by his associate John Breckenridge, and approved on November 16, 1798, they became known as the Kentucky Resolves. In his document, Jefferson made only two references directly to immigration. He pointed out that the Constitution did not say anything about aliens whose home countries were not at war with the United States. Under the principle of strict construction, that meant that Congress could pass no legislation regarding "alien friends." The states in which they lived passed any legislation necessary. The only power over migration that the Constitution gave Congress was in Article I, Section 9: "The Migration or Importation of such Persons as any of the States now existing shall think proper to admit, shall not be prohibited by the Congress prior to the Year one thousand eight hundred and eight." Jefferson knew this had been inserted as a compromise over the slave trade, but taken literally, the clause referred only to immigration. Fortunately for Jefferson, he was writing this in 1799, not after 1808, when this section expired and Congress had greater power. For the present, Congress had to follow state law. If a state admitted a person, Congress could not pass a law permitting the president to expel or detain that person.

It is worth emphasizing that immigration was of secondary concern in the Kentucky and Virginia Resolves. Jefferson used the Alien and Sedition Acts to show that Congress had exceeded its constitutional mandate. However, to say that immigration was of secondary importance is not to say it was of no importance. When he became president, Jefferson, like the Federalists he criticized, used the powers of the office to urge action on immigration issues.

On December 8, 1801, Jefferson delivered his first annual message to Congress, assessing his presidency and laying out plans for the future. He suggested action on the remaining sore point from the Alien and Sedition Acts, the Naturalization Act:

Considering the ordinary chances of human life, a denial of citizenship under a residence of fourteen years is a denial to a great proportion of those who ask it, and controls a policy pursued from the first settlement by many of these States, and still believed of consequence to their posterity. And shall we refuse the unhappy fugitives from distress that hospitality which the savages of the wilderness extended to our fathers arriving in this land? Shall oppressed humanity find no asylum on this globe? The Constitution, indeed, has wisely provided that, for admission to certain offices of important trust, a residence shall be required sufficient to develop character and design. But might not the general character and capabilities of a citizen be safely communicated to everyone manifesting a *bona fide* purpose of embarking his life and fortunes permanently with us?[14]

Congress obliged, restoring the previous requirement of five years' residence in order to become a U.S. citizen.

During his second administration, Jefferson had one last chance to act specifically on behalf of immigrants, and his actions showed his consistent adherence to his earliest principles. France and Great Britian were at naval war. The British had the stronger navy. British naval ships stopped other nations' ships, naval and commercial ships, even ships from countries with which England was not at war. The commanders ascertained where the ships were going. If they were going to England's enemies, the commanders had the ships searched and carried off any contraband or materials that would directly aid the enemy war effort. The commanders also searched the ships for people who could be subjected to British impressment laws. Life in the British navy was so notoriously harsh that the navy faced a constant labor shortage. This is where the issue of immigrants again came in. The British did not permit native-born men to abandon their citizenship and take on that of some other country. They considered any English-born man, even one who had become a naturalized U.S. citizen, to be English and thus subject to impressment laws. The United States, though, followed the Jeffersonian principle that an individual could leave one country and become a citizen in a second, that naturalized English-born sailors were Americans, and thus the sailors should not be impressed into the British navy. These conflicting issues of citizenship were as much an issue as neutral rights on the high seas.

The issue was still unsettled when Jefferson finished his second term as president; eventually, it contributed to the War of 1812. By then, James Madison was almost ready to run for his second term. Jefferson had watched his successor take the oath of office in 1809, then returned to Monticello. Much of the rest of his life was taken up with the founding of the University of Virginia, which he thought of as a "wonderful hobby for a septuagenarian," and his personal affairs. Jefferson was constantly in debt. He sold his library to the federal legislature (where it became the basis for the Library of Congress) and was supposed to use the money to pay off debts and start afresh, but soon he was back to his old habits of buying books, redesigning Monticello, experimenting with new plants in his garden, and ignoring the effect of his discretionary spending on his budget. He slipped back into debt and never emerged from it.

Jefferson never again dealt with immigration as a public issue. Having worked out his thoughts in the 1770s, he stuck to these principles throughout his life. On June 12, 1817, in a private letter, he gave them one last expression: "If [God] has made it a law in the nature of man to pursue his own happiness, he has left him free in the choice of place as well as mode; and we may safely call on the whole body of English jurists to produce the map on which Nature has traced, for each individual, the geographical line which she forbids him to cross in pursuit of happiness."[15]

This was indeed a radical position in that it was based on an analysis of the root issues of which rights took precedence, the rights of nations or the rights of individuals. It was also radical in that it was one of Jefferson's basic principles to which he adhered through fifty years of political activity as a writer, partisan leader, and president. In fact, it may have been Jefferson's consistency that gave rise to the charge that he was actually inconsistent, impractical, unable to see the real issues involved. Many other people, contemplating the immigration of people who might not make good citizens, would unhesitatingly protect those people from their own inevitable mistakes in self-government, and protect the nation, by prohibiting immigration. Jefferson, too, flinched at the prospect of immigrants bringing in strange languages and stranger political principles. However, he reminded himself that all men are, indeed, created equal and that this was the moral basis on which he should act.

NOTES

1. [Thomas Jefferson], *A Summary View of the Rights of British America* (Williamsburg: Clementin A. Rind, 1774), in Paul Leicester Ford, comp. and ed., *The Works of Thomas Jefferson*, 12 vols. (New York: G. P. Putnam's Sons, 1904), 2: 64.

2. David N. Mayer, *The Constitutional Thought of Thomas Jefferson* (Charlottesville: University Press of Virginia, 1994), pp. 338–339.

3. Jefferson, *A Summary View*, p. 79.

4. "The Declaration of Independence," in Henry Steele Commager, ed., *Documents of American History*, 8th ed., 2 vols. (New York: Appleton-Century-Croft, 1968), 1:101.

5. Samuel K. Padover, comp., *The Complete Jefferson* (New York: Duell, Sloan and Pearce, 1943), p. 659.

6. Thomas Jefferson, 1776 draft of constitution for Virginia, in Ford, *The Works of Thomas Jefferson*, 2:176, 180; Merrill D. Peterson, *Thomas Jefferson and the New Nation: A Biography* (New York: Oxford Univerity Press, 1970), pp. 153–154.

7. John Sharp Williams, *Thomas Jefferson: His Permanent Influence on American Institutions* (New York: Columbia University Press, 1913), p. 91.

8. William Eleroy Curtis, *The True Thomas Jefferson*, The "True" Biographies and Histories Series (Philadelphia: J. B. Lippincott, 1901), p. 302; Peterson, *Thomas Jefferson and the New Nation*, pp. 153–154.

9. Thomas Jefferson, *Notes on the State of Virginia*, ed. William Pedan (Charlotte: University of North Carolina Press, 1954; reprint, New York: W. W. Norton, 1972), pp. 83–84 (page citations are to the reprint edition).

10. Ibid., pp. 84–85.

11. Padover, *The Complete Jefferson*, p. 55. Jefferson's notes on the article were written on June 22, 1786.

12. Peterson, *Thomas Jefferson and the New Nation*, p. 310.

13. An example is the community of Anglo-Irish lawyers that migrated to New York. See Walter L. Walsh "Religion, Ethnicity, and History: Clues to the Cultural Construction of Law," in *The New York Irish*, ed. Ronald H. Bayer and Timothy J. Meagher (Baltimore and London: Johns Hopkins University Press, 1996), pp. 48–69.

14. Padover, *The Complete Jefferson*, p. 393.

15. Thomas Jefferson to John Manners, n.p., June 12, 1817, cited in Mayer, *The Constitutional Thought of Thomas Jefferson*, p. 80.

BIBLIOGRAPHY

Jefferson's own writings are available in several formats, including Paul Leicester Ford, comp. and ed., *The Works of Thomas Jefferson*, 12 vols. (New York: G. P. Putnam's Sons, 1904); Andrew Lipscomb and Alber Ellery Bergh, eds., *The Writings of Thomas Jefferson*, 20 vols. (Washington, D.C.: Thomas Jefferson Memorial Association, 1904); and Samuel K. Padover, comp., *The Complete Jefferson* (New York: Duell, Sloan and Pearce, 1943). Jefferson himself wrote one book; the edition used here was *Notes on the State of Virginia*, ed. William Pedan (Charlotte: University of North Carolina, 1954; reprint, New York: W. W. Norton, 1972). Jefferson also has many biographers. The most recent is Joseph J. Ellis, *American Sphinx: The Character of Thomas Jefferson* (New York: Alfred A. Knopf, 1997). Two others useful here were Dumas Malone, *Jefferson and the Ordeal of Liberty* (Boston: Little, Brown, 1962); and Merrill D. Peterson, *Thomas Jefferson and the New Nation: A Biography* (New York: Oxford University Press, 1970). Jefferson worked out his thoughts on immigration in the context of his general work on law, and there is a useful monograph on this subject, David N. Mayer, *The Constitutional*

Thought of Thomas Jefferson (Charlottesville: University Press of Virginia, 1994). A helpful monograph on the historical context in which Jefferson worked out his ideas is Stanley Elkins and Eric McKitrick, *The Age of Federalism: The Early American Republic, 1788–1800* (New York: Oxford University Press, 1993).

LYMAN BEECHER
(1775–1863)

The No-Popery Crusade

Lyman Beecher was born into one world on October 2, 1775, and died in another on January 10, 1863, and the evidence suggests he wasn't altogether happy with the transition. The world of his childhood in Connecticut (he was born in New Haven and raised in Guilford) was homogeneous, full of people who were, like himself, descendants of New England settlers and heirs of various forms of their Puritan faith. As an adult in New York, Connecticut, Massachusetts, and Ohio, he encountered immigrants of different ethnic backgrounds and a different religious faith, Irish and German Catholics. He developed an argument against Catholic migration that shaped the immigration debate of his day.

Esther Beecher, Lyman's mother, died of tuberculosis two days after Lyman's birth. His father, David, married again (Esther had been his third wife, and he married five times) and was a blacksmith by trade, but he could not take care of his baby boy and so sent him to live with his uncle, Lot Benton, a self-sufficient farmer. In adult life, Beecher was the tradition-minded sort of conservative who liked to recall the times when people grew what they ate and wore what they made rather than lusting after store-bought luxuries. However, as a youngster on the farm, he could not keep his thoughts on simple tasks such as ploughing in straight lines. Guessing

---

that Beecher's mind was insufficiently challenged, rather than overly challenged, by farming, Benton offered to send his nephew to what was then called Yale College. Off he went in 1793, when he was eighteen years old.

Beecher's intellectual development began in 1795, after he had already been at Yale for two years. That year, Timothy Dwight arrived to become the college's new president. From Dwight, Beecher learned some important concepts in religious doctrine. The English who arrived in New England in the seventeenth century brought with them a faith commonly known as Calvinism, after its founder, John Calvin, or Puritanism, from its avowed goal of purifying Christianity. An element that Puritans were particularly interested in was clarifying one part of the process by which individuals were "saved," or admitted to heaven. New England Puritans held to double, thick, supralapsarian predestination. "Predestination" meant that God picked out a particular fate for each human being. "Double" predestination meant that God chose either heaven or hell for each soul. "Thick" meant that the choice was made without reference to whether the individual, as humans judged it, "earned" it by good behavior. "Supralapsarian" meant that God had settled each individual's fate before the Original Sin had been committed in the Garden of Eden (the "lapse" buried in the middle of the word). In short, there was no way individuals could work their way to heaven. People could, though, know whether they were among the saved. This knowledge usually came in a series of emotional experiences: conviction of personal sinfulness, sense of helplessness to change one's condition, awareness of God's love and mercy. Dwight guided Beecher through these steps and produced what was known as a "conversion experience."

Dwight also introduced Beecher to questions of church polity, or organization. Another aspect of the church that the Puritans wished to purify was that the Church of England had bishops, a position for which there was little precedent in Scripture. The Bible, though, was unclear as to what the proper form of the well-established church should be. Before Beecher was born, there had been a split within Puritanism. The Congregationalists thought that the most important authority was the local congregation, with all congregations maintaining doctrinal unity because they shared a common scriptural faith. The Presbyterians thought that each local congregation ought to have lay elders who would gather in local groups called presbyteries (from the Greek word for *elder*), that the local ministers should gather into synods, and that these groups would oversee doctrinal unity and provide organizations for unified action. As an adult, Beecher moved between the Congregationalist and Presbyterian denominations with no problems. His first job, in 1798, was as minister of a Presbyterian congregation on East Hampton, Long Island.

Soon Beecher was a leading light in East Hampton, presiding over a revival, with people realizing that they were indeed among the saved and formally joining his congregation. Beecher's success in inspiring religious revivals was not universally appreciated among his ministerial colleagues, who accused him of watering down difficult doctrines to attract people to his church. Whether he ever formally challenged the double, thick, supralapsarian predestination of orthodox Calvinism became a question that dogged his heels.

Like a patriarch of old, Beecher had a large family. Two children, a daughter named Harriet and a son named Frederick, died in infancy. Another son, George, grew up to become a minister but died of an accidental gunshot wound at age thirty-four. Catharine became an educator and a promoter of using professionally trained women as elementary schoolteachers. William and James Chaplin were ministers whose chief work was with their congregations. Edward, Charles, and Thomas were ministers, authors, and educators. A second Harriet, better known by her married name of Harriet Beecher Stowe, wrote *Uncle Tom's Cabin* and other novels and short stories. Henry Ward was the prized preacher of the most popular church in midnineteenth-century Brooklyn, the Plymouth Congregational Church. Isabella Beecher Hooker was a suffrage advocate. Daughter Mary Foote Beecher Perkins led a quiet life, but she contributed to the family's fame as well; she was the paternal grandmother of feminist author Charlotte Perkins Stetson Gilman. With such a family, Beecher was glad to take a better-paying position at the First Church in Litchfield, Connecticut, which he did in 1810.

Litchfield was also a more prestigious location, one in which a rising star was more likely to be noticed. However, it had certain challenges that were, in a way, the defects of its virtues. Litchfield was a sophisticated place. People had more money and more education, less incentive to stick to the traditional faith, and more options when they sought new faiths. People for whom revivalism was important were better served by the Baptists, Methodists, and New School Presbyterians than by orthodox Congregationalism; those faiths rejected double, thick, supralapsarian predestination. Those who needed more than sermons gravitated toward the Protestant Episcopal Church, with its Gothic architecture, stained-glass windows, instrumental music, choral singing, and elaborate ritual. Those who found the traditional faith too complex joined the Unitarians; the local joke was that all they believed in was the fatherhood of God, the brotherhood of man, and the neighborhood of Boston. Switching denominations was a serious issue, not just for theological reasons but because it was the orthodox Congregational faith that was the established church in Connecticut, deriving its income from state funds generated by taxation. If people joined other churches, they might begin to question why their tax money should go to the Congregationalists. Could Beecher use the revival technique to save the traditional faith? He tried. In terms of saving the traditional tax-supported system, he was unsuccessful; Connecticut separated church and state in 1818. He did, though, help Congregationalism hold its own among the new competing faiths, using his lively preaching style to attract new members to the First Church. And, again, he did well for himself, attracting an offer from a more prestigious place. In 1826, he became pastor of the Hanover Street Congregational Church in Boston, the historic heart of Puritanism.

Beecher came to Boston as a locally famous soul-stirring preacher. The next year, he extended his reputation to New York. In the northern part of that state, Charles Grandison Finney was having tremendous success gathering congregations and, like Beecher, firing them with the will to perfect themselves and to reform the world. Finney's success seems to have brought on some professional jealousy that was expressed in theological terms. Finney, other ministers pointed out, lacked credentials. He was a lawyer who had a conversion experience and then persuaded the local Saint Lawrence presbytery to give him a license to preach; he hadn't been trained for the ministry. Other clergy also accused Finney of winning his converts by bending eternal truths, telling people they could be saved if only they asked to be, privileging free will over divine power. These preachers hoped to rein in Finney by having an accepted leader in the field—a trained minister who was also a famed preacher, Beecher's description, precisely—talk to him and make him more respectful of the traditional ministry. On July 18, 1827, a group of ministers, including Beecher and Finney, met at the Presbyterian church in New Lebanon, New York, and the outcome was not what the traditionalists expected. Finney protested that the public exaggerated his doctrinal unorthodxy and sensationalized reports of his revival meetings. For their part, the other ministers were reluctant to condemn Finney out of hand, because they agreed with him that revivals, increased church attendance, personal efforts at good behavior, and reducing the sins of the world were good things. The result was that two men's reputations were enhanced. Finney was accepted as a revivalist among the ministers, and Beecher was accepted as the man who bridged the gap between the traditional learned ministry and the new evangelism.

Again, Beecher's abilities attracted attention. A pious and wealthy group, led by Ebenezer Lane, gathered money to erect what would become Lane Theological Seminary, a Presbyterian training school for ministers. One donor, a devout New York merchant and reformer named Arthur Tappan, pledged $60,000 on the condition that Beecher accept the position as first president of the seminary. In 1832, Beecher moved to Cincinnati. One of a seminary president's duties was to raise money for the school. In 1834, Beecher traveled back east to Boston. There, on August 3, he began a series of evening sermons intended to inform Bostonians of the progress of the Gospel on the frontier and to inspire them to contribute to Lane Theological Seminary. This time, some charged, his fiery rhetoric had fiery consequences.

About two miles north of Boston, between Cambridge and the Mystic

River, was Mount Benedict, an Ursuline convent in Charlestown, Massachusetts. It was founded partly with money left by John Thayer, a Congregationalist minister who had converted to Catholicism. It included among its staff a number of converts, including some from New England families. The mother superior, Mary Anne Ursula Moffatt, in religious life Mother Saint George, did not have the shy, retiring personality so valued by early Victorians.[1] The convent had originally been located next to the cathedral, and the sisters had worked by teaching the poor Irish children who lived in the neighborhood. Bishop Benedict Fenwick thought they deserved better housing and arranged for their removal to Ploughed Hill in Charlestown. Charlestown had too few Catholic children for a school, so the sisters turned to running a girls' boarding school. They had some success attracting wealthy, Unitarian parents looking for a solid education for their daughters. And about the time Beecher came to Boston, they had a prisoner in their convent, or so people thought.

On July 28, Elizabeth Harrison, in religious life Sister Mary John, the convent music teacher, showed up at the Cutter farm near the convent, showing signs of overwork and mental distraction. At first she refused to see anyone, but on July 29 Bishop Fenwick came to visit her, and after their conversation she returned to the convent. On July 30, a group of men showed up at the convent to see if Sister Mary John was being kept there against her will. Mother Saint George told them that Sister was not seeing visitors, which only heightened their suspicions. On August 9, Edward Cutter, to whose farm she had gone, asked to see her and had a conversation with her. On Monday, August 11, a group of selectmen, elected representatives charged with Charlestown's management, came to Mount Benedict, toured the building, and saw Sister Mary John. About 9:00 P.M. that same night, a mob gathered around the convent. A group from the mob demanded to be let in and was turned away. At 11:00 P.M. a pyre of tar barrels in a nearby field was lighted. This was apparently a signal for action, for then a gang of men stormed the convent. The sisters woke the students and led them down a back staircase, across the yard and to the back fence, where they lifted them over. The sisters then tore a hole in the fencing material and squirmed through. Two sisters paid a last visit to the chapel and carried out the tabernacle, which contained reserved communion bread, thus protecting it from desecration. Then they abandoned their convent. The mob went through the building, destroying its contents before setting it afire. On August 12, a smaller mob finished the job by burning the property's fences and trees.[2] Beecher remembered that for some days after that the militia patrolled Boston to prevent a similar outbreak there.[3]

Historians have long linked Beecher's preaching, specifically a sermon on the evils of Catholicism that he gave on Sunday, August 12, with inciting the mob. There is some evidence that the mob action had been planned before Beecher arrived.[4] Beecher himself disavowed responsibility: "The sermon of mine to which the mob was ascribed was preached before my presence in the city of Boston was generally known, and on the very evening in which the riot took place, two or three miles from the scene, and not an individual in the mob, probably, heard the sermon or knew of its delivery."[5]

On the other hand, Beecher did complain about the event, especially about the humiliation of the founding city of Calvinism depending for protection on its Catholic bishop, Benedict Fenwick, who preached on the sin of vengeance and advised Catholics to depend on the law courts for redress. (The courts convicted only one person, whose sentence was overturned, and never compensated the Ursulines for their losses.) The matter could be cleared up if it was known what Beecher actually said. Unfortunately, Beecher's sermon for August 12, 1834, has not been preserved. And the writing Beecher published soon after the Mount Benedict burning may have been amended to include some new ideas he got later that same August by reading **Samuel F. B. Morse.**

Students may know Morse as the inventor of the telegraph. He was also an artist. The same year that Beecher moved to Cincinnati, Morse was studying art in Rome, not remarking on the Catholicism there until it nearly literally hit him over the head. He was standing pressed against his residence, watching a papal procession pass, when a guard marching by him swung his bayoneted musket over Morse's head, sending his hat flying several yards. The guard cursed and moved on without apology or effort to see if Morse was all right or to retrieve his hat. For Morse, that one incident summed up a world of difference between the egalitarian, democratic United States and the hierarchical, autocratic Vatican. Morse returned to the United States a dedicated opponent of Catholicism. From August 20 to November 22, 1834, the New York *Observer* published a series of a dozen articles by Morse, using the epistolary form and a pseudonym Brutus, about the Catholic threat. In his letters, Morse broached the idea that the Catholics were organizing to send legions of immigrants to the American frontier to take over the country and hand it over to the pope.[6]

There are similarities between Beecher's and Morse's conspiracy theories, although it is not clear whether Beecher came up with his ideas independently of Morse or adopted Morse's as his own. It might be enough to note that the ideas were in circulation and convincing to intelligent, educated individuals. That was why the public took seriously Beecher's most elaborate statement of the twin—and related—evils of Catholicism and immigration, *A Plea for the West*, which he published in 1835.

In *A Plea for the West*, Beecher described the opposition between Protestantism and Catholicism as a war for souls raging all over the world. In the Protestant Reformation, Catholics had lost the allegiance of half of Europe. At that point, it mattered only a little; at the same time, Catholics were outpacing Protestants in converting natives and settling Europeans in Spanish and French America. Recently, though, Beecher claimed, Catholicism had suffered more setbacks, this time due to the rise of democratic republics. Beecher theorized that both the papacy and the conservative monarchies of Europe, headed by Austria, saw a need to make up for lost territory and lost adherents. He argued that they set their sights on the American frontier, with its fresh lands and its vast spaces. He then described their supposed two-pronged program to conquer the United States.

First, Roman Catholic priests, brothers, and sisters offered to teach non-Catholic pupils, as the Ursulines were teaching Unitarian girls in Charlestown. (Beecher didn't mention women's education specifically; he was much more concerned about a Jesuit conspiracy to educate boys.) This was not just education, Beecher claimed; it had insidious side effects:

They cannot help interfering with the religion of their pupils. The known opinions and kind attentions of instructors sedulous to please, and a constant familiarity with their example and religious instruction and the doctrines, prayers, ceremonies and worship of the church, cannot fail to affect the mind of Protestant youth—allaying apprehension, conciliating affection, inspiring confidence and undermining their Protestant education—until they become either sceptics or devotees, or at least the friends and apologists and auxiliaries of Catholics.[7]

Beecher argued that Catholic education, if it did not convert the Protestants, as John Thayer and some of the nuns at Mount Benedict had been converted, at least lulled them into complacency while the combination of Vatican and Austrian forces implemented the second phase of their plot. Using funds gathered from pious Catholics in Europe by an association called the Leopoldsverein, they would encourage impoverished Catholics to migrate to the United States. Once there, of course, the migrants would become citizens with the right to vote. However, being Catholic, they would vote as their clergy told them, for Catholics were merely robots, slaves to their priests. The result was they would take over the country, establish a union of church and state such as existed in Austria, and would then threaten everyone else's freedom of worship. Beecher did not add the crowning touch that other conspiracy theorists produced. When, finally, every empire in Europe collapsed, these Catholics would welcome the exiled pope to a refuge in the Mississippi Valley.

If there be no such design, the facts in the case are as adverse to our safety as if they were the parts of a settled plan. The number of the immigrants, who lack information, their unacquaintance with the principles of our government, their superstition and implicit confidence in their ecclesiastical teachers, and the dependence of these on Rome, and of Rome on Austria,—all constitute an influence of dangerous actions in themselves, and offer to the powers of Europe, easy and effectual means of disturbing the healthful action of our institutions, which if it did escape their design to contrive, cannot be expected long to escape their power to employ.[8]

Not much could be done in America to break up the Vatican–Vienna conspiracy in Europe, and, besides, Beecher was confident the papacy and its monarchical allies were fighting a losing battle against the advances of self-government. However, Beecher had his own three-point program to oppose Catholic immigrant influence in the United States. First, he wanted to fund Protestant education so that parents wouldn't be tempted to send their children to Catholic schools. This was the mission that had brought him east to Boston.

Second, he wanted the government to limit certain types of immigration. He took pains to avoid a blanket condemnation, writing that "the language of indiscriminate discourtesy towards immigrants, calculated to wound their feelings and cast odium on respectable and industrious foreigners is carefully to be avoided." However, "an immediate and energetic supervision of our govermnment is demanded to check the influx of immigrant paupers, thrown upon our shores by the governments of Europe, corrupting our morals, quadrupling our taxation, and endangering the peace of our cities, and of our nation."[9]

Third, the United States should be more careful about whom it admitted to citizenship. Again, Beecher was careful to make clear he did not want to deny any European immigrants "participation in the blessings of our institutions and ample territory." However, the United States should regularize naturalization so that it would not "outrun the possibility of intellectual and moral culture," meaning the government should not naturalize those not fully assimilated, lest "the unregulated action of the European population bring down destruction on ourselves and them."[10]

Like any conspiracy theory that holds explanatory power for a large number of people, Beecher's plot rested on diverse facts that were lying around, waiting for someone to connect the dots and discover the hidden picture. In Beecher's case, there were four main groups of facts. First, some important events in European history occurred in the years before Beecher wrote *A Plea for the West*. On July 27, 1830, Parisians rebelled against their absent (he was hunting at his chateau) king, Charles X, with the result that Charles abdicated in favor of Louis-Philippe, the duke of Orleans, who was to govern France as a constitutional monarch. On November 29, 1830, the Polish military revolted and fought an ultimately unsuccessful war for independence from tsarist Russia. In May 1832, Greece was recognized as an independent country. That same year saw the "Long Diet" in Hungary, the first effort to challenge Austria's rule of that state, and the rise of Louis Kossuth.

Second, Beecher was correct that changes in European government affected the papacy and that the Vatican was not ready to make the transition smoothly. As it happened, Italy did not establish its capital at Rome until 1871. However, even though this was some time after the beginning of the nationalist movement, the Vatican still had no plans for adapting to a world of national governments and still insisted on independence for the papacy. The matter remained unsettled until the 1929 Lateran Treaties.[11]

Third, Beecher was correct that European Catholics were raising money to spend on the United States. Bishop Edward Fenwick, a member of the same family as Bishop Benedict Fenwick of Boston and himself bishop of Beecher's Cincinnati, solicited wealthy Europeans for aid for his frontier diocese. A response came in 1829 with the establishment of the Leopolds-verein. Another organization, the Society for the Propagation of the Faith, was founded in Lyons in 1832. The latter actually spent more money and was more influential, but the first seemed more suspicious because its patron was the heir of the Hapsburg family, the crowned head of the Austrian Empire. The one mistake Beecher made was in charging that these groups used their money to fund immigrants. There were other groups for that purpose, including the German Auswanderungs Gesellschaft and the Irish Colonization Association. The Leopoldsverein really spent its money on helping bishops to build churches, schools, and eleemosynary institutions and on to recruit clergy and religious orders.

Finally, Beecher was quite perceptive about an underlying moral problem. All the religious people of his day claimed their faith outweighed any earthly authority and that there was, in the words of Beecher's contemporary, politician **William Henry Seward**, "a higher law than the Constitution." It is still a much-debated topic as to how to balance church and state and what to do when one's religious beliefs conflict with the law.

Beecher's allegations of a Vatican–Vienna plot to take over the frontier sounded plausible to contemporaries because it fit in with other nasty rumors about Catholicism. The other anti-Catholic stories common in the Boston area had to do with sex. They were summarized in a novel published in 1836, *Awful Disclosures of the Hotel Dieu Nunnery of Montreal*. Its author was Maria Monk, who had never even been inside the famous Ursuline convent. The closest she had come to it was that she had spent time at a Magdalene asylum, or home for prostitutes and wayward girls, that was run by Catholic sisters. However, she knew what the public wanted, and she spun a tale in which she cast herself as a Protestant girl enrolled in the Hotel Dieu's convent school who felt a call to the holy life she thought the nuns were living. When she became a young widow, she determined to enter religious life. The day she received her habit she also heard explicit instructions from the convent superior to "obey the priests in all things." She soon found out what *that* meant. The nuns were supposed to provide sexual services for the priests. Impregnated by one of the clergy, she became curious about what would happen to her unborn child, and thus she found out about the huge pit in the basement into which strangled newborns were thrown. It was right by the tunnel connecting convent and rectory. Determined to save her child, she took a different route out, walking briskly by a guard to make him think she was going on an important errand. *Awful Disclosures* was a huge success and had many imitators.[12] The Charlestown mob that concerned itself with whether Sister Mary John really wanted to return to Mount Benedict after her night at the Cutter farm was reacting to tales such as these.

Although the tales of the *Awful Disclosures* genre weren't true, they did point to a gap between Protestantism and Catholicism. Protestantism had one path for young women: into marriage and motherhood. Catholicism offered the convent, which might sound confining but which provided more opportunities than Protestant women had. Catholic sisters in the United States could travel to exotic places, such as the frontier or into Indian territory. They could be pioneers in education, health care, and other forms of human services. And while not free of male priests and bishops, they were free of male relatives and husbands. There is some evidence, such as the burning of the Charlestown convent, that the Catholic model of women's choices was at least as problematic to the working-class Protestant New England men as were fears of priests seducing young women or of the pope settling in the Mississippi Valley.

The threat of immigrants bound to obey papal teaching voting as a bloc led the nativist movement into politics. In New York City, the *Courier and Inquirer* called for the formation of a party to combat the Catholic immigrant threat. By June 1835, the Native American Democratic Association had developed a platform opposed to Catholicism, to the immigration of criminals and paupers, and to office holding by foreigners. In 1836, they ran their first candidate for mayor, Samuel F. B. Morse. They lost that election. The next year they were more successful, partly because they used the 1837 depression, caused by a fall in western land values and by government decisions regarding how to handle the money supply, to complain that immigrants were competing with native workers for scarce jobs. In 1841, Morse tried one more time to run on an anti-immigrant issue, to prevent Catholics from receiving a share of tax monies for parochial schools. Thereafter, though, the nativist party foundered. Throughout the 1840s, nativism was the sort of issue that could get a local group together for a short while. In the early 1850s, however, after the Irish potato famine sent a great number of impoverished Catholic Irish to the United States, it emerged as a national issue.

Even for Beecher, anti-Catholicism competed with other issues. During the same period he was out fund-raising, he was also facing a crisis at Lane. The seminary had accepted as a student Theodore Dwight Weld. This young man had been converted by the same Charles Grandison Finney whose acceptance as a revivalist had been engineered at a meeting with

Lyman Beecher. Weld came to Lane to study for the ministry, of which he had an enlarged view. Ministers ought to work not just for personal salvation but for reform of the world. Particularly, they ought to work for the abolition of slavery, which Weld thought was the most serious social sin facing the Republic. He soon found Lane too conservative on the issue of abolition and began to criticize his teachers. The trustees voted to discipline him. He then walked out, taking like-minded students with him, and enrolled in another institution of higher education where he could get his bachelor of divinity degree. The new school was Oberlin College, which had been founded in 1834. Its president was Charles Grandison Finney. The revival movement was splitting up on the issue of how thoroughgoing the revival ought to be, how far human beings could alter the condition of human sinfulness.

In that quarrel, Beecher cast himself as the moderate, protesting to the trustees against their quashing of student debates. To others, he was still the most dangerous reformer. Besides being president of Lane Theological Seminary, Beecher was also pastor of the Second Presbyterian Church of Cincinnati. As such, he was under the supervision of the local elders in the presbytery and the local ministers in the synod. In 1835, the same year that Beecher issued *A Plea for the West*, a ministerial colleague, Dr. Joshua L. Wilson, formally charged him with heresy. In his enthusiasm for conversion, he had gone too far. Wilson thought that Beecher's preaching conceded too much to free will and not enough to divine power. He was preaching to people about the need to be converted to reach heaven but neglecting to remind them that ultimately God had already decided who was going to heaven and who was going to hell, and what humans really ought to be doing was waiting for signs of what that decision was. Beecher was found innocent of all charges. This, though, seems to have been a tribute to his success in increasing church membership as much as to his ability to explain in what ways his preaching conformed to Presbyterian doctrines.

By now, it is hard to find a religion that preaches double, thick, supralapsarian predestination. Questions of the most pressing reform of the middle of the nineteenth century were settled not by religion but by the Civil War. Beecher's children eclipsed him in fame, and they did not preserve his faith. They rejected double, thick, supralapsarian predestination. Most remained Congregationalists or Presbyterians, although Catharine eventually attended the Episcopalian Church. In terms of his personal achievements, Beecher remains most notable as the preacher of nativism, opposition to Catholics and to immigrants, and this particular interest of his seems not to have been based on reality. There are no documented cases of Protestant (or Catholic) girls pressured into lives of immorality at convents. Even the demise of European monarchies did not send the papacy into exile in America. The antagonism between Protestantism and Catholicism has been

matched by occasions in which religious people of all faiths worked together on common causes. What caused Beecher to so misinterpret the
facts?

Historians have come up with several possible answers. Ray Allen Billington pointed out that Beecher was raised in an intellectual atmosphere
of anti-Catholicism inherited from the Reformation that produced his Cal-
vinist faith, from the settlement of New England and its emphasis on a
purified faith, and from the American Revolution and its sense that its
democratic Republic and separation of church and state were incompatible
with Catholic traditions.[13] David Brion Davis studied anti-Catholic, anti-
Masonic, and anti-Mormon literature and concluded that the "antis' " motives were not ideological but psychological. They faced vast social,
economic, and political change, but they could not accept that these
changes were caused by impersonal forces. They took comfort in conspiracy theories. Paradoxically, by turning to conspiracy theories as explanations for social change, and by insisting on complete and absolute loyalty
to the past as they constructed it, they became as rigid and undemocratic
as they claimed their enemies to be.[14] **John Higham**, who studied nativism
between 1860 and 1925, produced two theories that are relevant for the
earlier period. To Billington's anti-Catholicism, he added two other ideologies with long intellectual roots, opposition to radical political philoso-
phies and racism. He observed that while these were always present in
American culture, they entered popular discourse and political life at moments of crisis, in times of depression and war. At first, he thought that it
was because at times of crisis nativism performed a function. Nativism was
a way of defining the United States by defining what it was not, of identifying the American people by sorting out who could and could not qualify.[15] Later, Higham put forth a second theory. Nativism is more noticeable
during a crisis because it is at these points that people undergo personal
crises in their social, economic, or political status. Readjustment in the
status of various groups goes on all the time in American society, as the
economy changes from agricultural to industrial or as manufacturing cities
become more important than seaport ones.[16]

One can see how the status-loss theory would make sense for Beecher.
He had the advantage of a college education and ministerial training. Yet
his authority was undercut by people making up their own minds about
religion. His professionalism was challenged by untrained but highly successful preachers such as Charles Grandison Finney. He certainly put on
paper his fears that the Catholics and immigrants—two groups to which
he didn't belong—were gaining ascendancy in the West.

Another school of thought focuses on economics. Religion in Lyman
Beecher's day was developing some of the aspects of the marketplace. Numerous denominations were emerging, and people were moving, as Beecher
himself did, from small towns to the larger cities, where they could choose

among denominations.[17] In the early 1830s, Beecher was in a high-stakes competition, raising money for Lane Seminary. Given the importance of securing the funds, the excitement in Boston seemed to Beecher a godsend:

The Catholic effervescence, though it obstructed for the moment, aided us on the whole. It was a favorable providence, which called me back to speak in undaunted tones, when, without someone to explain, and take correct ground, and inspire courage, all were likely to quail and be carried away. Before I left the tide turned, and Catholicism forever in New England must row upstream, carefully watched, and increasingly understood and obstructed by public sentiment.[18]

In a letter to a close friend, he was more direct: "Nearly twenty thousand have been raised already in money, and agencies, and the right spirit is wide awake, and strong to preoccupy the Valley before his Holiness. So much good is to come out of popery, though it meant not so." As one of Beecher's biographers observed, "In order to raise the energy and the money he required an enemy, and he found an authentically American one in the fear of Catholicism. He played it shamelessly."[19] Even some Catholics were aware of it. Beecher's contemporary **John Joseph Hughes**, then a priest of the Diocese of Philadelphia and later an archbishop of New York, said that "the fact is, the doctor wanted money, and like some of his brethren knew that he could extort more by denouncing Popery than by preaching the gospel."[20]

Lyman Beecher's anti-Catholic and anti-immigrant conspiracy theories, then, were functional, rather than important to him in and of themselves. His biographies generally agree that "[p]rejudice was incidental to his character, not integral to his passion."[21] Beecher's means, though, became other people's ends. He had popularized a new reason to oppose immigration.

NOTES

1. James J. Kenneally, "The Burning of the Ursuline Convent: A Different View," American Catholic Historical Society of Philadelphia *Records and Studies* 90 (1979), pp. 15–22.

2. Jeanne Hamilton, O.S.U., "The Nunnery as Menace: The Burning of the Charlestown Convent, 1834," *U.S. Catholic Historian* 14:1 (Winter 1996), pp. 35–65.

3. Lyman Beecher, *A Plea for the West*, 2nd ed. (Cincinnati, OH: Truman and Smith, 1835), pp. 94–95.

4. Ray Allen Billington, *The Protestant Crusade, 1800–1860: A Study of the Origins of American Nativism* (New York: Macmillan, 1938; reprint, Chicago: Quadrangle, 1964), p. 73 (page citation is to the reprint edition).

5. Beecher, *A Plea for the West*, p. 65.

6. Edward L. Morse, *Samuel F. B. Morse, His Life and Journals* (Boston, 1914), 1:353; quoted in Billington, *Protestant Crusade*, p. 123.

7. Beecher, *A Plea for the West*, pp. 97–98.

8. Ibid., p. 115.

9. Ibid., pp. 175–176.

10. Ibid.

11. Sandra Yocum Mize, "Defending Roman Loyalties and Republican Values: The 1848 Italian Revolution in American Catholic Apologetics," *Church History* 40:4 (December 1991), pp. 480–492.

12. Colleen McDannell, " 'The Devil Was the First Protestant': Gender and Intolerance in Irish Catholic Fiction," *U.S. Catholic Historian* 8:1–2 (Winter–Spring 1989), p. 55.

13. Billington, *Protestant Crusade*, pp. 1–25.

14. David Brion Davis, "Some Themes of Counter-Subversion: An Analysis of Anti-Masonic, Anti-Catholic, and Anti-Mormon Literature," *Mississippi Valley Historical Review* 67:2 (September 1960), pp. 205–224.

15. John Higham, *Strangers in the Land: Patterns of American Nativism, 1860–1925*, 2nd ed. (New Brunswick, NJ: Rutgers, the State University, 1963; reprint, New York: Atheneum, 1969), pp. 1–11 (page citations are to the reprint edition). To be fair, Higham claims racism is different from anti-Catholicism and antiradicalism because it focuses on who can became an American and limits admission to Anglo-Saxons. It would seem this implies the reverse. Racism also delineates who cannot become an American—those from non-Anglo-Saxon backgrounds.

16. John Higham, "Another Look at Nativism," in *Send These to Me: Jews and Other Immigrants in Urban America* (New York: Atheneum, 1975), pp. 102–115.

17. Nancy T. Ammerman, "Denominations: Who and What Are We Studying?" in *Reimagining Denominationalism: Interpretive Essays*, ed. Robert Bruce Mullin and Russell E. Richey (New York: Oxford University Press, 1994), p. 123.

18. Charles Beecher, ed., *Autobiography, Correspondence, Etc., of Lyman Beecher, D. D.*, 2 vols. (New York: Harper and Brothers, Publishers, 1865), 2:336.

19. James W. Fraser, *Pedagogue for the Kingdom of God: Lyman Beecher and the Second Great Awakening* (Lanham, MD: University Press of America, 1985), p. 39. The letter quoted is an undated one from Beecher to his son William.

20. Richard Shaw, *Dagger John: The Life and Unquiet Times of Archbishop John Hughes of New York* (New York: Paulist Press, 1977), p. 98.

21. Stuart Clark Henry, *Unvanquished Puritan: A Portrait of Lyman Beecher* (Grand Rapids, MI: William B. Eerdmans Publishing Co., 1973), p. 157.

BIBLIOGRAPHY

Charles Beecher edited his father's papers to produce the *Autobiography, Correspondence, Etc., of Lyman Beecher, D.D.*, 2 vols. (New York: Harper and Brothers, Publishers, 1865). A modern edition is Barbara Cross, ed., *Autobiography of Lyman Beecher*, 2 vols. (Cambridge: Harvard University Press, 1961). The fullest surviving statement of Beecher's combination of anti-immigrant and anti-Catholic sentiments is in *A Plea for the West*, 2nd ed. (Cincinnati, OH: Truman and Smith, 1835). Modern biographies and monographs on Lyman Beecher are James W. Fraser, *Pedagogue for the Kingdom of God: Lyman Beecher and the Second Great Awakening* (Lanham, MD: University Press of America, 1985); and Stephen H.

Snyder, *Lyman Beecher and His Children: The Transformation of a Religious Tradition*, Chicago Studies in the History of American Religion No. 21. (Brooklyn: Carlson Publishing Company, 1991). Stuart Clark Henry, *Unvanquished Puritan: A Portrait of Lyman Beecher* (Grand Rapids, MI: William B. Eerdmans Publishing Company, 1973), is especially useful for its family tree and its appendix describing the fate of the Beecher offspring. Lyman himself, Charles, Edward, Henry Ward, and Thomas Kinnicut have entries in the *Dictionary of American Biography (DAB)*: Catharine Esther, Charlotte Perkins Stetson Gilman, Harriet Beecher Stowe, and Isabella Beecher Hooker are in both the *DAB* and Edward T. James, Janet Wilson James, and Paul Boyer, eds., *Notable American Women*, 51 vols. (Cambridge, MA: Harvard University Press, 1971). Henry Ward, Catharine Esther, Charles Perkins Stetson Gilman, and Harriet Beecher Stowe also have modern biographies, and there is one book that treats the famous Beecher sisters together: Mary Kelley Boydston and Anne Margolis, *The Limits of Sisterhood: The Beecher Sisters on Women's Rights and Women's Sphere* (Chapel Hill: University of North Carolina Press, 1988). For the anti-immigrant and anti-Catholic context of Beecher's career, see Ray Allen Billington, *The Protestant Crusade, 1800–1860: A Study of the Origins of American Nativism* (New York: Macmillan, 1938; reprint, Chicago: Quadrangle, 1964). For the burning of the Ursuline's Mount Benedict convent in Charlestown in 1834, see Jeanne Hamilton, O.S.U., "The Nunnery as Menace: The Burning of the Charlestown Convent, 1834," *U.S. Catholic Historian* 14:1 (Winter 1996), pp. 35–65; and James J. Kenneally, "The Burning of the Ursuline Convent: A Different View," American Catholic Historical Society of Philadelphia *Records and Studies* 90 (1979), pp. 15–22.

JOHN JOSEPH HUGHES
(1797–1864)

Definitions of "Assimilation"

John Joseph Hughes was an immigrant who, denied a chance in his native Ireland, rose to the top of his field in the United States. From 1838 to 1864 he was spiritual leader of the Catholics of New York City and is most closely identified as a leader of Irish Catholics. What he led the Irish to was a method of assimilation that remains both useful and controversial to the present day.

Hughes was born on June 24, 1797, in Annaloghan, County Tyrone, Ireland. His parents, Patrick and Margaret, were farmers and weavers who did well enough so that when John showed an interest in the priesthood, they were able to keep him in school. Then, in 1814, the harvest went badly and the end of the Napoleonic War reopened competition between weavers of various nations. The parents had to pull John from school and apprentice him to a gardener. Even that wasn't enough, and the father and one brother went to the United States to scout the field for the others. John went in 1817, joining his brother Patrick in Maryland. In 1818, he found a new way to get to the priesthood. By chance, he found work in Emmitsburg, Maryland, site of Mount Saint Mary's Seminary. He became acquainted with the clergy there, and also with Mother Elizabeth Ann Seton, whose Sisters of Charity had their motherhouse in the same town. She interceded for him with the seminary's rector, the Reverend John DuBois. DuBois, dubious of Hughes's abilities, hired him as a gardener in exchange for tutoring to compensate for the gaps in his education. By 1820, DuBois had changed his mind, and Hughes was a regular member of the student body. He was ordained to the priesthood for service in the Diocese of Philadelphia on October 15, 1826, and worked there for several years. On January 7, 1838, he was appointed coadjutor, auxiliary bishop with the right of succession, to the Bishop of New York. That bishop was the same John DuBois who had admitted him to Mount Saint Mary's. Upon Du-Bois's death on December 20, 1842, Hughes automatically became bishop. When on July 19, 1850, the Diocese of New York was reconstituted an archdiocese, he was made its first archbishop. He held that position until his death on January 3, 1864. He is buried beneath Saint Patrick's Cathedral on New York City's Fifth Avenue, the construction of which he initiated.

In his position, Hughes had the opportunity to integrate a generation of immigrants into the United States. In 1820, the federal government began requiring ports to report on the number of passengers debarking. The statistics collected annually thereafter showed a steady stream of people, mostly from the British Isles. This was the easiest place to migrate *from*, as it was the United States' largest trading partner, with many ships going to the United States from London, Southampton, Liverpool, and Queenstown. The numbers of French, German, and Italian migrants were smaller, but if even a minority of the people who landed in New York City stayed there, the numbers would add up. There is no way to tell from the passenger lists how many people were Catholics. Respecting the separation of church and state, the United States never inquired into ship passengers' religion. However, scholars do know the established religions of the European states, and which were the popular religions, and can make inferences from these. England itself was a Protestant (Church of England) country. Scotland was also Protestant, although there were exceptions; James Gordon Bennett, a Scot who founded the *New York Herald*, was Catholic. Northern Germany, whence many early migrants came, sent mostly Protestants. Hughes, though, was aware from his work that there were Catholics in the mix.

The late 1840s and early 1850s saw a huge jump in Catholic migration. The reason was summed up in one phrase, the Irish potato famine. In back of that reason, though, was a complex situation. The entire island of Ireland was a British colony in the nineteenth century; the Republic of Ireland became independent in 1922. The British tried to control Ireland by removing any independent economic, political, or cultural base. As part of the effort to remove the economic base, tracts were given to people who supported the British crown, and the Irish were reduced to tenants who rented from the same landowners for whom they worked and had only a little time and space with which to raise food. Potatoes were almost the only crop that grew under these conditions. In 1845, and for several years thereafter, the potato crop was attacked by a virus that wiped out each year's yield. The landlords refused to use their own crops to feed their tenants, sending the food to English markets instead. The English refused to do more than permit voluntary charity to try to take care of the people. The result was an absolute loss of population. The 1841 census found 8,175,124 people in Ireland. In 1851 those tho took the census expected to find 9,018,799 but instead found only 6,552,385. The estimate was that 2.5 million died or fled for England, Canada, and the United States.[1] Most migrants to the United States in the early nineteenth century could make plans. Even the Hughes family, coming a generation earlier, had made plans, sending first the father, then some sons; finally, the one son who had stayed behind to tend the family's last crop escorted his mother and sisters to Chambersburg, Pennsylvania, the new home base. However, the famine Irish came fleeing disaster, with no plans and with no means to carry out any plans they may have made.

The colonization that contributed to the famine also contributed to the state of religion in Ireland. Most of the southern Irish were Catholics. One tactic used in the British conquest of Ireland was suppressing the local culture so that it could not be used as a basis of resistance to imperial rule. This meant outlawing the local language, Gaelic, and the local religion, Roman Catholicism. The result was that Catholicism meant a great deal to the Irish people, but they had little opportunity to practice it.

The Irish made the U.S. seacoast cities necessary—and possible. When they arrived in the United States, the cities were small. There was not enough housing for the immigrants, not enough water, not enough urban utilities. The immigrants provided them. They dug the Erie Canal that connected the Port of New York to the hinterland, making it the busiest port in the United States, and then they took jobs loading and unloading the ships. They paved the streets and laid the rails for the routes to the suburbs and built the houses there. When those who could afford to had moved out, the immigrants rented the remaining houses in the city. When they had filled those houses, they jammed second houses onto cramped city lots and erected buildings specially designed as multiple-family dwellings—the first tenements. They built the Croton Dam and laid the pipes that brought water to the thirsty, flammable city.

Americans cleared out to better neighborhoods as fast as the Irish moved in and took a dim view of their new compatriots. Their prejudices are preserved in the artifacts of popular culture. Popular theater featured comedy sketches of stereotypical Irish characters in unflattering situations. Newspapers and mass-circulation magazines ran pages of character sketches, cartoons, and jokes in barely readable dialect. Natives relied on Irish women for domestic service but routinely characterized them as unable to perform the simplest household tasks. Both sexes were supposed to drink to excess. Under the influence, the men might become amusingly boisterous, but the women became slovenly, and both sexes might become violent. The men were accused of corrupting politics. Even the average man was assumed to have become a citizen illegally and to vote only for those who promised him something in return. The men who were more heavily involved in politics were supposed to be routinely connecting votes and favors. Either they delivered their friends' votes to candidates who helped them renew their saloon liquor licenses, or they ran for office themselves and took kickbacks from buddies to whom they directed contracts for city services. Their religion had no dignity and no sense.

Antipathy to Irish Catholicism was linked to a more general anti-Catholicism. Americans thought of their heritage as being Protestant. During the 1820s, when Hughes was a young priest, revivals fostered by men such as **Lyman Beecher** and Charles Grandison Finney swept the Northeast. By the 1830s, the theological arguments were joined by riots by mobs who could not argue with Catholicism but who could demonstrate through action that they disapproved of it. From there, nativism became more political, with candidates running for office on anti-Catholic and anti-immigrant platforms. Political nativism reached a peak in the 1850s Know-Nothing movement.

Hughes first came to the attention of his superiors, and of the general public, as a defender of the faith. Even as a seminarian, he wrote letters to local editors who printed anti-Catholic articles. Late in 1829, when he was a guest preacher in New York, he came across a paper, *The Protestant*, devoted entirely to anti-Catholicism. He noted that most of what it printed were outright lies. He tried his hand at writing such lies himself and sent them to the editors under an assumed name. (He chose "Cramner," after Henry VIII's archbishop of Canterbury.) Soon, he was sending a steady supply of "news" regarding the Catholic takeover of Pennsylvania. He continued to send material until July 3, 1830, when he published an article in a Catholic newspaper revealing how he had tricked the nativists. Throughout his life, Hughes engaged in debates against Protestants, in the press and in person.

The topic of debate most pertinent here was the relation between religion and government. Contemporary historians see this matter differently than did antebellum Americans, stressing the Enlightenment origins and the political situation that gave rise to the First Amendment.[2] In the antebellum period, American Protestants traced religious liberty to their own branch of Christianity. American Catholics traced the American Revolution back to principles of natural law, which, they claimed, Catholics had preserved and developed so that eventually thinkers such as **Thomas Jefferson** could read them. Actually, the discussion seldom reached this level of scholarship.[3]

On January 29, 1836, he appeared on the debating platform with John C. Breckinridge. At the start, Breckinridge had all the advantages. He was well born; his father, also John C. Breckinridge, had been Thomas Jefferson's attorney general during 1805–1806. He was well educated, having graduated from Princeton. He had done something his age respected a great deal; after a conversion experience, he had abandoned his plans to study law and had entered the Presbyterian ministry. Hughes, though, could turn all of Breckinridge's advantages against him. At the first insult, Hughes complained that Breckinridge was no gentleman after all. When Breckinridge talked about how Protestantism always produced religious liberty, Hughes pointed out how Protestant England had denied the religious liberty of Catholic Ireland and how recently Protestants in Charlestown, Massachusetts, had deprived a convent full of Ursuline nuns of their religious liberty by burning down their house. In this case, Hughes either did not get or did not take the opportunity to outline the Catholic theory as to the origin of religious liberty. He did, though, make it clear that if American Protestants congratulated themselves on their invention of religious liberty, then they should make good on their boast by improving their treatment of Catholics.

When words wouldn't work, Hughes took action. On May 6, 1844, a confrontation between Protestants and Catholics in Kensington, outside of Philadelphia, escalated into a riot in which two parish churches and a convent were attacked. There was a rumor that a gang of Philadelphia Protestants was coming to New York. Hughes, then bishop of New York, published a warning to Catholics to stay away from public meetings. He also warned municipal authorities to take seriously their obligation to protect the property of all their citizens, including Catholics. "If a single Catholic Church is burned in New York," he wrote, referring to Napoleon's expedition into Russia, "the city will become a second Moscow." He followed that up with a visit to Mayor Robert Morris. New York City had recently had a mayoral election in which the winning candidate, James Harper, had received a large nativist vote. Hughes suggested Harper be called in to calm his nativist followers and do his share to keep order. Nothing happened—which was what Hughes wanted. It was by such tactics as defending his faith on every occasion that Hughes made it clear that Catholicism was going to be part of American life.

Part of American life, but Catholicism was also going to be itself. During the antebellum period, what sociologist E. Digby Balzell called the "Protestant establishment" was at its most established.[4] While city officials and private philanthropists couldn't control what people did in their own homes, they could control what people did when they had to be institutionalized. Private hospitals run by different denominations accepted Catholics as patients but prohibited their clergy from visiting them. Nor could priests visit city institutions such as hospitals, almshouses, or jails.

Hughes was most concerned about the public schools. Public schools had a Protestant flavor to them. The school day featured reading from the King James Version of Scripture, which had been authorized for use in the Church of England in 1611; it was not an ecumenical, let alone a Catholic, translation. Students were read passages of Scripture "without note or comment," that is, without an explanation as to what they meant. Evangelical Protestants assumed that as long as Scripture was in the listener's language, its commonsense meaning would shine through. Students learned Protestant hymns and recited Protestant versions of the Ten Commandments and the Lord's Prayer. Hughes had seen some of the textbooks and thought they were shot through with anti-Catholic bias.

In the early 1840s, Hughes thought he had an opportunity to do something about the situation. New York City didn't really have public schools. It taxed its people for public education, but turned the monies over to a philanthropy, called, confusingly, the Public School Society. This society set up schools that it claimed were nonsectarian. However, teachers read from the King James Bible, without note or comment. They used textbooks that characterized Catholics as intolerant torturers of heretics and Protestants as mild-mannered champions of freedom of conscience. In 1840, New York State Governor **William Henry Seward** suggested restoring the old system, at least to the point of giving tax money to Catholics for the education of their children.

Catholics themselves were divided on the issue. Seward was a Whig, and New York's Catholics were mostly Democrats. Was it worth changing parties to get a share of the tax money? Non-Catholic voters were largely against Seward's proposal. One, **Samuel F. B. Morse**, organized a party to run against it. In the 1841 election Morse's party fielded a slate of candidates who promised to bury Seward's proposal. On October 29, 1841, Hughes chaired a meeting that proposed its own slate of candidates, all of them expected to support Seward's proposal. Ten of Hughes's thirteen candidates had also been nominated to the Democratic ticket. Those were the only ten Democrats elected. Alerted by the election results that the public was unhappy with the system, the state legislature changed it. It abolished the connection with the Public School Society and set up truly public schools controlled by people who in turn answered to elected officials. The new system left to each school the task of determining how to handle religion. Hughes did not think this was enough protection. In response, he pressed for the development of a parochial school system.

Hughes supplemented the parochial school system by adding high schools and institutions of higher education. He invited religious institutes that specialized in education to staff institutions in New York. Thus, in 1846, the Society of Jesus came to staff Saint John's College, which grew into Fordham University. That same year, the Ladies of the Sacred Heart came to start institutions of higher education for elite young women. In

1853, the Christian Brothers arrived and started schools for poor and working-class young men.

While education was Hughes's paramount concern, he also interested himself in health care and social service. His sister Ellen entered the Sisters of Charity of Emmitsburg, Maryland, and became Mother Mary Angela in religious life. She was assigned to the Sisters of Charity's work in New York, where her brother was bishop. In 1846, she carried out the actual work of starting Saint Vincent's Hospital. That same year, Hughes precipitated a crisis among the Sisters of Charity. The sisters had informed him that their leadership in France wanted the American members to conform to the general rule that prohibited care of boys over a certain age. Hughes was upset about this news, as it meant he would have to find another religious order to care for orphaned boys. It must have also caused some division among the sisters. The result was that some of the Sisters of Charity left New York to remain with the main body of the community, whereas the group that remained in New York started a separate community. Later, in 1853, Hughes invited another order of women religious, the Sisters of Mercy, to come to the diocese to carry out their specialized ministries of caring for the poor, especially poor women, through teaching and institutional work.

Hughes's work was part of a larger process of developing a separate Catholic system of cradle-to-grave service. The cradle part, the New York Foundling Asylum, didn't open until after his death (in 1869). The orphanage, which took in children who were old enough to care for themselves and kept them until they were old enough to work, had been started before he arrived (by the Sisters of Charity in 1817). Hughes performed a major service by fostering education. Parochial schools, high schools, colleges, and universities touched more Catholics than any other institution, save parish churches. Later bishops could fill in the missing pieces, fostering the development of specialized institutions for the delinquent, handicapped, and elderly.

On the one hand, Hughes insisted that Catholics were equally American. On the other hand, his system of education and social services worked to keep them separate from other Americans. How to evaluate this combination? One can see how Hughes might be just what Catholicism needed at that point in time: someone to defend it from nativists and to protect its people from proselytization.

One could also take the same facts and apply the opposite interpretation, as did Catholic priest, sociologist, and novelist Andrew M. Greeley. "At precisely the time when the crises of the immigration experience were most severe, Hughes's influence can only be considered a major disaster."[5] Greeley pointed out that earlier American bishops had been more open to American influences. Catholicism had always interacted with the culture around it; they wanted it to interact with the new culture developing in the United

States. They wanted to emphasize the freedom of conscience of individuals within Catholicism and also to permit people some choice in those who held office over them. They advocated worship services that reflected the worshippers' culture (at that time, Catholics used Latin for public worship and for most of the rituals involved in administering the sacraments). For later generations of Catholic historians, especially for those who were interested in the Second Vatican Council, these bishops were pioneers, and Hughes was the one who brought their pioneering to an end.

Greeley was most concerned with what Hughes had done to Catholicism, erasing other bishops' influences and replacing them with "[t]his self-image of the bishop as father and protector of a flock not able to care for itself and surrounded by hostile enemies" that "was to persist in the Church for at least a century after Hughes's death."[6] Historian John Tracy Ellis noticed that more than a century after Hughes launched his effort to build educational institutions for them, Catholics lagged behind members of other religious groups in entry into the learned professions and into the top levels of American business.[7] Ellis's findings, originally delivered as a speech in 1955, opened up a flood of complaints. The separatist system left Catholics at a disadvantage vis-à-vis other Americans. It retarded their entry into the fullness of public life. It insulated them from the world and also prevented them from having any effect on it. It appeared to give some validity to the complaints of the anti-Catholics still around in the 1950s.[8]

Historian David O'Brien suggests Hughes's separatism was not all that thorough.[9] Jay P. Dolan has shown how New York's Catholics were rather like other Americans in staying away from the extremes of social reform.[10] Hughes erected a separate educational system, but the system did not always and everywhere teach subjects or values that were that much different from those of the surrounding society. To use the sociological terms of Milton M. Gordon, who established a vocabulary for discussing the assimilation of immigrants and ethnoreligious minority groups, Catholics did not undergo *structural assimilation*, in which many of them entered into the "cliques, clubs, and institutions of [the] host society, on [a] primary group level." Rather, Catholics created a system of *parallel structuralism*, whereby they and the host society each had separate but similar institutions: Both had schools, hospitals, and so on. However, Catholics did undergo *cultural or behavioral assimilation*, adapting specific cultural patterns of the host society; their schools conveyed much the same information as other schools; and their hospitals treated patients according to the same theories of medicine as other hospitals.[11]

Hughes's most recent biographer, Richard J. Shaw, thought Hughes's attitude toward immigration and assimilation came through most clearly in Hughes's treatment of minority Catholics. During Hughes's administration, Germans formed the largest linguistic minority in his diocese. They had practical reasons for wishing to have German clergy: They needed priests whose sermons they could understand and who could in turn understand them. Over and above this practical issues, though, there was a value system. Catholicism was something Germans had brought from their home country. If they changed any aspect of it, they would lose it. They were so devoted to the idea that they had to preserve their faith in its original form that they were willing to alter another aspect of that faith, the acceptance of episcopal authority. German parishes challenged Hughes's claim to control church property. Hughes in turn insisted the Germans accept his leadership. The conflict between Hughes and the Germans in his care had consequences for Catholic history. It also had ramifications for immigrant history: "As a naturalized citizen sensitive to the word 'foreigner,' Hughes constantly preached upon the need of the citizens 'by choice' to make themselves patriotic Americans. Because assimilation into the mainstream of life in the United States meant so much to Hughes, he balked at what he felt would be regression into a cultural ghetto."[12] He insisted the Germans become more like the Irish, setting a precedent for how religions cared for multiple groups that claimed the same faith but came from different linguistic and cultural backgrounds.

Hughes was not much more supportive of his own Irish ethnic group. During his episcopacy, U.S. bishops debated the wisdom of resettling Irish immigrants in ethnic enclaves on the frontier. The prelates thought that pioneer Irish would fare better economically, because they would be landowners and farmers rather than renters and wage earners, and also that they would preserve their culture and faith isolated from the secular and Protestant influences of the city. Hughes denied the frontier provided better opportunities either for economic well-being or for the preservation of the faith. Similarly, Hughes held aloof from Irish nationalist movements in his day. During the 1840s, Irish voters rallied to Daniel O'Connell, who ran for Parliament on a platform of altering laws to benefit Ireland; Hughes thought this was wishful thinking. It turned out Hughes was right that Parliament did not provide much legislative relief for Ireland, and by the 1860s, some Irish had changed tactics. The Fenian movement argued that the Irish should fight for what the British would not give. Hughes condemned such a violent approach.

One could also point to Hughes's support of the Civil War. As soon as war broke out, he began to fly the American flag from the steeple of Saint Patrick's Cathedral which was then located in New York's immigrant quarter. Hughes urged his people to volunteer for the armed forces and to accept conscription. He hoped to stress their American patriotism in doing so. At that time, people could volunteer for the armed forces in groups. People of the same ethnic group signed up together and formed their own units. Hughes preferred to use numbers or letters to refer to the units, for, what with "Irish brigades, German brigades, Scotch brigades [and] Garibaldian [Italian] brigades in our army, there will be trouble among the troops even before the enemy comes in sight."[13] Hughes also supported the Union effort in a more personal way. President Abraham Lincoln appointed him an unofficial representative to Europe. From October 1861 to August 1862, he traveled to Paris, Rome, and Ireland (and was willing to go to Saint Petersburg, then the capital of czarist Russia) as a goodwill ambassador presenting the Union's cause to people who might be lukewarm toward it. Catholicism taught subordination to proper authority, and to Hughes, the Civil War was a case of insubordination: Confederates refused to recognize the results of a constitutionally conducted presidential election.

Finally, one could point to Hughes's attitude toward slavery. Catholicism had little to say about slavery as it was practiced in the antebellum United States; the clearest statement was Pope Gregory XIV's 1838 criticism of the international slave trade of his day. Hughes did, though, have personal experience with slavery. One condition for his acceptance at Mount Saint Mary's was that he oversee the seminary's slaves. He didn't care for the work and even wrote some antislavery poetry. Later, he made the acquaintance of William Rodrigue, an architect who became his brother-in-law by marrying his sister Margaret. Rodrigue had survived slave revolts in Santo Domingo, and his stories tipped Hughes's sympathy toward slaveholders. Hughes had personal ties to Catholic bishops in the slaveholding South. He had one personal tie to the antislavery forces; he was friends with New York's antislavery politician, the same William Henry Seward who championed tax dollars for Catholic schools. Mostly, though, Hughes was suspicious of the antislavery forces. Reformers interested in antislavery were Protestants who tended to be interested in temperance, nativism, and anti-Catholicism as well.

When the Civil War came, the small amount of Catholic teaching on the subject was no match for Hughes's personal experience. He warned the government, "The Catholics so far as I know, whether of native or foreign birth are willing to fight to the death for the support of the constitution, the Government, and the laws of the country. But if it should be understood that, with or without knowing it, they are to fight for the abolition of slavery, then, indeed, they will turn away in disgust from the discharge of what would otherwise be a patriotic duty."[14]

Slavery and Civil War could not be kept separate for long. Blacks themselves took advantage of the situation, escaping to Union lines. Lincoln's supporters pointed out the advantages of denying Confederates their labor force and of swelling the Union army by accepting blacks for military service. Lincoln himself may have seen an opportunity to do well by doing good. On September 22, 1862, Lincoln used his power as commander in chief of the armed forces to announce the emancipation of the rebels' slaves. Critics have pointed out that such a proclamation freed no one. However, the document convinced the Irish Catholics of New York.

During the first half of 1863, the war went badly for the Union. The

Army of the Potomac was in some ways a showcase army. Journalists could follow it easily and then use the new telegraphs to send reports to their papers. Lincoln went through general after general, and most of them lost. High numbers of wounded and dead made even victories seem to be losses. The Union won at Gettsyburg during the first few days of July 1863, but at the cost of three days of fighting and 25,000 casualties.

People ceased volunteering to be slaughtered. As Hughes had predicted, the issuance of the Emancipation Proclamation depressed volunteering still more. Federal authorities then began to draft young men. In New York, the city was divided into districts. Each district registered every man of the proper age residing within the area, then held a lottery. Those whose names were drawn did not have to serve personally; they could pay $300 for a substitute. But $300 was more than most Irish Catholic working men could afford.

The lottery began on Saturday, July 11. Sunday was a day of rest and a day when some men laid plans. On Monday, July 13, small mobs began to gather and then to converge. First, they halted the draft lottery. They cut the telegraph wires to the police station, thus slowing response time. Then they began to attack everything that represented anyone who seemed to be getting something out of the Civil War. The homes of the wealthy—symbols of those who could buy substitutes—were ransacked. The *Tribune*, whose editor, Horace Greeley, had advocated emancipation, was besieged. Businesses that stood to make money out of the war—Brooks Brothers had a commission to supply uniforms—were vandalized. Attendants at an orphanage for black children hustled their charges out as rioters burned the building to the ground. Individual blacks were hunted down and lynched, an atrocity which for generations afterward was held up as proof of the racism of the Irish Catholic urban working class. The gangs dissipated in the evening, only to reassemble the next day.

Horace Greeley asked in his editorial columns: Where was the shepherd while the flock was proving itself to be wolves in sheep's clothing? Hughes was at home, suffering from several chronic physical ailments. Most seriously, he could not stand for long. Just before the riots started, he had tried to say mass and had been unable to remain standing; thereafter he contented himself with attending his secretary's mass. It was not just the illness that slowed him down. He thought Greeley's suggestion out of line. As he had said when the riots were directed against Catholics, keeping the peace was the city's job, not his.

The riot had already begun to wind down when Hughes agreed to give peacekeeping a try. On Thursday, July 16, he had posters distributed announcing that he would speak at his home at two o'clock in the afternoon the next day. About 5,000 people came. Looking out at them from the seat on his balcony, Hughes remarked that "I cannot see a rioter's face among you." Probably not. If they had been rioting, they were not now. Their energy for that was spent. Besides, they were in the presence of their long-time and respected archbishop. And it was clear that he was an old man with only a little time before his day's—his life's—energy gave out. He spoke for about an hour, then went inside. His audience cheered until he reappeared. He gave his blessing, then went back in. They went home.

For years afterward, the draft riot was a byword for the city, an example of how easily the impoverished Irish Catholic working class could get out of control. Historians have made great strides in pointing out the context in which the Irish acted. The rioters were caught between two forces that they saw as linked. The wealthy, Anglo-Saxon Protestant Republican reformers of New York had overlooked the city's own crying needs and had given their sympathies to slaves. Now, through the instrument of war, they were going to free the slaves, raise them up in status, and make it possible for them to migrate throughout the nation, competing for jobs. Who was going to do the actual fighting and dying in this war? The same overlooked poor Irish Catholic worker. To outsiders, Hughes might be a big fish in the little pond of American Catholicism, but to the urban, working-class Irish, he was a champion.

Hughes set the pattern for the method of assimilation that, allusions to melting pots notwithstanding, immigrants actually used. His separate institutions preserved a group identity. It was a group identity that complemented, rather than competed with, the general American identity. Within the walls of their different institutions, each different group of Americans behaved pretty much alike. The combination of group identity and shared values had ramifications outside religion. In their classic study of urban ethnic politics, *Beyond the Melting Pot*, **Nathan Glazer** and **Daniel Patrick Moynihan** made the point that ethnic groups "melted" only so far and that urban politics really consisted of organizing voters into blocs of sufficient size as to be powerful, which generally meant along ethnoreligious lines. Through their voting blocs, each group could protect its own interests, and because the groups did, after all, adhere to the same rules of the political game, each would understand the necessity for respecting others' interests.[15]

Hughes performed one final service. He set a high standard for discussing the process of assimilation. He placed his greatest emphasis on working out the truly difficult issue of assimilation as it related to religion, which he valued above national loyalties. If one is going to end up with the reputation for pigheaded combativeness that John Hughes had, one had better be arguing about the most important thing in one's life.

NOTES

1. Cecil Woodham-Smith, *The Great Hunger* (New York: E. P. Dutton, 1980), pp. 411–412.

2. For a recent examination of the history of liberty of conscience, see Leonard

W. Levy, *The Establishment Clause: Religion and the First Amendment* (New York: Macmillan, 1986).

3. The major exception came in 1848–1849, when revolutionaries in Italy temporarily overthrew papal power and launched a short-lived republic. Sandra Yocum Mize considers Hughes among the prominent Catholic writers in "Defending Roman Loyalties and Republican Values: The 1848 Italian Revolution in American Catholic Apologetics," *Church History* 40:4 (April 1991), pp. 480–492.

4. E. Digby Balzell, *The Protestant Establishment: Aristocracy and Caste in America* (New York: Vintage Press, 1964).

5. Andrew M. Greeley, *The Catholic Experience* (Garden City, NY: Doubleday, 1969), p. 103.

6. Ibid., p. 107.

7. John Tracy Ellis, *American Catholics and the Intellectual Life* (Chicago: Heritage Foundation, 1956).

8. One can get a sense of the debate from Thomas F. O'Dea, *American Catholic Dilemma*, with an introduction by Gustave Weigel, S.J. (New York: New American Library, 1958).

9. David J. O'Brien, "John Hughes and the Formation of the Ante-Bellum American Catholic Church" (paper delivered at the American Catholic Historical Association meeting in conjunction with the American Historical Association meeting, New York, January 4, 1997).

10. Jay P. Dolan, *The Immigrant Church: New York's Irish and German Catholics, 1815–1865*, foreword by Martin E. Marty (Baltimore, MD: Johns Hopkins University Press, 1975), pp. 121–140.

11. Milton M. Gordon, *Assimilation in American Life: The Role of Race, Religion, and National Origins* (New York: Oxford University Press, 1964), pp. 71, 159. One should note that one will find Catholics who deny having adopted the mores of the surrounding society.

12. Richard Shaw, *Dagger John: The Unquiet Life and Times of Archbishop John Hughes of New York* (New York: Paulist Press, 1977), pp. 178–179. For Hughes's relations with Italian immigrants, see Silvano Tomasi, *Piety and Power: The Role of Italian Parishes in the New York Metropolitan Area* (New York: Center for Migration Studies, 1975), pp. 63–71.

13. Hughes to William Henry Seward, New York, September 12, 1861, cited in John R. G. Hassard, *Life of the Most Reverend John Hughes, D.D., First Archbishop of New York* (New York: D. Appleton and Co., 1866), p. 443.

14. John Hughes to Simon Cameron, New York, October 15, 1861, cited in ibid., p. 437.

15. Nathan Glazer and Daniel Patrick Moynihan, *Beyond the Melting Pot: The Negroes, Puerto Ricans, Jews, Italians, and Irish of New York City* (Cambridge, MA: MIT Press, 1970).

BIBLIOGRAPHY

The archives of the Archdiocese of New York at Saint Joseph's Seminary, Dunwoodie, Yonkers, New York, has material from Hughes, and the Catholic University of America has microfilm. One biography, with documents reproduced, appeared shortly after Hughes's death: John R. G. Hassard, *Life of the Most Reverend John Hughes, D.D., First Archbishop of New York* (New York: D. Appleton and Co., 1866). A modern biography is Richard Shaw, *Dagger John: The Unquiet Life and Times of Archbishop John Hughes of New York* (New York: Paulist Press, 1977). Biographical sketches of Hughes appeared in Andrew M. Greeley, *The Catholic Experience* (Garden City, NY: Doubleday, 1969), pp. 102–126; and in Charles R. Morris, *American Catholics: The Saints and Sinners Who Built America's Most Powerful Church* (New York: Times Books, 1997). For Hughes and Ireland, see Charles P. Connor, "Archbishop Hughes and the Question of Ireland, 1829–1862," American Catholic Historical Society of Philadelphia *Records and Studies* 95 (March–December 1984), pp. 15–26. For his conflict with the Public School Society, see Michael F. Perko, "Two Bishops, the Bible, and the Schools: An Exercise in Differential Biography," *Vitae Scholasticae* 3:1 (1984), pp. 61–93; and Diane Ravitch, *The Great School Wars, New York City, 1805–1973: A History of the Public Schools as Battlefields of Social Change* (New York: Basic Books, 1974), pp. 3–76. For the intersection between the values of capitalism and Catholicism, see Joseph P. Chinnici, "Spiritual Capitalism and the Culture of American Catholicism," *U.S. Catholic Historian* V:2 (1986), pp. 131–161. Hughes's involvement in Civil War diplomacy is in Bruce Steiner, "The Prelate and the Politicians: Archbishop John Hughes, William Henry Seward and Thurlow Weed," *The Annual Collection of Essays in History* (Charlottesville: University of Virginia Corcoran Department of History, Winter 1957), pp. 5–34. Although Hughes plays no major role in this account, a useful narrative and analysis of the New York City draft riot is Adrian Cook, *Armies of the Streets: The New York City Draft Riots of 1863* (Lexington: University Press of Kentucky, 1974). Hughes has a cameo appearance in Peter Quinn's historical novel *Banished Children of Eve* (New York: Viking, 1994). The story characterizes him as a man of fierce pride but seems too optimistic about his health in the summer of 1863.

DENIS KEARNEY
(1847–1907)

"The Chinese Must Go!"

Open a survey of Chinese-American or California history to the index, and one will probably find "Kearney, Denis," or "Dennis," followed by one reference. Go to that reference, and one will probably find out that Kearney spearheaded a campaign that ultimately led to the 1882 Chinese Exclusion Act. The ubiquity of this information is matched by the paucity of any other. There is no modern biography of Kearney, and the one biography that ever was in book form consisted of 3 pages in a 100-page political pamphlet, with one of those pages being devoted to a picture of him.

Yet Kearney shaped the U.S. debate on immigration in numerous ways. He shifted the debate geographically, moving it from the East Coast and Old Northwest to the West Coast, from a discussion of Irish and German migration to a discussion of Chinese migration. Being Irish himself, he changed the sides in the debate from natives versus immigrants to one group of immigrants versus another. He was the first since the debate over the importation of slaves to raise the issue of immigrants of different races. To get across his viewpoint, Kearney had to involve himself in other issues. He had to break up the regular two-party sytem and to convince voters to support a third party, the Workingmen's Party of California (WPC). He had to organize his party so that it followed his guidance and not that of rival would-be leaders. And then he had to be on the winning side in a series of other conflicts: the power of the state legislature versus that of a constitutional convention, state power versus federal power, and the power of one country against another.

Denis Kearney was born in Oakmont, County Cork, Ireland, on February 1, 1847. He was the second of seven boys in a family so poor that they did not send him to school. Then the family situation worsened. When Denis was eleven years old, his father died. His mother sent him to sea to earn his living. At some point early in his career, he began to work under the American flag. He worked his way up from cabin boy to first officer. He sailed into San Francisco in 1868 as first officer aboard a coastal steamer, the *Shooting Star*, decided to make the city his home base, and took a job with Messrs. Holladay and Brennan, a steamship firm. In 1870 he married a Miss Mary Ann Leary, by whom he eventually had four children. In 1872, he gave up seafaring and purchased a dray business. A dray was a low wagon, without sides, used for heavy loads such as full beer barrels. He eventually acquired three drays and hired others to help do all the hauling that came his way.[1]

Since some might consider him an entrepreneur, it is worth emphasizing that Kearney called himself a workingman. Nor was he unusual in this. Those who worked with him in the Workingmen's Party of California had similar backgrounds. Frank Roney was born in Ireland and had been active in Irish trade unions and in the movement to liberate Ireland from England; he migrated to the United States when he was threatened with arrest and execution in Ireland. William Wellock, second vice president of the Workingmen's Party of California, was born in England and apprenticed to a boot and shoemaker; he immigrated to the United States in 1872 and to California in 1876. Henry M. Moore, the party secretary, was born in New York State, apprenticed to a tailor, and later became a lawyer. Thomas Donnelly was born in County Tyrone in 1848 and emigrated in 1857; at the time he was involved in Workingmen politics he was in the coal business. Lawyer Clitus Barbour was the son of Irish, German, and Welsh immigrants, although he himself was born in Illinois. Also a lawyer was Charles J. Beerstecher, who was born in Urach, Württemberg, Germany, and came to the United States when his father's involvement in '48er politics meant the family had to leave the country. Grocer John P. Dunn was born in County Cavan, Ireland, but raised in the United States.[2] Critics charged that the adoption of the workingman identity was politically motivated; Kearney attracted voters by claiming, falsely, to be one of them.

Political opportunity does not seem to have been Kearney's reason for calling himself a workingman. Kearney was involved in the Draymen and Teamster's Union. The business he owned was the Irish immigrant equivalent of the stereotypical Chinese laundry, a business that did not require a great deal of capital to start or a great deal of skill to operate. Kearney truly relied on his own labor. He inherited nothing from his family and apparently did not marry into wealth. And he would work for a long, long time to support himself, as he had no retirement earnings. In fact, critics charged that Kearney's interest in politics stemmed from a failed effort to enhance his own earnings; some people claimed he invested his savings in the stock market and lost all.[3] In short, even though he owned his own business, Kearney's life was as insecure as it would have been had he worked for wages, and in that sense he was a workingman.

Work, though, whether in one's own business or for wages, was not the core of self-definition for Kearney and his colleagues. Their pamphlets explained why they were "real" workingmen and the Chinese, who seemed equally industrious, were not:

The intelligent American laborer in seeking employment in California, for the purpose of providing for his wife and children the necessary raiment for covering their nakedness, food for their mouths, and education enough to enable them to successfully fight the battle of life after him, contends with a race who know nothing of these necessities in their lives, who live upon the very refuse of the land, and who make this very absence of responsibilities and the low depravity of their own lives the means of successfully underbidding the labor of our own people.[4]

For the "intelligent" workingmen, work was not an end to itself but a means to an end. It was the way to earn money to achieve middle-class status, measured by the acquisition of comforts for one's self and by one's ability to secure more education and more options in terms of careers and professions for one's offspring. Ironically, the workingmen resembled the Chinese more closely than they knew; it was just that the Chinese had their families back home in China, where the overall cost of living, and their own families' standard of living, was indeed lower. Rather than reach across the races, though, and form one large union, Kearney and his associates turned to familiar and traditional tools, to their trade unions and to politics, to preserve their status in society.

The conditions that led Kearney into politics started in 1873. That year, the New York Stock Exchange collapsed, partly because financier Jay Gould tried to corner the gold market and drove up prices with his purchases. When the stock market crashed, investors held on to their money until more secure investments presented themselves. That meant that businesses couldn't get the capital to start up or to expand, and thus they couldn't hire new workers. Businesses that depended on other businesses' expansion, such as forges that turned out steel for railroads, had to lay off their workers. There was no safety net for these workers, no unemployment insurance. What saved the situation for a while was that the same year the stock market crashed, the Comstock Lode silver vein was discovered in

Nevada. For a few years, renewed mining opportunities drew more people west. By 1877, the West was sharing in the depression that ground on year after year. In January of that year, the Comstock Lode missed paying a dividend to its stockholders. Its stock slipped. The stock market sank, and the economy started to unwind: no business expansion, no new jobs; soon, the existing jobs disappeared, too.

Unemployment was not an either/or situation. During the good weather, men fanned out across California. Periods of employment planting a crop or filling in on a railroad gang alternated with periods of tramping to the next possible work site. As the weather turned bad, workers began to drift, like autumn leaves falling off a tree, down the hills and into San Francisco. They competed against each other for jobs that were only as numerous as the city's normal population. Consistent losers sank into hunger and homelessness. Winners lived from job to job, working a few days here and there, eating from day to day and paying the rent nightly or weekly. The semi-employed filled up any spare space in the city, presenting an opportunity for more settled families to make fast money by taking in a boarder or lodger. They spent their time together, sharing information on job possibilities, spending money when they had it, discussing what it was that had brought them to this condition.

The Workingmen's Party of the United States put forth one attractive theory. This party had been formed a year earlier on the East Coast. Its members had previously been involved in the First Internationale, Marxism, and other socialist groups. However, it would be premature to see the Workingmen as equivalent to the Communist Party of the twentieth century. The most communistlike thing that could be said about them was that they thought that the government was stacked against the workers. They parted with the communists in that they thought it was still possible to use the political system to restack the government in favor of the workers. The next summer, the Workingmen's Party became interested in a labor-state conflict taking place in Pittsburgh. On July 16, 1877, the Baltimore and Ohio railroad announced a 10 percent wage cut. Baltimore and Ohio workers at Martinsburg, West Virginia, responded by halting railroad traffic through their town. The Baltimore and Ohio managers asked the governor of West Virginia for assistance, and the governor called out the state militia. When state troops proved ineffective, and the strike spread to other cities, President Rutherford B. Hayes authorized the use of the United States Army. Truly, the government seemed to favor the railroad over the workers.

On July 23, some people who were interested in starting a San Francisco unit of the Workingmen's Party of the United States called an open-air meeting to show support for the Baltimore and Ohio workers. About 6,000 people came to the meeting.[5] The meeting was held near city hall at a sandlot, a tract cleared for construction and covered with sand until a building could be erected on it. Speeches about the Baltimore and Ohio workers, even speeches about the dangers of capital and a capitalist-dominated government, that could apply more directly to the San Franciscans, were insufficiently compelling. Groups hived off from the audience and went marauding in nearby Chinatown. On July 23, they attacked Chinese laundry rooms. The next night, they set fires and murdered Chinese before the police intervened. The third night, they set fire to a lumberyard near the docks of the Pacific Mail Steamship Company, which transported many Chinese to California. Apparently, the rioters were attempting to burn down the docks. When firefighters arrived, the arsonists tried to prevent them from doing their work, and the result was a riot in which several men were killed.

City officials regained control with the aid of a volunteer, an entrepreneur who had helped out in previous anti-Chinese violence, William T. Coleman. Coleman formed a Vigilance Committee to patrol the streets for several weeks to discourage rioting. He also prepared a report on the causes of the riot and made suggestions for preventing another one. His chief proposal was that the federal government seek to amend the Burlingame Treaty with China so as to exclude Chinese immigration to the United States. Coleman's report came out the day before the state elections scheduled for early September. The effect was to give the voters a new task to impose on their elected officials. It was at this point that Kearney burst upon the scene. As Kearney later explained:

In September, 1877, immediately after the general State, municipal and congressional elections, I called a meeting of working men and others to discuss publicly the propriety of permanently organizing for the purpose of holding the politicians up to the pledges made before the election. . . . I made up my mind that if our civilization—California civilization—was to continue, Chinese immigration must be stopped, and I saw in the people the power to enforce that "must." Hence the meeting. This meeting resolved itself into a permanent organization, and "resoluted" in favour of a "red-hot" agitation. I was, in spite of my earnest protests, elected president of this new organization, with instructions from the meeting to "push the organization" throughout the city and state without delay. Our aim was to press Congress to take action against the Chinese at its next sitting.[6]

On August 18, 1877, the nucleus of the San Francisco branch of the Workingmen's Party held a small meeting at Charter and Oak Hall. They announced a platform party members were dedicated to promoting. Its key features were abolishing assessments on candidates for office, holding state and local officials accountable for their action, establishing a bureau of labor statistics, regulating the hours of labor, and pressing the state legislature to create a convention on labor with its headquarters at San Francisco. On Sunday, September 16, the leaders called a meeting for the sandlot by city hall in order to appeal to the masses and attracted about 500 people. Considering the meeting reasonably successful, the leaders called a second meeting for Friday, September 21. At this meeting, Kearney changed the direction of the entire political movement by making racism a reasonable response to capitalist exploitation, claiming that "the capitalists who employ Chinese are robbing the working people with their system."[7]

On October 4, word reached San Francisco that a group of Chinese at Rocklin had murdered a group of whites. Kearney used the resulting spike in the anti-Chinese fever to call a meeting for Dashaway Hall for October 5. He led the audience in forming a Workingmen's Party of California. Its first party platform plank showed its affinity for the Workingmen's Party of the United States, proposing "to wrest the government from the hands of the rich and place it in the hands of the people where it naturally belongs." The second plank added a specifically California twist: "We propose to rid the country of cheap Chinese labor as soon as possible, and by all the means in our power, because it tends still more to degrade labor and aggrandize capital."[8]

The Workingmen's Party embarked on a series of open-air meetings. Critics complained that the choice of the open-air format indicated that Kearney was nothing more than a demagogue attracting unemployed loiterers. Kearney replied: "It was only when the city authorities, who while persecuting us, either hired all of the halls or frightened their owners or lessees into not allowing us to hire them, that we were driven to the Sand Lots."[9] When Kearney's claim is balanced against the actual meeting record, a pattern appears that indicates the secret of his success. Others vying for party leadership often met indoors, hiring a variety of halls. Kearney, though, excelled at sandlot addresses, dominated the open-air meetings, and sometimes used the crowds he mobilized there to back him in getting the other would-be leaders to agree to do things his way.

During the month of October, the Workingmen's Party of California became the talk of San Francisco and the specter that haunted the city's officials. On Sunday, October 7, a sandlot meeting attracted 4,000, eight times the number that came in mid-September. By the end of the month, the mob had moved off the sandlots and closer to the homes and offices of the well-to-do and the entrepreneurs. On Monday, October 29, Kearney addressed a crowd at the city's Nob Hill. Kearney himself later complained that the newspapers distorted his speeches, but in this case, parts of the speech were reprinted in a Workingmen's Party of California pamphlet, and one can see that it was replete with slurs upon the Chinese and with reminders of previous acts of violence visited upon capitalists who oppressed the workers. On November 1, All Saints' Day for himself and his many Irish Catholic followers, he addressed another crowd at the Irish-American Hall. Kearney's remarks were not recorded, but the officials either heard it or heard about it. On November 3, they issued a warrant for his arrest for "using language tending to incite his hearers to deeds of violence." Bringing the warrant with them, the police found Kearney speaking at a street-corner meeting and carried him off in midsentence.[10]

Instead of solving their problems, the city officials created a martyr. On November 14, officials had to release Kearney because the ordinance under which the arrest warrants were issued was ruled illegal. They immediately rearrested him under a different charge, inciting a riot. A judge heard the case November 15–21 and acquitted Kearney on the grounds that there had in fact been no riot following Kearney's address. On January 9, 1878, Kearney was arrested a third time, for violating a new law, another attempt to ban language tending to incite public disorder. This time the case went to a jury, which, on January 22, found Kearney not guilty. Each time he was cleared, it was an occasion for celebration and for attracting new adherents to the Workingmen's Party of California.[11]

The appearance of one third party encouraged yet another, the Grangers, who found support in rural California. The Grangers also criticized the regular politicians and parties for being in the pay of the corporations. Railroads, the Grangers complained, charged farmers more for hauling their produce than they charged the big corporations for hauling their larger shipments of industrial goods. Grain elevator owners similarly gave price breaks to big customers and gouged the small ones. Banks lent money at low interest to big industries but charged high rates to farmers. If the Workingmen and Grangers could get together and discuss their economic programs, perhaps they could unite and form a stronger party movement that would benefit them both.

During the 1875–1876 legislative session, the state legislature had decided to have voters elect delegates to a convention to write a new state constitution. California was operating under a constitution drafted in 1849. The Civil War and its attendant constitutional amendments, state population growth, the completion of the transcontinental railroad, and the development of the economy made a new one desirable. The legislature's action was a boon for the Workingmen and the Grangers, giving both a chance to guide public policy. At this point, the Workingmen's Party of California had to organize itself so as to create a united front at the California constitutional convention and to ally itself with the Grangers so that the two groups could dominate the convention. However, efforts to create unity nearly broke down over Kearney's insistence on retaining power.

By early 1878, Kearney had a serious rival for power in the Workingmen's Party of California, Frank Roney. Roney wanted an organization that reflected his experience in Ireland and in San Francisco. He proposed that the Workingmen's Party structure itself by creating a statewide central committee composed of five representatives from each senatorial district and one from each trade union in the state. This, he thought, would strike a balance between competing goods: allowing the diverse voices in the party to be heard and their various interests to be aired and securing leadership from experienced, competent people who could choose among themselves who would run for available political offices. Kearney objected that all Roney's plans simply guaranteed more politics as usual. The district and trade union representatives would be more interested in their positions, and in the lucrative bribes and kickbacks industries routinely offered political leaders, than they would be in representing their constituents. Kearney proposed that no one already an officer in the party should accept a position as a candidate for office. Kearney won, mostly on the strength of his superior skills at rousing oratory and ad hoc leadership; he would speak at a local political meeting, give a speech, and the next thing Roney knew, his experienced and competent leaders were being dumped for putting their personal advancement above party concerns and were being replaced with leadership loyal to Kearney. Maybe Roney's system of carefully building a disciplined party whose leadership represented diverse views would have prevailed, but time was too short for him to fight back. Roney was so thoroughly routed that he abandoned his political efforts and left the city.

Why was it so important to Kearney to dominate the Workingmen's Party of California? Perhaps he was simply power hungry. But there is another possible explanation, and that is that Kearney did not trust anyone else to give the same priority to anti-Chinese legislation that he did. People like Roney would be too willing to work with the Grangers on general economic issues and would not press for anti-Chinese laws. Support for this view comes from a look at the constitution the delegates drafted in September 1878.

Rather than cooperation between the Grangers and the Workingmen's Party of California on legislation important to both, there was a division. The economic laws written into California's constitution were of particular concern to the Grangers. The Grangers thought government was corrupt, and they tried to prevent such corruption by putting elected officials on short leashes, by limiting the state legislature to enacting laws that carried out priorities set in the constitution, and by making it a felony to attempt to bribe a state official. The Grangers distrusted big business even more than big government and so introduced regulations for the stock market, the telegraph business, the gas business, the water business, and the railroad and established in the constitution the principle that the government could legislate to prevent corporations from conducting business in such a way as to infringe on public welfare. Finally, the Grangers thought the previous constitution distributed the tax burden unfairly and so legislated a different system, authorizing a state study of property holdings for tax purposes, taxing uncultivated land (which corporations had been holding as investments), and authorizing the state to levy an income, in addition to a real estate, tax.

The Workingmen got their anti-Chinese legislation. Their program was spelled out in the four sections of Article XIX. Section 1 was directed at immigrants generally. It listed the categories of immigrants for which the state could enact legislation and described the kinds of things the state could do. The second section spoke directly to the Workingmen's most pressing concern, job competition:

No corporation now existing or hereafter formed under the laws of this State shall, after the adoption of this Constitution, employ, directly or indirectly, in any capacity, any Chinese or Mongolian. The Legislature shall pass such laws as may be necessary to enforce this provision.

Section 3 also discussed job competition, this time in the public sector: "No Chinese shall be employed on any State, County, municipal, or other public work, except in punishment for crime." Section 4 indicated that the Workingmen's anti-Chinese sentiment drew strength from racism as well as from economic concerns:

The presence of foreigners ineligible to become citizens of the United States is declared to be dangerous to the well being of the State, and the Legislature shall discourage their immigration by all means within its power. Asiatic coolieism is a form of human slavery, and is forever prohibited in this State; and all contracts for coolie labor shall be void. All companies or corporations, whether formed in this country or any foreign country, for the importation of such labor, shall be subject to such penalties as the Legislature may prescribe. The Legislature shall delegate all necessary power to the incorporated cities and towns of this State for the removal of Chinese without the limits of such cities and towns, or for their location within prescribed portions of those limits; and it shall also provide the necessary legislation to prohibit the introduction into this State of Chinese after the adoption of this Constitution. This section shall be enforced by appropriate legislation.[12]

Upon completion of its work, the convention called for a statewide referendum to ratify or reject the drafted constitution. The ratified constitution became California's fundamental law in 1879. Almost immediately, the state constitution came into conflict with the federal Constitution. Pursuant to Article XIX, Section 2, the 1879–1880 California state legislature made it a misdemeanor for a corporation to employ Chinese. The Sulphur Bank Quicksilver Mining Company challenged the law. The case went to the Supreme Court, which ruled that Article XIX was an unconstitutional violation of the recently (1868) ratified Fourteenth Amendment to the federal Constitution, which guaranteed equal protection under the law.[13]

Thus, all the anti-Chinese provisions that the Workingmen's Party of California had managed to have added to the California state constitution became null and void. In response, the party became even more thoroughly anti-Chinese. Frank Roney, for example, had earlier had his doubts about the party's anti-Chinese thrust. According to Roney, when the anti-Chinese issue first took over San Francisco politics, "[I] agreed to sail under the flag so emblazoned in order that I might in time have other and real subjects considered by the people, which I deemed to be of far greater importance to their permanent well-being."[14] However, later in his career, Roney borrowed a leaf from Kearney's book. After his quarrel with Kearney cooled, he returned to San Francisco and organized forty labor unions into a League of Deliverance that called on employers to discharge Chinese workers and asked consumers to boycott goods made by Chinese immigrants. Kearney had demonstrated that being anti-Chinese was the way to get ahead in California politics.

Kearney now rode astride two horses, one being the Workingmen's Party of California and the other the effort to participate in the national anti-Chinese movement. After the ratification of the constitution, Kearney busied himself selecting California Workingmen's Party candidates for the 1879 elections. As candidate for mayor of San Francisco, Kearney chose a former New England abolitionist named Isaac Kalloch. Kearney's choice caused a split among his followers. Charles De Young, editor and publisher of the San Francisco *Chronicle*, had wanted to promote his own candidate. De Young tried to achieve his goals by shooting candidate Kalloch. Kalloch survived the assassination attempt, won the election, and continued the anti-Chinese agitation locally.

For his part, Kearney began to campaign nationally. After the summertime election of the constitutional convention delegates in 1878, Kearney headed east to campaign against the Chinese there. He returned to California in 1879 to stump the state on behalf of the constitution and to prepare for the September elections. In January 1880, after Kalloch was installed as mayor, Kearney went back east. He recalled these trips as "a brilliant success. In less than a year I had succeeded in lifting the Chinese from a local to a great national question."[15]

Kearney was correct that the Chinese had become a national issue, although making it so came at a cost. While Kearney was reaching new audiences in the East, he was losing them in California. He missed the winter in San Francisco, when the unemployed gathered in the city. When they went to the sandlots, the unemployed heard new speakers, a Mr. L. J. Gannon and a Mrs. Anna Smith. The Workingmen's Party also suffered a scandal. When Kalloch recovered from his assassination attempt, judicial officials concluded there was no further reason to hold his would-be assassin and freed De Young. Kalloch's son then distributed the sort of rough justice frontier California had been famous for, shooting, and this time killing, De Young.

Kearney also should have shared with others the credit for making opposition to Chinese immigrants a national cause. A quarter century of anti-Chinese legislation and agitation in California had not been lost on the federal government. In 1877, a Joint Congressional Committee to Investigate Chinese Immigration interviewed numerous Californians and concluded that economics indicated continued Chinese immigration was indeed undesirable. In 1880, the Chinese imperial government and the United States signed an agreement to revise the Burlingame Treaty, with new provisions for the limitation or temporary suspension of Chinese immigration. The next year, the U.S. Congress tried to suspend Chinese immigration for twenty years; it was prevented from doing so by President Chester Alan Arthur's veto. On May 6, 1882, Congress got its way, passing the first of a series of laws that excluded Chinese immigration almost entirely.

Anti-Chinese sentiment did have its opponents. Two years after the Joint Congressional Committee to Investigate Chinese Immigration issued its report, an anonymous minority report appeared; rumor had it the report was authored by the Joint Committee's chair, the late Oliver Morton, who had been active in Reconstruction. The report charged that the real opposition to Chinese migration stemmed not from the supposed economic concerns but from racism. An editorial in the *New York Times* fairly dripped with sarcasm trying to communicate its theory that the reason the Chinese were so mistreated was because their government was too weak to enforce its treaty claims. The United States, the *Times* claimed, honored its agreements with France and England, countries strong enough to force such respect. When there was no one around to compel respect, when it was a matter of dealing with Indians or Chinese, the United States showed its true attitude toward the importance of its treaties.[16]

Some critics of the anti-Chinese movement found it ironic, or perhaps fitting, that Kearney should be so thoroughly identified with it. Racial discrimination was so contrary to the Declaration of Independence proclamations of equality, so un-American, that it had to come from somewhere else. William Lloyd Garrison heaped on Kearney the venom he previously reserved for slaveholders and their supporters: "that most ignorant, profane, strike-engendering and besotted declaimer Denis Kearney—himself a foreigner, or of foreign descent, and much more entitled to be in a lunatic asylum than running at large."[17] W. H. Barton of the *California Independent* saw "a Historic Parallel." At the same time as the anti-Chinese excitement, Germany experienced an outbreak of anti-Semitism, with prominent Germans calling for Jewish exclusion on the grounds that Jews filled the universities and colleges, worked their way to the top in business, and excelled in the arts. Similarly, Kearney and his companions "say the Chinese are intemperate, industrious, economical, ingenious and apt in intellectual acquirement, and are, therefore proving themselves more the equal in the race of life with the Irish; hence the cry: 'The Chinese must go!' "[18]

Kearney himself thought he had nothing to apologize for. When critics taunted that his star fell as rapidly as it had risen, and that he had no career in politics, he answered them serenely:

I stopped agitating after having shown the people their immense power, and how it could be used. The Chinese question was also in a fair way of being solved. The plains of this State were strewn with the festering carcasses of public robbers. I was poor, with a helpless family, and I went to work to provide for their comfort. Common sense would suggest that if I sought office, or the emoluments of office, I could easily have formed combinations to be elected either governor of my State or United States Senator.[19]

Kearney was correct that he spent the rest of his life out of the public eye. He remained interested in his reputation; most of the quotes from him cited above come from a long letter he sent to Lord Bryce when he saw a chapter on "Kearneyism in the United States" in Bryce's case study of American political science, *The American Commonwealth*. Kearney died at Alameda, California, on April 24, 1907.

Kearney's influence on the debate over immigration continued long after him. The laws against Chinese migration remained on the books until 1943. When the Republic of China was allied with the United States in order to defeat the Empire of Japan in World War II, it seemed contradictory to regard the Chinese as suitable allies but not suitable immigrants. Accordingly, the Chinese were given a "national quota" of 105 immigrant visas per year. The Chinese achieved parity with other nations in 1965, when all national restrictions on migration were lifted. Even then, questions remained about the desirability and possibilities for assimilation of immigrants of different colors and races.

NOTES

1. J. C. Stedman and R. A. Leonard, *The Workingmen's Party of California: An Epitome of Its Rise and Progress* (San Francisco: Bacon and Co., 1878), p. 95.

2. Ibid., p. 103ff.

3. James Bryce, *The American Commonwealth*, 2 vols. (New York: Macmillan Company, 1910), 2:432; "The Anti-Chinese Movement—Important Statements, Letter from a Trades Unionist," *Labor Standard*, June 23, 1878, reproduced in Philip S. Foner and Daniel Rosenberg, eds., *Racism, Dissent, and Asian Americans from 1850 to the Present* (Westport, CT: Greenwood Press, 1993), pp. 173–174.

4. Stedman and Leonard, *Workingmen's Party*, p. 11.

5. Elmer Clarence Sandmeyer, *The Anti-Chinese Movement in California* (Urbana: University of Illinois, 1939; reprint, Urbana: University of Illinois, 1991), p. 64 (page citation is to the reprint edition).

6. Bryce, *American Commonwealth*, 2:937–938.

7. Stedman and Leonard, *Workingmen's Party*, pp. 16–19.

8. Ibid., pp. 20–21.

9. Bryce, *American Commonwealth*, pp. 938–939.

10. Ibid., pp. 22–27.

11. Ibid., pp. 31–33, 49–53.

12. "The Constitution of the State of California, 1879," quoted in William L.

Tung, *The Chinese in America, 1820–1973: A Chronology and Fact Book* (Dobbs Ferry, NY: Oceana Publications, 1974), p. 57.

13. Mary Roberts Coolidge, *Chinese Immigration* (New York: Henry Holt and Company, 1909; reprint, New York: Arno, 1969), p. 124 (page citation is to the reprint edition).

14. Frank Roney, *Frank Roney: Irish Rebel and California Labor Leader*, ed. Ira B. Cross (Berkeley: University of California Press, 1931), p. 287, quoted in Alexander Saxon, *The Indispensable Enemy: Labor and the Anti-Chinese Movement in California* (Berkeley: University of California Press, 1971), p. 122.

15. Bryce, *American Commonwealth*, p. 938.

16. "The Chinese Must Go," *New York Times*, February 26, 1880, reprinted in Foner and Rosenberg, *Racism, Dissent, and Asian Americans*, pp. 106–108.

17. Letter to the editor, William Lloyd Garrison, Boston, February 15, 1879, reprinted in ibid., p. 105.

18. W. H. Barton, "A Historic Parallel," *California Independent*, March 13, 1880, reprinted in ibid., pp. 109–110.

19. Bryce, *American Commonwealth*, p. 938.

BIBLIOGRAPHY

Kearney had no biography but is represented in the *Dictionary of American Biography*. Besides coverage in the newspapers of the day, useful primary material is in J. C. Stedman and R. A. Leonard, *The Workingmen's Party of California: An Epitome of Its Rise and Progress* (San Francisco: Bacon and Co., 1878); and Philip S. Foner and Daniel Rosenberg, *Racism, Dissent, and Asian Americans from 1850 to the Present*, Contributions in American History No. 148 (Westport, CT: Greenwood Press, 1993). James Bryce, *The American Commonwealth*, 2 vols. (New York: Macmillan, 1910), includes excerpts from a letter from Kearney to the author and cites the author's own interviews in San Francisco in 1880. It discusses Kearney from the perspective of political science. Useful secondary material includes Mary Roberts Coolidge, *Chinese Immigration* (New York: Henry Holt and Company, 1909; reprint, New York: Arno, 1969); Elmer Clarence Sandmeyer, *The Anti-Chinese Movement in California* (Urbana: University of Illinois, 1939; reprint, Urbana: University of Illinois [Illini Books], 1991); and Alexander Saxon, *The Indispensable Enemy: Labor and the Anti-Chinese Movement in California* (Berkeley: University of California Press, 1971). A useful chronology of anti-Chinese legislation in California is in William L. Tung, *The Chinese in America, 1820–1973: A Chronology and Fact Book* (Dobbs Ferry, NY: Oceana Publications, 1974). Ronald Takaki, *Strangers from a Different Shore: A History of Asian Americans* (New York: Penguin, 1989), offers good coverage on Chinese, and other Asian, immigration from a perspective other than Kearney's; unlike most such surveys, he's not even in the index.

BOOKER T. WASHINGTON
(1856–1915)

"Cast Down Your Buckets Where You Are"

African-American leader Booker T. Washington approached immigration with his own priorities firmly in mind. When immigration could be made good for blacks, as in the case of not forbidding migration from Africa, he was all for it. When it seemed harmful to blacks, as in the case of job competition, he watched it warily. It was the African American that was important to him, not immigration per se. However, Washington's commitment to African Americans could also make him a fascinating commentator on immigration.

Washington's views have become more important in the past generation. The 1970s saw a rise in interest in white ethnicity. This white ethnic revival took place in the context of the late civil rights movement. In some ways, white ethnic leaders were reacting to the civil rights movement, and in other ways they were borrowing from it. Thus, there has long been scholarly interest in white immigrant and white ethnic perceptions of African Americans. In order to get a complete picture, it is important to do similar research into African-American perceptions of white immigrants and ethnic groups.

Since 1965, the United States has had many immigrants coming from new sources. Unlike nineteenth-century and early twentieth-century immigrants, the newcomers are less likely to be European background. Some are African Asian; people from the Caribbean, Latin America, and South America often have ancestors from more than one race. There are several possible scenarios for the integration of new immigrants. They could follow the pattern established by previous generations of immigrants, or they could follow the pattern set by indigenous racial minorities. One force determining the pattern of integration new immigrants will follow is the reception they receive from all Americans, of every race. Thus the particular history of the African-American response to immigration becomes more important than ever. How have African Americans seen immigrants? economic competition? people from another culture, whose culture would change in the U.S. environment? people from another race, whose racial traits would not change even after generations in the United States? This chapter cannot answer these questions for all African Americans, but it can introduce the subject by focusing on the thought of Booker T. Washington.

Booker Taliaferro Washington was born into slavery on April 5, 1856, the son of a white man whose identity he never learned and of a slave woman named Jane Burroughs, who had a husband who was a slave on another plantation and also another son, also by a white man. Washington was only nine years old when slavery ended in 1865. He experienced emancipation as moving from one kind of poverty to another. His family moved from his parents' slave cabins to Malden, West Virginia, where his stepfather took a job in a salt mine. Young Washington worked full-time in a mine and then as a houseboy. In 1872, at sixteen, he worked his way diagonally across West Virginia and Virginia to the Hampton Normal and Agricultural Institute, and thereafter education was his life. He completed the program at Hampton, then briefly taught there and served as a dormitory supervisor. On July 4, 1881, at age twenty-five, he became president of the new Tuskegee Institute in northern Alabama. He built Tuskegee into an institution offering black men and women a basic education and vocational training or preparation for teaching. He pushed himself to the limit to ensure Tuskegee's survival, to the point where he took fatally ill while on a fund-raising trip. Informed of the hopelessness of his condition, he insisted on going home to Tuskegee, where he died on November 15, 1915. Tuskegee built upon the firm foundation he laid and has grown into a university.

Washington's work at Tuskegee led to an invitation to give a speech at the Cotton States and International Exposition held at Atlanta, Georgia, in 1895. His speech, given September 18, is sometimes known as the Atlanta Compromise because in it Washington claimed that "[i]n all things that are purely social we can be as separate as the fingers yet one as the hand in all things essential to mutual progress," rejecting the notion of immediate legal, political, and social equality between blacks and white in favor of an emphasis on opportunity for blacks in the Southern economy. Other prominent blacks, such as William Monroe Trotter and W.E.B. Du Bois, have since become more attractive examples of black thought in the Progressive Era, but in his day Booker T. Washington was the most important African-American leader.

His role as a black spokesperson supplemented Washington's role as a political insider. Washington connected white Northern and Southern entrepreneurs, philanthropists, and politicians. He identified black institutions to which philanthropists might donate their money, and blacks who might be the beneficiaries of political patronage. To black rivals, he seemed a powerful machine politician. But Washington himself knew how limited his power was. He had to pick his priorities, husband his strength, and not squander his ammunition shooting at unimportant targets.

Washington dealt with the issue of black migration on several separate occasions. The most highly publicized occurred near the end of his life. In January 1915, Senator James A. Reed, a Democrat from Mississippi, secured an amendment to a general immigration bill that would have barred African immigration. Had it passed, Africans would have been excluded by congressional action solely on account of their ethnic origin. The bill would also have had more far-reaching consequences than the word "African" might suggest. It was drafted in such a way that every person of African descent was excluded, no matter where the person was actually born, thus also excluding much migration from the Caribbean and South America. It also contributed to the generally negative attitude toward blacks born of several generations of Americans.

Washington swung into action. On this issue, he joined forces with Du Bois and with Trotter, African-American leaders who questioned Washington's leadership and his goals. The three of them used whatever influence they had, and Washington was the one with the most political connections at the federal level. He even planned a personal appeal to President **Woodrow Wilson**. Washington also wrote editorials and newspaper articles under his own name and sent information to others, urging them to write. He pointed out that African exclusion was unnecessary, as few people immigrated from any predominantly black nations. More to the point, he claimed it was unfair. Characteristically, he based his accusation of injustice not on the abstract notion of equal rights but on the idea that blacks had done so much for the United States that they deserved better treatment. In this case, Caribbean blacks had performed most of the labor of building the Panama Canal, a ten-year project that had been completed in 1914. Surely, the United States could not turn around and forbid former canal construction workers and their co-nationals from migration. The bill was defeated.

Throughout most of his career, though, Washington was not so concerned that blacks might want to come from Africa as he was that U.S. blacks might want to go to that continent. Historically, U.S. migration to

Africa has been small, but Washington was in no position to see the big historical picture. What he did know was that before he was born, white Americans had thought to end slavery by sending even U.S.-born blacks "back" to Africa and had founded Liberia as a place to which U.S. blacks should relocate. In Washington's day, people such as **Henry McNeal Turner**, a bishop of the African Methodist Episcopal Church, preached that racism made black life impossible in the United States and promoted black migration to Africa. (In 1916, after Washington's death, the Jamaican-born **Marcus Garvey** came to New York to revive interest in black migration to Africa.) In 1913, a missionary named Joseph Booth wrote Washington regarding a plan to raise money to assist U.S. blacks who wished to relocate to South Africa. Washington replied with a reference to the one part of Africa that had seen substantial white immigration. His words sounded like deadpan humor: "For my part, I cannot help feeling that any funds that were raised to assist Negro emigration to Africa might better be used in sending back home the class of white people in South Africa who are making the most trouble."[1]

Washington also worried that U.S. blacks might try to move around the United States. The late 1870s and early 1880s saw an internal migration known as the Exoduster movement, in which Southern blacks who could do so tried to escape Southern racism and poverty by moving to the frontier to claim their own farms and to live in communities that had not yet passed segregation ordinances. During the late nineteenth century, African Americans participated in the worldwide movement from country to city. At the end of Washington's life, in World War I, Southern blacks moved north to take jobs that would normally go to white immigrants, had not the war cut off European immigration. Washington tried to discourage this black migration. He opened his Atlanta speech with a story about a ship becalmed at sea. Upon sighting another vessel, it sent a signal for water. The answer came back: "Cast down your buckets where you are." The message had to be transmitted twice more before the captain actually did it—only to find that all this time his ship had been stuck in a stream of fresh, clean, potable water pouring into the ocean from the nearby Amazon. From this parable, Washington drew a moral: black Americans should cast down their buckets where they were, in the rural South.

Regarding black migration, Washington seems inconsistent. He worked to make it possible for blacks to migrate from Africa, but he also worked to discourage blacks from moving out of, or around, the United States. Yet both positions were consistent with Washington's priorities. An advocate for black people, he did not want the humiliation of having black migration barred. His discouragement of internal migration was another sort of advocacy for blacks, this time mixed with self-protection. Whites might have objected to a black spokesperson who urged blacks to migrate, depriving the South of labor and raising the specter of racial mixing elsewhere. Washington had built Tuskegee on the idea that blacks' best opportunity was to stay in the South; to suggest blacks could also better their condition by leaving the South would undermine his work at Tuskegee. Finally, whether one agrees with Washington on this point or not (and historians generally haven't), he did sincerely reject immigration in favor of Southern blacks building an economic community that was integrated into the economy of the South.

Similarly, Washington dealt with white migration from Europe on several separate occasions. The most public was probably the Atlanta Compromise, in which he urged Southern whites also to cast down their buckets: "[A]mong my people, helping and encouraging them as you are doing on these grounds, and to education of head, hand, and heart, you will find that they will buy your surplus land, make blossom the waste places in your fields, and run your factories."[2] In other words, don't bring in white immigrants to supplant native blacks.

When asked directly about immigration, Washington responded politely. In 1915, the *Jewish Immigration Bulletin* solicited his thoughts and received a response that said in part:

While I do not claim to be a special student of this subject it appears to me that the immigrants of today as well as those of yesterday are contributing much to American life. While I write there comes to mind the great work which **Jacob Riis** did, the splendid lessons which **Mary Antin** is teaching us. The European peasant and the Negro, however, I believe are at present contributing most to American life by teaching the lessons of helpfulness, patience, tolerance, forbearance, brotherliness, in fact all those things which are comprehended under what is characterized as the broader humanity.[3]

It was so brief and bland that one cannot blame the *Jewish Immigration Bulletin* for not printing it.

Washington was equally opaque when a student who was associate editor of a University of Alabama student publication asked him for his opinion:

I am not at all opposed to European immigrants coming to the South. What I have said from time to time in advising the colored people [is] to see to it that they must take advantage of their opportunities in the South or else they will be crowded to the wall by others who will come in and get more out of the soil than they get out of it. I have some personal feeling, however, as to how well European emigrants and our native Southern people will get on together, but this has nothing to do with the direct matter of European emigrants coming to the South.[4]

Occasionally, the mask slipped. Washington once wrote about education in the Austro-Hungarian Empire, which, in the early twentieth century, was engaged in a project of teaching all children in the languages they used in their homes and small villages. The result was that the Austrian side of the empire had some 8,000 German schools, 5,578 Czech schools, 645 Italian schools, 162 Romanian schools, 5 Magyar schools and 6,632 schools teaching various mutually unintelligible Slavic languages. Even then, Washington confined himself to widely held sentiments, claiming that if each of these groups migrated to the United States and attempted to preserve its distinctive language and culture, "we might have a racial problem in the South more difficult and more dangerous than that which is caused by the presence of the Negro."[5]

Washington's approach to the connection between immigration and criminality was similarly commonplace. He noted that of 112 unsolved murders committed in and around New York City between 1906 and 1909, 54 involved Italian victims. He claimed that the victims either were objects of extortion rackets who had failed to pay their protection money, or they were people whom someone else feared might go to the police. Their murders were unsolved because other Italians observed the code of *omertà*— rather than identify the killers to the police, they avenged the murders themselves, producing another round of unsolved cases. The preponderance of Italians "suggests, at least, the manner in which our own country is affected by the conditions of the masses in southern Italy and Sicily."[6]

In private, Washington was more interested in certain aspects of immigration. One of these, job competition, was a widespread concern. Washington received letters from people who thought that as a leading black spokesperson he should know how immigration affected African Americans. One correspondent informed him that "ten years ago all the barbers in Richmond were Negroes, and they were good ones, too. Now nine tenths of them are Italians. The Richmond Locomotive Works is supplanting its Negro laborers with Italians."[7] Washington's friends also kept him informed. Belton Gilreath, a Birmingham coal executive and Tuskegee trustee, had his secretary send Washington's secretary a clipping showing Italians remitted $400 million to their home country in 1907. "[S]uch figures show the importance of encouraging and developing our own people here to the highest extent, who are investing all of their earnings here among us, as your race do."[8]

Washington made use of such information. He ran a redoubtable public relations effort and was always placing news where it would be used, as in this letter to Oswald Garrison Villard, son of the abolitionist William Lloyd Garrison, a reformer himself, and also editor of the *New York Post*.

You may recall there has been considerable talk from time to time in the South about securing Italians to take the place of the Negro as a cotton farmer. You may also recall that Mr. Alfred Holt Stone in his book [*Studies in the American Race Problem*] and in all of his lectures on the subject has laid considerable emphasis upon what the Italians have done on a certain farm in Arkansas in replacing the Negro.

Because of all Mr. Stone has said, I thought perhaps you could make some use of the enclosed marked article from the Daily Graphic of Pine Bluff, Arks., which shows that Mr. John M. Gracie, the man who employed the Italians to which Mr. Stone refers, has gotten rid of the Italians and replaced them by Negro labor.[9]

Again, Washington acted inconsistently, even deviously, professing to have no opinion while showing his disapproval of white migrants taking plantation jobs. Again, the two seemingly opposite actions were consistent with Washington's own priorities. He wanted to make sure no one stole black jobs, but he didn't dare say so openly, for fear of jeopardizing his work at Tuskegee and his position as the black leader to whom whites listened.

One can see where Washington's heart really lay in two other statements he made regarding immigration. One was in a private letter in which he made another deadpan-sounding comment:

There are reasons—I shall not venture to say how valid they are—why some restrictions should be put upon all forms of immigration to this country. There are, perhaps, other reasons in the case of the Japanese and other oriental [*sic*] people, why immigration should be even more restricted. One of these is the very fact that there is a prejudice, in some parts of this country, against people who are not white.[10]

The other communication, also private, came in the course of a project Washington participated in for *The Outlook*, a monthly magazine with which he was affiliated. (It serialized the chapters of the biography that became his best-known book, *Up from Slavery*.) *The Outlook* opposed unrestricted immigration. However, it was also a magazine of integrity, and it tried to provide a forum for differing views, at one point soliciting writers who would contribute articles questioning its position on immigration. Washington notified an acquaintance that the latter had been accepted as contributor to that forum, and then he passed along what he considered the really important news: "I have gotten *The Outlook* thoroughly committed to use the capital 'N' for Negro in the future."[11]

Did Washington ever look at immigration itself, without trying to determine whether it was good or bad for blacks? He did have one opportunity to do so. From August 20 to October 9, 1910, Washington and a companion, **Robert Ezra Park** (who later became a pioneering sociologist at the University of Chicago), traveled through Europe. The board of trustees of Tuskegee had insisted Washington get some rest and relaxation and had offered to pay for the trip. Washington agreed to go, but only on the condition that he be allowed to study the people whose social, economic, and political status most closely resembled that of African Americans.

The itinerary of Park and Washington began in England, with a side trip to Scotland to visit **Andrew Carnegie**, one of Tuskegee's major benefactors, at Skibo Castle. They went across Europe by rail, seeing Berlin, Prague, Vienna, Budapest, Belgrade, Sofia, and Constantinople; they even got over the border to see a village in the Russian empire. Then they sailed through the Greek islands to Sicily and to Naples. At Naples, they switched back to the train and rode up through Rome and northern Italy to France, Berlin, and Copenhagen. They boarded a ship for England and there boarded another for the United States. Through it all, Washington studiously avoided cathedrals, museums, art galleries, palaces, historic ruins, and other tourist sites and went out of his way to see the most oppressed and exploited workers he could find.

During long train rides, Park and Washington discussed what they saw. Washington then thought over their conversation and formed a text in his head. When they reached major cities, Washington dictated his thoughts to a stenographer while Park gathered the books and official papers that supplied supporting documentation and expanded their observations. On their return to the United States, Park edited Washington's dictation into a book-length manuscript. The two published their observations in a series of articles in *The Outlook* in 1911 and in a book titled *The Man Farthest Down* in 1912.

Parts of *The Man Farthest Down* indicated Washington did not take full advantage of his opportunity to study immigration firsthand because he was still trying to be a black who pleased U.S. whites. Nearly everything he saw in Europe reminded him of the advantages U.S. blacks had. For example, he toured a new kind of establishment in England, an ancestor of the modern laundromat, where the urban poor could wash their clothes. He mused that Southern blacks could wash their clothes at home—which was true enough, except that it involved making soap, building a fire, heating the water, pounding the dirty clothes against rocks or washboards, rinsing them by hand in cold water, wringing them in a mechanical wringer, drying them outdoors on fences or branches, and ironing them with heavy irons (more like weights with handles) heated on top of stoves, tasks so time-consuming and arduous they seldom got done.

Other parts of *The Man Farthest Down* indicated that even when he wasn't conscious of how whites might interpret his writings, Washington was still unable to take full advantage of his opportunities because he himself shared some of the stereotypes of other Americans. When they visited Palermo, Washington temporarily turned into the thrill-seeking tourist. He saw the exact spot where New York Police Detective Lieutenant **Joseph Petrosino** was gunned down. He wove together the influence of the Catholic Church and the mafia in order to create a system that produced impoverished, and degraded, peasants.

However, *The Man Farthest Down* also showed how Washington's own preconceptions and experiences could help him to make sensitive obser-

vations regarding the people who became immigrants. Consider his conclusion that in Europe "the man farthest down is woman": "Men have
profited by the use of machinery more than women. The machines have
taken away from the women the occupations they had in the homes, and
this has driven them to take up other forms of labour, of more or less
temporary character, in which they are overworked and underpaid."[12] Immigration increased women's burdens, driving them into the fields to replace the absent men, while not offering them relief from cooking, cleaning,
and child care, the traditional women's jobs of their respective cultures.

Washington was also sensitive to the working class and particularly to
child laborers. When he heard there were mines in Sicily, he went out of
his way to find them, pushing his carriage driver into unfamiliar territory
high in the hills. Once there, he headed down hundreds of feet beneath the
earth, where he observed the relative temperatures and took meticulous
notes of how the work was done and who was doing it. His description of
little boys staggering as they lifted their loads, reeling to maintain their
balance under the weight, clambering to carry their packs to the surface—
and his comparison of how machinery made this a relatively light task in
West Virginia—makes for harrowing reading.

In many of the places Washington visited, it seemed that no person or
institution with any power was making any effort to improve the life of
the working class. When the upper classes or government officials did benefit the poor, that was an unintended side effect. He told the story of the
agricultural college in Hungary that did indeed attract a number of students
and train them to be more productive farmers. However, the agricultural
college had to be closed because it was too close to a liberal arts college
that served the aristocracy; the authorities feared that such close contact
with the upper class would unfit the lower one for its position. The tartness
of Washington's comment comes through his efforts to frame his thoughts
as a visitor's humble opinion: "In short, I think I might sum up the situation
by saying that Hungary is trying the doubtful experiment of attempting to
increase the efficiency of the people without giving them freedom." He
pointed out the obvious response to a government that feared the rise of
its own citizens: "[T]he masses of the people are emigrating to America in
order to better their condition."[13]

In places where the government was not actively frustrating people with
its efforts to improve them, neglect functioned as another kind of oppression. Italy, for example, had laws against child labor, but they were seldom
enforced. The government ran in a traditional manner, including the collection of many regressive taxes on consumer goods. "[T]he only way the
poor Italian can get free is by going to America, and that is why thousands
sail from Palermo every year for this country."[14]

In general, Washington judged immigration by the standards of black
welfare. He treated it warily, because he knew that employers would hire

almost anyone before they hired blacks. However, he was also wary about criticizing migration, because a crusade to prevent immigrants from entering the United States would probably turn to exclusion on racial grounds, and any more racism would also be bad for blacks. Only occasionally, as in *The Man Farthest Down*, did Washington let his guard down a little, to indicate that he knew that not everyone could cast down their bucket where they were.

NOTES

1. Booker T. Washington to Joseph Booth, Tuskegee, November 13, 1913, in Louis R. Harlan, ed., *The Booker T. Washington Papers*, 14 vols. (Urbana: University of Illinois Press, 1974), 12:330.

2. Booker T. Washington, *Up from Slavery* (1901), reprinted in John Hope Franklin, *Three Negro Classics* (New York: Avon, 1965), p. 148.

3. Harlan, *Booker T. Washington Papers*, 13:369–370.

4. Washington to Wyatt Rushton, Tuskegee, January 14, 1915, in ibid., 13: 222.

5. Booker T. Washington and Robert E. Park, *The Man Farthest Down* (Garden City, NY: Doubleday, 1912; reprinted with a new introduction by St. Clair Drake, New Brunswick, NJ: Transaction Books, 1984), pp. 83–84 (page citations are to the reprint edition).

6. Ibid., p. 180.

7. W. B. Watkins to Washington, Richmond, April 24, 1908, in Harlan, *Booker T. Washington Papers*, 9:508–510.

8. George A. McQueen to Emmett Jay Scott, Birmingham, June 12, 1908, in ibid., 9:571.

9. Washington to Oswald Garrison Villard, Huntington, New York, August 7, 1910, in ibid., 10:363–364.

10. Washington to J. Harada, Tuskegee, November 10, 1913, in ibid., 12:329.

11. Washington to Kelly Miller, New York City, February 1, 1911, in ibid., 10: 572.

12. Washington and Park, *The Man Farthest Down*, pp. 316–317.

13. Ibid., pp. 221–222.

14. Ibid., p. 145.

BIBLIOGRAPHY

Washington wrote several books; the two most helpful here were *Up from Slavery* (1901), reprinted in *Three Negro Classics*, with an introduction by John Hope Franklin (New York: Avon [Discus Books], 1965), pp. xxv–205); and with Robert E. Park, *The Man Farthest Down* (Garden City, NY: Doubleday, 1912; reprinted with a new introduction by St. Clair Drake, New Brunswick, NJ: Transaction Books [Black Classics of Social Science], 1984). Washington's other writings are in Louis R. Harlan, ed., *The Booker T. Washington Papers*, 14 vols. (Urbana: University of Illinois Press, 1974). Harlan also has a comprehensive two-volume biography of Washington: *The Making of a Black Leader, 1856–1901* (New York: Oxford University Press, 1972), and *The Wizard of Tuskegee, 1901–1915* (New York: Oxford University Press, 1983). For more on the subject, see D. J. Hellwig, "Black Leaders and United States Immigration Policy, 1917–1929," *Negro History Bulletin* 65 (July–September 1982), p. 65; Arnold M. Shankman, *Ambivalent Friends: Afro-Americans View the Immigrant* (Westport, CT: Greenwood Press, 1982); Silvia Pedraza and Ruben G. Rumbaut, eds., *Origins and Destinies: Immigration, Race, and Ethnicity in America* (Belmont, CA: Wadsworth, 1996); and Jeff Diamond, "African American Attitudes Towards United States Immigration Policy," *International Migration Review* 32:2 (Summer 1998), pp. 451–470.

JACOB A. RIIS
(1849–1914)

How the Other Half Lives

It must have been quite a show. The audience was usually composed of middle-class urbanites, some of them reformers and some of whom were drawn by their own reading or by announcements at their church. On the screen in front of them the magic lantern combined two slides, sometimes black and white and sometimes tinted, to produce a three-dimensional picture that both revolted and attracted them. They could almost step into the picture's narrow alley, squeezing between tenement house walls and lifting their skirts over the litter and garbage. From the stoops and windows, people peered back at them: men with shabby, ripped, and patched jackets, shirts, and pants and women with disheveled hair and huge aprons. Did the audience really want to get to know these people? Oh, yes, the lecturer assured them and proceeded to take them on a whirlwind tour, full of graphic details, lively anecdotes, comments about ethnic characteristics, warnings about impending class warfare, and finally, impassioned pleas for reform, complete with detailed suggestions. And all of this delivered by an irrepressibly optimistic fair-haired man with gold wire-rim spectacles. It is unknown exactly *how* he spoke, and it is interesting that no one mentioned one detail. This group of middle-class Americans was being led on its photographic tour of immigrant slums by someone who himself might be expected to speak with a foreign accent. Jacob A. Riis was born in Denmark and immigrated to the United States as an adult.

Riis's was a show historians are still trying to analyze. Through his writings and photographs he had a profound impact on a nation's views of immigrants, both at the time and since. He has been criticized for using, and thus perpetuating, the stereotypes of his day regarding Irish, Germans, Italians, Jews, Bohemians, Chinese, and African Americans. However, he also subverted the stereotypes, embodying and bolstering the argument that immigrant problems were due not to the immigrants themselves but to the environment in which they lived.

Riis was born on May 3, 1849, in Ribe, Denmark. As far as he was concerned, his first memorable event occurred when he was fifteen. He caught a glimpse of nearly thirteen-year-old Elisabeth, the niece and foster daughter of the owner of Ribe's only factory. Thereafter, he thought of his life story as being shaped around her. Other people might also note his father's influence. A member of the faculty of a preparatory school in Ribe, Mr. Riis may have recognized his son's talents early on, or he may have been vain enough to want someone to follow in his footsteps; either way, he wanted his boy to be a man of letters. Jacob, though, hated being stuck indoors at a desk and wanted to be a carpenter. This choice of a career brought physical proximity to Elisabeth; he helped to build a new factory for her father. However, it was not calculated to bring him into her social orbit. When he asked for her hand, her foster parents pointed out he had no steady work. Riis emphasized unrequited love rather than economics in his story of his decision to emigrate: He would make enough money to impress Elisabeth's foster parents. He arrived in New York harbor on June 5, 1870, a month after he turned twenty-one.

Riis had learned English in school in Denmark, and so could seek work easily, but he was so anxious to get back to Elisabeth that he would not settle down. He drifted from one place to another, always returning to Manhattan. He experienced some aspects of the tramp life he later wrote about: futile searches for work followed by equally unsuccessful searches for food and for places to sleep, a stray person whose only companion was an equally stray dog. He reached a personal nadir one night when it was too cold and rainy to sleep outdoors, and he had to leave his dog outside and seek shelter at a police station lodging house. The police exercised their responsibility for New York's vagrants by opening rooms in certain station houses where the homeless might sleep. The room Riis slept in was bare of all furniture, save a platform on which planks rested. The men slept on the planks—or, in other stations, on the floor—in their clothing. Most of them had not had recent opportunities for baths or laundry, and some smelled of liquor. One stole the gold locket containing a curl from Elisabeth's hair that Riis wore around his neck. When Riis complained, the sergeant on duty accused him of having stolen the locket from someone else and ordered him thrown out as a thief. When he appeared at the door, his dog rose up to greet him—only to be clubbed to death by the irate police officer. Riis shook the dust of the city from his feet and resumed his transient ways. Then he received a more severe blow: Elisabeth was engaged to a cavalry officer.

The news knocked the wind from Riis's sails. The next time he returned to Manhattan, he resolved to stay. He used his savings from his last itinerant job to take a course in telegraphy, with the idea of qualifying for a good skilled job. He dropped the course to follow what seemed a better opportunity, an entry-level position as a newspaper reporter. He had helped his father work on a newspaper in Ribe, and he liked the idea of being a reporter. It turned out the newspaper was in serious financial trouble and balanced its books on the backs of its employees, not paying them in a timely manner. Soon Riis was back on the street, homeless, hungry, reduced to peddling books on the corner by the Cooper Institute. As he told the story, his telegraphy teacher happened by, saw him, and mentioned that there was a job at a news-gathering agency. The next day, Riis showed up for it. He did well enough that by May 1874 he could advance himself by leaving the agency and taking a better job as a reporter for the *South Brooklyn News*. He did well enough to buy the newspaper. The crowning touch was he received another letter from home, mentioning that Elisabeth's fiance had died.

Overlooking the morbid circumstances that permitted him to resume his persistent courtship, Riis wrote Elisabeth and received a favorable answer. He sold his newspaper for five times what he had paid for it, sailed to Copenhagen, boarded a train for Ribe, and went to visit Elisabeth's family, this time successfully. He and Elisabeth were married in Ribe's Lutheran church on March 1876. Soon thereafter they set off for the United States. The only problem was that now Riis needed another job.

Riis returned to the newspaper he had sold, this time as editor. However, he had sold it to a group of politicians who were less reform-minded than he was. He gave up editing in favor of opening an advertising bureau. He purchased a magic lantern at a rummage sale, and he used it to develop slide shows, mixing slides of interesting scenery with those advertising consumer products. In 1877, Riis talked one of his neighbors, who was city editor for the New York *Tribune*, into giving him a job. He moved from his starting position to a staff job at police headquarters and then, in 1890, to similar work with the New York *Sun*. His father had been correct: Riis had it in him to be a man of letters, albeit one who got outdoors a lot.

On a typical day, Riis left his Brooklyn house in the afternoon, walked or took the "cars," or public transportation, to the foot of Brooklyn's Fulton Street, ferried over to Manhattan's Fulton Street, and got up to the police station on Mulberry Street as quickly as possible. He checked his messages and then began nosing about the police station, alert for tips. He spent the rest of the afternoon and evening turning the tips into stories, chasing down and interviewing police officers, city officials, witnesses, and victims. During the evening, there might be some late-breaking news, in which case Riis would go along with the police to cover events firsthand and then hustle back to his desk to prepare his story. His workday wound down in the early morning. Now there was no real hurry, and so he would walk back to the ferry.

He could have gone from the police station over to the Bowery to take public transportation, but he preferred to walk. So between two and four in the morning, he started down Mulberry Street, then a vast Italian neighborhood. He headed to the "Bend" or curve in the street at its southern terminus. He crossed Five Points, where several streets converged, passed City Hall, and ended up at the Fulton Ferry. During the day, when he was in the same neighborhood chasing down stories, he saw people acting tough or unconcerned or like big shots in their small circles of acquaintances. "It is a human impulse, I supposed," he mused. "We all like to be thought well of by our fellows. But at 3 A.M. the veneering is off and you see the true grain of a thing."[1]

What he saw on Mulberry Street was disturbing enough that Riis put some distance between himself and it. In 1886, he moved his family to Richmond Hill, Long Island, where "[t]he very lights of the city were shut out. So was the slum, and I could sleep."[2] But Mulberry Street also reinforced Riis's commitment to reform: "It was not fit for Christian men and women, let alone innocent children, to live in, and therefore it had to go." The lectures on reform that Riis covered as a reporter helped him to analyze current events, and the sources he had cultivated for his newspaper stories he now began to press for assistance in understanding slum conditions. He planned a book on slums and even copyrighted the title, *How the Other Half Lives*. But he feared mere words would not convince people of what he saw nor stimulate them to action.

A solution to the inadequacy of words presented itself one morning in 1887. Riis was sitting at his breakfast and going over the newspaper when a little four-line news item caught his eye. Someone in Germany had figured out a way to make an artificial light by which one could take photographs. Riis immediately saw the implication. If he could take such photographs, he could bring the public with him to the midnight slums. This was not as easy as it sounded. Riis's first photographic outfit consisted of a box camera, a tripod on which to steady it, and a stack of glass plates, each covered with the emulsion necessary to take the pictures. To make the light, he at first used a pistollike gadget that lit a magnesium cartridge but abandoned this in favor of a wick saturated in alcohol that he touched with a match and then used to light a thin film of magnesium he had spread across a frying pan. He did not have an easy time of it. He once set fire to the shreds of wallpaper clinging to the walls of a room in which six blind people lived, high atop a tenement building that had no fire escape. He managed to smother the flames before the situation became serious, and he was forced to try to lead the residents down the steep, rickety steps.

Riis tried to get better photographs by having someone else take them. However, few other people wanted to be in Mulberry Bend at 3:00 A.M. Perhaps also few wanted to engage in some of the tactics Riis used to get his pictures. To get a picture of overcrowding in tenement flats, he and his companions knocked on doors and then burst through, set up the camera, set off the flash, and took the picture before the sleepers could figure out what was going on. One person Riis paid to take photographs then tried to further increase his profit by selling the negatives. Occasionally, Riis could not take the photograph he wanted and so bought something similar from the Health Department or took a photograph of the photographs of criminals in the police station's Rogues' Gallery. For some, Riis's hiring photographers and borrowing photographs disqualifies him from being a photographer. For others, the important point is that without his direction the photographs would not have been taken and would not have been used for reform purposes.

Riis did not think he was a good photographer, and there is plenty of evidence in the surviving negatives to back him up. He has overexposed plates, underexposed plates, and plates with blurs on them, indicating someone moved during the exposure. Some of the technical problems would have challenged a more experienced photographer. Riis brought his camera to places that were so narrow that it was difficult for him to position himself for a good picture. The most troubling questions concern composition, or placement of subjects in the photograph. Critics have accused Riis of posing his photographs in order to get what he wanted. Riis did pose his subjects. He told stories on himself about a tramp whom he paid to sit for a photograph, only to have the tramp ask for more money when Riis wanted to include his picturesque pipe in the portrait, and about the gang that insisted on being photographed demonstrating, with wildly exaggerated gestures, its pickpocketing technique. He saw nothing wrong with posed shots. He knew what he wanted to bring out in his subjects, and sometimes he had to pose them to do it. But did he *im*pose as well, using his photographs to communicate his ideas about the slums rather than the reality? If so, it might be important to remember one thing: Riis's ideas regarding slums may have been different from reality, but they were also different from the ideas of many of his contemporaries.

The technology of the times did not permit many photographs in newspapers. Riis therefore developed a slide show. He switched his work hours from night to day and made the rounds of churches and organizations, offering to deliver talks on tenement life and possible reforms. One evening an editor from *Scribner's* magazine was in his audience and approached him about doing a story based on the lecture and the photographs. The story, with line drawings based on the photographs instead of reproductions of the photographs themselves, appeared in the Christmas 1889 issue of the magazine. From that came an offer to write the book Riis had been planning for years, *How the Other Half Lives: Studies among the Tenements of New York*, which appeared in 1890.

How the Other Half Lives, and the photographs he took for it, made Riis's reputation. The book itself was a striking innovation. Like the *Scribner's* article, it had line drawings based on Riis's photographs, but it also had a number of the photographs themselves. They were reproduced for the book by the half-tone process, on special shiny white paper. The photographs, and the text that accompanied them, reflected Riis's immersion in his times. He knew the techniques of advertising, of newspaper journalism, and of mass-market magazines. He used them to get across a particular point of view.

It was a point of view that differed from conventional wisdom, which taught that poverty was a personal failing. Many of Riis's contemporaries argued that people were poor because they were idle, lazy, shiftless, thriftless, drunken, ignorant, and libidinous, not given to industry, punctuality, or sobriety, squandering what they had on drink, on a good time, on their vices. And they probably couldn't be cured of these faults. Science in the late nineteenth century indicated many traits were inherited. Although the phrase "gene pool" hadn't been coined yet, there was a sense that different groups of people had different characteristics. In a country already used to racial issues and experiencing heavy immigration, it was a logical step to think that different ethnic groups had different characteristics. Given that these traits were supposed to be inherited, it was logical to keep charity to a minimum. Why do anything that encouraged the survival of the unfittest?

Riis used these stereotypes to shape *How the Other Half Lives*. The book begins with a couple of chapters on the housing problem, then turns to a long section divided into many chapters describing the various population groups. This section starts with an imaginary map of Manhattan's ethnic populations, with different colors for the Irish, Germans, Italians, Jews, Chinese, Bohemians, Arabs, and French. Riis then takes his readers into several of these neighborhoods, with chapters on Italians, Chinese, Jews, Bohemians, or Czechs and "the color line in New York." (There is also a chapter on "street Arabs," but that was really a colloquialism for homeless children.)

Riis's verbal walking tours all followed the same outline. He began on a dark note, referring to Bohemian anarchists, Chinese opium smoking, and Jewish moneygrubbing. Then he described the living conditions of these people and, for those that worked in the tenements, their work conditions as well. Finally, he finished with another passage on the characteristics of the ethnic group under question. Some passages fall all over themselves in an effort to sound favorable:

With all his conspicuous faults, the swarthy Italian immigrant has his redeeming traits. He is as honest as he is hot-headed. There are no Italian burglars in the Rogues' Gallery; the ex-brigand toils peacefully with pickaxe and shovel on American ground. His boy occasionally shows, as a pick-pocket, the results of his training with the toughs of the Sixth Ward slums. The only criminal business to which the father occasionally lends his hand, outside of murder, is a bunco game, of which his confiding countrymen, returning with their hoard to their native land, are the victims. The women are faithful wives and devoted mothers. Their vivid and picturesque costumes lend a tinge of color to the otherwise dull monotony of the slums they inhabit. The Italian is gay, lighthearted and if his fur is not stroked the wrong way, inoffensive as a child. His worst offense is that he keeps the stale beer dives.[3]

How one reacts to that statement depends on how one evaluates the stereotyping behind it. Given the vicious stereotypes about the Italian mafia then circulating, Riis's assertions about Italians are pretty mild. However, any stereotype tends to obscure individuals. What about Italians who couldn't be gay and lighthearted, couldn't live up to the stereotype Riis assigned them?

Riis's chapters on Jewish and Chinese immigrants were structured differently. Instead of the upbeat conclusion about positive group characteristics, he suggested ways to help the immigrants. He had two chapters on Jews, one a general introduction to their neighborhood and the other on their work habits. Neither of these had any paragraphs praising any Jewish characteristics, and both had nasty asides about how Jews undermined their own health and oppressed their children with work beyond their years in their search for economic security. Nevertheless, none of these supposed characteristics were so ingrained that they couldn't be changed. The Jews, Riis wrote, "must be taught the language of the country they have chosen as their home, as the first and most necessary step."[4] He had no doubt "the people be both willing and anxious to learn" and that they could do it if they had time: "As scholars, the children of the most ignorant Polish Jews keep fairly abreast of their more favored playmates."[5] Riis did not think the Chinese were so hopeless they had to be excluded. "Rather than banish the Chinaman, I would have the door opened wider—for his wife; make it a condition of his coming or staying that he bring his wife with him. Then, at least, he might not be what he is now and remains, a homeless stranger among us."[6]

In both types of rhetoric, Riis aimed at the same conclusion: Immigrants were not naturally bad. What seemed naturally bad might be the result of their environment; the only way to find out was to change that environment. Riis definitely rejected the notion that extending charity to the poor only encouraged survival of the unfittest. In his discussion of African Americans, he saw the issues in a way not unbefitting of **Booker T. Washington**:

The [color] line may not be wholly effaced while the name of the negro, alone among the world's races, is spelled with a small n. Natural selection will have more or less to do beyond a doubt in every age with dividing the races; only so, it may be, can they work out together their highest destiny. But with the despotism that deliberately assigns to the defenceless Black [that's Riis's capital B] the lowest level for the purpose of robbing him there that has nothing to do.[7]

Another tactic Riis used further undercut the importance of heredity. He took photographs of every group he could find: Irish, Germans, Italians, Bohemians, Jews, Chinese, an English coal heaver with his wife and two daughters, a family circle of Mohawks. He put these pictures shoulder to shoulder. If one group had a particular undesirable trait, it seems everyone had it: African Americans had a gambling racket called policy, the Chinese had one called fan tan, and the Italians had their bunco games. Chinese tucked knives up the voluminous sleeves in their blouses, blacks hid razors in their boots, and Italians carried stilettos. If different races did the same things, how could these be ethnic traits? Pictured this way, it seemed doubtful ethnic background had much to do with poverty. Here were all the races of the world, all equally poor. It must have something to do with the environment in New York rather than with their heredity from the old country.

After his tour of ethnic neighborhoods established that ethnicity provided color but no substantial explanation for the horrendous conditions, Riis demolished one cornerstone of the traditional argument against the poor. His poor were anything but lazy. They worked, sometimes almost around the clock, sometimes seven days a week. Riis concentrated on those who worked in the tenements and documented the system that exploited recent immigrants, particularly Jews in the garment industry and Bohemians who worked rolling cigars. For example, coat manufacturing started in a factory, because the bolts of cloth from which the coats were cut were too expensive and heavy to move about and because cutting the pieces of cloth according to a pattern was a skilled job. However, the cut pieces went out to jobbers who promised to bring back semiassembled coats at a certain price. The jobbers either rented flats in tenements or used their own homes for tiny factories called sweatshops. They purchased sewing machines or, if they could, persuaded their employees to buy them on a kind of installment plan. Then they hired people, bearing in mind that their profit was going to be the difference between what they promised to make the coats for and what it actually cost them to have the coats made. They found it expedient to hire recent immigrants, who didn't have any money, didn't speak English, and thus had to find jobs fast but didn't have a way to find them. The sweatshop workers basted the coats, sewed the seams, stitched the linings, added the collars, and pulled the basting threads. Then the jobber returned the coats to the factory. The coats went out again, this time to someone who worked at home; such a person was paid so much per buttonhole cut, per button sewn. The coats went back to the factory again, then to the wholesaler or retailer.

An even more complete oppression could be found in cigar making, for there the roles of real estate owner and shop owner, tenant and employee, were conflated. Cigar capitalists purchased tobacco and tenement houses. They rented out the latter to people who were willing to work in the former trade. Usually these were Bohemians, whose women learned the trade in the old country and then taught it to their immigrant husbands when language barriers prevented the men from resuming their skilled trades. The possibilities for exploitation here were almost endless, as the same person could both raise the rent and lower the piecework rates, and those who complained lost both their homes and their jobs.

The system, Riis pointed out, had many evils. Sweatshop operators paid no attention to health or safety regulations. The employees were vulnerable to breathing in the lint from the cloth on which they worked or to sudden fires. Labor was oppressed, with people working long hours for low pay, with no benefits and no job security. Children were particularly oppressed. The law said that children had to be fourteen years of age in order to work in a factory. Riis, who had five children of his own, could tell by the little workers' growing teeth that some of these adolescents were no older then twelve. He also took a sobering photograph of a woman with one baby on her lap and six more young children seated or standing at a round table, all except the baby busily assembling artificial flowers: Mom the sweatshop operator.[8]

Middle-class householder that he was, Riis was interested in what happened when the laborers turned into consumers, when these hardworking people received and spent their pay. He was appalled at what their housing money bought. There were no single-family dwellings in immigrant neighborhoods. There were houses that had once been single-family dwellings, but the families had moved to less congested neighborhoods, selling their houses to those who would live off rental income or were living off rental income themselves. Landlords increased their income by renting the house out in parts, one floor to a family, or one room to a family, then letting out the cellar and the attic and building yet another rental unit in the rear. To these old houses were added modern tenements designed as multiple-unit dwellings. Whether old or new, the owners maximized their rent by neglecting their property, so that stairs sagged, plumbing leaked, and wallpaper shredded off the walls. Those who were willing to rent their houses to African Americans could increase their income by charging more than the going rate to a people who were as often shut out of decent housing by prejudice as by price.

The high rents, Riis complained, forced people to do things that worsened their housing conditions. Even the women worked, leaving no one free to do the housekeeping. If their combined income didn't meet the expenses, families took in lodgers (to sleep in their flat) and boarders (to sleep and to eat). They took in work or turned their home into a sweatshop. Still, the high rents squeezed people out of their homes. Young women who couldn't make enough money at their work were tempted to turn to prostitution to meet their expenses. Young men had a few more options. They could become boarders or lodgers. If they couldn't afford that, they could stay at lodging houses for twenty-five cents a night, in which case they got a little partitioned area in which to sleep, with a bed and chair. Those who could afford only fifteen cents got a dorm room with a row of beds, each with a locker at the foot to store clothes overnight. The ten-cent-a-night lodging house had no lockers. The seven-cent-a-night lodging house had no beds. The room had two sets of parallel wooden bars that served to anchor two tiers of hammocks. All of these were run by licensed operators. For five cents a night, one could crowd into an unlicensed tenement flat. For free, one could stay overnight at the police lodging house. Riis claimed to know real estate owners who cleared thousands of dollars in profit annually herding into lodging houses men who, if the rents were more reasonable, wouldn't be homeless.

The centrifugal force of the rent pulled families apart. Children were crowded out of their households, literally, by the high numbers of people in the small space and, in an emotional sense, by the feeling that no one there noticed or cared for them. Again, boys had more options than girls. They could pick up work on the streets, blacking boots or fetching buckets of beer for construction workers. And they could reduce their expenses to almost nothing by stealing food from pushcart peddlers and by sleeping in sheltered spots. One wonders if Riis's employers were embarrassed that he photographed boys napping on the floor of the room at the *Sun* office where they would later pick up newspapers for sale.[9] Boys might fall into gangs and would thus go on to street fighting and criminal activity. Or they might grow up to be tramps, roaming the city streets, occasionally indulging in petty theft but most often begging and trying to get by.

Riis concluded his section on housing conditions and their effects with the story of a man, a husband, father, and unskilled laborer, who stood at the corner of Fifth Avenue and Fourteenth Street watching carriages full of wealthy and fashionable people roll from their uptown homes to their downtown shopping sprees. The contrast between their luxury and his penury grew too great for him to bear. He unsheathed a knife, perhaps a tool he would use for work—if he could get any. He plunged into the traffic with the knife in his fist. "The man was arrested, of course, and locked up. To-day he is probably in a mad-house, forgotten. And the carriages roll by to and from the big stores with their gay throng of shoppers. The world forgets easily, too easily, what it does not like to remember."[10] Riis himself thought the man mad in using his knife but not in his analysis. The poor were not poor only through their own fault but through the action, and inaction, of others.

Riis then turned to describing efforts at amelioration. Balancing out his story about the man with the knife, he mentioned several wealthy individuals who interested themselves in alleviating poverty. He also discussed the role of religion. Riis himself was baptized into the Lutheran faith, attended a Methodist Mission when he was first learning the newspaper business and before he married Elisabeth, and then settled into Episcopalianism, but he frequently mentioned the work of the Catholic clergy. Catholicism was set up on a territorial basis, with clergy responsible for particular areas, so some of them did live among the poor and knew how to help them. Riis also described institutions: the New York Foundling Asylum for babies; the Five Points Mission, Five Points House of Industry and Children's Aid Society for youngsters; the Newsboys' Lodging House on Duane Street; and agencies devoted to the concerns of working women. Yet these were not quite enough, as he noted when he told the story of the mother and her adult daughter who were found "sewing and starving" in an Elizabeth Street attic. Benevolent folk found the two women a job in New Jersey and a place to live there. Three weeks after being settled in their new home, the two were back in their wretched neighborhood. Another example of the ungrateful poor, who didn't know what was good for them? Not at all. Riis was listening when the younger woman said, "We do get so kind o' downhearted living this way, that we have to be where something is going on, or we just can't stand it." And he answered those who argued that the poor were different from the middle class: "[T]here was sadder pathos to me in her words than in the whole long story of their struggle with poverty; for unconsciously she voiced the sufferings of thousands misjudged by a happier world, deemed vicious because they are human and unfortunate."[11]

New York was, in Riis's phrase, "a city of a thousand charities where justice goes begging." It needed fewer people to rescue the unfortunate and more to exercise ordinary humanity in their everyday dealings. In fact, the final point of *How the Other Half Lives* was that New York needed people who would not attempt to make a killing in the real estate market but would accept a reasonable profit and in turn provide reasonable housing. Riis closed the book with a few chapters describing model tenements, complete with maps showing how the buildings were laid out and how they were surrounded by gardens.

To reinforce his point that model tenements would find model tenants, Riis photographed tenement dwellers. The photographs were a good example of how he got people to see beyond the standard image of the slum. Some of the photographs showed the kind of nuclear family in which Riis himself lived: husband, wife, children. Photographs of people living alone showed how they made their dwellings homelike. Mrs. Benoir, a Mohawk woman, sat in her tiny dormer room braiding rugs, with just enough space to put her chair between her bed and her stove.[12] A Jewish man celebrated the Sabbath in a cellar with a single loaf of challah on a table devoid of even a cloth.[13] An Italian woman posed amidst the paraphernalia of the ragpicker's trade, a swaddled baby on her lap, a Madonna of the slums.[14]

Riis did well by doing good. He remained in demand as a writer and lecturer the rest of his life. He turned out numerous magazine articles, more books on the need for reform, still more books on his native Denmark, and a campaign biography of **Theodore Roosevelt**. (His family published a collection of his Christmas stories posthumously.) He did well enough that he could afford to quit his job at the newspaper and to devote himself to freelance writing and to lectures.

Riis did more than just write. He wanted to enact some of the reforms he wrote about. After *How the Other Half Lives* came out, then-Police Commissioner Theodore Roosevelt left his calling card, and the two struck up a friendship. Riis told Roosevelt the story of his miserable night at the police lodging house; Roosevelt had the power to order the entire system shut down, which he did in 1896. He and Riis were more impassioned than thoughtful, as this action meant there was then no place at all for homeless people to stay. Riis succeeded in getting the block of tenements on the western side of Mulberry Bend condemned and then in getting the City of New York to turn the vacant lot into Columbus Park. This was another action that was more impassioned than thoughtful, as there were no plans to build replacements for the houses thus demolished.

Riis went on to become the chief advocate of small parks for neighborhood use, even serving as secretary of the Small Parks Commission. He helped to add to the modern notion of park use. Traditionally, a park was a green space where city dwellers renewed themselves by contact with nature. Riis championed the erection of children's playgrounds where youngsters could indulge what people at the time thought was their natural propensity for activity. He was so supportive of the charitable work of an Episcopalian women's group, the King's Daughters, that they named their settlement house after him. Riis's reporting on tenement house conditions influenced housing reform in New York in the 1890s. His enjoyment of the Christmas holidays made him a promoter of Christmas events: setting up a Christmas tree at Madison Square, holding a community carol sing (to give one more example of Riis's command of the technology of his time, the words to the songs were projected on big screens around the park), and selling Christmas seals to raise funds for research into tuberculosis.

By 1901, Riis had been married to Elisabeth for twenty-five years. Their family had grown to include grandchildren. Theodore Roosevelt had succeeded to the presidency upon the assassination of William McKinley, raising the possibility that the Progressive urban reforms the two had championed locally in New York could now become national policy. It was a propitious time for an autobiography. *The Making of an American* became, after *How the Other Half Lives*, Riis's most popular work.

The Making of an American provides another perspective on Riis's attitude toward immigration. He and Elisabeth, who wrote out a half a chapter on their courtship from her perspective, freely extolled the beauties of their native Denmark. For Riis, the transition to American life was difficult primarily because he missed Elisabeth and because he had trouble holding a job. Any problems he might have had with English or American customs were reduced to a story typical of the kind he told on himself; he heard a mother tease her daughter about the latter having "set her cap" for him, but he didn't know what that meant, and he sought to find out by asking the girl herself. He reported that Elisabeth was homesick on first coming to the United States. They remained attached to Denmark. The last chapter of the autobiography describes how Riis visited Denmark and lunched with its king. Riis summed up his attitude toward his own immigration with a familiar metaphor. The home country was his mother, the United States his wife. The love he bore one did not reduce the love he bore the other. Why did he not express similar sentiments in *How the Other Half Lives*? Perhaps because that wasn't his point. *The Other Half* was not about the importance of immigration and ethnicity; it took those for granted and went on to examine the American environment in which these people lived.

Riis also identified other crusades: eradicating child labor, designing better school buildings and placing those buildings in playgrounds, and setting up reformatories so that wayward boys were not mixed in with the hardened criminals of the city's penal system. But he had to leave these crusades to others. He himself was busy meeting the demand for his writings and lecturing and thereby meeting the financial demands of his family. Of the four children who had reached adulthood at the time of his death, three were still dependent on him financially, at least occasionally. He also suffered from personal tragedies. Elisabeth died on May 18, 1905. In 1907, Riis took a second wife, his longtime secretary Mary Phillips. He had one more child by her, a son who died soon after birth. Then Riis's own heart began to falter. On May 26, 1914, just weeks after his sixty-fifth birthday, his heart condition took his life.

Although Riis had been ill for some time, his death was unexpected and untimely. He and his second wife had planned his estate to the point of leaving it to his children. She had a small settlement that she used to build a long career as an entrepreneur on Wall Street. Most of his children were grown and living far away; his youngest son was still in school and too young to take responsibility for his father's legacy. They did not even attend to his collection of glass negatives. When another immigrant photographer, Alexander Alland, inquired about them, no one knew where they were. Riis's youngest son, Roger William, uncovered a box of lantern slides at the Barre, Massachusetts, farm his father had bought after his second marriage. When they were preparing to tear down Riis's former house in Richmond Hill, the new owners found the rest of Riis's materials under the eaves: 412 glass negatives, 161 lantern slides, and 193 prints.

The family donated the recovered material to the Museum of the City of New York. They have been used in exhibits and reproduced in photography books, new editions of *How the Other Half Lives*, and a variety of texts and monographs on the urban, ethnic working class at the turn of the century. Along with the photographs of the younger **Lewis Hine**, Riis's photographs have become the pictures of immigrant neighborhoods that people carry in their heads: ethnic groups with different costumes and customs, suffering under the same harsh living and working conditions, and striving toward the same goals of familial and economic stability.

NOTES

1. Jacob A. Riis, *The Making of an American* (New York: Macmillan, 1901), pp. 235–236.
2. Ibid., p. 287.
3. Jacob A. Riis, *How the Other Half Lives: Studies among the Tenements of New York*, with a new preface by Charles A. Madison (New York: Dover, 1971), p. 47.
4. Ibid., pp. 106–107.
5. Ibid., pp. 99–100.
6. Ibid., p. 83.
7. Ibid., p. 115.
8. Ibid., p. 123.
9. Ibid., p. 155.
10. Ibid., p. 233.
11. Ibid., p. 133.
12. Ibid., p. 190.
13. Ibid., p. 105.
14. Ibid., p. 45.

BIBLIOGRAPHY

Most of Riis's photographic negatives are on deposit at the Museum of the City of New York. They have been published in two editions of *How the Other Half Lives: Studies among the Tenements of New York* (New York: Charles Scribner's Sons, 1890; reprinted with a new preface by Charles A. Madison, New York: Dover, 1971); a second is edited with an introduction by David Leviatin (Boston: St. Martin's [Bedford Press], 1996). They are also in Alexander Alland, Sr., *Jacob A. Riis: Photographer and Citizen* (New York: Aperture, 1973). There is no published collection of Riis papers or collection of his books. Besides *How the Other Half Lives*, Riis's books include the following studies of immigration, its impact on urban neighborhoods, and the possibilities for reform: *Out of Mulberry Street* (1898;

reprint, Upper Saddle River, NJ: Literature House, 1970); *A Ten Years' War: An Account of the Battle with the Slum in New York* (1900; reprint, Freeport, NY: Books for Libraries Press, 1969); *The Battle with the Slum* (New York: Macmillan, 1902; reprint, Montclair, NJ: Patterson Smith, 1969); *The Children of the Poor* (New York: Charles Scribner's Sons, 1902; reprint, New York: Arno, 1971); *Children of the Tenements* (1903; reprint, Upper Saddle River, NJ: Literature House, 1970); *The Peril and Preservation of the Home* (New York: Macmillan, 1903); *Theodore Roosevelt, the Citizen* (New York: Outlook Co., 1904); and *Neighbors: The Life Stories of the Other Half* (New York: Macmillan, 1914). This was only part of his literary output, which also included magazine articles, Christmas tales, and accounts of Denmark. Riis also published an autobiography *The Making of an American* (New York: Macmillan, 1901). Besides the biographical information in the reprints of *How the Other Half Lives* and in Alland, there is a good young reader's biography, Edith Patterson Meyer, *"Not Charity but Justice": The Story of Jacob A. Riis* (New York: Vanguard Press, 1974).

JANE ADDAMS
(1860–1935)

Settling in the American City

Jane Addams contributed to the shaping of the U.S. debate on immigration in several ways. She was one of those people for whom immigration functioned as a metaphor, bringing out an otherwise hidden truth about her own life. She was a strong voice in favor of the idea that immigrants could be assimilated into U.S. culture. She also championed the idea, novel at the time, that the United States could learn something from immigrants. However, her support for immigrants had crucial limitations. She failed to address real clashes of culture between immigrants and natives, and she failed to appreciate how much the immigrants could do for themselves.

An immigrant is a literal outsider, someone who comes from another place. Addams was also an outsider, albeit in a less literal way. It was part of her genius that she did not let her sex, her family, her education, or anything else limit her. Instead, like an immigrant, she worked out a modus vivendi with the world around her.

When Addams was born, on September 6, 1860, girls and women led restricted lives. Girls whose families needed money worked in their youth, but girls didn't have career goals, nor were they educated to follow professions or trades. They were expected to marry, to have children, and to devote themselves to the care of their homes and families. They worked

Jane Addams from the Jane Addams Collection, Swarthmore College Peace Collection.

for wages only if the family was very poor. They usually did unpaid labor in the form of child care, cooking, cleaning, sewing, laundry, or the direction of servants in these tasks. They might be renowned hostesses or noted for their charity, but they weren't supposed to take a leadership role in public affairs. Being born a woman could have relegated Addams to the sidelines. Instead, by the time she died, on May 21, 1935, she had pioneered new roles for women, had lent her support to women suffrage, had participated in the forming of the National Association for the Advancement of Colored People (NAACP), and had won a Nobel Peace Prize for her activism in the Women's International League for Peace and Freedom.

Sometimes, Jane seemed to be the center for the Addams family, because as a young adult she was constantly busy helping family members. But this was not really her choice; rather, it was the expected role of the unmarried daughter. Jane's mother, Sarah Weber Addams, died in January 1863, when Jane was only twenty-eight months old. In 1868, when she was eight years old, her father, John Huy Addams, remarried, to a widow named Anna Hostetter Haldeman. Modern psychologists know how disruptive parents' new marriages can be to children. Addams had personal experience with that disruption. As she matured, she distanced herself from her stepmother and became an outsider in her own family.

Addams was educated in her birthplace of Cedarville, Illinois, until just before her seventeenth birthday. She knew that several institutions had been founded on the East Coast that educated women for the same bachelor's degrees that men earned at their colleges, and she wanted to go to one of those schools. However, her father preferred she attend Rockford Female Seminary in Illinois: He was a trustee there, and two of her older sisters were alumnae. Fortuitously, Rockford was preparing for college accreditation, allowing Addams to take a course of studies that ensured she would qualify for a Bachelor of Arts degree as soon as Illinois would let Rockford grant one. Addams left Rockford in 1881 with a diploma indicating she had completed the course. When in 1882 Rockford was elevated to college status, she returned to pick up her B.A. Now she was well educated and credentialed, but for what? Women were usually barred from the law and ministry and could enter medicine and higher education only in limited numbers. Education, then, further contributed to Addams's outsider status.

Addams may also have been an outsider because of her sexual orientation. Lesbianism is a historically constructed concept, one that has developed over time, and Addams's concept of her sexuality would not be the same as that of later historians. And Addams left no writing on the subject. However, there is circumstantial evidence aplenty. She rebuffed a stepbrother's romantic advances, she never mentioned an interest in men, and she had a close relationship with a woman, Mary Rozet Smith, that included sharing vacations, love letters, and rooms. Questions of homosexuality aside, *any* older unmarried woman was marginalized in a society that thought women should get married and have children.

In the 1880s, Addams found a way to end her outsider status and to become a community leader. At the time she graduated from Rockford, she intended to go to Smith College for another year of education. However, once she got home to Cedarville, she began to feel poorly. On August 18, 1881, John Addams died while traveling in Marquette, Michigan, with his wife and daughter Jane. His death made Jane independent financially, with an inheritance of about $50,000. It also left her in an awkward social position. Social mores prevented her from establishing herself apart from her family and encouraged her to stay with the stepmother with whom she had a tenuous relationship. Instead of going to Smith, she and her stepmother moved to Philadelphia, where Jane entered the Philadelphia Medical College for Women. In February 1882, she gave up her studies and entered the Hospital of Orthopedic and Nervous Diseases under the care of S. Weir Mitchell. While she was recuperating, her stepbrother George discussed their relationship; Jane's sister Alice and George's brother Harry had married, and Anna and George were hoping for another match between stepsiblings. Jane spent the summer of 1882 extricating herself from the possibility of a romantic relationship with her stepbrother. In the fall of 1882, stepbrother, brother-in-law, and physician Harry operated on her for curvature of the spine, which led to more bedrest. In the spring of 1883, she had to deal with the business affairs of her brother Weber, who suffered a mental breakdown. From August 22, 1883, to June 1885, she and her stepmother traveled in Europe. From her return until the fall of 1885, she stayed with her sister Mary while her preacher brother-in-law rode circuit. While the Johns Hopkins Medical School had its 1885–1886 session, George attended the school, and Jane and her stepmother lived in Baltimore with him. During the summer of 1886, she was in Cedarville. When the Hopkins Medical School opened its 1886–1887 session, she, George, and Mrs. Addams were back in Baltimore. She returned to Cedarville for the spring of 1887 but did not return to Baltimore that autumn. Instead, she and two friends toured Europe again. Two of the friends, Addams and Ellen Starr, were inspired to move to a working-class, immigrant neighborhood in Chicago and to "settle" among the poor. On September 19, 1889, after a period of planning and preparation, they opened a "settlement" called Hull House.

Hull House went on to become a great success. After an initial period of getting to know the neighbors and getting to be known by them, Addams and Starr began to involve themselves in life on the West Side of Chicago. They took care of preschool children for women who had to work. They sponsored girls' and boys' clubs for school-age children and for adolescents who had to leave school to work in shops and factories. They had area mothers over for tea and hosted lectures for people whose education was cut short by the need to work. More people came to live at Hull House, mostly single, white, middle-class daughters from small towns, who had good education but limited opportunities. These new residents developed projects according to their interests and community needs. Julia Lathrop, a Rockford friend of Addams, came and lived at Hull House while serving on the Illinois Board of Charities. Florence Kelley, who combined her family background in politics (her father was a congressional representative) with training in sociology obtained at the University of Zurich, became a special agent of the Illinois State Bureau of Labor Statistics. Sophonisba Breckinridge of Kentucky and Edith and **Grace Abbott** of Nebraska came to develop social work as a profession. Mary Kenny O'Sullivan came to link Hull House with the labor movement. Alice Hamilton, M.D., came to research the health and safety problems of factories and helped to found the field of industrial medicine.

Contact between Hull House and immigrants came naturally. When Addams and Starr first came to Hull House, the West Side still had old English, Irish, and German immigrant families. One of Hull House's early visitors was the daughter of a widowed English-born scrubwoman; she later married a lawyer and moved to the East Coast, where he climbed to the top of his profession, and she, too, took a giant leap in status. However, the old families were giving way to new groups. There were a small number of Greeks, a much larger number of eastern European Jews, mostly from places controlled by the Austro-Hungarian, German, and Russian Empires, and a huge number of Italians, mostly from the southern part of Italy or from Sicily.

Americans framed their debate on these "new immigrants," as the southern and eastern Europeans were called, in terms of nature versus nurture. Some of the most prominent opinion makers of Addams's day leaned toward the nature side of the debate. Forgetting that previous generations had bemoaned the impossibility of assimilating earlier immigrants, they instead argued that the earlier immigrants were easy to assimilate because they came from the same parts of Europe as the first colonists and settlers. (The Catholics of southern Ireland, who began to migrate en masse during the famine, were the exception that proved the rule.) New immigrants, though, came from nations that did not participate in the early settlement of the United States. These new immigrants had such different national characteristics from those of old stock Americans that assimilation was considered quite impossible and immigration restriction the only way to prevent the deterioration of the American way of life.

Addams argued that assimilation was a function of nurture, not nature. Immigrants needed to be in the proper environment in order to assimilate. However, the environment in which the immigrants were forced to live was not conducive to assimilation. What was most disturbing was that immigrants in a bad environment did not just go unassimilated. They became alienated, separated from both the Americans beyond their ghetto and from their own past.

Why were immigrants alienated? One reason was the pressure of poverty. Work was a matter of feast or famine. People could work long hours for many days in a row for weeks or months at a stretch and then suddenly be unemployed. And when there was work, it wasn't enough for living expenses, let alone enough to save for a rainy day. The solution was for all members of the family to take any job available. The results were almost always stressful. Mothers were pulled two ways, responsible both for supplementing family income and for maintaining the household. Parents took their children from school in order to put them to work, sacrificing future opportunities to present needs. Ironically, their children's education continued, albeit in shops, in factories, and on the street, in ways that separated children from parents. Sometimes, the search for money became not just stressful but tragic. In her memoirs, Addams told the story of a husband and father who lost his office job and then searched unsuccessfully for similar work. On Addams's advice, he took a job digging ditches rather than apply for "relief," or welfare. Not used to long hours of hard work outdoors, he contracted pneumonia and died.

Addams was more interested in the social and psychological side of alienation. She was especially sensitive to how these issues affected the lives of women and girls. She found a way to close the gap that had opened between immigrant women and their own pasts and also between immigrant women and their daughters. As she told the story, the idea came to her while she was walking down one of the streets in her neighborhood, thinking about this problem. Suddenly, she looked up to see an elderly female neighbor sitting in the sun on the steps of her tenement. She was spinning yarn the same way she had back at her home in a mountainous village in Italy, throwing her distaff down the steps and then reeling it back up in order to twist and stretch wool fibers into thread.

"The occupation of the old woman gave me the clew that was needed. Could we not interest the young people working in the neighboring factories, in these older forms of industry, so that, through their own parents and grandparents, they would find a dramatic representation of the inherited resources of their daily occupation."[1] The thread of thought Addams spun as she watched the Italian woman spin a more tangible thread bore fruit in 1900 in the Hull House Labor Museum. Addams searched the neighborhood and was able to find spinning and weaving equipment that showed the evolution of the technology of textile manufacturing, from the Italian woman's distaff through the spinning wheel to the spinning jenny, and from small hand-held looms to one powered by electricity. On Saturday evenings, women from Syria, Greece, Italy, Russia, and Ireland operated the traditional machines, and people walking through the museum could see how each piece of equipment was improved upon and refined in order to make the next piece.

The Labor Museum served two purposes. It reinforced the self-esteem of older women, who often seemed out of place in the modern, industrial city:

> I recall a number of Russian women working in a sewing-room near Hull-House, who heard one Christmas week that the House was going to give a party to which they might come. They arrived one afternoon when, unfortunately, there was no party on hand and, although the residents did their best to entertain them with impromptu music and refreshments, it was quite evident that they were greatly disappointed. Finally it was suggested that they be shown the Labor Museum—where gradually the thirty sodden, tired women were transformed. They knew how to use the spindles and were delighted to find the Russian spinning frame. Many of them had never seen the spinning wheel, which has not penetrated to certain parts of Russia, and they regarded it as a new and wonderful invention. They turned up their dresses to show their homespun petticoats; they tried the looms; they explained the difficulty of the old patterns; in short, from having been stupidly entertained, they themselves did the entertaining.[2]

Second, the Labor Museum helped daughters to understand their mothers. Addams told the story of an Italian girl and her mother who both came to Hull House on Saturday evenings, the former to a cooking class and the latter to do demonstrations at the Labor Museum. But they would enter the building by separate doors, for the girl didn't want her friends to know that this old-fashioned woman, with a kerchief instead of a hat, boots instead of shoes, and "short" (at least by the floor-sweeping standards of the fashion the daughter followed) skirts, was her mother. Then the girl happened to catch sight of her mother, surrounded by an admiring group of museum visitors. After that, she allowed her mother to take out from their hiding place at home the homespun clothing the mother had brought from Italy but that the daughter had rejected as unfashionable. And mother and daughter came to their different Saturday activities through the same entrance.

Hull House, then, developed a particular approach toward assimilation. Contrary to those who argued that immigrants couldn't assimilate because they were the "wrong nationality," Addams argued that assimilation was possible. In fact, given that the immigrant generation would die and the American-born one would grow up, assimilation was inevitable. The problem was not that of encouraging assimilation but of preventing this inevitable process from tearing generations apart.

Hull House also supported a social service organization, the Immigrants' Protective League. The League was founded in 1908. The settlement resident most fully associated with it was Grace Abbott, a Nebraska-born social worker who often collaborated not only with Addams but with her blood sister Edith; when Abbott succeeded Julia Lathrop as head of the federal Children's Bureau, Jessie Binnford took over her League work. The League performed a number of functions. Members of the League met immigrants in transit, particularly girls and young women traveling alone; the Hull House people fully believed in an extensive white slave traffic and did what they could to prevent females from falling into prostitution. The League also studied the conditions under which immigrants traveled, entered the United States, and lived and worked. It used these studies as the basis for lobbying for federal agencies to supervise the immigration process and for presenting the immigrants' cause to the sometimes suspicious public.

Addams's work to close the generation gap and the Immigrants' Protective League's work to assist newcomers were both geared to help immigrants adapt to U.S. life. Was there, perhaps, something immigrants could preserve of their own culture, something that they could contribute *to* U.S. life? At first, Addams did not think so. She recalled the experience of Hull House's kindergarten teacher, Jennie Dow. One of Dow's kindergartners habitually came to school drunk. It turned out her Italian-born mother was giving the girl wine for breakfast. Dow paid a visit to the mother to try to convince her to serve something else:

The mother, with the gentle courtesy of a South Italian, listened politely to her graphic portrayal of the untimely end awaiting so immature a wine bibber; but long before the lecture was finished, quite unconscious of the incongruity, she hospitably set forth her best wines, and when her baffled guest refused one after the other, she disappeared, only to quickly return with a small dark glass of whisky, saying reassuringly, "See, I have brought you the true American drink." The recital ended in seriocomic despair, with the rueful statement that "the impression I probably made upon her darkened mind was, that it is the American custom to breakfast children on bread soaked in whisky instead of light Italian wine."[3]

The longer she was at Hull House, the more Addams came to appreciate her immigrant neighbors' culture. Eventually, Hull House sponsored a calendar full of celebrations for every group in the community except Jews. (Addams had been baptized under the Presbyterian rite as an adult, attended a Unitarian church near Hull House whose minister shared her social concerns, and eventually went from a kind of Christian socialism to a kind of agnosticism; she had little contact with Jewish culture.) Some celebrations were tied to religious practice: There was a Mardi Gras party for the Italians and a Saint Patrick's Day cotillion for the Irish. Others were tied to patriotic occasions: Hull House observed the hundredth anniversary of the birth of Italian national leader Giuseppe Mazzini, and Addams also recalled a celebration of the achievements of Greek civilization.

Addams also fostered intercultural contact between immigrant groups. She recalled one time when the largely Irish Social Extension Club invited the Italian ladies of the neighborhood to a get-acquainted affair, only to find that the ladies were not used to going out by themselves in the evening and so all stayed home, and their husbands had come instead. It turned out to be a fun evening, as "untiring pairs of them [the men] danced the tarantella; they sang Neapolitan songs; one of them performed some of those wonderful sleight-of-hand tricks so often seen on the streets of Naples; they explained the coral finger of St. Januarius which they wore." One thing they did not do was snack on their native cuisine; Addams recalled that these same Italian gentlemen "politely ate the strange American refreshments."[4]

In the 1910s, philosophers began to develop theories of cultural relativism, cultural pluralism, and multiculturalism. Addams was way ahead of them. Her practical experience at the settlement led her to conclude that there were some values that Americans considered uniquely theirs but that really could be found in all cultures, just as republicans such as Mazzini were honored both by the Italians and by her own father. She had also learned that immigrants brought some new and different cultural traits to the United States, and these, she thought, added color and excitement to drab, industrial U.S. cities.

However, there were some limits to Addams's appreciation for other cultures. One limit has to do with the *kind* of culture Addams appreciated. As historian **John Higham** observed, "When examples of specific gifts came to mind, they turned out invariably to be things to which Americans attached slight importance: folk dances, music, exotic dishes, handicrafts, perhaps certain literary fragments. The contributions that charmed sympathetic progressives had no bearing on American institutions or ideals."[5] Gone was **Thomas Jefferson**'s fear that immigrants would bring political opinions incompatible with self-government or **Lyman Beecher**'s suspicion that immigrant Catholicism sought to undermine native Protestantism. Addams overestimated what immigrants and natives had in common and underestimated the extent of painful cultural clash.

A more serious problem was that Addams overlooked one particular immigrant "gift," the immigrants' ability to organize themselves and to oversee their own assimilation. The map of Chicago indicates that there was a huge Italian Catholic church right near Hull House, Holy Guardian Angel. The parish's history began when the Reverend Paul Ponziglione, S.J., came from a nearby Jesuit institution to say mass for the Italians. The Reverend Tommaso Moreschini, O.S.M., a Servite priest long active among Chicago's Italians, opened a chapel in 1894. The alumnae from the nearby convent of the Sacred Heart organized a Sunday School for Italian children; they were the first to use the name Holy Guardian Angel. In 1899, the archdiocese of Chicago erected a parish by that name and appointed as pastor the Reverend Edmund Dunne, an Irish-American archdiocesan priest who had trained in Rome and who spoke Italian. When he was promoted to chancellor of the archdiocese, Holy Guardian Angel was given to the care of the Society of Saint Charles-Scalabrinians, an order of priests and brothers who specialized in ministering to migrants. Under their administration, Holy Guardian Angel counted tens of thousands of parishioners. These people raised funds among themselves to provide a church, a parochial school, and many different spiritual and social activities. Holy Guardian Angel performed many of the same functions as Hull House. And even though it limited its ministrations to Italian Catholics, it attracted many more people than Hull House did.

Yet the only time the two institutions took note of each other was during Father Dunne's tenure at the parish. Hull House was lobbying for expanded public education on the West Side, and Father Dunne criticized public education as godless. Except for this brief confrontation, the two institutions stayed apart. They both missed the opportunity to work together for the good of the neighborhood. And Hull House missed the opportunity to see how the people it hoped to help assimilate were carrying out their own assimilation on their own terms.

The historian Rivka Shpak Lissak has noticed another group that Hull House did not. Lissak characterized these people as immigrants of the lower middle class. They had less money, education, or social status than Jane Addams and the other Hull House residents. However, they did generally speak English. They followed the professions, or they owned their own businesses. They had more money and status than poorly paid industrial workers without much education or English-language skills. One way immigrant leaders got ahead was by serving as mediators between American and immigrant cultures and societies. They helped the immigrants in various ways: finding jobs, banking, writing letters, sending money or mail to the old country, guiding them through the American bureaucracy. They also served as public relations officers, championing the immigrants and their ways to American audiences and promoting among the immigrants the strategies—acquisition of English, education, businesses—that helped them fit into the United States. Such service could be rewarded. The immigrants could form a base that could launch the ethnic leader into politics. Hull House, though, never tapped into this incipient political bloc. When Hull House worked with immigrant leaders, it was usually with people who could plan ethnic festivals for their co-ethnics, which would then be held at the settlement.[6]

Why did Hull House not form a coalition of native-born and immigrant leaders that worked together? Perhaps it was a power play, with the Hull House residents thinking they alone knew what was best for the West Side. Perhaps it was simply a lack on knowledge on Hull House's part regarding immigrant leaders and their institutions. Perhaps the immigrant leaders, like Father Dunne, did not wish to work with Hull House.

Addams's approach to assimilation was too complex to make her easy to categorize. If one focuses on the fact that immigrants developed assimilation processes of their own, Addams comes across, again, as a marginal, less important figure. However, compared to her Progressive contemporaries, she was central. She made a strong case for the possibility of assimilation. She added a new idea to the concept of assimilation, pointing out that it was a two-way street in which Americans learned from the newcomers. She developed practical programs for both immigrant-to-American and American-to-immigrant assimilation.

NOTES

1. Jane Addams, *Twenty Years at Hull-House, with Autobiographical Notes* (New York: Chautauqua Press, 1911), pp. 236–237.
2. Ibid., pp. 241–242.
3. Ibid., pp. 102–103.
4. Ibid., pp. 358–359.
5. John Higham, *Strangers in the Land: Patterns of American Nativism, 1860–1925*, 2nd ed. (New Brunswick, NJ: Rutgers, the State University, 1963; reprint New York: Atheneum, 1969), pp. 122–123.
6. Rivka Shpak Lissak, *Pluralism and Progressives: Hull House and the New Immigrants, 1890–1919* (Chicago: University of Chicago Press, 1989), Chapter 5.

BIBLIOGRAPHY

Jane Addams's papers are at the Swarthmore College Peace Collection; researchers can access them by starting at http://www.swarthmore.edu/Library/peace. Hull House's papers are at the University of Illinois Archives in Chicago. Addams wrote several books. The most useful for understanding her views on immigration and assimilation are: *Democracy and Social Ethics* (New York: Macmillan, 1902); *The Spirit of Youth and the City Streets* (New York: Macmillan, 1909); *Twenty Years at Hull-House, with Biographical Notes* (New York: Macmillan, 1910; reprint New York: Chautauqua Press, 1911); *A New Conscience and an Ancient Evil* (New York: Macmillan, 1912); and *The Second Twenty Years at Hull-House, September 1909 to September 1919, with a Record of a Growing World Consciousness* (New York: Macmillan, 1930). Addams also wrote extensively for the periodical press. Her articles concerning immigration include: "Immigrants and American Charities, Illinois Conference of Charities and Correction," *Proceedings* (1905), pp. 11–18; "Recent Immigration: A Field Neglected by the Scholar," *Education Review* 29 (March 1905), pp. 245–263; "The Public School and the Immigrant Child," National Education Association *Journal of Proceedings and Addresses* (1908), pp. 99–102; "Report of the Committee on Immigrants," National Conference of Charities and Correction *Proceedings* (1909), pp. 213–215; "Foreword," in Immigrants' Protective League *Annual Report* (Chicago: IPL, 1909–1910), p. 4; and "Americanization," American Sociological Society *Publications* 14 (1919), pp. 206–214. Some of Addams's articles, along with excerpts from her books, have been compiled into readers such as Allen F. Davis, ed., *Jane Addams on Peace, War, and International*

Understanding (New York: Garland, 1976), and Christopher Lasch, ed., *The Social Thought of Jane Addams* (Indianapolis, Ind.: Bobbs-Merrill, 1965). Useful biographies include Daniel Levine, *Jane Addams and the Liberal Tradition* (Westport, CT: Greenwood Press, 1971); and Allen F. Davis, *American Heroine: The Life and Legend of Jane Addams* (New York: Oxford University Press, 1973). Monographs concerned with the subject at hand is Rivka Shpak Lissak, *Pluralism and Progressives; Hull House and the New Immigrants, 1890–1919* (Chicago: University of Chicago Press, 1989); and Mina Carson, *Settlement Folk: Social Thought and the American Settlement Movement, 1885–1930* (Chicago: University of Chicago Press, 1990).

HENRY CABOT LODGE
(1850–1924)

Immigration Restriction as National Policy

Henry Cabot Lodge presents a divided face to American history students. Most encounter him when they study World War I, when he defeated **Woodrow Wilson** and his Versailles Peace Treaty. In this role, Lodge appears to be governed partly by personal passions and short-term considerations: his own dislike of Wilson, the rivalry between his Republicans and Wilson's Democrats, and his guardianship of Senate prerogatives in foreign affairs over and against an increasingly powerful presidency. However, even if one grants these issues figured in Lodge's opposition to the treaty, one still has to concede that Lodge and Wilson had substantial differences in the field of foreign affairs, with Wilson arguing for international equality and cooperation and Lodge defending the United States from the limits to its independence that he feared in the League of Nations covenant.

On the other hand, if one reads monographs about immigration legislation, Lodge appears to base his work almost wholly on personal prejudices and passions. Lodge is presented as someone who was well born, well off, and well educated but whose social status was slipping as other people came to dominate U.S. politics and economics. He projected his fears of status loss onto the immigrants, as if the lowly, impoverished, illiterate foreign-born might topple the elite from their places. To this end, he led an early, and underhanded, effort to legislate the exclusion of particular immigrants on the basis of ethnicity, race, or national origin.

It might be possible to develop a unified field theory of Henry Cabot Lodge, one in which immigration restriction and his other accomplishments—in U.S. tariff policy as well as in foreign policy—can be brought together. Lodge was a "protectionist" in the largest possible sense of the word.[1] He aimed to bring the United States to the status of a Great Power, which required attention to the economy, to international affairs, and to population characteristics. In this scenario, the fact that immigration restriction had a personal appeal for Lodge becomes less important. After all, certain aspects of the defeat of the Versailles Treaty—the opportunity to put Wilson in his place, for example—had a personal appeal, too.

There's a quatrain that used to be well known in Boston:

> And this is good old Boston
> The home of the bean and the cod
> Where the Lowells talk only to Cabots
> And the Cabots talk only to God.

That, silly as it is, might be helpful understanding Lodge. He was born in Boston on May 12, 1850. His father, John Ellerton Lodge, was a prosperous merchant who owned a fleet of clipper ships and engaged in the China trade. His mother Anna was the one who connected him to the Cabots; she was the granddaughter of Federalist politician George Cabot. Lodge was so pleased with that connection that he preferred using his middle name. If a proper Bostonian can be pictured jumping through hoops, Lodge jumped through all the proper ones. He was educated at E. S. Dixwell's Latin School in Boston, where he met other young boys of good family and comfortable income. He then moved on to Harvard. Upon graduation, he married his cousin, Anna Cabot Miller Davis, the daughter of Rear Admiral Charles H. Davis. During 1871–1872, the couple spent a year in Rome. Upon their return to Boston, the young husband entered Harvard Law School. None of this was done with any firm plan in mind; these were all steps other men of his class took. In most cases, the young men's ancestors had already achieved status and money. Keeping up the family reputation wasn't quite as exciting as making it, and it wasn't as easy. One could always slip up and lose it all. Young men such as Lodge had no reason to hurry and good reasons not to. The result was some failed because they didn't even try; they kept waiting for opportunities appropriate to their station to come along, or kept bemoaning the passing of the "good old days," when their family name, their wealth, their education, and their cultured backgrounds automatically commanded respect.

In Lodge's case, an assist came from a man like himself. Henry Adams had also been born in Boston. (The opening pages of his *Autobiography*, while not so quotable as the rhyme above, are a far more elegant evocation of the same notion of being born to the head of society.) He also had famous relatives; his great-grandfather was President **John Adams**, his grandfather was President John Quincy Adams, his father was Civil War Minister to England Charles Francis Adams, and his brother was railroad regulation pioneer Charles Francis Adams, Jr. The family home was in Quincy, but Charles Francis Adams maintained a town house on Beacon Hill. The Adamses had money: John Adams had bequeathed John Quincy land, John Quincy bequeathed Charles Francis more real estate and some canal stock, and Charles Francis invested in the modern industries of his age, the railroads. Charles Francis's sons were also faced with the problem of how to hold on to their status as social and political leaders, and at one point Henry Adams chose to exercise his influence through journalism. He was the editor of *The North American Review*, a monthly magazine that printed thought-provoking articles on the issues of the day. In 1873, Adams asked Lodge to be his assistant. Lodge received his law degree in 1874 and was admitted to the bar in 1875 but never practiced his profession, preferring his career in editorial work and then in doing research and writing on his own. In 1876, Harvard granted him the first doctorate in political science it ever awarded. Characteristic of his interest in preserving his heritage, he produced a dissertation entitled "The Anglo-Saxon Land Law." From 1876 to 1879 he lectured at Harvard, and throughout the 1880s he produced a series of historical and biographical works on the Revolutionary and Federalist periods of U.S. history, including an 1877 biography of his great-grandfather.

In 1879, Lodge moved into politics. On the one hand, it was a tradition; the Boston "Brahmins," as the town's elite were called, had come to their position partly through their leadership during the Revolution, the Federalist period, the development of the abolitionist movement, and the Civil War. On the other hand, it was not a tradition that many of Lodge's peers took personal steps to preserve. Most of them went into business, law, college and university education, or publishing or lived off their family income while writing or pursuing cultural or philanthropic interests. They disdained politics. Gilded Age politics was the antithesis of ancestor worship. Candidates were judged on how they personally appealed to voters, not on the basis of what their ancestors had done in the past. In the Boston area, it was even necessary to appeal to the Irish Catholic working class; shortly after Lodge began his political career, Hugh O'Brien became the first Irish-American Catholic mayor of the English Puritan's city on a hill, and Lodge served a term in Congress with John Fitzgerald, **John F. Kennedy**'s maternal grandfather, as a colleague. Lodge, though, turned out to be a canny, shrewd, partisan young man who could play the political game as if he were one of the Irish ward heelers he so much disliked. He built a considerable personal power base in his voting district and used it to sustain a long career.

Lodge won election to the Massachusetts State House of Representatives in their election of 1879. He was reelected in 1880 and also elected one of the delegates to the Republican National Convention, where he participated in nominating James Abram Garfield for what turned out to be a successful presidential candidacy. The next year, he left his House seat for an unsuccessful bid for the Massachusetts Senate and the year after that saw another setback, as he was defeated in a try for the U.S. House of Representatives. Then, in 1883, he became campaign manager for the Republican candidate for governor of Massachusetts, George D. Robinson. Lodge helped Robinson to defeat Benjamin F. Butler. Butler was a tough opponent because he had a Civil War record (it helped in Massachusetts that people in New Orleans, where Butler served, referred to him as "General Beast Butler"), and he was a Democrat who could command the vote of numerous Irish throughout the commonwealth.

The year after that, Lodge really proved his political savvy. Elected delegate-at-large to the 1884 Republican National Convention, he went to the meeting fighting the candidacy of James G. Blaine. Boston Brahmins thought of themselves as being on the morally correct side of political questions ranging from the Revolution to the labor-capital disputes of the Gilded Age, and Blaine had an unsavory reputation for showing favoritism to railroad magnates. Lodge opposed Blaine—until Blaine won the majority necessary to become the Republican presidential candidate. A group of Republicans bolted the party to bolster the support of the Mugwumps, a splinter political group that criticized both major parties as corrupt. Lodge closed ranks and remained a regular Republican. Because the Republicans divided into regulars and Mugwumps, Blaine lost his campaign to Democrat Grover Cleveland. Lodge also lost his race for a congressional seat in 1884. But because he had been loyal, the Republicans nominated him again in 1886, by which time the Mugwump revolt was over. He won by a narrow majority and was reelected in 1888 and 1890, serving from 1887 to 1893.

During Lodge's tenure in the House, the definition of a regular Republican changed. One of the early bills Lodge drafted and tried to get through Congress was the 1890–1891 "Force Bill." Had it passed, this legislation would have established federal control over polling places, thus breaking southern opposition to black voting. This would have been a way of standing up for traditional Republican interests and also increasing Republican votes. However, instead of having his legislation become law, Lodge found that even Bostonians had given up on helping southern blacks to secure the vote. Lodge was also well known for supporting the Sherman Anti-Trust Act and for promoting civil service reform, specifically for getting

Theodore Roosevelt to serve on the federal Civil Service Commission. These activities showed that he did indeed understand the Republican agenda at the end of the Gilded Age and the beginning of the Progressive Era. The new Republican conscience combined a critique of politics and economics with snobbery and partisanship. A properly run civil service would sabotage machine politics, patronage, and favoritism, which would help the Republicans' chances. Antitrust legislation would undermine the basis on which the nouveau riche were building their fortunes, thus preventing them from challenging the most established Republicans for leadership. There were other challenges to the American way of life. Lodge began addressing them as early as 1888, when he gave a speech imploring, "[L]et us have done with British-Americans and Irish-Americans and German-Americans, and so on, and all be Americans."[2]

In 1891, an event prompted a major consideration of immigration. The story begins in New Orleans, with Police Chief David Hennessey. On the night of October 15, 1890, Hennessey was honored at a banquet for his assistance in controlling organized crime among the city's Italians. As he headed up his street at 11:30 that night, he was assassinated by a group of men that had been hiding behind a parked cart. He died on October 16. People watching at his deathbed heard him say that "the dagoes" had got him. Officials concentrated their efforts on the Italian community, particularly among the people who felt oppressed by Hennessey's anticrime activities. On November 9 of that year, the city indicted nineteen Italians. On March 13, 1891, a jury acquitted thirteen and reported it could not render a decision regarding the other six. Although cleared in the case, those on trial were returned to jail pending the completion of the necessary legal forms. The next night, March 14, a mob broke into the jail and summarily executed every Italian it could find. Eleven Italians died in the lynching, seven connected with the trial and four who were in jail that night on other charges.

Lodge wrote an article on "Lynch Law and Unrestricted Immigration," explaining why the massacre took place. He offered one minor reason, that corrupt government in New Orleans gave people good reason to distrust even jury decisions. Then, ignoring anything he had learned in law school, he skipped over the question of whether the accused had murdered Hennessey to point out that there was indeed a mafia operating in New Orleans, established by criminals migrating from Sicily. For good measure, he then went on to accuse the immigrants of bringing diseases and of increasing the pool of unskilled labor and thus lowering wages. He leapt over the last logical barrier to present his solution to problems immigrants presented: "Some such fair and restrictive test as that of the ability to read and write."[3] Specifically, the idea was that every adult male immigrant had to be able to read and write in the language of the country from which he came.

Lodge got the idea for a literacy test from Edward W. Bemis, who lectured on this subject in 1887. An economist, Bemis was concerned with the problem of competition between immigrants and native workers for jobs. The law of supply and demand suggested that the sheer numbers of job seekers would lead employers to conclude they could keep wages low. Immigrants were also widely suspected of having an additional advantage. Their lack of culture and refinement gave them a competitive edge in the job market, for they would accept wages that were too low to support a good lifestyle and never realize what they were missing. A literacy test would solve two problems. It would reduce the pool of eligible immigrants by about half. The remaining immigrants and natives would compete on a more level playing field, as the literate immigrants presumably had a standard of living closer to that of the natives. Bemis, though, was not just an economist. Like many people in his day, he was convinced of the importance of heredity. It was for him a happy coincidence that the places with the least desirable national groups—Italy, Poland, Greece, Russia, and so on—also had the least inclusive educational systems and that many immigrants from these places were unable to read.

Over the years, Lodge considered, and dismissed, other ways to limit migration. A high head tax would seem to be the most direct way to eliminate the impoverished immigrants, but, Lodge claimed, "it would have excluded the desirable as well as the objectionable immigration," that there was no necessary corollary between wealth and citizenship qualifications. Lodge also investigated the idea of having U.S. consular officials examine the potential immigrants while they were still in their homelands and issue certificates for those who passed the examination. However, it turned out that most countries objected to having U.S. officials exercise that much authority outside their own national boundaries. Also, the countries that were willing to cooperate were most interested in having the United States help them prevent the young men of military age from immigrating, whereas it was in the best interest of the United States to admit such healthy young men at the peak of their labor power. The literacy test, though, would bar exactly the kind of people Lodge wanted to limit, without his having to come right out and object to any immigrants on the grounds of national origins or poverty.[4]

In all this, Lodge sounds like he either was, or was trying to pose as, a friend of the worker. Immigration restriction was a variant of the protective tariff. The tariff supposedly preserved American jobs at decent wages by keeping cheaply made foreign goods off the American market. Restriction kept the same foreigners from manufacturing the cheaply made goods in the United States. (This was before potential immigrants could stay in their home countries and compete with U.S. workers by manufacturing inexpensive goods in U.S.-owned plants there.) However, one should also note that Lodge had grounds for complaint. Mass immigration gave a boost to employers, allowing the captains of industry to reduce costs, rake in more profits, move up in society—and challenge Henry Cabot Lodge and his Boston Brahmins for social leadership much faster than a bunch of recently arrived illiterates ever could. Immigrants' votes fueled Lodge's political rivals' campaigns.

Lodge had identified a new issue, but he had no time to press it in the House. In 1892, Lodge declined to run for Congress again, partly because a window of opportunity had opened for a higher office. Henry Laurens Dawes was getting too deaf to fulfill his duties as a U.S. senator, and under the rules that applied until the Seventeenth Amendment to the Constitution replaced them, the commonwealth's legislature had to elect a successor; it chose Lodge early in 1893. It is worth comparing Dawes and Lodge. They were both born in Massachusetts of New England families. They both went to Ivy League schools, Dawes graduating from Yale. Both had editorial experience, were admitted to the state bar, started their political careers in the state legislature, and moved to the U.S. House of Representatives and then to the Senate. They had slightly different legislative records. Dawes is best known for the Dawes Severalty Act of 1887. The law is controversial in American history, for it was based on the idea of breaking up Native American tribes and weaning individual Indians away from their inherited identities. The point here is that Dawes did not see a need to protect his own heritage from pollution. While it may have been chauvinistic of him to think others *should* assimilate into it, it is, in the light of his successor's career, interesting to note that he thought others *could* assimilate. Lodge was less optimistic about the possibility that others could assimilate and more concerned about setting boundaries between himself and outsiders.

Lodge was not the only one who doubted the possibility of assimilation and desirability of immigration. In the spring of 1894, about a year after Lodge replaced Dawes, the Immigration Restriction League of Boston formed. The Restriction League was founded by a group of Bostonians much like Henry Cabot Lodge, albeit somewhat younger; they were just finishing their studies at Harvard's graduate or professional schools and were trying to preserve their places near the top of society. Charles Warren, the one who gathered the others into the organization, was the descendant of a colonial family and the son of a politician who had gotten as far as port collector of the Port of Boston before his personal advance and his reform proposals were blocked by local Irish Democratic politics. Robert DeCourcy Ward's mother was Anna Saltonstall, another descendant of a colonial famiy that remained politically active through the twentieth century, and his father was Henry Veazie Ward, a merchant whose middle name indicated his ancestors had come to Massachusetts in the seventeenth century. Prescott Farnsworth Hall was the son of merchant Samuel Hall and Elizabeth Farnsworth. The Immigration Restriction League advocated a literacy test before the public and in the halls of Congress. It was so effective that it aroused opposition. Hull House, a Chicago settlement headed by **Jane Addams** and famous for its interest in its immigrant neighbors, organized the Immigrants' Protective League, which lobbied Congress and the public on behalf of generous immigration laws.

Lodge continued to write against immigration and in favor of a literacy test as the fastest, fairest way to reduce it. He combed the census for figures to support his contention that immigrants were a burden on the taxpayer. The foreign-born and native-born of foreign parents (second-generation immigrants) accounted for only 38 percent of the national population in 1890 but supplied 52 percent of all penitentiary inmates, 61 percent of all juvenile delinquents, and 59 percent of all almshouse residents.[5] Lodge was not above manipulating his data to get the desired effect. In 1890, police reporter **Jacob A. Riis** published *How the Other Half Lives*, a lengthy indictment of New York City's officials and landlords for overcharging impoverished and uncomprehending immigrants for tenements in which they lived in squalor. Lodge ignored the forces of law and economics and blamed the immigrants themselves:

Anyone who is desirous of knowing in practical detail the degrading effect of this constant importation of the lowest forms of labor can find a vivid picture of its results in the very interesting book just published by Mr. Riis, entitled *"How the Other Half Lives."* The story which he tells of the condition of a large mass of the laboring population of New York is enough to alarm every thinking man; and this dreadful condition of things is intensified everyday by the steady inflow of immigration, which is constantly pulling down the wages of the working people of New York and affecting in a similar way the entire labor market of the United States.[6]

As Lodge moved from the House to the Senate, the political climate changed and thwarted his restrictionist ambitions. Any anti-immigrant sentiment unleashed by the New Orleans episode had dissipated by the 1892 congressional elections. These went heavily Democrat. The depression of 1893 had a longer effect; voters still remembered it in 1894, when they replaced Democrats with Republicans in many districts in the fall elections. However, the rules in force at the time meant that the Congress elected in November 1894 didn't sit until December 1895, by which time it faced an issue it, at least, considered of pressing importance: the 1896 elections. The election of William McKinley as the next president in November 1896 gave Lodge confidence, and he got the literacy bill through the House and the Senate and to lame-duck President Grover Cleveland. Cleveland vetoed it. He was a Democrat, but he was more than that. He was a conservative, and legislation that compromised the American tradition of relatively free migration offended his conservatism. He didn't like the idea that someone might be pulling the wool over his eyes, and this bill seemed clearly designed to do that, legislating a literacy test when supporters speechifying about it usually skipped right over literacy and promised the law would limit the immigration of undesirable races. Finally, he didn't like the invidious distinctions between different types of European-descended peoples.

During the late 1890s and early 1900s, Lodge tried to get the literacy test into law several times but was blocked by his colleagues on Capitol Hill. Once McKinley had actually taken the oath of office and would be available to sign the bill into law, Lodge tried to send the bill through Congress again, but opponents to the bill had been alerted by the first campaign and were now mobilized against it. McKinley's assassination brought the subject of immigration restriction up again. The assassin, Leon Czolgosz, was himself born in the United States, but his parents had been born elsewhere, and that was close enough. Also, Czolgosz professed to be an anarchist, and there seems to have been a sentiment that he couldn't have picked up such ideas just through reading; he must have learned the ideology by contact with foreign-born anarchists. In 1902, Congress went to work on a bill prohibiting immigrant anarchists. Lodge got his literacy test appended to the bill, but his amendment had to be removed in order to get the law passed. The antianarchism bill became law, without his literacy test, on March 3, 1903.

The issue of literacy tests came up again during the period when Theodore Roosevelt was in the White House. Whether Roosevelt would have signed such a bill is open to question. He considered Lodge a close friend, and they were in agreement in other matters, such as the direction they wanted U.S. foreign policy to take. Although the president did not deliver a formal State of the Union address then, Roosevelt did mention the literacy test favorably in his constitutionally required written State of the Union message. As president, though, Roosevelt was the lightning rod attracting the protests of those opposed to the literacy test. He understood that he was president only because McKinley had been assassinated. If he wanted to be elected president in his own right, he had to avoid gratuitously antagonizing big voting blocs. Whether Roosevelt would have signed the bill remains academic. Speaker of the House Joseph G. Cannon, a Republican from Illinois, prevented an immigration bill from being reported to the floor of the House with the literacy test as a component. Yet the bill did contain other clauses Lodge wanted to see enacted, such as a requirement that Japanese immigrants present passports to American officials at their ports of entry. (There was a diplomatic understanding with the Empire of Japan that the government would issue passports only to the very few Japanese the United States wanted to admit.) Lodge removed the literacy test to get the rest of the bill through, and it became law on February 20, 1907.

Behind Cannon's actions was a complicated assessment of voting behavior. Cannon's home district was a mining area, composed of wealthy mineowners and largely ethnic miners. Cannon already had ties to the mineowners, and he knew they were interested in a large labor pool that would allow them to set low wages. However, he knew the miners had votes, too, and he wanted to avoid antagonizing them. In this case, it so happened that the mineowners' interest in a large labor pool coincided with the ethnic voters' interest in relatively open immigration.

That ironic agreement hides another layer of issues. Pehaps the reader could draw a stick figure representing one of Cannon's mineworker-constituents. Draw a circle around that miner such that the miner appears at the extreme right of the circle, then label the circle "worker." Draw a second circle, also around the stick figure, but this time making the circle so that the figure is on the extreme left. (In other words, a Venn diagram with the figure in the overlap.) Label the second circle "ethnic." Cannon's mineworkers—and millions of other voters—belonged to both circles, claimed both identities. They were workers and might presumably be expected to vote their pocketbooks, that is, for candidates and legislation that raised their wages, provided them with public schools, and made their socioeconomic advancement easier. They also identified with their particular ethnic group, and that brought another set of interests: They wanted to see a member of their group receive political honors, they wanted to practice their home religion freely (which might mean sending their children to denominational schools), they wanted their compatriots to be free to migrate, and if their home country went to war, they wanted it to emerge victorious. When Lodge wrote against immigration, he appealed to the "worker" identity and acted as if he opposed immigration chiefly because it pushed down wages. This was partly a ploy, but it also reflected Lodge's deepest values: He wanted to emphasize American economic interests. Politicians like Cannon either used the opposite ploy or sincerely held opposite values. Either they were willing to appeal to the voters as the voters indicated they wanted to be appealed to—through their ethnic pride—or they thought the United States could easily accommodate people with pride in their ethnic heritages.

After 1912, Lodge had gained sufficient control over Congress that he was able to get literacy test bills through the House and Senate. By then, however, the presidency was against him. Lame-duck President William Howard Taft vetoed a literacy bill in 1913, on the grounds that the United States needed as many laborers as it could get. Woodrow Wilson vetoed a literacy bill in 1915 on the grounds that during his campaign he had indicated to foreign-born voters he would do so. Still operating on the theory that his campaign promises meant something, Wilson vetoed the law a second time in 1917. This time, though, the House and Senate overrode the veto and the bill became law on February 5. The difference that led to victory in 1917 was the new concern about the depth of foreign-born loyalty in the event of war, and Wilson did ask Congress for a declaration of war against imperial Germany on April 2.

Evaluations of the 1917 literacy test law agree that it was nearly useless as soon as it passed but differ as to why. One line of thought emphasizes the low standard of literacy and the exemptions. Europe had made some progress in literacy since the law was first proposed in the early 1890s. Yet the law required only that every immigrant over sixteen years of age be able to read one fifty-word passage in the language of the immigrant's choice. There was a provision that if a family was migrating together, one person could take the test for all family members, so one school-age child who could read secured admission for a family of illiterate adults. There was also an exemption for groups fleeing religious persecution, which Russian Jews, not one of Lodge's favored groups, used heavily. A second line of thought emphasizes the timing. The same war that secured passage of the literacy test law also did more to reduce migration than the law ever could.

On the other hand, one might ask not what the law accomplished but what it intended to accomplish. It intended to shape migration along the lines of national origins, disguising the real criteria with a literacy test that members from undesirable groups weren't expected to pass. It reflects a shift from exclusion on a case-by-case basis (an anarchist here, a trachoma sufferer there) to exclusion on prejudicial grounds (reducing the immigration of undesirable groups without worrying about the merits of particular individuals). Viewed this way, Henry Cabot Lodge had finally helped to effect a major change in immigration policy.

Lodge, though, was not in a position to rest on his laurels. The United States was at war, and he was a member of the Senate, the branch of Congress the Constitution charges with the role of "advice and consent" in foreign affairs. By 1919, he was the senior member of the Foreign Relations Committee (the committee member with the longest tenure in the Senate) and thus its chair. Soon after he entered the Senate, he had taken part in important episodes in international affairs and always with a view to making the United States a Great Power, with a sphere of influence extending from the Western Hemisphere to the Pacific Rim and the ability to stand up to European Great Powers. Wilson's proposals for the basic equality of nations threatened Lodge's long-term commitment to making the United States *un*equal, to making it a Great Power.

Immigration was an element in the debate over the League of Nations in two ways. First, Lodge argued, perhaps simply to scare people, that if the United States joined the League, it would no longer be able to govern itself, but would have to abide by League rulings. What if the League followed **Thomas Jefferson**'s logic, and ruled in favor of the worldwide freedom to migrate? The Chinese Exclusion Act would then be unenforceable, the United States would be swamped with cheap labor, and wages and living standards would go down.[7]

Second, different ethnic groups had varied and sometimes conflicting agendas. Jews, aware of the anti-Semitic tendencies of Tsar Nicholas II and his court and advisers, did not want Russia to win the war. Poles hoped that their birthplace could be reconstituted as an independent state. The

Italians wanted to use the war to further their policy of reclaiming the irridenta, the Italian-speaking populations living just over the Italian border in the Austro-Hungarian Empire. The Irish tried to use the fact that the British were engaged elsewhere to their advantage and staged an uprising in the spring of 1916. When this Easter Rebellion failed, they pinned their hopes on postwar negotiations. His experience dealing with ethnic expectations "served to confirm Lodge in his opinion that the composition of the American population placed a severe limitation on the country's ability to pursue a consistent foreign policy."[8] Lodge wanted to identify and pursue American interests, but he could not continue to hold political office without at least acknowledging some Americans had multiple interests and as yet saw no reason to choose between them.

It is a measure of Lodge's political ability that although he disapproved of groups of citizens putting their particular interests in Fiume or Free Ireland ahead of the U.S. national interest, he still found a way to turn this regrettable state of affairs to his advantage. He encouraged the ethnic groups when he could. Privately, he worried that Irish agitation for independence might antagonize the British, with whom he hoped to cooperate. Personally, he thought the Italians a bit chauvinistic in their insistence on Fiume. However, he could use their agitation to call attention to issues in the postwar negotiations that he thought important. And, after all, Wilson had set himself up as *the* negotiator of the Versailles Treaty, going to Paris without Lodge, without any senators, and with few Republicans. Let ethnic voters bring their complaints to Wilson. Let them nibble away at the treaty day after day, week after week. Let them plant in the minds of the general public the notion that the treaty was flawed. This was not the whole of Lodge's strategy, but it didn't hurt. In 1920, he managed to defeat the Versailles Treaty in the Senate and to have his counterparts defeat it in the House.

It was at this point that immigrant quotas, the kind of national origins legislation that Lodge had disguised with literacy tests, dropped their disguise and came out in the open. Lodge, though, was not a champion of them. It is difficult to determine cause and effect at this point. Did Lodge's sense that other people were getting ahead of him in political leadership depress him and further the aging process, or was Lodge getting old and therefore irrelevant, even to the rather conservative 1920s?

It is a fact that Lodge's role in politics diminished after 1920, right at the peak of his most famous victory. Other factions of the Republican Party secured the nomination of Warren G. Harding of Ohio as a Republican candidate for president in 1920. The Republicans did nominate Calvin Coolidge, also of Massachusetts, as vice president, but Coolidge came from a different wing of the Republican Party. Harding died in office, Coolidge took his place as president, and in 1924 the Republicans nominated Coolidge for a presidential term in his own right.

While other Republicans were convening, Lodge was in the Charlesgate Hospital in Cambridge, Massachusetts, in failing health. He never left the hospital. On October 20, his physicians performed surgery. On November 9, he suffered a stroke that killed him that same night.

NOTES

1. William C. Widenor, *Henry Cabot Lodge and the Search for an American Foreign Policy* (Berkeley: University of California Press, 1980), pp. 57–58: "To Lodge immigration restriction was an integral part of any intelligent protective policy, and protection transcended the interests of individual manufactures and had a national purpose."

2. Karl Schriftgiesser, *The Gentleman from Massachusetts: Henry Cabot Lodge* (Boston: Little, Brown, 1944), p. 114.

3. Henry Cabot Lodge, "Lynch Law and Unrestricted Immigration," *North American Review* 152 (May 1891), pp. 602–612.

4. Henry Cabot Lodge, "A Million Immigrants a Year, Part I," *Century* 67 (January 1904), pp. 466–469.

5. Henry Cabot Lodge, "The Census and Immigration," *Century* 24 (September 1893), pp. 737–739.

6. Henry Cabot Lodge, "The Restriction of Immigration," *North American Review* 152 (January 1892), pp. 27–36.

7. Schriftgiesser, *Gentleman from Massachusetts*, p. 290.

8. Widenor, *Henry Cabot Lodge and the Search for an American Foreign Policy*, p. 342n.

BIBLIOGRAPHY

Lodge's papers are at the Massachusetts Historical Society. Lodge produced one pamphlet on his thought on immigration, *The Question of Immigration: A Lecture before the Massachusetts Society for Promoting Good Citizenship* (Boston: Massachusetts Society for Promoting Good Citizenship, 1892). He also produced articles for the periodical press, including "The Census and Immigration," *Century* 24 (September 1893), pp. 737–739; "Lynch Law and Unrestricted Immigration," *North American Review* 152 (May 1891), pp. 602–612; "A Million Immigrants a Year, Part I," *Century* 67 (January 1904), pp. 466–469; and "The Restriction of Immigration," *North American Review* 152 (January 1892), pp. 27–36. Lodge's biographies include: John Garraty, *Henry Cabot Lodge: A Biography* (New York: Alfred A. Knopf, 1953); Charles Stuart Graves, *Henry Cabot Lodge: Statesman* (Boston: Small, Maynard and Co., 1925); and Karl Schriftgiesser, *The Gentleman from Massachusetts: Henry Cabot Lodge* (Boston: Little, Brown, 1944). There's also a helpful monograph of a specific aspect of Lodge's career, William C. Widenor, *Henry Cabot Lodge and the Search for an American Foreign Policy* (Berkeley: University of California, 1980). A monograph helpful for the anti-immigration aspect of Lodge's work is Barbara Miller Solomon, *Ancestors and Immigrants: A Changing New England Tradition* (Chicago: University of Chicago Press, 1956). Lodge also figures in a helpful political case study, Richard M. Abrams, *Conser-

vatism in a Progressive Era: Massachusetts Politics, 1900–1912 (Cambridge, MA: Harvard University Press, 1964). A helpful article is John Higham, "Another Look at Nativism," in *Send These to Me: Jews and Other Immigrants in Urban America* (New York: Atheneum, 1975), pp. 102–115. For a monograph on the 1891 New Orleans lynching, see Richard Gambino, *Vendetta* (New York: Doubleday and Co., 1977). Lodge often charged that "birds of passage," or transient workers, impoverished the United States by taking their wages out of this country to spend or invest elsewhere; for more on this, see Neil Larry Shumsky, " 'LET NO MAN STOP TO PLUNDER!' American Hostility to Return Migration, 1890–1924," *Journal of American Ethnic History* 11:2 (Winter 1992), pp. 56–76.

THEODORE ROOSEVELT
(1858–1919)

Race Suicide

Theodore Roosevelt was a man of many accomplishments. Born in New York City on October 27, 1858, he entered public life in 1882 with his election to the New York State Assembly. He then held many and diverse offices, including police commissioner of the City of New York, assistant secretary of the navy, colonel in a volunteer regiment in the Spanish-American War, vice president of the United States, and from 1901 to 1909, president of the United States. He was also the first presidential candidate of an important third party, the Progressive Party.

His achievements as president were equally diverse. He prevented the powerful banker J. P. Morgan from acquiring a monopoly over the nation's railroads, made the Panama Canal possible, promulgated the Roosevelt Corollary to the Monroe Doctrine, won the Nobel Peace Prize for his mediation of the Russo-Japanese War, supported the passage of the Pure Food and Drug Act and the Hepburn Act to regulate railroads, promoted conservation of natural resources, and sent U.S. naval ships on a round-the-world cruise to display U.S. military might. In private life his activities included the hands-on management of a ranch he owned in the Dakotas, authorship of books and articles about historical and contemporary events, big-game hunting in Africa, and the exploration of previously unknown

Theodore Roosevelt at his home of Sagamore Hill at Oyster Bay, Long Island.
Theodore Roosevelt Collection, Harvard College Library.

areas in Brazil, which named one of its rivers after him. Ironically, his adventurous life ended when he died quietly in his sleep at his estate on Oyster Bay, Long Island, on January 6, 1919.

Roosevelt's presidential administration could have been a turning point in the debate over U.S. immigration. His personal contacts put him in touch with the leading theoreticians of his day, the people whose ideas had implications for national immigration policy. His political clout gave him the power to press for laws. Yet he took the ideas of the intellectual leadership of his time in a wholly different direction, one that ended up putting off immigration restriction for a generation. How that happened is a story that encompasses the intellectual history of the day, politics, and Roosevelt's own personality.

The story starts with the research of **Francis Amasa Walker**, an economist and sometime president of the Massachusetts Institute of Technology and the person who supervised the taking of the 1870 federal census. Walker was comparing that census's results with those of later censuses when he noticed that immigrants had higher birthrates than did native-born Americans. He explained this phenomenon in terms that came readily to an economist. By the late nineteenth century, industry was replacing agriculture, and urban living replacing rural. The shift to industry and urbanization increased the cost of living for several reasons. People were now paying for consumer goods, such as food, they used to raise on the farms. They were paying more for consumer goods they had bought even when they did live on the farm; their city houses were on more expensive real estate than their farm homesteads. There were more things they could buy: No one needed to buy light bulbs until there was electricity, but once the house was wired, one might as well buy not only light bulbs but books and magazines to read under the new lights. Finally, there was more to want in the city: more store windows, posters, newspaper advertising, other people with their stylish clothes. And it cost more to pass one's social status on to the next generation. Each child had to be carefully educated to find its place in the urban economy. The native-born realized they had to limit the number of children they had and to spend more on each child's education in order to maintain their place in society.

By contrast, Walker continued, immigrants made different economic calculations. They clung to economic strategies developed in rural agricultural societies, where more children meant more hands for farmwork. Even after they transferred from farm to factory and from country to city, they continued to take their children out of school early and to put them to work, preferring the pittance children brought in to the prospect of better future income from well-educated young adults. They either did not understand or did not care that they were undermining their own position by increasing the pool of cheap labor and lowering the overall wage rate.

Why did the immigrants have a different strategy than the natives? Walker argued that the immigrants were "beaten men from beaten races."[1] They were inherently, genetically, "racially," as Walker said, different from the natives. They were incapable of the kind of moral thought that would lead the natives to care so much for their children as to provide the best future for them. They were also incapable of rational economic calculations, of reasoning that if they temporarily forswore the earnings of their unskilled children, they could later count on greater earnings from highly educated children. Given that this is what Walker and other economists thought, it is no wonder immigration restriction had some support.

Another pioneer economist, **John Rogers Commons**, took Walker's analysis a step further. Commons was a paradoxical figure. He was interested in economic reform and particularly in making sure that economic prosperity reached the farm population and the industrial working class. However, he also thought that immigrants were incapable of reform, that they were racially different from native whites, further down on the evolutionary scale. However, Commons pointed out, this primitive nature meant the immigrants actually had the better survival plan. The native strategy sounded better in that it produced higher family income through education and in that it avoided the moral evil of child labor. However, the natives were still going to lose population. They were producing fewer children, while the immigrants were producing more. Eventually, the natives would lower their birthrate below the point of replacing themselves. They would then die out, leaving the country to the more numerous sons and daughters of immigrants. This replacement of native offspring by immigrant offspring was called "race suicide."

Here, the characterization of immigrants as members of primitive races came into play again, this time with disastrous consequences for U.S. history. Walker, Commons, and other social scientists and natural scientists argued that all the good characteristics of the United States were inherited. They denied that immigrants could assimilate, that is, acquire these characteristics through schooling or exposure to U.S. society. They further denied that immigrants could acquire these traits through intermarriage and the production of children of mixed parentage, for, they argued, mixing advanced people and primitive ones would dilute the traits of the advanced people. When the natives died out, then, all the good qualities of U.S. life would disappear with them, and the immigrants' invidious traits would take over. Thus, there was a second reason for restricting immigration. Not only were the immigrants themselves considered undesirable; their offspring could not be brought up to U.S. standards, and so the whole group should be barred at the outset.

Roosevelt knew about the economists and natural scientists. He had a lifelong interest in natural history. As a child, he terrorized the household servants by using the kitchen ice box to store the corpses of birds and small animals until he could mount them. He received his early education at home but entered Harvard College in 1876, came in contact with scientists there, and for a time seriously considered a scientific career for himself. As an adult he retained an interest in natural science. He knew one leading advocate of immigration restriction, **Madison Grant**, from their work together at the Boone and Crockett Club in Manhattan and from their mutual interest in the American Museum of Natural History. Roosevelt had fewer connections with the social scientists. He preferred history and politics to sociology and economics. However, he did know some restrictionists among the historians and politicians. The only reason he wasn't on a first-name basis with biographer, editor, politician, and restrictionist **Henry Cabot Lodge** was because Lodge used his middle name, which linked him to an old New England family. Lodge referred to Roosevelt as "Roosevelt," and Roosevelt referred to Lodge as "Cabot."

Roosevelt could have brought the social scientists' and natural scientists' racist notions to the presidency. He could have used the "bully pulpit" of the presidency, a phrase he coined, to push for immigration restriction. He was popular with the public, and he had what politicians call long coattails, the ability to get everyone else running on his party ticket elected. He could have led the way to restricted immigration. Instead, his record regarding immigration and race was mixed.

In one instance, Roosevelt refused to press for a racially restrictive immigration law. Roosevelt had been vice president for seven months when, on September 6, 1909, an anarchist shot William McKinley while the latter shook hands in a receiving line at an exposition in Buffalo, New York. Although the anarchist was native born, he had a foreign-sounding name, Leon Czolgosz. Congress drafted a bill prohibiting the migration of anarchists.

The bill included a number of other immigration-related provisions. It continued the prohibition on the importation of contract labor, extended to three years the grace period during which authorities could double-check to see that each immigrant had been properly admitted to the United States, provided for the deportation of those improperly admitted, and permitted deportation of those who became public charges (went on welfare) within two years of their arrival. Most important, the bill required each immigrant (or one person in a family) to be able to read a fifty-word passage in a modern language of the immigrant's choice. This last provision was a Trojan horse. The places that scientists thought sent undesirable immigrants also had low literacy rates. Requiring literacy would thus exclude the racially undesirable.

Immigrants and immigration advocates realized the literacy test was being used to sneak racial restrictions into immigration law. They demanded that the proposal be dropped from the bill. Even though one of the literacy test's supporters was Roosevelt's good friend and political colleague Henry Cabot Lodge, Roosevelt advocated compromise, and the literacy test was dropped from the final version of the law, which Roosevelt signed in 1903. There was no literacy test, and thus no racial restriction of Europeans, until 1917, fourteen years after Roosevelt signed the law and eight years after he left office.

While Roosevelt did not support a literacy test for incoming immigrants, he did support raising the standards for naturalized citizens. In 1906, Roosevelt signed a law regulating the naturalization process. The law created a Bureau of Immigration and Naturalization, the ancestor of the Immigration and Naturalization Service. It set up a standard process for applying for citizenship, with forms used throughout all the states and with fixed fees for processing those forms. Included in the requirements for naturalization was one that all candidates for citizenship who were between childhood and old age have some ability to speak English.

Other Roosevelt actions recognized the role of immigrants in U.S. political life. In 1906, newspaper entrepreneur William Randolph Hearst ran for governor of the state of New York on the Democratic ticket. In his campaign, Hearst called for generous immigration laws. Hearst could not have carried out this particular campaign promise. Even if he had been elected, immigration law was a federal, not a state, affair. Nevertheless, he seemed to be on his way to winning—and in Roosevelt's home state. Roosevelt did the Republicans back home a favor. He called on Jacob Schiff, a German Jewish immigrant, entrepreneur, and philanthropist, and asked him for suggestions for candidates for a new office, secretary of the Department of Commerce and Labor. On Schiff's recommendation, he gave the job to Oscar Straus. Roosevelt's act undermined Hearst's claim that the Democrats were the immigrants' best friend and helped to defeat Hearst. It may also have been of real help to immigrants, as Straus headed the cabinet department charged with supervising immigration. It definitely broke new ground in patronage. Previous presidents had balanced their cabinets by selected members based on their geographical background. By appointing Straus, a Jew, Roosevelt pushed the idea to include balancing the cabinet with representatives from various ethnic and religious groups.

In another instance, Roosevelt did make a racial exclusion, but he did so in order to halt racism at another level of government. In 1906, the state of California began to segregate Asian children into separate classrooms in its public schools. The government of the Empire of Japan protested this treatment of its citizens and their offspring. Roosevelt explained to imperial diplomats the difference between federal and state government, hoping to buy some time. In February 1907, he brought the Californians to a meeting in Washington and bought some time from them, too, convincing them to desegregate their schools in exchange for his promise to work toward federal legislation limiting Japanese migration. That October, Roosevelt sent William Howard Taft to Japan to work out the details of the "Gentlemen's Agreement," whereby the United States agreed not to issue passports to citizens bound for Japan whom the Japanese would find objectionable, and Japan agreed not to issue passports to subjects bound for the United States whom the Americans would find objectionable. This diplomatic agreement was intended to limit Japanese immigration. It was backed up by legislation. Roosevelt again sacrificed a clause for a literacy test in order to get through Congress a 1907 bill containing a provision preventing the Japanese who had gone to the American possession of Hawaii to work in the sugar fields from coming to the United States.

The most support Roosevelt gave those who wanted to restrict European immigration on racial grounds came in 1907, when he signed an omnibus immigration law. The law concretized the 1907 Gentlemen's Agreement with Japan, prohibited the immigration of people with various sorts of mental handicaps (the exact wording of the law referred to imbeciles, the feeble-minded, and the mentally defective, each of which had a precise meaning to the mental health professionals of the day). The law also established a commission to study immigration. Under the care of **William Paul Dillingham**, the commission produced a multivolume study rigged to prove that immigrants coming from southern and eastern Europe were inferior to those coming from northern and western Europe, which strengthened the restrictionists' cause and contributed to the passage of restrictive laws in 1917 and in the 1920s.

Roosevelt did not do as much as he could have to promote immigration restriction. None of his work on immigration mentions race suicide or the ideas associated with it. Perhaps Roosevelt was simply a shrewd politician, unwilling to risk immigrant votes by coming out openly against immigration. However, Roosevelt's published writings suggest another reason why Roosevelt did not urge immigration restriction. He had a different solution to the perceived problem of race suicide. He called not for fewer immigrants but for more American babies.

Shortly after his second inauguration, on March 13, 1905, Roosevelt addressed the National Congress of Mothers. He laid out ideas that he would return to again. The first was the relationship between the individual and the state. Individuals, he claimed, had responsibilities to the state. (This was very different from the idea expressed in the Declaration of Independence that "governments are instituted among men, deriving their just powers from the consent of the governed," meaning the people didn't owe the government as much as the government owed the people.) Women, Roosevelt told his audience, had a responsibility specific to their sex. Only women could bear and rear children. On them, then, population increase depended, and on population increase depended settlers for the frontier, the labor force for the economy, and the soldiers for the army. Thus, it was women's responsibility to have as many children as possible.

The problem was, women weren't. Roosevelt asserted, correctly, that the birthrate was declining. He also asserted, correctly, that it was declining fastest among the well educated and well-off. He further asserted that this was because women preferred to do other things rather than to have children. In this case, Roosevelt made a break with other theorists of race suicide. Walker and Commons thought of the lowered birthrate as a *family* strategy, done to better provide for each child. Roosevelt saw it as a *woman's* strategy, something that gave women more options in life than motherhood.[2]

Roosevelt also differed from Walker and Commons in his solution to the problem of declining birthrate. Rather than advocate immigration restriction, he urged women to have more children. Throughout his presidency, *The Ladies' Home Journal*, a leading women's monthly magazine of the day, carried short essays from Roosevelt on the importance of motherhood. One might argue that Roosevelt's writings for *The Ladies' Home Journal* were public relations pieces. Mrs. Roosevelt was of the opinion that a lady's name should appear in the press only at birth, marriage, and death. Since the ladies' magazines couldn't get much out of her, they had to content themselves with the material her more voluble husband was always eager to supply.[3] There is other evidence, though, that Roosevelt was really interested in boosting the U.S. birthrate. In April 1907, he was reading an article about "The Doctor in the Public School," another idea Progressive reformers championed, in the *Review of Reviews*. The article concluded that the physician's experience showed the importance of maintaining a low birthrate so that people could have fewer children and take better care of them. Roosevelt called the editor, long-distance, with a rebuttal that appeared in the next issue:

There are countries which, and people in all countries, who, need to be warned against a rabbit-like indifference to consequences in raising families. The ordinary American, whether of the old native stock or the self-respecting son or daughter of immigrants, needs no such warning. He or she needs to have impressed upon his or her mind the vital lesson that all schemes about having "doctors in public schools," about kindergartens, civic associations, women's clubs, and training families up in this way or that are preposterous nonsense if there are to be no families to train.[4]

After leaving the White House, Roosevelt continued to advocate parenthood. In 1917, he published a collection of essays entitled *The Foes of Our Own Household*. Among the essays were "The Parasite Woman; the Only Indispensable Citizen" and "Birth Reform from the Positive, Not the Negative, Side." Roosevelt used these later essays to answer objections to his theory that had been raised in the eight years since he first voiced it. One of the most serious was the complaint that he was urging women to have children only in order to have cannon fodder. This was especially problematic by 1917, when the United States entered World War I. Roosevelt stuck to his guns, writing, "If we now had war, these four boys [his sons] would all go. We think it entirely right that they should go if their country needs them."[5] They did go, and they, and Roosevelt, paid a high price. Theodore was devastated when on July 20, 1918, he received word that his son Quentin had died when his airplane went down behind German lines. (Roosevelt would lose two other sons to war. His son Kermit died while on duty in Alaska in 1943 and another son, also named Theodore, died on July 12, 1944, of a heart attack while serving as military governor of Cherbourg, recaptured from the Nazis shortly after the D-Day invasion.)

Urging women to have large families may make Roosevelt sound as retrograde regarding sex as Commons, Walker, and other restrictionists were regarding race. Actually, Roosevelt was ahead of his time in some matters related to women's place. While physicians argued too much education drained a woman's energy toward her brain and away from her reproductive organs, leaving her unfit for childbearing, Roosevelt declared "the woman is entitled to just as much education as the man, and it will not hurt her one particle more than it hurts the man."[6] When law and custom barred women from traditional male professions, Roosevelt proclaimed: "[A]ny woman should be allowed to make any career for herself of which she is capable, whether or not it is a career followed by a man."[7] When other people argued that if women were allowed to vote, they would forsake their homes for politics, Roosevelt wrote "The right to vote no more implies that a woman will neglect her home than that a man will neglect his business."[8] When he bolted the Republican Party and fostered the development of a third party, the Progressive Party, it was a woman, **Jane Addams,** who seconded his nomination as the party's candidate for the presidency in 1912, eight years before women got the right to vote nationwide. Regarding more intimate forms of male domination, Roosevelt was a Victorian gentleman. He opposed men siring large families simply to show off their virility: "[T]he imposition on any woman of excessive childbearing is a brutal wrong; and of all human beings a husband should be most considerate of his wife."[9] In an age that practiced a sexual double standard, Roosevelt held himself to the higher standard usually considered appropriate for women. He was very proud that he had not engaged in sex before marriage and therefore had nothing to hide from his wife.

Roosevelt's vehement attitude toward women's role in "race suicide" might have stemmed not from any ideas about competition between natives and immigrants, or from any ideas about women, but from personal experience. Biographers make much of two events of Roosevelt's childhood. Roosevelt was born shortly before Lincoln's election. His father, also Theodore, did not fight in the Civil War. He was married to Martha Bulloch, a native of Georgia, and he didn't want to upset her by going to war against her home state and her relatives. Their son, by contrast, went out of his way to involve himself in the Spanish-American War. When World War I broke out, President **Woodrow Wilson** had to find a tactful way to turn down the fifty-nine-year-old Roosevelt's offers to resume command.

Besides a father who didn't fight in the war, the young Roosevelt had precarious health. He always had poor eyesight and wore thick spectacles. (Years later, when he was drawing pictures of himself for his preliterate children, he always made sure to draw the eyeglasses.) During his youth, he had asthmatic attacks. His father turned the back of their house on East 20th Street into a home gymnasium so the youth could build himself up. Some of his body-building exercises included learning how to box. In adult life, he sought out physical challenges. Biographers argue that Roosevelt's father's lack of a military record and his own sickly childhood gave him obstacles to overcome. These incidents gave him an early start in the belligerence that one can see in many incidents of his life.

Insofar as race suicide is concerned, the pertinent experiences seem to be those of adulthood. Early in 1879, when he was in the second semester of his junior year at Harvard, Roosevelt met seventeen-year-old Alice Hathaway Lee and fell for her completely. He spent eight months energetically campaigning for her to marry him. He was so involved with her that his friends worried about what might happen to him if she turned him down. She agreed to marry him on January 25, 1880. They announced their engagement on Saint Valentine's Day, and then Roosevelt launched an equally vigorous campaign directed at her parents, to permit them to marry as soon as possible. Their wedding took place on his twenty-second birthday (she was eighteen), October 27, 1880. Shortly thereafter, the young Roosevelts bought property on Long Island on which to build a big house for the large family they both hoped to have; Theodore wanted to name it Leeholm, in honor of Alice's family.

There was some problem starting that large family. Alice had to consult doctors and even undergo surgery to improve her prospects for becoming a mother. However, plans for a family seemed well under way on February 13, 1884. Roosevelt was at work in the capitol building in Albany when a telegram reached him notifying him Alice had given birth to a daughter. At that time, there was no reason for him to be at her bedside. Women of Alice's class were attended by physicians and nurses, and women who couldn't afford or didn't want a male doctor could still get a midwife and some female friends. Later that day came news that Alice was ill, and Roosevelt took the train south from Albany to New York City. He found not only that Alice was dying of Bright's disease but that his mother was also dying of typhoid fever. Martha Bulloch passed away first, in the early hours of February 14. Alice died that afternoon.

In those days, it was not unusual for someone who had suffered the loss of a close family member to withdraw for a period of time. Roosevelt, though, withdrew all the way to the Dakotas. After the end of the legislative session and the Republican convention, Roosevelt used his inheritance (his

father had died while he was at Harvard) to purchase a ranch in the Dakotas, which he managed himself from 1884 until 1886. His ranching came
to an end when the blizzard of 1886 wiped out his ranch.

Roosevelt did make trips back east, though, and it was on one of those
trips that he found a second wife. During his adolescence, Roosevelt had
become acquainted with his sister Corinne's best friend, Edith Carow, and
they may have become close. At some point after Alice's death, Roosevelt
resumed his friendship with her. They became engaged on November 17,
1885. On December 2, 1886, the two married in a quiet ceremony in London.

Alice's daughter, whom Roosevelt had named Alice Lee in her mother's
honor, joined Theodore and Edith at the Long Island estate, which Theodore renamed Sagamore Hill. Edith and Theodore had five more children:
Theodore, Jr. (born 1887), Kermit (1889), Ethel (1891), Archibald (1894),
and Quentin (1897). Roosevelt's move to the White House brought his
family to public attention. At that point, his six children were, respectively,
in their seventeenth, fourteenth, twelfth, tenth, seventh, and fourth years.
They brought to the White House a stable of horses and a menagerie of
pets. They tried out all their toys; the stilts were particularly well suited to
the high ceilings in the formal rooms. They livened up the White House in
a way not seen since Abraham and Mary Todd Lincoln brought their boys
there and not seen again until **John F. Kennedy** and Jacqueline Bouvier
Kennedy brought Caroline and John-John. And they were not alone. Roosevelt's letters to them indicate that he was, in some ways, one of them.
When he went on trips, he wrote them letters. If they were too young to
read, he drew them pictures. Upon his return, he brought them animals for
their menagerie. He played with them and through play guided them to
adult skills such as horseback riding.[10] Edith's poise and distant, detached
demeanor reinforced the general perception that her lively, playful husband
was in some ways another one of her children.[11]

It's hard to read Roosevelt's oft-repeated line that "the pangs of motherhood put all men in women's debt" and not hear the voice of a husband
whose wife died shortly after childbirth. When reading his praise of good
mothers, the image of Edith comes to mind: a woman who raised several
children and spent her time on caring for them, her household, and her
husband. Altogether, there's something autobiographical about Roosevelt's
writings on race suicide, a sense that Roosevelt was preaching about what
he was practicing. Perhaps that is what makes his writing more compelling
than the scientific treatises or the anti-immigrant rantings of people who
made race suicide part of the debate on immigration.

Ironically, it was that same passion that brought the issue of race suicide
to the public. During Roosevelt's presidency, there was a burst of interest
in his argument that the lowered birthrate was a problem and that it
stemmed from women's reluctance to have children. The issues Roosevelt
raised continue to be of concern to those interested in women's issues.

However, during Roosevelt's presidency, this shifting of the debate over race suicide to a focus on women was a diversion. After Roosevelt left the presidency, leadership in the discussion of race suicide returned to the social scientists and natural scientists who regarded it as a problem only insofar as immigrants tended to increase faster than natives. Therefore, they saw it as a problem that could be solved through immigration restriction.

NOTES

1. Francis A. Walker, "The Tide of Economic Thought," *Publications of the American Economic Association* 6 (January–March 1891), p. 37.

2. Linda Gordon, *Woman's Body, Woman's Right: Birth Control in America*, rev. and updated (New York: Penguin, 1990), pp. 136–158.

3. Betty Boyd Caroli, *First Ladies*, exp. ed. (New York: Oxford, 1995), pp. 120–121.

4. "A Letter from the President on Race Suicide," *Review of Reviews* 35 (May 1907), pp. 550–551.

5. Ibid., p. 551.

6. Theodore Roosevelt, *The Foes of Our Own Household*, vol. 19 of *The Works of Theodore Roosevelt* (New York: Charles Scribner's Sons [National Edition], 1926), p. 143.

7. Ibid., p. 141.

8. Ibid., p. 145.

9. Ibid., p. 165.

10. Theodore Roosevelt, *Letters to His Children*, vol. 19 of *The Works of Theodore Roosevelt* (New York: Charles Scribner's Sons [National Edition], 1926).

11. Caroli, *First Ladies*, pp. 118–124.

BIBLIOGRAPHY

Elting E. Morison and John M. Blum, eds., *The Letters of Theodore Roosevelt*, 8 vols. (Cambridge, MA: Harvard University Press, 1951–1954), and Hermann Hagedorn, ed., *The Works of Theodore Roosevelt*, 20 vols. (New York: Charles Scribner's Sons, 1926), bring together Roosevelt's writings. Among these, the most useful are Volume 19 of the National Edition set, which contains a reprint of *The Foes of Our Own Household* (1917), chapters eleven and twelve of which are on women and birth control. Another useful volume is Willis Fletcher Johnson, ed., *Theodore Roosevelt: Addresses and Papers* (New York: Sun Dial Classics, Co., 1908). One can also consult Roosevelt's pieces in the periodical press, specifically "A Letter from the President on Race Suicide," *Review of Reviews* 35 (May 1907), pp. 550–551; and essays in *The Ladies' Home Journal* 20 (July 1905), pp. 3–4; 23 (February 1906), p. 21; and 24 (June 1908). For useful one-volume biographies, see William H. Harbaugh, *The Life and Times of Theodore Roosevelt*, new rev. ed. (New York: Oxford, 1975), and Nathan Miller, *Theodore Roosevelt: A Life* (New York: William Morrow and Company, 1992). Regarding the effect of the "race suicide" debate on U.S. women's history, see Linda Gordon, *Woman's Body, Woman's Right: Birth Control in America*, rev. and updated (New York: Penguin, 1990), esp. chapter 7, pp. 136–158.

JOSEPH PETROSINO
(1860–1909)

International Criminal Conspiracies

Joseph Petrosino was an immigrant success story, an American hero. Paradoxically, he was also involved in creating an immigrant stereotype he himself didn't believe in and in pinning it firmly to his own ethnic group. Petrosino himself was born in Italy, and his success discredited those who saw Italians as a dangerous lot. What happened to him, though, lent weight to those who questioned the desirability of open-ended migration from Italy and who sought to limit the number of Italian immigrants on the grounds that they were criminally inclined.

Giuseppe Michele Pasquale (later Americanized to Joseph or Joe) Petrosino was born on August 30, 1860, to Prospero Petrosino and his wife, Maria Giuseppa Arato. He was born and grew up in Padula in the province of Salerno in the southern part of Italy. Prospero and Maria had two other children, a girl named Caterina and a boy named Vincenzo. Mrs. Petrosino died, and Mr. Petrosino subsequently married another woman named Maria, Maria Mugno. He and his new wife had three more children, Antonio, Giuseppina, and Michele. Mr. Petrosino was a tailor and made a sufficient living. He was able to send his sons to elementary school. However, long-term prospects looked better in the United States. In the summer of 1873,

---

Bust of Joseph Petrosino at his grave at Calvary Cemetery, Queens, New York, Section 22, Range 9, Lot K, Grave 16.

the Petrosinos left Padula for Naples, where they boarded an oceangoing vessel for New York City.

Had he remained in Padula, Joe would have probably entered the workforce at about age thirteen. It may not have seemed remarkable to him that he did the same in New York, but the fact was later incorporated into the legend of a rags-to-respectability story. At the age of thirteen, Joe, and his friend Pietro Jorio became petty entrepreneurs. They ran a combination shoeshine and newspaper stand. They had a good spot for their little business, in front of a store at 300 Mulberry Street, which was across from police headquarters. There were a lot of men who needed to keep up their appearance by having their boots blacked and a lot of people who had a little time on their hands to kill with a newspaper. And it was a spot with a future. Across the street paraded constant examples of men who had achieved economic stability and community respect.

In the evenings, Joe attended night school. Having learned to read and write Italian, he learned English, which he would need to rise above the unskilled jobs within the Italian community and try for a job in the larger U.S. economy. Once his English was sufficient, he found himself an office job working for an Italian-American stockbroker named DeLuca, who had an office on Broome Street in the heart of the Lower East Side Little Italy. In 1876, Mr. Petrosino became a U.S. citizen. Joe, his minor son, became a citizen when his father did.

In 1878, at age eighteen, Petrosino made an important economic advance. He got a full-time job as one of New York's "white wings," or street cleaners. This may sound like a fairly low-level, unskilled job, but it was steady work, with little chance of unemployment even in an economic downturn. It also turned out to have possibilities for advancement. After about a year on the job, his superiors promoted Petrosino to foreman and assigned him to supervise the loading of the garbage scows that carried the city's refuse out into the harbor and dumped it in the ocean. Cleaning the streets had the potential for an even greater kind of advancement. The street cleaners were under the control of the police department, with police inspectors checking on the street cleaners' work. When he was promoted to foreman, Petrosino came under the direct supervision of Police Inspector Aleck Williams.

Coincidentally with Petrosino's promotion, Italian migration to the United States increased. The Italian migration had some characteristics that might concern police. First, few police spoke Italian. Second, the majority of the migrants were young working-age males traveling apart from their families, hunting for low-skilled, low-paid work and making do when such work wasn't available—just the kind of population that might turn to crime. Third, about four fifths of the Italians that came to the United States hailed either from the part of the mainland that lay south of Rome or from

Sicily, and this was important because those parts of Italy had a reputation for criminal activity.

Italian criminal activity went by various names. The names originally had different meanings. The Black Hand, the most popular name during Petrosino's day, was originally an anarchist organization. The camorra was the name for extralegal organizations in the area around Naples. The mafia was the name for similar extralegal organizations on the island of Sicily. Americans used the three names as synonyms. For Americans, one important element in the history of Italian crime was the political history of southern Italy. The southern peninsula and Sicily had been owned by the Bourbon royal family of Spain, which tried to get as much money as possible from the area without providing much in the way of government protection. Into the vacuum of government authority stepped extralegal criminal organizations that established their authority over an area and engaged in kidnapping for ransom, blackmail, and extortion. To make their threats real, the criminals murdered victims who did not pay them. They also murdered gang members who betrayed the group's secrets.

Given these factors, it is natural that the New York Police Department would consider making connections with the Italians in the city. It is not clear whether Petrosino took the initiative and volunteered his services or if Williams realized Petrosino had the necessary intelligence and character and recruited him. By the early 1880s, there was a relation between the two men. Williams used Petrosino as an informer (or "auxiliary," as Petrosino phrased it), nosing about the Italian community and reporting on possible criminal activities. In exchange, Williams promised to help Petrosino get a regular appointment to the police force. Later in his career, Petrosino became famous for his ability to go undercover, but when he was young and inexperienced, he failed to maintain sufficient secrecy. By 1883, those he was informing on knew he was an informer. At that point, Williams made good on his promise to press his superiors to hire Petrosino. It required some suspension of regulations. Police were supposed to be taller than Petrosino, who was five feet three inches tall, and if they were short, they weren't supposed to weigh 200 pounds. The physical requirements were waived, and on October 19, 1883, Petrosino became a police officer.

Petrosino began his job as a patrolman, walking a beat on 13th Street. This was general police work, but Petrosino retained his interest in the connection between Italians and crime. When on October 15, 1890, New Orleans Police Chief David Hennessey was assassinated, Petrosino speculated that the chief was right when he said "the dagoes got me"—that Hennessey had been targeted by a gang whose control of the city's produce market he had thwarted. Even without his hobbylike interest in organized crime, Petrosino was a useful and competent police office. On July 20, 1895, New York City Police Commissioner **Theodore Roosevelt**, who was devoted to the merit concept, promoted Petrosino to detective. Now Petrosino could really follow his particular interests and use his talents. Not only was he bilingual in Italian and English; he understood the spoken dialects of southern Italy. In some settings, he was able to disguise himself as a common laborer, pushcart peddler, or petty entrepreneur, at least until his distinctive short, squat physique gave him away. He also had a memorable face, scarred from a childhood bout of smallpox. He tried to fade into the crowd by wearing dark business suits and building up his height with tall derby hats and double-soled shoes.

To his competence, Petrosino added a sense of how to work with the public. He demonstrated his public relations ability during a 1901 rash of assassinations of heads of state. On July 30, 1901, Umberto I, King of the Italians, was assassinated. Italian police arrested the culprit, Gaetano Breschi. Investigation disclosed that Breschi had been living in Paterson, New Jersey, and had been part of an anarchist circle there. The anarchists had plotted the assassination and had drawn lots to choose the assassin. Breschi had sailed from Paterson to Italy to carry out the mission. Italian authorities asked the United States for assistance in tracking down Breschi's co-conspirators. The new vice president of the United States, Theodore Roosevelt, knew just the man, the Italian American he had promoted to detective in the New York Police Department. Petrosino disguised himself as a laborer, complete with a job, rented a room in a cheap boardinghouse in Paterson known as an anarchist meeting place, and let people think that he was sympathetic toward anarchism. He managed to sit quietly through meetings, to secure introductions to prominent people within the group, and to listen to them describe their exploits. Eventually, he had to get out. He had been introduced to Breschi's wife, an Irish-American anarchist named Sophie Knieland, and questioned her a little too closely. (And perhaps a little too roughly; this was before the potential for police brutality was closely monitored, and Petrosino had a reputation for getting physical in the heat of interrogations.)

Rather than make his report to his superiors in New York, Petrosino traveled to Washington to speak to President McKinley and Vice President Roosevelt. He had uncovered something he thought they should know. The assassination of King Umberto I was part of a much larger plot to assassinate as many heads of state as possible, including the president of the United States. McKinley and Roosevelt thanked Petrosino for the information but did not take it seriously. Perhaps they need not have; the Paterson circle never seems to have attempted to assassinate the president. But on September 6, 1901, an anarchist unconnected to the Paterson group, a non-Italian named Leon Czolgosz, did shoot McKinley. After McKinley's September 14 death, Petrosino was talking to reporters, claiming he had warned the president about the possibility of anarchist assassination. Petrosino was stretching the truth a bit; he had not warned McKinley about

Czolgosz. However, the incident became part of the legend of Petrosino, the good (skillful) detective and the good (patriotic) American.

In New York, a morbid boost to Petrosino's career came on April 14, 1903. Early that morning, a man's body was discovered stuffed into a barrel in a vacant lot on East 11th Street. The man had been stabbed to death, then mutilated, his sex organs amputated and stuffed into his mouth. The police inspector supervising the neighborhood called Petrosino. Petrosino set about solving the mystery. He used the trademark on the barrel to figure out what company had packed its original contents (which, he guessed by tasting the remnants stuck between the barrel staves, was sugar). He then had someone contact the sugar refinery to determine to whom it had shipped the barrels. When it turned out that one of the places that bought sugar from the company was a bar called the Star of Italy, he went there, took a table, sat quietly, and gathered information. Eventually, he pieced together a story. The victim was one Benedetto Maduena or Madonnia. The murderer was probably Tomasso Petto ("Petto the Ox"), a hit man for the gang that used the bar as a headquarters. Their main motive was probably to prevent Madonnia from turning informer. However, the killer had also used the corpse to send a signal to others considering the same course. Stuffing the dead man's genitals in his mouth was a way of advertising that this is what would happen to those who betrayed secrets.

Petrosino became famous for cracking the case, but it was not an entirely successful piece of detective work because he failed to obtain a conviction. As nearly as he could reconstruct it, this was because the gang was one step ahead of him. When the gang realized Petrosino had identified Petto as the killer, it sent Petto into hiding and substituted for him another man of similar physique. When Petrosino went back to the Star of Italy to arrest the murderer and conspirators, he picked up a man who looked like Petto. However, when the case came to trial, the man proved he was not in fact Tomasso Petto and was not connected with this murder. Without a murderer, there could be no one for the conspirators to support, and the case fell apart. Even though Petrosino could not prove it in court, he himself was convinced Petto was the killer, and, later he found at least one other person thought so, too. At the time of Madonnia's murder, his brother-in-law, Giuseppe Di Primo, was doing time in Sing Sing. Shortly after Di Primo's release from prison, the real Tomasso Petto, who was living under an assumed name in the mining town of Wilkes-Barre, Pennsylvania, was murdered at his own front door.

Not getting a conviction might have been fatal to Petrosino, because the case was actually more significant than the rubbing out of a potential stool pigeon. Petrosino hypothesized that Madonnia's jailed brother-in-law, Di Primo, had been part of the Star of Italy bar gang and had been sacrificed by his cohorts. He was the only member of the gang who had been caught, convicted, and imprisoned. From his prison cell, he sent his brother-in-law

Madonnia to the gang's headquarters to retrieve his share of the gang's profits. The gang refused to give Madonnia Di Primo's portion, at which point Madonnia threatened them with exposure, with fatal results to himself. The murder suggested the Star of Italy gang had important secrets to keep. Other evidence Petrosino collected pointed to gambling and counterfeiting. In short, it seems Petrosino stumbled upon racketeers at the beginning of what could have been a highly lucrative career. He was unable to end their activities through arrest. He was so sure he had the right killers that when the justice system did not convict the culprits, he undertook to do justice, as he saw it, personally. He harassed the gang with obvious police surveillance (intended to send a warning rather than to really monitor them) and with arrests for petty crimes. The gang had to disperse. But its members lived—for revenge.

The second failure connected with the Barrel Murder was a failure in public relations. While working on the Barrel Murder mystery, Petrosino held press conferences and answered such questions as would not compromise the investigation. The most frequently asked was whether this was a Black Hand crime. Petrosino kept explaining that there was no such thing as an international criminal conspiracy with headquarters in Sicily and branch offices in New York. Individuals with criminal experience in Sicily and southern Italy migrated and plied their trade in New York, but they acted as individuals or as small gangs, not as part of a giant conspiracy. They confined their criminal activity to the Italian neighborhood. They posed no general threat to the United States.

The public failed to buy Petrosino's reassuring story. The number of Black Hand stories indexed in the *New York Times* increased steadily after 1903, and the *Times* even then prided itself on not being a yellow journalism scandal sheet. Similarly, the turn of the century saw an increasing number of articles on the Black Hand in English-language periodicals devoted to serious discussion of national issues, such as the *North American Review*. The Italian-language press had a different perspective on the issue and criticized Petrosino, at least partly because his efforts to arrest and prosecute gangsters reinforced the general notion that all Italians were criminals. However, it was the English-language press that concerned Petrosino and his superiors. That was the part of public opinion that had to be reassured the police were in control.

As the outcry against the Black Hand grew, Police Commissioner **Theodore Bingham** took action. On January 20, 1905, Detective Petrosino held the first meeting of the department's five-person Italian squad. Every member of the squad was of Italian background and bilingual. Fairly soon thereafter, the squad had its first big case. A young man named Frank Lo Cascio came stumbling out of the woods between the New York City line north of the Bronx and the adjacent City of Yonkers, alerting the first police officers he saw that he had found a body in the woods. The officers thought Lo Cascio himself had committed the murder and arrested him. Petrosino cleared Lo Cascio right away: The corpse had multiple stab wounds and bore the signs of a struggle to the death, whereas Lo Cascio was unscathed. Then Petrosino identified the corpse and tracked down the murderer. The victim was Antonio Torsiello. The perpetrator was Antonio Strollo. The motive, apparently, was money. Strollo and Torsiello worked together in the same small town in Pennsylvania. Strollo found out that Torsiello had come to the United States to track down his brother Vito but that he couldn't read or write. Strollo then "helped" Torsiello place advertisements in the papers. He then pretended to have received a written response from Vito inviting his brother to come live with him in Yonkers. Excited, Torsiello emptied his bank account in Pennsylvania. Strollo "kindly" offered to accompany him to the unfamiliar town of Yonkers and, when they reached a forsaken stretch of the route, stabbed him to death and took all his cash.

The informal Italian squad was sufficiently successful at cracking cases such as the Torsiello murder that Police Commissioner Bingham formalized it as the Italian Legion. The stolid Petrosino was becoming the talk of the town. The *New York Times* sent a reporter to interview him at Legion headquarters on Elm Street in Lower Manhattan just above city hall. Although the reporter described Petrosino as "noted for an unusual degree of taciturnity even for a member of the Secret Service branch of the Police Department of New York," the interviewee was voluble enough to provide a cohesive theory of Italian crime. He still denied the existence of a truly organized criminal syndicate and maintained that what Americans were seeing was the activity of individuals who had learned how to be criminals in Italy and who carried those techniques to the United States but who were not all part of one organization. These criminals were dangerous not so much because of what they themselves were or could do but because of circumstances. Back in Italy, the legal system was capricious and seemed to favor the rich and well connected. The average Italian assumed the same was true in the United States and did not even think of going to the police when threatened by the Black Hand:

What they need is a teacher, someone who will make them realize that they are missing the greatest of all blessings this country affords, equal rights. If you tell them casually that any one of them before the law of the land is as good as the richest and the proudest of the native born they will laugh at you. They must be instructed so that the humble organ grinder, the shopkeeper and even the laborer on the tracks of the Subway will know that when the Black Hand picks him out for blackmail and possible destruction, the Black Hand is not only attacking him but is also seeking to break down and destroy the laws built by Americans to protect their sacred rights, rights in which he shares equally.[1]

When Bingham announced the upgrading of the Italian Force to the status of an Italian Legion, Petrosino and some friends from the police force celebrated with dinner at Vincent Saulino's restaurant at the corner of Lafayette and Spring Street in the Lower East Side's Little Italy. Petrosino had been frequenting the restaurant for some time. Vincent Saulino had come to the United States in about 1871 from Agnoni, Campobasso; he knew how to make the dishes his southern Italian compatriots appreciated.[2] Mr. Saulino also had a daughter, Adelina. She had been married to an Edward Vinti but had been left widowed and childless and had returned to her parents' house. On this night, after bolstering his courage with a couple of bottles of Chianti, Petrosino took Adelina aside and said something to the effect that they were two lonely people who might get along together.

Adelina accepted, and the two were married on the first Sunday of April 1907, at Petrosino's parish church, Saint Patrick's Old Cathedral, between Mott and Mulberry, Prince and Houston streets, at the northern end of Little Italy. Monsignor Michael J. Lavelle, who had been born and raised in the neighborhood when it was a predominantly Irish area and who had gone on to become the rector of Saint Patrick's new cathedral on Fifth Avenue and the archbishop of New York's liaison with Italian Catholics, presided at the wedding. The couple moved into a four-room apartment near Adelina's father's restaurant, at 233 Lafayette Street. Their only child, a daughter named Adelina Bianca Giuseppina, was born November 30, 1908, and baptized at the old cathedral.

The only thing that was not going well in Petrosino's life at this point was that he appeared to be fighting a losing battle with crime. The public was convinced there was a Black Hand, and Petrosino himself was seeing evidence that criminals in Italy and in New York had some kind of ongoing connection. It was not just a matter of individuals migrating but of groups coordinating activities. Also, the migration situation presented an easy way to evade the consequences of criminal behavior. Individuals could commit crimes in the United States, leave the country, and evade extradition proceedings. What was frustrating to Petrosino was that these people should never have been in the United States in the first place. U.S. immigration law barred the migration of persons with serious criminal records. Yet these people were slipping past Italian and U.S. authorities and becoming problems for local law enforcement.

Petrosino shared his frustrations with his superior, Police Commissioner Bingham. The commissioner went before city officials to see if he could get a secret service invested with the power to eradicate Black Hand activities. His presentation raised questions as to whether the police would stick to constitutional and legal measures in their campaign against organized crime. City officials, fearing Bingham would be creating a rogue agency, refused to fund his project. Bingham then went outside city politics, outside the city's treasury, to private individuals and groups. The Italian Chamber of Commerce, eager to clear the Italian name, contributed. There were rumors that non-Italian wealthy philanthropists such as **Andrew Carnegie** and John D. Rockefeller also gave money. As the phrase "there were rumors" might lead one to suspect, the new agency was hardly a secret. The story was in the papers by December 1908.

What Petrosino and Bingham thought of the lack of secrecy is unknown. Both of them paid attention to the press and were aware of the newspapers' ability to create among the public the comforting feeling that something was being done about crime. For Bingham, this may have been a major consideration. His position was a highly political one; he served only as long as the mayor regarded him as a help. Petrosino had to balance his appreciation of good public relations with another concern. Newspapers did, after all, give out news—and sometimes news criminals could use.

Sometime in January 1909, Bingham told Petrosino that the latter was going to Italy. There he was to make contact with U.S. and Italian officials but was not to rely on them for information. He was to make his own investigation into Italian police files. These were, after all, part of the public record and thus available to anyone with an interest in them. Particularly, he was to check into the criminal records of individuals known to be in the United States. With those records in hand, the New York Police Department could initiate deportation proceedings of people who had come into the United States supposedly innocent of any crimes. Petrosino was also to supplement the official records by establishing his own network of informants and gathering data from them.

Petrosino left New York at 4:00 P.M., February 9, 1909, in a first-class cabin aboard an Italian liner, the *Duca di Genova*. He immediately took seasick. When he felt better, he roamed the ship a little. Although he was traveling under an assumed identity, as an Italian-Jewish merchant, a few people recognized him, and he did not feel the need to tell them to keep his identity confidential. It probably would not have mattered if he had. About the time that Petrosino left New York, two of the suspects whom he had arrested in the Barrel Murder case and whom he had chased out of New York after breaking up their profitable gambling and counterfeiting operation boarded another ship, the *Romanic*. Was this only a coincidence, or did they know Petrosino was on his way to Italy? The timing of their trip suggests these two had some information. As of February 20, everyone had information. On that day, the *New York Herald* carried a story in which Police Commissioner Bingham described Petrosino's "secret" mission in some detail.

The *Duca d Genova* reached Genoa at 6:00 A.M. on February 21. That same day, Petrosino boarded the southbound Paris-Rome express at the Genoa railroad station. He got off at Rome, rented a hotel room, and settled down. The next day, he tried to see some officials but faced a barricade of holidays. At that time, the United States observed George Washington's birthday on February 22, and that year February 22 fell on the Tuesday before Ash Wednesday, and so was the last day of celebrating before Catholic Italy observed its penitential season. Petrosino turned tourist for a day, then tried again. By February 27, he had visited U.S. and Italian authorities. On that day, he boarded a southbound train out of Rome, stopped briefly to visit relatives in Padula, boarded the train again, and went to Naples. There, he took a mail boat for Palermo, the capital of the island of Sicily. The two men who had sailed on the *Romanic* were busy, too. Their ship docked in Naples, from which they went to their hometown, Partinico, on the island of Sicily. From Partinico, one sent a telegram back to the United States. Either the message was in code, or the combination of Italian and English rendered it obscure to people for whom it was not intended. However, knowing the name of the recipient was enough to arouse suspicion. He was yet another man arrested and released in the Barrel Murder case.

The mail boat pulled into Palermo early on February 28. Petrosino checked into the Hotel de France. Like most Italian cities, Palermo had a series of plazas, open squares around which were the facades of public buildings. The square in front of the Hotel de France was a little different. It wasn't completely open. In the center of the square was another square, the Garibaldi Garden. The garden had thick trees and a high iron fence around it. One could not cross the square diagonally by cutting through the garden; one had to walk around the perimeter of the iron fence. The usual plaza was reduced to a sidewalk around the garden fence. The Hotel de France was on the south side of this square. By going east to the corner and then north to the next corner, Petrosino found a good restaurant, the Cafe Oreto.

From February 28 to March 6, Petrosino followed the same routine: up and out of the hotel in the morning; to the police office of Palermo or to a police office in one of the many surrounding small towns; take notes and maybe make connections with a few informants; dinner at the Cafe Oreto in the early evening; then back to the hotel to type up the day's notes. Occasionally, Petrosino took a break from this routine to visit the post office, where he mailed letters to his wife and documents to Bingham.

On Saturday, March 6, Petrosino visited Palermo Police Commissioner Baldassare Ceola. At this meeting, he expressed his opinion that Italian police were deliberately concealing the criminal records of individuals applying for passports. Ceola tried to explain that there was no deliberate deception involved, that under certain circumstances Italian law rehabilitated criminals by suppressing their past records. Ceola also introduced Petrosino to one of his own subordinates, a Cavalier Poli, who talked with the American detective at length about his mission. Taciturn by American standards, Petrosino talked just enough for the Italians. Comparing notes on their separate interviews with Petrosino, Ceola and Poli realized the detective's informants had access to confidential information in Italy's judicial system. Ceola asked Petrosino not to leave Palermo without letting the police know; he implied that this was for Petrosino's safety. When he was alone with his subordinate, Ceola asked that Petrosino be let to work undisturbed but that he be watched. It is not clear whether Ceola's orders were followed, for Petrosino resumed his schedule of researching at the Palermo police office and visiting small towns outside the city.

Friday, March 12, Petrosino finished another day of research, which included a trip outside Palermo to the small town of Caltanissetta and a 4:00 P.M. meeting, probably with an informant. He returned to the Hotel de France about 5:00 P.M., bought a copy of the newspaper in the lobby, and went to his room. There was a rainstorm about 6, but it probably didn't affect Petrosino's schedule; Italians ate their last meal of the day later than that. At 7:30, Petrosino put on his derby and coat, picked up his umbrella, left the Hotel de France, and walked over to the Cafe Oreto. By 8:45, his dinner was over.

The evidence suggests that Petrosino had an appointment. He did not exit the Cafe Oreto, walk south to the end of the square, and then turn west to go back to the Hotel de France. He went the long way around the Garibaldi Garden. He walked along the north side of the garden until he had almost reached the northwest corner. Then, did he see who he expected to see? If so, he may have been surprised. He hadn't expected violence. He had left his police pistol back in the hotel room. But now, some persons produced guns and advanced on Petrosino until his back was to the iron fence, just as one would stand for an execution by firing squad. Then came three rapid gunshots and a slightly delayed fourth shot.

Just north of the Cafe Oreto was the terminal of one of Palermo's trolley lines. A trolley was waiting to begin its rounds, and a number of people were already seated in the trolley waiting for it to go. One of them, an Italian sailor named Alberto Cardella, jumped out of the trolley and ran west to the end of the street to see what had happened. He saw a stocky man, who had been standing against the garden fence, topple over. He saw two other men run away across the street, to an alley between two buildings, the Church of San Giuseppe dei Miracoli and the Palazzo Partanna. He heard a carriage drive away. Then he looked down and realized someone had dropped a gun.

The Palermo police arrived and took over the case. One of them searched the pockets of the victim, realized it was Petrosino, and had Commissioner Ceola summoned from his evening at the theater. The police began questioning employees working around the trolley terminal. They admitted to hearing the shots and seeing "a man and a girl" run off but could not recall anything else. The employees of the Palazzo Partanna, right across the street from the shooting, heard and saw even less. Fortunately, the deceased supplied his own list of suspects. Petrosino was carrying a notebook with a list of those whose criminal records he was checking. The police began to arrest them, and a pattern emerged. The suspects knew each other. All had at one point or another been involved in syndicate crime in Italy, had migrated to the United States, and had compiled criminal records there. Some had only recently returned from the United States, recently enough that they might have been inspired to return because they knew Petrosino was sailing to Italy. It looked as though there had been an international plot to eliminate a man seen as the scourge of the mafia.

As the police reconstructed the execution, they determined that there had been one gunman, Vito Cascio Ferro. One of the conspirators provided a detailed account of how Cascio Ferro conceived the plot, infiltrated Petrosino's informants with double agents, finally presented himself as an informant, gained Petrosino's confidence, then lured him to the northwest corner of the Garibaldi Garden and shot him. Many years later, long after it would have mattered to anyone, Cascio Ferro himself took credit for the crime. Usually, Cascio Ferro wasn't the type to actually kill someone. He was sufficiently high in the ranks of criminals that he sent other people to kill for him. However, he had a special animus against Petrosino. He had been one of those involved in the gambling and counterfeiting ring Petrosino had closed in on during the Barrel Murder. Although no one had been convicted for that crime, Cascio Ferro had been one of those hounded out of New York, and in his case, it really did close off an opportunity. Cascio Ferro was the kind of person who could have made a fortune in many honest lines of work. Having chosen crime, he still did well, directing syndicate operations in parts of Sicily. He had even been back in New York once since the Barrel Murder. But Petrosino had bested him once and had kept him from doing business in his city, and Cascio Ferro wanted revenge.

Police arrested Cascio Ferro in his hometown on April 3, 1909. He was held in jail while the police gathered evidence. Their case, though, began to fall apart on July 17, 1909, when Palermo's police commissioner, Baldassare Ceola, was transferred to Rome and then forcibly retired. The suspects charged with conspiracy were set free, and the investigation was closed on July 22. Cascio Ferro was never convicted of this particular crime. He seems to have died in 1943, while he was in fascist custody for his mafia activities and they were attempting to shift prisoners from a vulnerable prison to a more protected one during the Allied invasion of Italy.

The *New York Herald* broke the story in the United States, receiving information before Mrs. Petrosino or the New York Police Department heard anything. This was the beginning of the end for Commissioner Bingham. Although it would seem from the timing of their trips to Italy and their telegrams to each other that the conspirators had some other source of information, the publicity Bingham gave to Petrosino's work (and to his own efforts to stamp out the Black Hand) seemed to have placed the detective's life in danger. Plus, Bingham aroused other controversies regarding other ethnic groups and regarding his general handling of the city's crime. The mayor removed Bingham from office that July.

The city was concerned about the widow and infant Petrosino had left behind. At that time, there was no regular arrangement to provide for the dependents of a police officer who died in the line of duty. Assembly representative J. Oliver introduced a bill providing for a pension for Mrs. Petrosino. The bill passed the state assembly, received Mayor George B. McClellan's endorsement, and on May 30 went to Governor Charles E. Hughes for signature.[3] Friends also held at least one benefit that raised $2,500 for the family.[4]

The city also comforted the widow with a tremendous outpouring of respect for the slain detective. In Italy, Petrosino's body was kept at the morgue at the Rotoli Cemetery until Thursday, March 18, when it was moved to the Hostel for the Poor at Corso Calatafimi for embalming. On March 19, the Feast of Saint Joseph and thus Petrosino's name day, the church attached to the hostel held a funeral mass for him.[5] A funeral procession brought the body to the harbor to be sent back to New York aboard a British ship, the Cunard Line's *Slavonia*. The ship left on March 23 and arrived in New York a bit behind schedule, on April 9. Monsignor Michael J. Lavelle, who had married the Petrosinos, was the homilist at a second funeral mass, held at Saint Patrick's Old Cathedral on April 12, despite threats from criminal elements that they would blow up the church.[6] Another funeral procession went a few blocks east from Saint Patrick's to Broadway, north to 23rd Street, where Broadway cuts diagonally west of Fifth Avenue, and then north on Fifth Avenue to 42nd Street, where it turned east. At the East River, the funeral party boarded a ferry for the ride to Calvary Cemetery in Queens. The procession brought the city to a halt, as 200,000 mourners lined the sidewalks and watched the casket pass by.

It did not, though, stop the presses. Through the year, the newspapers reported on efforts to track down the criminals. Both newspapers and magazines used the murder to blow apart Petrosino's long-held theory that there was no international mafia. Not only was there a mafia, but it now loomed as incredibly dangerous. Typical was the comment of the *Outlook*: "The crime should at least have one good result: it should concentrate municipal, national and international action to eradicate and crush the type of criminal conspiracy against which Petrosino fought bravely and skillfully for many years and through which he died."[7] The Petrosino murder did what Petrosino least wanted it to do: It fixed firmly in the public's mind that immigrants, particularly Italian immigrants, and criminals were one and the same.

NOTES

1. "Petrosino, Detective and Sociologist," *New York Times*, December 30, 1906, pt. 3, p. 3, cols. 2–5.

2. Arrigo Petacco, *Joe Petrosino*, trans. Charles Lam Markmann (New York: Macmillan, 1974), p. 70, wrote that Saulino had been in the United States thirty-five years as of 1906.

3. *New York Times*, March 16, 1909, p. 2; April 6, 1909, p. 18, col. 2; May 8, 1909, p. 6, col. 7; and May 30, 1909, p. 8, col. 7.

4. Ibid., March 15, 1909, p. 2, col. 2; May 3, 1909, p. 6, col. 5.

5. At baptism, Catholics take the names of saints. In some cultures, the saint's feast day functions as a kind of birthday, with one's friends sending good wishes on that day instead of one's own birthday. This was the case in late nineteenth-century Italy.

6. *New York Times*, April 12, 1923, p. 19, col. 5.

7. "Blackmail and Murder," *Outlook* 91 (March 27, 1909), p. 656.

BIBLIOGRAPHY

Joe Petrosino has one biography that was originally in Italian, Arrigo Petacco, *Joe Petrosino*, trans. Charles Lam Markmann (New York: Macmillan, 1974). The English translation has several small errors in its description of the New York situation, so it might be best to check any specific fact against other accounts insofar as that's possible. Petrosino's death is also an element in the stories told in Thomas Monroe Pitkin with Francesco Cordasco, *The Black Hand: A Chapter in Ethnic Crime* (Totowa, NJ: Littlefield, Adams and Co., 1977); and Humbert Nelli, *The Business of Crime: Italians and Syndicate Crime in the United States* (New York: Oxford University Press, 1976). Petrosino has no papers in the sense that others described in these biographies do. However, the *New York Times* covered the story; one can retrieve the citations to the articles through its index and then check the rival newspapers for the same dates for more details. More background is available in the articles indexed under "Black Hand" in *The Reader's Guide to Periodical Literature* for the 1900s.

MADISON GRANT
(1865–1937)

The Passing of the Great Race

New York sums up what some people mean by "city," but it also has a healthy and vigorous Wildlife Conservation Society. Its largest conservation site is the Bronx Zoo. The zoo is a fascinating place, with acres of animals, some of them there because their natural habitats have been destroyed, all of them there to encourage greater appreciation for the animal kingdom. It is also a poignant, thought-provoking place. If being one of the zoo's founders was all that Madison Grant did, he might be remembered as a pioneer in his field. Yet Grant is better known for his views on human beings. He divided them, like animals, into different categories, and he wrote and lobbied to keep the categories he considered inferior from migration to the United States.

Grant was born on November 19, 1865. Both his parents descended from old colonial families. His father's people were Scots. They inherited money. Grant was born in his maternal grandfather's house on East 33rd Street and Madison Avenue; financier J. P. Morgan's brownstone was a few blocks north. Grant's father was a well-educated professional, a physician and surgeon who served in the Civil War. Grant had a thorough education under the auspices of private tutors. His father took him on tours of Europe and the Near East. Upon his return, he entered Yale as a sophomore and graduated with a B.A. in 1887. He took an LL.B. at Columbia, opened a law office, and practiced law, but he never really had to earn his living. He could divide his time between his two favorite activities.

During the good weather, Grant was out in the wilderness, hunting and exploring. During the winter, he was in the city, where he joined all the elite social, political, and philanthropic clubs. He helped to organize another institution, the Society of Colonial Wars, which preserved the history of pre-Revolutionary warfare in the territory that became the United States. He was also a member of a club that bridged the field and the city, the Boone and Crockett Club. The club was named for American explorers and pioneers Daniel Boone and Davy Crockett; its members were active outdoors and also in conservation and in natural history. By the 1890s, his experiences in the field and in the city began to come together. Grant never married. His home was the entire city. He saw himself as, in the words of a review of one of his books, a "strong-willed idealist," who had the best interests of New York and its people at heart.[1]

His breakthrough year came in the mayoral election of 1894. This was the last election of its kind; only Manhattan voted. By the next election the city boundaries had been redrawn to create five boroughs: Manhattan, Brooklyn, Queens, the Bronx, and Staten Island. The leading contenders for mayor were Hugh John Grant and William Lafayette Strong. A common last name and New York City birthplace was all Hugh J. and Madison Grant shared. Although he had a decent record of using government power to shape urban development—laying water and sewer pipes, paving streets, and building fire houses—Hugh was an Irish-American Roman Catholic who rose through the ranks of Tammany Hall. Old-stock Protestants of Republican background and progressive leanings supported Strong, and he won.

The Boone and Crockett Club lobbied Strong for a wildlife park that would allow people to see the animals that hunters and explorers were privileged to see in the wild. Strong in turn appointed a committee to develop the project. On the committee were Grant, architect C. Grant La Farge, the future president (and lifetime big-game hunter) **Theodore Roosevelt**, the future cabinet member and Nobel Peace Prize winner Elihu Root, and the Columbia University biologist and American Museum of Natural History (AMNH) director Henry Fairfield Osborn. In 1895, this committee secured a charter from New York State incorporating the New York Zoological Society (NYZS) and empowering it to build an animal park. The NYZS hired William Hornaday, founder of the National Zoological Park in Washington, D.C., to direct their park. Grant was one of the NYZS's founders, its secretary from 1895 to 1924, the chair of its executive committee from 1908 to 1936 and its president from 1925 to his death. Along with the Bronx Zoo/Wildlife Conservation Park, the NYZS took responsibility for the Central Park Zoo Conservation Center (from a zoo that grew up independently), the Flushing Meadows–Corona Park Zoo, and the Prospect Park Wildlife Conservation Center. In 1902, it took responsibility for the New York Aquarium. Eventually, the only New York animal park it did not manage was the Staten Island Zoo, which is directed by the Staten Island Zoological Society.

By 1899, when the Bronx Zoo opened, Grant was an acknowledged authority on large land mammals of North America. In 1895, he published a report on caribou in Alaska. Later, one species of Alaskan caribou was named *Rangifer granti* in his honor, and Grant donated a diorama of the "Grant caribou" to the AMNH's collection of dioramas showing North American land animals in their natural settings. Some of his works were intended for general-interest reading; the Boone and Crockett Club published his *The Vanishing Game of Yesterday* in 1933. One may think that the New York Zoological Society was simply doing its most faithful supporter favors by publishing his monographs: *The Caribou* came out in 1901, *Origin and Relationship of the Large Mammals of North America* in 1904, and *Condition of Wild Life in Alaska* in 1909. However, the NYZS and others took Grant's work seriously. *The Smithsonian* reprinted *Condition of Wild Life in Alaska* in its 1909 annual report, and New York State's Fish and Game Commission published his *Moose* in 1902 and also his *Notes on Adirondack Mammals, with Special Reference to the Fur-Bearers*. The AMNH also took his expertise seriously. In 1907, it funded an expedition that sent Grant and others to Alaska; the group came back with photographs showing the remains of a wooly mammoth projecting from the frozen earth. The AMNH elected Grant a trustee in 1911; he remained with the AMNH until his death.

Grant worked to preserve endangered species of animals and plants. In 1905, he helped to found the American Bison Society. In 1907, the Bronx Zoo sent fifteen of its bison to the new Wichita National Bison Reserve in Oklahoma. There, they would preserve a species that at one time covered the prairies. In 1919, Grant, Osborn, and John C. Merriam organized "Save the Redwoods" to conserve the trees synonymous with the northern California landscape. In 1931, the California State Board of Parks dedicated the tallest redwood it could find to Grant, Osborn, and Merriam in recognition of their work. (It might be a comment on Grant's subsequent reputation that later generations attributed the tree's name to Ulysses S. Grant.)

Besides organizing the Bronx Zoo, Grant organized ways to get to the zoo. From 1907 to 1925, Grant was the president of the Bronx River Commission, overseeing a watershed that ran through the New York Botanical Garden, on a tract of land adjacent to the Bronx Zoo. He was a member of both the Bronx Parkway Commission and the Taconic Parkway Commission, both of these entities being charged with building roadways linking cities to suburbs. Such roads have proved useful for commuting to and from work, but in Grant's day, there was another reason for them. They were for the middle-class families that had cars but did not have the time to drive them too far. Such people could still go out to the parkway and drive along the curving roads past the woodlands. Thus, they could take a nice drive that ended at the zoo.

Grant's interest in human beings was not quite the same as his interest in trees or animals. He never did the same kind of field research that he did on large land mammals of North America. He did, though, have friends and colleagues in the Boone and Crockett Club, the NYZS, and the AMNH who were researching and writing about how the human species and its various races evolved. He also had friends and colleagues at the Society for Colonial Wars and the other elite clubs of New York who were particularly interested in this scholarship. They were the old-stock, old-money, native-born people facing the annual arrival of hundreds of thousands of foreign-born poor and working-class people from a different ethnic stock, from southern and eastern Europe. Grant joined these two worlds together in a book he published in 1916, *The Passing of the Great Race*.

The "Great Race" of the title is the Nordic race, which Grant considered "the white man par excellence."[2] Nordics came from a territory in northern Europe that extended from Scandinavia to the British Isles and included northern Germany. They were not so easily distinguishable by skin color. The two other main European races, the central European Alpines and the southern European Mediterraneans, were darker, but they were still white people, with different pigmentation than races indigenous to Africa, Asia, the Western Hemisphere, or Australia. The physical characteristics Grant used to tell European races apart were height, with Nordics being the tallest; hair and eye color, with Nordics being the lightest in both categories; and the proportion between length (chin to forehead) and width (ear to ear) in the skull, Nordics being long heads, whereas the Alpines and Mediterraneans were round heads.

According to Grant, the Nordics' most important traits were mental and moral:

The Nordics are, all over the world, a race of soldiers, sailors, adventurers and explorers, but above all, of rulers, organizers and aristocrats in sharp contrast to the essentially peasant and democratic character of the Alpines. The Nordic race is domineering, individualistic, self-reliant and jealous of their personal freedom both in political and religious systems and as a result they are usually Protestants. Chivalry and knighthood and their still surviving but greatly impaired counterparts are peculiarly Nordic traits and feudalism, class distinctions and race pride among Europeans are traceable for the most part to the north.[3]

The Nordics' passing was caused partly by their supposed racial traits. At the time Grant wrote, Nordics were warring against Nordics in northern

Europe, wiping out a generation on the battlefields of World War I. There wouldn't be enough Nordics left to produce another large generation, whereas the Alpines and Mediterraneans would survive the war to breed again.

Grant was relatively restrained in his use of evidence. This was not his field of expertise, and he was properly cautious. One example is the way he described the recent unearthing of remains in Sussex, England. They were different from any paleontologists and anthropologists had seen in England, and they were tentatively assigned the identity of Piltdown Man, a preliminary to fitting the bones and skull into the scheme of human evolution. Grant reported that the findings were "highly aberrant" and reserved judgment on them.[4] He died not knowing he was justified; Piltdown Man was later proven to be a fake. Cautious as he was, Grant placed his faith in evidence that later generations have proved false. He regarded physical height as the sure sign of a Nordic. Even when he wrote that, cultural anthropologist **Franz Boas** (ironically later also affiliated with AMNH) was busy proving that height reflected environment as well as heredity. The better the nutrition, the taller the people.

Despite his warnings about the limits of the evidence, Grant had an unmistakable preference for the Nordics. He thought so much of them that he attributed everything to them. When it came to the Italian Renaissance, an outpouring of literary, scientific, and artistic advances on a peninsula populated mostly by Mediterraneans, he claimed that

[t]he chief men of the Cinque Cento [fifteenth century] and the preceding century were of Nordic blood, largely Gothic and Lombard, which is recognized easily by a close inspection of busts or portraits in northern Italy. Dante, Raphael, Titian, Michael Angelo, Leonardo da Vinci were all of Nordic type, just as in classic times many of the chief men and of the upper classes were Nordic.[5]

At least there was one Lombard in the group, da Vinci. In other cases, all the evidence seems to run against Grant. Consider, for example, his handling of the Normans. "The descendants of the Danish and Norse Vikings who settled in Normandy as Teutonic-speaking heathen and who as Normans crossed over to Saxon England and conquered it in 1066 are among the finest and noblest examples of the Nordic race." However, "This Norman strain, while purely Nordic, seems to have been radically different in its mental make-up, and to some extent in its physical detail from the Saxons of England and also from their kindred in Scandinavia."[6] If Nordics are characterized by certain physical and mental traits, and if Normans have different physical and mental traits, one has to wonder how Normans qualify as Nordics.

Perhaps Grant could wriggle the Normans into the category of Nordics. What about cases in which people clearly seem to be Nordic but didn't act it? Appalachian whites descended from English or Scots-Irish pioneers. But they were terribly poor. Extreme changes in climate might affect the expression of racial characteristics, but the weather in Appalachia was mild. Ignoring the possibility of social or economic forces or malnutrition, Grant went right to his favorite explanation: "There are probably other hereditary forces at work there as yet little understood."[7]

Grant's tendency to claim every accomplishment for the Nordics was fueled not by the historical record but by his understanding of the importance of race. *Everything* depends on race. There is nothing one can do to escape the fate mandated by the gene pool. Grant simply denied that all men were created equal. If that was antidemocratic, so be it. Grant preferred republicanism (upper- and lowercase *r*) to democracy (upper- and lowercase *d*). In his view, a small-*r* republic, or political system in which voters elected a representative who had a free hand to govern, was the same as an aristocracy, "government by the wisest and best, always a small minority in any population. Human society is like a serpent dragging its long body along the ground, but with the head always thrust a little in advance and a little elevated above the earth."[8]

Education, in particular, was wasted on people who could not appreciate it. If one was born of Alpine stock, one needn't bother. Grant thought the Alpine race short on both stature and intellectual attainment. Mediterraneans did better; in the field of art, they did better than even Nordics. Nordics, though, did the best in the most important areas of literature and scientific research.[9]

Nor did religion help improve immigrants. Grant complained particularly about Christianity. Early Christianity "was at the outset the religion of the slave, the meek and the lowly while Stoicism was the religion of the strong men of the time."[10] The rise of Christianity meant the increase of these racial and class inferiors. The consolidation of Catholic Christianity completed the revolution of unfit over fit. "In the Middle Ages, through persecution resulting in actual death, life imprisonment and banishment, the free thinking, progressive and intellectual elements were persistently eliminated over large areas, leaving the perpetuation of the race to be carried on by the brutal, the servile and the stupid."[11] In the French and Spanish colonies, Catholicism contributed to losses of the Nordic race: "The Church of Rome has everywhere used its influence to break down racial distinctions," permitting marriages between Europeans and natives, which diluted the strength of the European gene pool.[12] Grant was appallingly frank about the shortcomings of religion in his own day. "Mistaken regard for what are believed to be divine laws and a sentimental belief in the sanctity of human life tend to prevent both the elimination of defective infants and the sterilization of such adults as are themselves of no value to the community."[13]

Perhaps one should admit defeat for one's self but seek to improve one's children by marrying into a better gene pool and giving the next generation an infusion of good genes. Grant denied this strategy would work. First, he did not think much of women as carriers of the proper genetic material. "Women in all human races, as the females among all the mammals, tend to exhibit the older, more generalized and primitive traits of the past of the race. The male in his individual development indicates the direction in which the race is tending under the influence of variation and selection."[14] Even mating with one's own race, then, ran the risk of producing a throwback, for even within their own race superior males would be siring offspring by slightly inferior women.

More important to Grant's argument, when races intermarried, the traits of the lower one always dominated those of the higher one. "The cross between a white man and an Indian is an Indian; the cross between a white man and a Negro is a Negro; the cross between a white man and a Hindu is a Hindu; and the cross between any of the three European races and a Jew is a Jew."[15] As far as Grant was concerned, the Alpine French and the Mediterranean Spaniards had already demonstrated this principle during their colonization efforts. When they came to the New World, the French and Spanish did not bring their own women with them but intermarried with those they found in the lands they conquered. Instead of strengthening the aboriginal races, they had weakened their own.[16]

One has to wonder why Grant thought the Nordics were so intelligent, since they seemed to be ignoring what he considered plain fact. The United States had started with the best possible race, the Nordics. They had the best kinds of Nordics, hardy and vigorous people who crossed the ocean and who survived the rigors of the early colonial era. They had brought their own women with them, so there were few intermarriages, and the ocean cut off the possibility of mixing with other races.

What happened? The American Nordics threw away their chance at racial superiority. Throughout their history they admitted every possible race of immigrant. Grant called for an end to indiscriminate immigration:

We Americans must realize that the altruistic ideals which have controlled our social development during the past century and the maudlin sentimentalism that has made America "an asylum for the oppressed," are sweeping the nation toward a racial abyss. If the Melting Pot is allowed to boil without control and we continue to follow our national motto and deliberately blind ourselves to all "distinctions of race, creed or color," the type of native American of Colonial descent will become as extinct as the Athenian of the age of Pericles, and the Viking of the days of Rollo.[17]

The Passing of the Great Race received mixed reviews.[18] *The American Historical Review* considered it a work of scholarship and, as such, not a replacement for the standard work in the field, W. Z. Ripley's 1899 *Races*

of Europe. Some reviewers were more interested in the political implications of the work. **Emily Balch,** herself a liberal Progressive and the author
of a book entitled *Our Slavic Fellow Citizens* and who reviewed *The Passing of the Great Race* for *The Forum*, a monthly journal on contemporary
affairs, didn't think much of Grant's racial hierarchy. **Horace Meyer Kallen,** who created the concept of multiculturalism and who reviewed the
book for *The Dial*, also lambasted the racism. *The Nation*, which later
became more interested in racial equality, was in 1917 more complimentary
of Grant's careful attention to the problems of racial mixing. *The Yale
Review* gave favorable reviews both to its alumnus and to his proposal for
immigration restriction along national lines.

Grant also put his views directly before the politicians who could incor-
porate them into legislation. The years immediately after World War I were
a propitious moment for immigration legislation. Public opinion was shifting to oppose immigration. Organized labor had long opposed open immigration because of the fear of a huge labor market and depressed wages.
Now, capitalists began to join labor. It wasn't that they were uninterested
in low wages, but they were beginning to equate immigrants with the prom-
ulgation of labor unions and political radicalism. Also, there was a large
proportion of Anglo-Saxons among the entrepreneurs. If they valued their
ethnic group rather than their business opportunities, they would realize
their ethnic group would be outnumbered by new migration from southern
and eastern Europe. The first openly racial limitation on European immigration passed in this atmosphere. Proposed by Senator **William Paul Dillingham,** a Republican from Vermont, it assigned each European state a
quota that was equal to 3 percent of the number of immigrants from that
state counted in the 1910 U.S. census. Congress passed the law in May
1921 as a temporary measure.

The next year, Grant became a vice president of the Immigration Restriction League, an organization created in Boston in 1894 to lobby for
immigration restrictions. He was already acquainted with **Albert Johnson,**
Republican congressional representative from Washington State and chair
of the House Committee on Immigration. He offered Johnson his advice
on how to frame a more enduring immigration law. The new law passed
on May 26, 1924, reflected his advice. Temporarily, it assigned each nation
a quota equal to 2 percent of that nation's nationals present in the U.S.
population in the 1890 census. Using the 1890 census rigged the system to
the disadvantage of ethnic groups from southern and eastern Europe, which
had begun arriving in large numbers only after that date. After 1927, the
total annual quota of immigrants was set at 150,000. Each country was
permitted a national quota that bore the same relation to 150,000 that the
nation's nationals had borne to the total U.S. population in the 1920 census. Thus, countries with more recent immigration, the nationals of which
were few in number and who did not yet have numerous descendants,

received small quotas. Countries that had been sending immigrants for a longer period of time, and whose nationals had numerous descendants, received large quotas.

The national quota law, though, was not what Grant himself would have called a "Counsel of Perfection," the best law there could be. In *The Passing of the Great Race* he had noted that race and nationality were two different things. Nationality was determined by the government one lived under (all people living in the boundaries of France were French), but gene pools determined race (within France there were a few Nordics, many Alpines and Mediterraneans, and Jews and other smaller racial groups). Because of continental migration and the rise of empires, there were no places in Europe where racial and governmental boundaries coincided. The Nordic race had spread everywhere but were the majority in only a few places; it was possible the Italian government might issue a passport to a citizen who happened to be a Nordic but, given the percentage of Nordics in the Italian population, unlikely. However, it would have caused great logistical difficulties for the United States to specify that only Nordics could migrate. The United States instead adopted *national* quotas, admitting people by the passport they held, not the race of which they were supposedly a member. Grant would have preferred passports that identified racial groups so the United States could include or exclude immigrants.

Nor was Grant out of advice. From the 1920s to his death, he published several works that reinforced anti-immigration sentiments, almost as if he wanted to inspire Americans to administer the laws they had passed. In 1925, *The Forum* ran his article on how the new laws would secure "America for the Americans." He collaborated with Charles Stewart Davison, a colleague on the board of trustees of the AMNH and the president of another anti-immigrant group, the American Defense Society, on two works. In 1928, they published *The Founders of the Republic on Immigration, Naturalization and Aliens*, a slender volume containing anti-immigrant quotes from **John Adams, Thomas Jefferson,** and other signers of the Declaration and Framers of the Constitution, all without any context or interpretive material. In 1930, they published a larger work, *The Alien in Our Midst, or "Selling Our Birthright for a Mess of Pottage": The Written Views of a Number of Americans (Present and Former) on Immigration and Its Results.*

In 1933, Charles Scribner's Sons published *The Conquest of a Continent, or, The Expansion of Races in America.* This was Grant's last full-length book. As he aged, he developed problems that hindered his enjoyment of the outdoors: arthritis, heart ailments, nephritis. It's difficult to determine which was the most important cause of his death, which took place at his Park Avenue apartment home on May 30, 1937. Overlooking or forgiving his nasty comments on Christianity, he was given an Episcopalian funeral. Befitting his devotion to his colonial roots, he was buried in a place redolent of New York's colonial past, the Sleepy Hollow Cemetery in Tarrytown, New York.

The Conquest of a Continent was in some ways a fuller development of Grant's racial theories than his previous works. The first two chapters provide an abbreviated, updated account of some of the material in *The Passing of the Great Race*, on the evolution of human beings and the rise of the Nordics, first in Europe and then in the United States. Chapters three through ten are a more detailed narrative of the Nordics in North America, describing how they began exploring, settled in New England and Virginia, and then spread out across the frontier to the Old Northwest, the Pacific Northwest, and the part of the Southwest that previously belonged to Mexico. Chapters eleven through thirteen covered events in which Grant himself participated. He recounted the events leading up to immigration restriction, assigning people like himself the greatest credit:

The most active voices in its [immigration restriction's] favor were, primarily, organized labor, which wished no more competition from floating aliens with a wholly un-American standard of living, and, most of all, the native American groups, eugenists and others who were far-sighted and unwilling to see the racial character and national unity of America destroyed and republican ideals endangered and undermined.[19]

In their effort to halt immigration, "[a]n investigation was ordered to find the proportion of the various national (not *racial*) groups in the United States at the time of the 1920 census."[20] Having lobbied for the 1924 law, Grant was aware of its shortcomings. In his chapter on "the Nordic Outlook" in *The Conquest of a Continent*, he made recommendations to remedy those shortcomings.[21]

Grant's recommendations may be divided into three categories. The first consisted of suggestions for plugging the remaining holes in the immigration law. The United States should suspend all immigration. Included in this suspension would be all immigrants from U.S. colonies, especially the Philippines. Other Asian nations, particularly Japan, were complaining that members of their race were forbidden to migrate to the United States. A suspension of Filipino immigration, indeed of all immigration, would put the sensitive Japanese on par with the rest of the world. Grant also proposed suspending naturalization procedures, so that immigrants could not become citizens, which meant that they would never be able to vote or run for office in the United States. *That*, perhaps, would leave the political arena to those descendants of Nordics best fitted to it. Nonnaturalized immigrants would also not have the same rights that citizens did regarding the sponsorship of close relatives, and that would further reduce the immigration of people Grant considered undesirable.

A second category of suggestions had to do with dealing with the races already in the United States, particularly the African race. Grant noted with satisfaction that blacks were a smaller proportion of the population in 1933 than they had been during the early days of the Republic. (He neglected to point out that this was due to the immigration of European whites and to their reproduction.) However, he thought the black birthrate was still high.[22] To reduce it, he suggested promoting birth control and, if that didn't work, imposing sterilization. As with immigrants, he also thought it best if blacks be denied U.S. citizenship.

A third proposal moved this kind of racism out into the larger world. The British Empire, Grant thought, was faltering. The British had suffered from World War I and from the depression. Also, a wave of sentimentality and of consideration for the natives was leading the British to relax their grip on the native populations in the colonies. Grant called on the United States to end its historic policy of isolation, not to join the world as an equal but to pick up where Great Britain might be compelled to leave off and to assume the "white man's burden" of supervising dark-skinned peoples. Anti-immigration was not just anti-immigration. It was part of a larger program of establishing a secure racial hierarchy in the United States and over the world. Grant was not only dangerous to immigrants but also to citizens of the United States and to people who would never come near the country.

By the time he wrote *The Conquest of a Continent*, Grant had already pushed the immigration debate in a particular direction. He had provided a rationale for racially and ethnically restrictive immigration laws. U.S. immigration law reflected his influence from 1921 until 1968, when the 1965 amendments were finally fully implemented.

Although the laws Grant lobbied for have been repealed, Grant's racism continues to shape the immigration debate. His work firmly yoked together two different concepts, immigration restriction and racism. He inadvertently made it difficult for subsequent restrictionists to argue for the limitation of immigration on any other basis. Later opponents of immigration could talk about overpopulation, environmental degradation, labor competition, and other ill effects of immigration, but it was difficult to shake off the fear that underneath these charges lurked the racist history of restriction.

NOTES

1. Review of *The Passing of the Great Race* in *The Yale Review*, n.s. 6 (April 1917), p. 670.

2. Madison Grant, *The Passing of the Great Race*, new edition, rev. and amplified, with a new preface by Henry Fairfield Osborn (New York: Charles Scribner's Sons, 1918), p. 27.

3. Ibid., p. 228.

4. Ibid., p. 106.
5. Ibid., p. 215.
6. Ibid., p. 206.
7. Ibid., p. 39.
8. Ibid., p. 7.
9. Ibid., p. 229.
10. Ibid., p. 221.
11. Ibid., p. 53.
12. Ibid., p. 85.
13. Ibid., p. 49.
14. Ibid., p. 27.
15. Ibid., p. 18.
16. Ibid., p. 75.
17. Ibid., p. 263.
18. A bibliography of reviews, with excerpts from the longest ones, is found in *Book Review Digest*, thirteenth annual cumulation (New York: Henry Wilson, 1917), p. 229.
19. Madison Grant, *The Conquest of a Continent, or, The Expansion of Races in America*, with an introduction by Henry Fairfield Osborn (New York: Charles Scribner's Sons, 1933), p. 269.
20. Ibid., p. 272.
21. Ibid., pp. 348–352.
22. Linda Gordon has pointed out that the African-American birthrate was quite low. See Linda Gordon, *Woman's Body, Woman's Right: Birth Control in America*, rev. and updated (New York: Penguin, 1990), p. 154.

BIBLIOGRAPHY

The Wildlife Conservation Society, the successor to the New York Zoological Society, has files showing Grant's activities in his capacity as secretary, chair of the executive committee, and president; the time period covered is 1895 to 1937. The American Museum of Natural History has a biographical file and includes Grant's publications in its library. Grant has an extensive list of publications on large mammals. The publications that are relevant for immigration include *The Passing of the Great Race, or, The Racial Basis of European History* (New York: Charles Scribner's Sons, 1916); *The Passing of the Great Race*, new edition, rev. and amplified, with a new preface by Henry Fairfield Osborn (New York: Charles Scribner's Sons, 1918); "America for the Americans," *Forum* 74 (September 1925), pp. 346–355; *The Founders of the Republic on Immigration, Naturalization and Aliens*, with Charles Steward Davison (New York: Charles Scribner's Sons, 1928); *The Alien in Our Midst*, with Charles Steward Davison (New York: Galton Publishing Co., 1930); *The Conquest of a Continent, or, The Expansion of Races in America*, with an introduction by Henry Fairfield Osborn (New York: Charles Scribner's Sons, 1933). For more on Grant's intellectual milieu, see Ronald Rainger, *An Agenda for Antiquity: Henry Fairfield Osborn and Vertebrate Paleontology at the American Museum of Natural History, 1890–1935*, History of American Science and Technology Series (Tuscaloosa: University of Alabama Press, 1991).

A. MITCHELL PALMER
(1872–1936)

Red Scare

During 1919–1920, Americans turned their attention from the end of World War I to the possibility that the Bolshevik Revolution might extend to the United States. Their focus was broad enough to include various kinds of radicals, not just the communists who overthrew czarist Russia and erected the Union of Soviet Socialist Republics but also anarchists. It narrowed, though, on one particular point, targeting foreign-born alleged radicals for deportation. The efforts to eradicate foreign radicalism led to gross violations of civil and human rights. By 1920, concern about the potential for revolution among foreign-born radicals had declined. Generations later, history texts summarized the event as a kind of spasm of national hysteria called the Red Scare. It's also summed up as the product of the personal hysteria, and ambition, of Alexander Mitchell Palmer. Without denying that Palmer had a personal interest in, and bore some responsibility for, the Red Scare, it might be possible to use this entry to place him in the context of the social, legal, and political forces of his time.

Palmer was born in Moosehead, Pennsylvania, on May 4, 1872. He was the third child and second boy, out of a total of six children, of Samuel Bernard Palmer, descendant of Quakers that had originally settled in New York, and Caroline Albert, descendant of Quakers in Luzerne County. He was named after the president of the Lehigh Valley Railroad, for whom Mr. Palmer occasionally worked building bridges; as an adult, he used A. Mitchell. He was educated at Stroudsburg High School, at the Moravian Parochial School, and at the Quaker's Swarthmore College. Biographers and historians often point to the irony of someone with such a thoroughly Quaker education, living in such a part of the country with such a mixed population as Pennsylvania had, heading up an antiradical campaign that abused people's civil liberties and sometimes threatened them physically. While Palmer himself took his Quaker background seriously on some occasions, he did not see it as providing moral guidance on immigration. Nor was he influenced by the heterogeneity of his environment.

Upon graduation from college, Palmer laid a foundation for realizing his greater ambitions. He returned to Stroudsburg, where his family was already well known and studied to become a court reporter. Once he had a steady job, he used his work to finance his study of the law at the offices of John B. Storm. When he became a lawyer, he used his profits to invest in local businesses. He also joined local social clubs and became known as an attractive speaker. He became active in the Democratic Party, then not the majority party in Pennsylvania but the one with which his family affiliated. In 1898, he made an advantageous marriage. His wife, Roberta Bartlett Dixon of Maryland, belonged to a prosperous and politically active (albeit Republican) family. From such a base, Palmer developed a political career. He began by running for the House of Representatives and ultimately served three terms, being elected in 1908, 1910, and 1912.

Palmer's opposition to local captains of industry, particularly Charles Schwab of Bethlehem Steel, gave him a reputation for solicitude for the mass of voters in the working class. Palmer gravitated toward the Progressive faction of the Democratic Party. Progressive Democrats committed themselves to breaking down monopoly and to reducing the power of large social institutions so as to give individuals opportunities for advancement. Thus, rather than regulate businesses, as say, Progressive Republicans regulated the meat and drug industries, they forced businesses to stay small and to compete with each other. Their characteristic legislation included the Clayton Anti-Trust Act and the Federal Trade Commission. However, it is worth noting that Progressive Democratic interest in fostering democracy and individual opportunity did not extend to their own leadership. Their leader, **Woodrow Wilson,** was notorious for his refusal to compromise when he thought a principle was at stake. Thus, the relationship between Palmer's adherence to the Progressive wing of the Democratic Party and his subsequent antiradical campaign is obscure. Was he a Progressive because progressivism reflected his own principled opposition to the consolidation of wealth and power in the hands of a few? Or was he a Progressive because that seemed the most expeditious way to topple, and replace, the local leadership? Or did he pick up one element of the Progressive personality, the assumption that he knew what was best for society as a whole?

In 1912, the Democrats won the presidency. Palmer's efforts did not affect the outcome. The plurality of Pennsylvanians voted for **Theodore Roosevelt**, who then got all of Pennsylvania's electoral votes; Pennsylvania was one of only eight states Wilson *didn't* carry. However, Palmer had supported Wilson from the start of the campaign and had made TR fight for Pennsylvania. He hoped to be rewarded for his efforts with the post of attorney general. Wilson offered to make him secretary of war, but Palmer declined, claiming it was incompatible with his Quaker faith. Palmer's 1912 election to the House meant he still had a job, though, and a position from which he could further prove his loyalty to Wilson. Until the next Congress sat, which, under the rules then in effect meant until December 1915, Palmer helped to enact Wilsonian legislation, at the cost of his support among more conservative Democrats in Pennsylvania. In the 1914 election, he was defeated by a more conservative Democrat, Boise Penrose. In 1916, Palmer again supported Wilson for president in Pennsylvania and again failed to carry the state for him, even though this was the election in which Wilson was supposedly so popular for keeping the United States out of World War I.

Still, Palmer wanted to advance in his career, and his only hope was to convince Wilson that his services were, if not effective, at least loyal enough that he deserved a reward. And Wilson now had more offices to give. On April 2, 1917, Wilson asked Congress for a declaration of war against Germany. The government had to expand to direct the war effort. One need was for someone to take over the property that Germans, either German citizens living in the United States or investors living in Germany, had in the United States and manage it until hostilities ceased and normal relations between the two countries resumed. In October 1917, Wilson asked Palmer to be the Alien Property Custodian. In November 1918, when the war ended and the attorney general, Thomas Watt Gregory, decided to return to private life, Palmer began angling for the position he had wanted all along. On February 26, 1919, just before he left for France to negotiate the Versailles Treaty, Wilson appointed Palmer to the coveted position.

It was as attorney general that Palmer faced the full effects of the war and postwar situation. In some ways, Palmer scapegoated immigrants and made them bear the major responsibility for postwar radicalism. In some ways, history has scapegoated Palmer and placed on him blame that fell on more impersonal forces. These forces included international events, ideology, radical action, what the law permitted, what politicians proposed—and what ordinary Americans sanctioned.

Antiradicalism had a long history in the United States. Proponents of the French Revolution claimed they were imitating the American one. Americans rejected the comparison and considered the French to be not just altering their form of government but calling into question every social institution. However, the chain of cause and effect known as the Red Scare begins in 1917, at a point in World War I at which the French, British, Russians, and Italians were leading an alliance against the Central Powers of Germany, Austria-Hungary, the Ottoman Empire, and Bulgaria. One reason the Central Powers had their name was that they were in the middle. The French, British, and Italians on one side, and the Russians on the other, were forcing the Central Powers to fight a multifront war.

Then one front collapsed. The Russians had not been as well prepared for the war as Czar Nicholas II thought. Soon the czar was fighting a multifront war himself. Germany attacked him in the summer of 1914. Other nobles, and Russia's tiny educated elite, complained that the czar was an ineffective leader. The masses resisted serving in an underequipped army and were supported in their resistance by radicals who encouraged them in their belief that World War I benefited the upper classes at the expense of the lower ones. In March 1917 (February on the Russian's Gregorian calendar) Czar Nicholas II abdicated. A coalition of his elite critics under the leadership of Alexander Kerensky tried to form a "liberal" government, that is, one characterized by having the leadership elected. In other ways, the liberal government resembled the czarist one in its determination to fight World War I. In November 1917 (October by their calendar) the liberals were overthrown by the communists, who were at that time such a small part of the political spectrum that their name, Bolshevik, identified them as the minority party. In March 1918 Lenin surrendered to Germany, even giving up territory, in order to take Russia out of the war and concentrate on social revolution.

Russia's departure from the Allies had complicated consequences. On the one hand, Wilson could more easily convince Americans to enter the war, because the remaining Allies were either republics (France) or constitutional monarchies (Italy and the United Kingdom). On the other hand, Russia's collapse did put more pressure on the United States to enter the war in order to shore up the remaining Allies. Instead of being an ally, revolutionary Russia became a problem for the Allies. The Allies mounted an expeditionary force to enter Soviet territory to prevent the Germans from taking advantage of the situation. There was much anger at the Soviets for taking Russia out of the war and breaking up the international coalition against the expansion of imperial Germany.

The anger was even greater because of ideological factors. Theoretically, Russia wasn't just changing the party in charge of government. To the communists, the real issue was class. Every other aspect of society had been constructed by the upper classes to facilitate the exploitation of the laboring classes. National boundaries were just ways of keeping the working class divided. Religion was just a way of pacifying them, preaching pie in the sky when you die. Education brainwashed the poor with hopes that hard work and right living would lead to personal advancement. Police removed from social circulation those who would not be brainwashed. Multiparty republics were elaborately rigged to fool people into thinking they could vote for someone who represented their interests; actually, all politicians colluded with the economic elite, selling out their constituents to enrich themselves. Also, it wasn't enough to overthrow czarist Russia and to create the Union of Soviet Socialist Republics, the name the government took in 1922. Some communists advocated an immediate worldwide class revolution, and all of them expected the entire international system to fall at some point. Although Wilson, in accord with his general principle of national self-government, called for permitting Russia to work out its own destiny, he had no intention of having the communist system spread to the United States. There were some in his administration who wanted to end Russia's own experiment with communism.

This wasn't just a theoretical debate conducted in political science class. A small party of Bolsheviks had indeed changed the world. And there were activists in the United States as well. At the time of the Bolshevik Revolution, the United States had various types of radicals. To provide some short, handy definitions, socialists thought that the best economy was one controlled by society as a whole, rather than by permitting individuals to control private property. Socialists were divided as to just how much control society ought to have and how to go about getting it. Communists were socialists inasmuch as they agreed that the group, rather than the individual, should control the economy. However, communists departed from socialists in that they wanted not just to alter the form of government to make it more responsive to the working class; they thought *any* government would become a tool of an upper class and so advocated ultimately dismantling government in favor of community (hence the name) control over the economy. Followers of the communist theoretician Karl Marx departed from socialists in being more consistent advocates of violence; arguing that every social institution was stacked against the working class and thus could not be relied upon to protect proletarian interests, and that the elite would not give up power, it must be seized from them. After Lenin led the Bolshevik Revolution, communism had two other distinguishing features. Lenin advocated party leadership—having a well-indoctrinated party that directed the proletariat in furthering the revolution. Lenin's success also made communism the most important radical movement, at least temporarily. However, there was one more category of radicals. Anarchists agreed with communists that social institutions were tools for class exploitation. However, they parted company with the communists in that they included the Communist Party as one of those tools; the party, too, could be an oppressive institution. Also, there were differences between anarchists as to whether a violent or a pacifist approach would be the fastest way to reform society, whether to work through labor unions, or whether to eschew all groups except those of anarchists.

When the major countries of Europe entered World War I, the United States had no intention of following them. When the United States did enter the war (Wilson asked for a declaration on April 2, 1917; the Senate voted on the proposal April 4 and the House on April 6), everything had to be done at once. The United States had to raise an army, train it and ship it overseas, and provide food and manufactured goods for it. Then, nineteen months later (the armistice went into effect on November 11, 1918), everything went into reverse. The United States canceled the orders for the food and equipment for the troops, demobilized the troops, and sent veterans back into a chaotic job market. There were more people in the labor market than usual, because African Americans of both sexes had been drawn out of the South and white women drawn out of traditionally female jobs to take the places of men in the military. And there was less to do than usual because the government had just canceled its war contracts, and wartime inflation limited people's spending. There were plenty of opportunities for labor disputes in 1919. Sixty thousand workers in Seattle, Washington, went on strike starting on February 6. The entire Boston Police Force went on strike on September 9. Steelworkers went on strike on September 22. Coalminers walked off the job on November 1. It was a short, slippery slope from these discrete actions to rumors of a grand conspiracy orchestrated by the Bolsheviks.

On top of the strikes, which enjoyed radical support, there was a bombing campaign that was assumed from the beginning to be a radical plot. Thirty bombs were put into the mail somewhere near the New York City General Post Office, timed to reach their targets by May 1, 1919, the anniversary of the 1886 Haymarket bombing in Chicago and an annual observance of the international radical community. Several bombs did reach their destinations, and one blew the hands off the maid who opened it, but the general campaign failed because the majority of bombs were held for insufficient postage. Then the bombers tried delivering the bombs to people's houses by hand. On the night of June 2, 1919, bombs went off in cities all around the Northeast, Mid-Atlantic, and Midwest regions.

The bombing campaign touched Palmer personally. One of the package bombs being held for insufficient postage was addressed to him. A bomb on his doorstep the night of June 2 damaged the front of his Washington, D.C., home. It also created a grisly scenario. The bomb went off before the bomber could let go of it. The bomb blew him to pieces and scattered chunks of human remains in a block-wide radius around the Palmer household. Exactly how this affected Palmer is disputed. Franklin Delano Roosevelt, who lived across the street from Palmer and could still walk at this time, ran upstairs to check on his own son and then across the street to check on his neighbor. He recalled that Palmer was so shaken that he had regressed to the Quaker speech of his youth: "He was 'theeing' and 'thouing' me all over the place."[1]

After the bombing, Palmer requested, and received, an increase in funding for the Justice Department. He used it to reorganize the antiradical activity he had already started. On August 1, he created a General Intelligence Division and placed it under the command of J. Edgar Hoover, who was at the beginning of a lifelong career in federal law enforcement, including being the founding director of the Federal Bureau of Investigation. Hoover began compiling an index-card file on all newspapers that espoused radicalism, all organizations that fostered it, and all individuals associated with it in any way.

It is doubtful that anyone would have tolerated Palmer using his position to conduct a personal vendetta against his attackers. Here, general public frustration enters into the picture. Leaflets mailed with the bombs, or left with them at the houses, indicated that a group of anarchists had orchestrated the bombing. The police traced the wrapping paper for bombs back to a supplier. They pieced together the person killed placing the bomb at Palmer's house. Eventually, the determined that the deceased was Carlo Valdinoci, an anarchist who lived in Stoughton, Massachusetts. But they couldn't figure out who his confederates were. This was worrisome because they couldn't predict when or where or how the anarchists might strike again.

Citizens called for action. One important incident took place at Centralia, Washington, on November 11, 1919. The town had an American Legion. The organization was open to anyone who had served the U.S. military overseas, but it also had a reputation for an intolerant brand of patriotism. It organized an Armistice Day parade that was routed to go past the hall of the International Workers of the World (IWW), a radical labor organization. Fearing an attack on their property, the IWW defended it by posting armed members along the parade route. A clash between the American Legion and the IWW ensued. Four Legionnaires were shot and killed. A mob apprehended one of those who shot a Legionnaire, IWW member Wesley Everest. The police intervened, arrested Everest for murder, and put him in jail. That night, a mob broke into the jail and carried Everest away to his death. They castrated him, tied a noose around his neck, tied the other end to a bridge, pushed him off, twice hauled him back up in order to use a longer rope, stamped on his fingers to force him to let go of the bridge, and finally riddled his hanging body with bullets.

Had Everest lived, he would have been tried for the killing of the Legionnaire, but he could not have been tried for his membership in the IWW; that was not illegal. However, had Everest not been born in the United States, he might have run afoul of numerous laws. The Immigration Act of March 3, 1903, proscribed anarchists. The Immigration Act of February

5, 1917, dropped the statute of limitation on deportations. This meant that immigrant radicals could be deported no matter how long they had been in the country. Theoretically, not only radicals who entered as radicals could be deported; those who developed radical opinions in the United States could be deported as their opinions changed. There was also an Entry and Departure Control Act of May 22, 1918, which permitted the president, in times of war or other national emergency, to proscribe or deport aliens whose presence threatened public safety. Because the United States was no longer at war, this law was not necessarily useful. However, the point is that there was more that one could do to radical immigrants than one could do to native-born radicals. Thus, immigrants, rather than natives, would bear the brunt of antiradical activities.

This leads to the question of which government leaders were in charge. The president of the United States at that point was Woodrow Wilson. On September 25, 1919, though, Wilson suffered a stroke. Under the Constitution at that time, he remained president, but he was so ill that Mrs. Wilson wouldn't let him transact much business. When he was well enough, he was focused on a futile effort to get the Senate to ratify the Versailles Treaty. Leadership in domestic affairs fell to other people. The main responsibility for immigrant radicals was shared by the Department of Justice and the Department of Labor. Palmer could arrest the immigrants, but he had to depend on the Labor Department to carry out the penalties and deport them.

Presidential aspirations also figured into Palmer's calculations.[2] There was a precedent allowing presidents only two terms in office. Wilson was prepared to challenge that precedent. Generous people argue that he desperately wanted to pursue his vision of a better postwar world order and also that his mind was affected by his stroke. Cynics point to this as one more example of his messianic tendencies. Few insiders acted as if Wilson would really run again. However, one person had to, William G. McAdoo, who was not only an ambitious politician but Wilson's son-in-law. He had to wait until he got a signal from Wilson. Thus others, like Palmer, could get a jump on maneuvering for the Democratic nomination for the presidency in 1920.

So there *were* radicals, even if there weren't as many as the public feared. There were means for deporting the aliens among them. There was a great public outcry that this be done. And there was the possibility that the one who gave the public what it wanted could ride the resulting wave of popularity all the way to the presidency. The final push into action came from the Senate. Fifty-four alien radicals had been apprehended in Seattle in the wake of the strike there and entrained for Ellis Island and deportation, amid much national praise. This had been a local initiative. On October 19, the Senate formally requested Palmer "to advise and inform the Senate whether or not the Department of Justice has taken legal proceedings, and if not, why not, and if so, to what extent."[3] On November 7, Palmer gave them their answer.

That day, Department of Justice officials assisted by local police in twelve cities went to the meeting places of an organization called the Russian Workers Union. Studies of the literature this group produced indicated it indeed espoused the violent overthrowal of all government, including that of the United States. And November 7 would be an excellent day for getting as many members as possible. It was the second anniversary of the Bolshevik Revolution, which, presumably, they would be celebrating. The raiding parties arrested everyone they could find on the premises at the time. Over the next few weeks, they worked to deport as many as possible. On December 21, an army transport ship, the *Buford*, sailed out of New York harbor for Finland, where the 249 anarchists aboard were transferred to local transportation for passage to the Soviet Union.

Palmer followed up this performance with a second series of raids starting on January 2, 1920. Again, Justice Department officials cooperated with police in a dozen cities, although this time the targets were the Communist and Communist Labor Parties.[4] This time, the raids continued for some days, as authorities rounded up party members in smaller cities. The raids netted over 3,000 suspects. Exactly how many is not clear, and that should be a signal alerting students to the fact that the most basic rights of citizens were not being observed. In Boston, authorities searched people's houses and papers without warrants.[5] Most raiding parties had arrest warrants but arrested more people than they had warrants for. In Boston, they arrested more people than they had room for in jail. Of 800 suspects, 400 could be accommodated in Boston. The remaining 400 were transported to windswept Deer Island in the middle of the harbor, where there was no heat and two suspects died of pneumonia before it could be determined whether they should have been detained at all. Detroit also ran out of room. Eight hundred suspects were detained in a corridor in the city's federal building, without windows or furniture; the inmates spent most of their time standing in line waiting for the lone toilet. After holding people for up to six days without informing them of the reasons for their being held and without permitting them to communicate with lawyers or family members, authorities had to release 300 of them when interrogations revealed they were not alien radicals.[6] In Philadelphia, most of the 500 people arrested had to be let go for the same reason.

This still left 3,600 people whom the Justice Department thought had violated immigration laws by their advocacy of the overthrow of the U.S. government and thus should be deported.[7] Accordingly, the Justice Department prepared dossiers and sent them to the Labor Department, which had the power to draw up the actual deportation orders. Secretary of Labor William B. Wilson was ill, so from January until March 1920, Acting Secretary John B. Abercrombie presided over deportation proceedings. Then

Abercrombie resigned to run for senator from Alabama. Assistant Secretary **Louis F. Post** became acting secretary. Post took his responsibilities seriously, carefully checking each dossier before filling out deportation forms. By April 1, he had considered 1,600 cases and dismissed 71 percent of them.[8] He began by throwing out the cases of individuals for whom there was no arrest warrant, those who had not received the benefit of a lawyer before they made incriminating statements, and those against whom evidence had been seized illegally. He differentiated between the Communist Party and Communist Labor Party, which were organizations with two different origins and ideologies, and automatically freed all those who had joined the latter. The Justice Department took membership in the Communist Party at face value; Post dismissed those cases involving individuals who belonged to groups that had affiliated with or transferred members to the Communist Party, reasoning the followers might not agree with what the leaders were doing. About the only people he deported were those who had willfully joined the Communist Party. It is likely that some alien radicals remained in the United States when he finished reviewing the cases. It is certain innocent aliens did. More than that, when the House Committee on Rules began holding impeachment hearings about Post, he appeared before the committee and defended himself convincingly. His performance went a long way to reassuring the public that competent civil servants were checking into the threat of radical aliens and would protect the country.

As May 1, 1920, approached, Palmer began to warn the public that the radicals would celebrate their Labor Day with strikes, uprisings, riots, bombings, and assassinations. When the day passed and nothing happened, Palmer began to lose credibility. Later that month, the National Popular Government League issued a sixty-seven-page pamphlet criticizing Palmer's methods in the crusade against foreign-born radicals. By June 1, the House Rules Committee was questioning Palmer as a preliminary to possibly censuring him for his conduct in office. The committee decided not to act, but by then Palmer was no longer carrying out his raids and deportation proceedings. What was left was a lingering link between immigration, radicalism, and violent terrorism that contributed to the passage of the national quota laws of the 1920s and to the anticommunist legislation of the 1950s.

Palmer never did get to be president. While he wasn't in as helpless a position as McAdoo, he couldn't announce his candidacy until Wilson renounced his. By the time Wilson did that, James Cox, an Ohio politician who was not part of Wilson's family or cabinet and could campaign openly, was far ahead in terms of securing delegates to the Democratic National Convention. Palmer did continue to be active in politics, though, last helping to draft the Democratic platform on which Franklin Roosevelt ran in 1932. He died of a heart attack in Florida on May 11, 1936.

There are some interesting sequels to the Palmer story. Police were still trying to figure out who had tried to send Palmer a package bomb and who had conspired to plant a bomb at his house. They finally got a lead about a Brooklyn printer who produced the leaflets that came with the bombs. Justice Department officials arrested two men, Roberto Elia and Andrea Salsedo, who were indeed anarchists and printers. They held the two men at the department's New York Office; Salsedo committed suicide under their watch. Word of their incarceration, and their possible confession, got out to other anarchists. Some of these anarchists took steps to leave the country, to hide incriminating materials, or to protect themselves by carrying firearms. Two of those anarchists were Nicola Sacco and Bartolomeo Vanzetti of Stoughton and Plymouth, Massachusetts, respectively. When police arrested the two the night of May 5, 1920, on charges of robbing a payroll and murdering the paymaster and his assistant, they did so because they thought Sacco and Vanzetti acted as though they were guilty of something. Historian Paul Avrich argued that they probably acted that way because they were aware the police were looking for anarchists like themselves and also because they had just been moving their anarchist equipment, including dynamite, to a safe hiding place.[9] Instead of being deported as alien radicals, they were executed for a robbery and two murders that have never been successfully linked to them.

Carlo Tresca escaped the Palmer raids unscathed. Tresca would have been a prize catch. Born in Italy in 1879, he became an anarcho-syndicalist (an anarchist who advanced his cause through work with labor unions) there. When in 1904 his radicalism got him into trouble with the Italian government, he escaped to the United States and was allowed to enter despite the laws prohibiting the immigration of anarchists. He continued to proselytize and was an important figure at the IWW-sponsored textile mill strike in Lawrence, Massachusetts, in 1912 and at the Paterson, New Jersey, silk mill strike in 1913. In 1917, he refused to support the Bolshevik Revolution but refused to support U.S. entry into World War I either. In the early 1920s, he was active in the effort to free Sacco and Vanzetti, although privately he was convinced that Sacco had a hand in the robbery and murders. Tresca, though, came to a different end than Sacco and Vanzetti. When in 1922 Mussolini came to power in Italy, Tresca was one of the first stalwarts of the antifascist coalition. As fascism spread, he broadened his work to include opposition to fascism in Spain and Germany. He also continued to oppose the Communist Party, which he feared might take advantage of the chaos that would wrack Italy after Mussolini left power. And he opposed the mafia. When he was assassinated, in New York City on the night of January 11, 1943, he was memorialized with a grudging respect for sticking to his anarchism and for opposing the evils of fascism, communism, and organized crime.[10] Had A. Mitchell Palmer still been alive, they would have been on the same side.

NOTES

1. Stanley Coben, *A. Mitchell Palmer: Politician*, Leonard W. Levy, general editor (New York: Da Capo Press, 1972), p. 206.

2. Ibid., pp. 252–253.

3. *Congressional Record*, 66th Cong., 1st sess., pp. 6871–6872, cited in Robert K. Murray, *Red Scare: A Study in National Hysteria, 1919–1920* (Minneapolis: University of Minnesota Press, 1955; reprint, New York: McGraw-Hill Book Company, 1964), p. 196 (page citation is to the reprint edition).

4. The difference between these two was the members' birthplace. When the Communist Labor Party was formed, in emulation of the Bolshevik Party in the Soviet Union, American-born communists broke from their foreign-born colleagues and started the Communist Party.

5. Coben, *A. Mitchell Palmer*, p. 228.

6. Murray, *Red Scare*, pp. 214–217.

7. Coben, *A. Mitchell Palmer*, p. 233.

8. Ibid., p. 232.

9. Paul Avrich, *Sacco and Vanzetti: The Anarchist Background* (Princeton, NJ: Princeton University Press, 1992).

10. Dorothy Gallagher, *All the Right Enemies: The Life and Murder of Carlo Tresca* (New Brunswick, NJ: Rutgers University Press, 1988). Officially, Tresca's murder went unsolved. Gallagher argued that Frank Garofalo, a New York Italian with connections to bootlegging, gangsters, and fascists, hired Carmine Galante to do the killing.

BIBLIOGRAPHY

Alexander Mitchell Palmer has no collection of papers. The papers for the period during which he was attorney general are among the Papers of the Department of Justice in the National Archives and Records Administration. He does, though, have a biography, Stanley Coben, *A. Mitchell Palmer: Politician*, Da Capo Press Reprint Series, Civil Liberties in American History, Leonard W. Levy, general editor (New York: Da Capo Press, 1972). For specialized studies on the general topic of monitoring radical activity among the foreign-born right after World War I, see Mark Ellis, "J. Edgar Hoover and the 'Red Summer' of 1919," *Journal of American Studies* 27:1 (1994), pp. 39–59; James J. Lorence, "Socialism in Northern Wisconsin, 1910–1920: An Ethno-Cultural Analysis," *Mid-America* 64:3 (1982), pp. 25–51; Robert K. Murray, *Red Scare: A Study in National Hysteria, 1919–1920* (Minneapolis: University of Minnesota Press, 1955; reprint, New York: McGraw-Hill Book Company, 1964); William Preston, Jr., *Aliens and Dissenters: Federal Suppression of Radicals* (Cambridge, MA: Harvard University Press, 1963; reprint, New York: Harper Torchbooks, 1966); and David Williams, "The Bureau of Investigation and Its Critics, 1919–1921: The Origins of Federal Political Surveillance," *Journal of American History* 68:3 (1981), pp. 560–579.

HENRY FORD
(1863–1947)

The Protocols of the Elders of Zion

Henry Ford was born on July 30, 1863, and died on April 7, 1947, a total of almost eighty-four years. He lived through many changes, some of which he helped to create. Yet in immigration he was most famous for extending the life of a hoary prejudice, anti-Semitism. In the context of the times, the 1920s and 1930s, this had tragic consequences.

Ford was born in Dearborn, Michigan, to a Protestant Irish immigrant, William Ford, and his wife, Mary Litogot, whom he had met when he was working for her adoptive father, Patrick O'Hern. Ford received his only formal education in Dearborn's local schools between the years of 1871 and 1879. At that point, he moved to Detroit. During 1879–1880, he worked at his apprenticeship at James Flower and Brother Machine Shop by day and took a second job repairing watches at night. In the summer of 1880, he finished his apprenticeship and took a new job that combined work and training, at Detroit Drydock, where he learned about engines.

For the next few years, Ford swung, pendulumlike, between his home on the farm and his work in the city, helping his father out as needed and then returning to Detroit during the off-season. His father hoped he would settle on the farm permanently, but Ford disliked that kind of work. In 1885, he met Clara Bryant, who, like him, had been raised in Dearborn.

The First Official Ford Motor Company Portrait of Henry Ford, 1904.
From the Collections of the Henry Ford Museum and Greenfield Village.

On April 11, 1888, he married her. Their only child, a boy named Edsel, was born on November 16, 1893. By then, Henry worked for the Edison Illuminating Company of Detroit, spending his days tending the steam engines that generated the electricity. As long as the engines were running smoothly, he had time to retire to a little workshop. At night, he and some friends met to talk, to engage in horseplay and goofing off, and to tinker.

During this period, other tinkerers were developing an interest in automobiles. The first automobiles were built in Germany by Karl Benz and Gottlieb Daimler and exhibited in 1886. The French took to the new technology at once, and France was the first country to establish an automobile industry. In 1893, the same year that Edsel was born, Charles and Frank Duryea of Springfield, Massachusetts, and Elwood Haynes of Kokomo, Indiana, working independently, built motor cars. R. E. Olds, who had been experimenting with automobiles powered by steam engines, switched to gasoline engines and built his first gas-powered car in 1895. That year, Chicago hosted an automobile race that raised interest in the subject. It seems to have raised Ford's interest; he not only concentrated on producing a functioning automobile; he also fixed upon automobile races as the way to get his cars before the public. On June 4, 1896, Ford took an axe and chopped a larger door in his workshop in order to drive his creation, the Quadricycle, out onto the street.

In order to produce enough cars even for the small market of the elite and upper middle class, Ford needed capital. In attracting capital, Ford depended on his natural public relations ability. As a young man, Ford was amiable, making friends on the job and off. When it came to reaching beyond his circle of friends, the early Ford intrigued the press, tantalizing them with demonstrations of new technological developments. He gave the impression of being progressive and forward-minded and also of being aware of how the average person lived and how that style of living might be improved. His persona made it seem possible that the average person, not just the wealthy, would want an automobile and that cars could become conveniences, not luxury items. Ford did not need to court banks in distant New York. He could find capital among the savings of a few friends in Detroit.

There were two false starts. In 1899, a number of prominent Detroit citizens combined with Henry Ford to organize the Detroit Automobile Company. They were to provide the finances, and he was to receive shares of the company in exchange for his automotive expertise. Ford unveiled a prototype on January 12, 1900. Then something went wrong. Ford may not have been able to figure out how to mass-produce his prototype. He may have deliberately not produced much in the hopes of getting out of his agreement so that he could negotiate one more favorable to himself. The exact reason is not documented, but the Detroit Automobile Company never produced any cars for the market and dissolved in 1901. On November 30, 1901, the Henry Ford Company was formed, along the same lines as the previous company. This time, though, the investors were less charitable. When it seemed that Ford was again not going to produce a car they could manufacture and sell, they dissolved the corporation and went on to form their own company, Cadillac Automobile Company, the corporate ancestor of General Motors, without him. Ford started his third, and most enduring effort, Ford Motor Company, in 1903. During the 1900s and 1910s, Ford bought out his backers and became the sole owner of the company. His financial maneuvering gave him the reputation of being a robber baron, willful and sneaky. His ownership of the company gave him great freedom to act.

For this third company, Ford developed a prototype, which he called the Model A. He then worked out a system for buying all the necessary parts for it from various suppliers. His factory assembled the car rather than making any parts. From the beginning, the Model A sold well. Then Ford began to reach out toward the mass market. During the early years of car manufacturing, there was a sense that the car, like the bicycle, was a kind of fad, or toy, for young people of at least middling means. Ford, though, with his background in farming, thought that people might want cars as conveniences if the cars were truly convenient and the price was right.

First, the company had to find the right car. Ford settled upon the Model T. It was lightweight, which meant that it used less gasoline and was less expensive to run. Although there were numerous jokes about its breakdowns, it was easier to keep in repair than more expensive models from other companies. Ford had variations of the Model T, such as small runabouts and larger sedans, but he minimized the number of options the buyer had in order to reduce the manufacturing costs. In his most famous act of economizing, he manufactured Model Ts in various different colors until 1914, when he decreed that customers could have the Model T in any color they wanted so long as it was black. Ford kept the Model T prices low, aiming for volume rather than for an enormous profit on each car. He succeeded. He jettisoned further model making and turned out Model Ts from 1908 until 1927.

To his reputation as a mechanical genius, Ford added another dimension, that of the brilliant business executive. He began his work in this field by organizing assembly lines at his factory. When Ford built his prototypes, he and his colleagues had all worked on every phase of the car. Now Ford laid out his factory so that partially assembled automobiles traveled on conveyor belts between rows of workers, each of whom had one specific task to do. As the worker finished the task on one car, another was moving along on the conveyor belt. Increased efficiency lowered the cost of manufacturing, allowing Ford to reduce prices while still making enough profits to become an extraordinarily wealthy man.

Ford cemented his reputation for administrative ability in 1914 with what became known as the "five dollar day." Biographers and business historians have identified numerous strings to Ford's deal for his employees. First, Ford wasn't actually proposing to pay his employees $5 a day. What he did was to calculate what the 1914 bonus was going to be, and instead of distributing it in one lump sum, he gave it out with the biweekly pay, so that it averaged out to $5 a day. Second, the money wasn't, like wages, something employees earned for their work. Employees under twenty-two years of age had to be supporting a family in order to qualify, because Ford suspected that young people might waste their money on frivolous luxuries. Even older employees could lose their bonuses if Ford discovered that they were living in ways of which he disapproved. The $5 a day was intended to help cut the tremendous turnover that developed at Ford's factory after the installation of the assembly line and to allow Ford to impose greater discipline on his highly paid workforce. Despite these problems, Ford made it possible for his workers to buy his cars, and he was regarded as a hero of both capital and labor.

From a pioneer in automobile manufacturing and an innovator in business management, Ford moved into public affairs. Here he had mixed results. To start with the successes, Ford, although he called history "bunk," started a new way of studying it. Ford admitted he disliked farmwork, but he appreciated the kind of communities and small town that existed before the people living on the farms began buying his cars. He worked to preserve that past, in a somewhat direct and simplistic way, but one that has had lasting effect. He began collecting U.S. farm implements and other items from bygone days. In 1923, he purchased the Old Wayside Inn at Sudbury, Massachusetts, to house his collection. In 1929, he dedicated the Edison Institute (named for Thomas Alva Edison, whom he knew and admired) in his hometown of Dearborn, a combination museum and restored schoolhouse, so that people could see what earlier times had looked like. In 1933, he opened a re-creation of a preautomobile small town, Greenfield Village, in Dearborn. Since then, many Americans have learned something about U.S. history by visiting colonial Williamsburg in Virginia (which had as its patrons another wealthy family, the Rockefellers), or industrial towns such as Lowell, Massachusetts.

At the other extreme from the success of Greenfield Village were the problems that began when Ford decided to intervene in World War I. The war began in 1914. At this point, the United States was not directly involved. It was, though, a horrified spectator. War, especially the brutal war of attrition that World War I quickly became, seemed such a primitive, barbaric, and uncivilized way to resolve international conflict that people who considered themselves Progressives sought another solution. Ford chartered a steamer, the Scandinavian-American line's *Oscar II*, and invited other peace workers to accompany him to Europe to deliver talks and to stir up public interest so that the people of Europe would demand their leaders end the war. The liner headed out on December 4, 1915, and arrived at Oslo, Norway, on December 18, 1915. Ford then turned around and went home, departing on December 23, 1915, and leaving the others aboard the "Peace Ship" to figure out what to do. He had taken ill with a bad cold. One person aboard the ship had already died of pneumonia, so Ford's cold probably seemed even worse than it was. Ford also seems to have concluded that he really couldn't bring about peace by Christmas, as he had promised in the newspapers.

The next year, the United States launched a "preparedness" campaign. Some argued the United States had to be ready in case it was pushed into the war by some international incident and that preparedness could actually prevent potential enemies from launching attacks. Others, including Ford, argued that preparedness was the first step down the slippery slope to war. On June 13, 1916, the Chicago *Tribune* published an editorial criticizing Ford's antipreparedness stance and calling him an anarchist and an ignorant idealist. Ford wasn't so ignorant that he missed the insult. He sued the *Tribune* for libel. During the trial, Ford took the stand in his own defense. This gave the *Tribune* lawyers a chance to cross-examine him in the hopes of demonstrating the truth of the newspaper's charges. The lawyers succeeded in establishing that Ford had numerous personal opinions but insufficient education to support them. In 1919, after World War I was over and after the public had begun to return to Ford's opinion regarding the folly of the war, the jury found the *Tribune* guilty of libel but awarded Ford only six cents in damages, its way of indicating the *Tribune* had not exaggerated Ford's ignorance by much.

At about the same time, Ford became involved in another public embarrassment. Nominally a Republican, his attitude toward war brought him closer to **Woodrow Wilson**'s position. In 1918, he ran for the position of senator from Michigan as an independent in order to support Wilson's principles where that support was most needed. He lost. Instead of taking the loss gracefully, he accused the winner, Truman H. Newberry, of underhanded campaigning. He hired detectives, who did enough work to finally find some campaign irregularities and to drive Newberry out of public life.

What is interesting about Ford's biography so far is that anti-Semitism, particularly as it influenced immigration, played no role in it. Indeed, the anti-immigrant sentiment of the 1920s and Ford's anti-Semitism seem to have developed on separate tracks. In 1921, Congress began passing laws that restricted the immigration of people according to the perceived desirability of their national origins. The laws did not specifically mention Jews. The national origins laws were drawn up so that individuals' national origins were usually determined by their passports, not by their own ethnic identity. There were exceptions: No matter what their passports said, Asians were excluded on the grounds that they came from the "barred zone," a geographic area established in U.S. law in 1917. Jews, though, were treated as members of various European countries. For example, the wife of Enrico Fermi was Jewish—indeed, that was why the Fermis wanted to leave fascist Italy—but as far as the United States was concerned, she was Italian, because she carried an Italian passport.

Yet the U.S. public identified Jews as an ethnic group, and there was anti-Semitism in U.S. life. Ford probably got his anti-Semitism from the Populist movement. *Populism* is one of those words that rides the currents of U.S. political history. The word itself comes from the Latin for "people." The most precise use of the word is to refer to the People's, or Populist, Party, a third political party active between 1892, when it nominated James B. Weaver as its first candidate for president, and 1896, when it endorsed Democratic nominee William Jennings Bryan and thus faded as a separate party. The geographic stronghold of the Populists was an L-shaped swatch of land going down the Midwest and then east across the Deep South. Economically, these two parts of the country were united by agriculture, and the Populists supported numerous proposals to aid those who owned farms. The most important of these proposals here had to do with the basis for the U.S. money supply and with banking. Culturally, the Populists were united by common interest in Protestant evangelical religions, such as the Baptist faith, Methodism, and William Jennings Bryan's Presbyterianism. (There were exceptions that proved the rule; one person who borrowed heavily from Populist economics and cultural was Charles Coughlin, a Catholic priest of Irish-Canadian descent.)

While not all the Populists were anti-Semites, there was a certain amount in the political movement that could be used for anti-Semitic purposes. The most important fertilizer for any cash crop is cash. Every farmer needs to borrow money to get the farm started. Hence, low interest rates are extremely important to farmers. During the last quarter of the nineteenth century, farmers thought that interest rates were too high. They also thought they knew the reason. Interest is the price one pays for money: Just as with any other commodity, when there is a lot of money available, the interest rates go down as banks compete to lend, and where there is little money available, the banks can charge interest rates as high as the market can bear. Thus, late-nineteenth-century farmers identified a solution to their woes, making more money available. Farmers proposed a variety of schemes for increasing the number of dollars in circulation, from continuing the Civil War practice of issuing greenbacks with government guarantees to back them up to using silver and gold—not just gold—as a basis for the money supply. When the farmers' suggestions were not taken, the farmers gathered that the bankers had control over the politicians and were using that control to arrange financial affairs to their own advantage.

Who were these bankers? In actuality, the most notorious U.S. bankers, men such as Jay Gould and J. P. Morgan, were gentiles. However, farmers who had heard even a little Shakespeare would have encountered the character of Shylock, the Jewish moneylender in *The Merchant of Venice*. If they read the newspapers, they would have seen the name Rothschild, the legendary Jewish banking family of Europe. Plus, there were a few well-known Jewish bankers in the United States, such as Joseph Seligman. From these few bits of reality, the stereotype of the Jewish banker got its credence. There was little to counter the stereotype. Their rounds of farmwork and travel to town brought farmers into contact with only the occasional Jewish peddler or shopkeeper, never with the Jewish factory worker.

A variation on the stereotypical connection of Jews and money began in the late nineteenth century. Pogroms swept Czarist Russia, forcing Jews to flee. At about the same time that Henry Ford moved to Detroit to study machine work, European Jews began to migrate to the United States. They were too poor to purchase farms, and they didn't really have the kind of farming skills that were needed, so they settled in cities. The jobs that were open to them, mostly in petty shopkeeping or light industry, didn't pay well. Most families wanted to save enough to get ahead; some probably also felt an obligation to family members left behind. The strong incentives to save money led to ruthless underconsumption. Another stereotype was born: No matter how poverty-stricken they seemed to be, Jews were actually hoarding their money and accumulating a great deal of wealth.

When Ford became a famous automobile manufacturer, he came into contact with other people who reinforced his anti-Semitism. Ford's confidential secretary, a man named Ernest G. Liebold (what an ironic surname!) was anti-Semitic. Thomas Edison was also known to put anti-Semitic comments on paper, although in the most frequently cited conversation between them, Edison hardly took the initiative.[1] Naturalist John Burroughs, who accompanied Ford, Edison, and tire manufacturer Harvey Firestone on a camping trip, recalled that Edison made some comment on the inefficiency of the U.S. Navy but that it was Ford, not Edison, who attributed this alleged inefficiency to Jews.[2]

Outside of Ford's own circle, there were other people who had their own rationale for anti-Semitism. In cities on the Eastern seaboard, people of old families and old money feared their historic position at the top of the social hierarchy was being undermined by a combination of new money and new immigrants. New immigrants threatened the elite indirectly, by supporting rival politicians at the polls. New money threatened the elite more directly, as they earned more in their businesses than the old elite ever earned in theirs. Sometimes, the threat of new immigrants and new money combined, as when an immigrant made good. Such fears crystalized into yet another anti-Semitic stereotype: Jews who made fast fortunes bought or built homes in exclusive neighborhoods, flaunted their wealth, vacationed at fancy resorts, and enrolled their offspring in the Ivy League or the Seven Sister schools. The anti-Semitism of these social leaders explains why Ford was able to be so open about his own.

There were two possible sources for Ford's anti-Semitism that must be discounted. There were Jewish bankers, whom Ford could have met and from that meeting developed his prejudices. However, Ford had a Populist's distrust of banks. Once he began to make money in cars, he bought out his partners, became sole owner of his company, and seldom worked with bankers. Second, it is possible that a person would exploit prejudices for money. The Ku Klux Klan of the late 1910s and early 1920s was organized by people who profited from it personally. Ford's ghostwriter for his anti-Semitic publications, William J. Cameron, was not an anti-Semite at first and seems to have developed a prejudice against Jews because he was paid to write articles against them. But Ford himself did not profit from his anti-Semitism. He was sinking his own money into the anti-Semitic campaign.

In November 1918, about the same time he lost his Senate campaign, Ford purchased a local newspaper, the *Dearborn Independent*. Its first issue as a Ford publication appeared on January 11, 1919. It had its own staff: Edwin G. Pipp as editor, Fred L. Black as business manager, Ernest G. Liebold as general manager, and William J. Cameron as the collaborator for "Mr. Ford's Own Page." Originally, Ford intended to use the publication to disseminate support for Wilson's internationalism, the Versailles Treaty, and the League of Nations. These issues were dead by 1920. Soon Ford and his staff were aware of the need to attract increased numbers of readers and purchasers. The latter were especially important, as Ford didn't accept any advertising, for fear of having sponsors dictate the paper's contents. The *Dearborn Independent* asked Joseph J. O'Neill, formerly with the nearby Mount Clemens News Bureau, for an analysis of the paper and its prospects. O'Neill pointed out that the *Dearborn Independent* wasn't living up to its masthead promise to tell "neglected truth" and even recommended "LET'S HAVE SOME SENSATIONALISM in order to raise the paper's profile."[3]

The "sensationalism" that Ford settled on was anti-Semitism. On May 22, 1920, the *Dearborn Independent* printed an unsigned article on "The International Jew: The World's Problem." From May until August, the articles were probably researched and written by William J. Cameron. In August, Cameron's research became easier. He began using a document called *The Protocols of the Elders of Zion* (sometimes the "Elders" is rendered as "Wise Men"). *The Protocols* was a pamphlet purportedly written in 1897 in Basel, Switzerland, by the Zionist Congress. It supposedly came out of a cabal of Jews who already controlled international finance. They planned to use their economic power as a base for overthrowing every government in the world and had written a series of twenty-four "instructions" or lectures to teach conspirators-in-training how to undermine governments and other social institutions and to prepare for the coming Jewish takeover. Thereafter, Cameron followed the format of juxtaposing highly selective accounts of world events with quotations from *The Protocols* that seemed to show how the conspirators were carrying out their instructions. Occasionally, he went further afield to link jazz music and sexy movies to a Jewish conspiracy to undermine public morals so as to soften up society for the final conquest. Cameron was not hindered a bit by general opinion that condemned *The Protocols* as a forgery. He didn't even take note of an August 1921 story by Philip Graves in the *London Times* showing that Serge Nilus, a Czarist agent, had plagiarized *The Protocols* from a nineteenth-century French political satire, *Dialogue in Hell between Machiavelli and Montesquieu* by Maurice Joly, in order to create a hoax suitable for fomenting pogroms.

The *Dearborn Independent* continued its anti-Semitic columns until January 1922. Cameron's story was that Ford met him on his way into the office one day and ordered the series stopped in favor of a new crusade. Ford wanted to change the basis of international currency to something more flexible and favorable to the agricultural sector, and he wanted Jewish cooperation on this new subject, so the anti-Semitic articles had to go. Biographers have identified other possible motives. The anti-Semitic campaign offended people close to Ford. His editor, Edwin Pipp, resigned in protest over the articles. His son, Edsel Ford, couldn't resign his position, but he could use it to press his father to abandoning his campaign. Ford didn't always respect his son's opinions, but Edsel wasn't the only one offended. **Louis Marshall**, president of the American Jewish Committee, contacted Warren Harding, who contacted a mutual friend, Judson C. Welliver, to pass on to Ford the president's request that the articles cease. The anti-Semitic campaign evidently contributed to a sales slump. Jews, and people interested in doing business with Jews, did not buy Fords. **Upton Sinclair** claimed Ford met his match in movie mogul William Fox, who threatened to show newsreels that made it look as though Ford cars were involved in a disproportionate number of automobile accidents. In 1922, when Warren Harding was performing poorly in the presidency, there was talk of dumping him from the 1924 presidential ticket and replacing him with Henry Ford; an anti-Semitic campaign wouldn't exactly help Ford with all segments of voters. Harding died in 1923, and Republicans were more supportive of his successor, Calvin Coolidge, but there were still political reasons for Ford to hold his anti-Semitic fire. During World War I, the government had begun to develop Muscle Shoals, Alabama, planning to dam the Tennessee River there, set up a hydroelectric plant, and open factories that would manufacture nitrates used in explosives in wartime and fertilizer in peacetime. Ford hoped to purchase the unfinished project, but Coolidge might be reluctant to sell to someone who stirred up the voting public with his anti-Semitism. (Ford's efforts to get Muscle Shoals were blocked by another friend of the farmer, Nebraska Senator George Norris; it eventually became part of the New Deal's Tennessee Valley Authority.) The political explanations have the virtue of explaining one other peculiar bit of timing, not only why Ford stopped his anti-Semitic campaign in 1922 but also why he restarted it in 1924.

When Ford reopened his anti-Semitism, his target was not the international Jew of finance and government upheaval but a particular Jew, Aaron Sapiro. Sapiro was a lawyer who had recently organized a series of farmer's marketing cooperatives, thus putting the farmers in a better position vis-à-vis the buying power of huge purchasers such as supermarket chains. Ford, though, charged that Sapiro treated the farmers unfairly, overcharging them for his legal advice and failing to get for them the best deal possible. In 1925, Sapiro sued Ford for $1 million for defamation of character.

The case went to trial. Ford had an interest in winning the suit and stooped to unworthy tactics to get his way, having detectives follow the jurors to see if there was a possibility of tampering or creating a situation for a mistrial. With his vivid memories of his humiliation at the hands of the Chicago *Tribune* lawyers, Ford also wanted to avoid being called to the stand. The plaintiffs had to sneak up on him and drop a subpoena almost into his lap. Even then, he claimed they didn't really serve it to him, as it had fallen between his knees to the floor. On March 31, 1927, the day before his scheduled court appearance, the car Ford was driving went off the road just beyond the gatehouse of his estate, Fair Lane, rolled down an embankment toward the Rouge River, and crashed into a tree. Ford claimed he had been sideswiped by two men in a Studebaker and thought the men had been watching him since the day before the accident. Biographers have not been above suspecting Ford staged the accident to avoid testimony, but it isn't necessary to go that far. Ford was nervous enough about the testimony to have had a genuine accident.[4] If it was staged, it was an unnecessary sacrifice. A few weeks after his accident, a juror made a casual remark to reporters that it seemed someone wanted to keep the case from going to the jury. The judge saw the comment, declared a mistrial, and set a date for a new trial. Ford chose to negotiate instead. He signed an apology for the anti-Semitic columns in the *Dearborn Independent* and promised to halt his anti-Semitic activities.

However, the damage was already done. Ford's anti-Semitism was already in print. Even though he did not run any new editorials in the *Dearborn Independent*, his past editorials were collected into a four-volume work called *The International Jew*. These volumes continued to be available and continued to be influential.

Ford had a particular following in Germany. During the Nuremberg Trial, Baldur von Shirach, leader of the Hitler youth movement, told his prosecutors, "You have no idea what a great influence this book [*The International Jew*] had on the thinking of German youth. . . . [T]he younger generation looked with envy to the symbols of success and prosperity like Henry Ford, and if he said the Jews were to blame, why naturally we believed him."[5] Von Shirach's remarks are a bit suspect. If one were on trial before a panel of judges that included Americans, it might make sense to stress the American origins of one's ideas. Von Shirach, though, has some support, from a person who was writing in the 1920s. In *Mein Kampf*, Adolf Hitler singled out Henry Ford for admiration: "Every year makes them [the Jews] more and more the controlling masters of the producers in a nation of one hundred and twenty millions [the United States]; only a single great man, Ford, to their fury, still maintains full independence."[6]

On July 30, 1938, Ford accepted the Grand Cross of the German Eagle, acquiescing to an honor from the Nazis. He did not have to accept the award. Thomas J. Watson, founder and president of International Business Machines (IBM), refused to accept an award from the Nazis in protest against their militarism. Ford also missed the signals that Adolf Hitler was sending along with the award. The award did not just honor Ford's contribution to the development of modern industry or to the welfare of individuals workers, or even to anti-Semitism. Hitler was already expanding the territory under his control and knew that sooner or later he would declare war. What better way to throw potential enemies off balance than to award the peacekeepers among them, particularly Ford, whose idea of keeping the peace was limited to keeping the United States out of wars?

Hitler invaded Poland on September 1, 1939, which brought England and France to Poland's defense and began World War II in Europe. Ford continued his efforts to keep the United States out of war, working with Charles Lindbergh and the notoriously anti-Semitic Charles Coughlin to do so. Only in June 1941 did Ford change his mind. June 22, Hitler broke a public nonaggression pact with the Soviet Union and launched a massive invasion of that country. Ford concluded that Hitler was drunk with power and probably could not be stopped without war. The United States entered World War II on December 7, 1941, with the Japanese attack on Pearl Harbor. Ford and his automobile factory supported the war effort.

Ford did not notice the international effects of his anti-Semitic campaigns. Instead, he focused on his own priorities. In 1927, he shut down his automobile plant to retool it for the first new Ford model since the 1908 Model T. This meant that the Great Depression started early at his company, for many workers were laid off in order to retool the plant. By the time Ford was ready with his new model (the N), the rest of the United States was in a depression, and car sales slumped. After 1933, when the New Deal tried to answer public demand for government action to ease the depression by supporting labor unions, there were some ugly confrontations between the antiunion Ford and his organizing employees.

Hitler's anti-Semitism sent many European Jews fleeing for safety. As he absorbed some countries and made war on others, it became clear that few places in Europe offered protection from him. Palestine was physically nearby, across the Mediterranean, but the British, fearful of tension between immigrant Jews and native Palestinians, closed the area to Jewish migration. When the Jews tried to get visas to immigrate to the United States, they were caught by laws that, while not anti-Semitic, worked against them. The United States issues only about 150,000 immigrant visas. The eastern European countries, where the Jewish population was centered, had only a small share of those visas. And there were no provisions for refugees. Two originally unrelated events, Ford's anti-Semitism and the restrictive immigration legislation of the 1920s, now combined to weave a net that trapped European Jews in Europe, where Hitler could get at them and destroy them.

Having made the point, it is important not to overemphasize it. There is no evidence that Ford gave direct support to the Nazis, ideologically or financially.[7] Also, there were important differences between Ford and the Nazis. It is difficult to imagine an American born in 1863 and raised in the shadow of the Civil War and adhering through his youth to the Republican Party, even one known for subjecting his workers to rigid discipline, accepting Hitler's idea of utilizing inferior races as slave labor, to be worked to death in the service of the master race. Ford did not have an elaborate hierarchy of superior and inferior races; Ford Motor Company hired both immigrants and African Americans (and for that matter, Jews). Nor did Ford ever convert to Hitler's militarism, although he tolerated it far longer than other people. Ford was as shocked as anyone else when in May 1945 he saw a newsreel documenting the Majdanek concentration camp—so shocked that he suffered a serious stroke, the effects of which contributed to his death.[8]

NOTES

1. Albert Lee, *Henry Ford and the Jews* (Briarcliff Manor, NY: Stein and Day, 1980), pp. 139–166.

2. Robert Lacey, *Ford: The Men and the Machine* (Boston: Little, Brown, 1986), p. 205.

3. David L. Lewis, *The Public Image of Henry Ford: An American Folk Hero and His Company* (Detroit: Wayne State University Press, 1976), p. 137.

4. Lacey, *Ford: The Men and the Machine*, p. 218.

5. Lewis, *The Public Image of Henry Ford*, p. 143.

6. Lacey, *Ford: The Men and the Machine*, p. 218.

7. It is difficult to prove a negative. Albert Lee, who focused on this topic most directly, observes that Ford and Hitler had common interests in anti-Semitism and that Ford had the means to give to the Nazis, even surreptitiously if he so chose: He kept up to a million dollars of cash on hand in the vaults of his office, and he knew people who could carry donations to the Third Reich (see Lee, *Henry Ford*

and the Jews). David L. Lewis, who balanced his thesis—the importance of the Ford image—against the goal of a comprehensive one-volume tome, reported that the Nazis solicited funds from Ford Motor Company but were rebuffed (see Lewis, *The Public Image of Henry Ford*, p. 149). Allan Nevins and Frank Ernest Hill have the most complete biography of Ford and do not credit the charges. See Allan Nevins, *Ford: Decline and Rebirth, 1933–1962* (New York: Charles Scribner's Sons, 1962), p. 182.

8. Lee, *Henry Ford and the Jews*, p. 137.

BIBLIOGRAPHY

The Henry Ford Museum and Greenfield Village in Dearborn, Michigan, house the Ford papers. One can commence one's research on them (and even see photographs of Ford and his industry) via the Internet at http://www.hfmgv.org. Ford also wrote one autobiography, at about the middle of his long life, *My Life and Work* (Garden City, NY: Garden City Publishing, 1927). The most complete biography is the three-volume work of Allan Nevins, with the collaboration of Frank Ernest Hill, *Ford: The Times, the Man, and the Company* (New York: Charles Scribner's Sons, 1954); *Ford: The Challenge of Expansion* (New York: Charles Scribner's Sons, 1957); and *Ford: Decline and Rebirth, 1933–1962* (New York: Charles Scribner's Sons, 1962). Recent substantial one-volume monographs include Robert Lacey, *Ford: The Men and the Machine* (Boston: Little, Brown, 1986); David L. Lewis, *The Public Image of Henry Ford: An American Folk Hero and His Company* (Detroit: Wayne State University Press, 1976). Anne Jardim, *The First Henry Ford: A Study in Personality and Business Leadership* (Cambridge, MA: MIT Press, 1970), is a shorter book, albeit one exploring a particular subject, attempting to produce a unified field theory of Ford's psychology. The book that most directly touches on Ford's anti-Semitism is Albert Lee, *Henry Ford and the Jews* (Briarcliff Manor, NY: Stein and Day, 1980). For general background on American anti-Semitism, see John Higham, *Send These to Me: Jews and Other Immigrants in Urban America* (New York: Atheneum, 1975), chapters 7, 8 and 9.

LAURA FERMI
(1907–1977)

Illustrious Immigrants

Laura Fermi's contribution to the immigration debates consists of a single phrase, the title of a book she published in 1968, *Illustrious Immigrants*. The "illustrious immigrants" were those who between 1920 (when World War I ended) and 1941 (when U.S. entry into World War II temporarily halted immigration) had to leave Europe because they opposed the rising communist or fascist dictatorships there or because they were classified as members of "inferior races" whom the Nazis marked for annihilation. They were fortunate in that their previous accomplishments and well-established reputations gave them some advantages in securing immigration visas to the United States. The United States was also fortunate, for their talents made the country a leader in many fields of human endeavor, including art, psychoanalysis, and physics. Ultimately, though, the story of the "illustrious immigrants" is a cautionary tale about the ethical basis on which immigration law rests.

Laura Fermi didn't plan to be an illustrious immigrant, or any sort of immigrant. She was born Laura Capon on June 16, 1907, the daughter of a rear admiral in the Italian navy. She and her sister Anna were raised in upper-middle-class comfort in Rome. She was just fifteen years old when, on October 28, 1922, Benito Mussolini launched his "March on Rome."

Laura and Enrico Fermi. Argonne National Laboratory Photo.
Courtesy of Fermilab Archives.

Over the next few years, Mussolini tightened his grip on power. In 1924, he arranged for the assassination of Giacomo Matteotti, a socialist leader and member of Italy's Parliament. He then began to round up and imprison his political opponents. In June 1925, authorities arrested scholar and activist Gaetano Salvemini for his resistance to the fascist regime. Released from prison in August, Salvemini eluded police surveillance and reached the Franco-Italian border. He eventually came to the United States and returned to Italy only after World War II. He became one of the first wave of refugees from fascism.

At first, fascism affected the Capon family only in minor ways. The most important for Laura came in 1926. The Capons planned to vacation abroad that year, but Mussolini launched his "battle for the lira." In order to keep money in the country, he forbade nonessential international transactions, vacations abroad included. Accordingly, the Capons went to Santa Cristina, a resort in the Dolomites. It was on that vacation that Laura became better acquainted with Enrico Fermi. They had met once before, in the spring of 1924, when they were both part of a larger group of young people hiking in the hills around Rome and stopping for a game of soccer. They inhabited the same milieu; Laura was a student in the general-science program at the University of Rome, and Enrico held an endowed chair in theoretical physics in the same university. However, they had never been in a classroom together, and as it turned out, they never would be. Instead, on July 19, 1928, they married.

If Laura had wanted to marry someone she could be proud of, she had married the right man. Born in Rome on September 29, 1901, to Alberto Fermi, a high-ranking railroad administrator, and his wife Ida de Gattis, an elementary schoolteacher, Fermi's abilities in mathematics and physics came to the attention of one of his father's colleagues when the boy was about thirteen. Enrico received his doctorate from the Scuola Normale Superiore of the University of Pisa magna cum laude in July 1922, a few months before his twenty-first birthday. Financed by a fellowship from the Italian Ministry of Public Instruction, he spent the 1922–1923 school year in Göttingen studying under prominent physicist Max Born with other rising young stars of the profession, Werner Heisenberg (formulator of the Heisenberg uncertainty principle) and Wolfgang Pauli. For the 1923–1924 school year, he received a Rockefeller fellowship and used it to study at Leiden with Paul Ehrenfest. When the fellowship ran out, he became Professor Fermi and spent the 1924–1925 school year teaching at the University of Rome and the 1925–1926 school year teaching at the University of Florence. While he was in Florence he produced what became known as the Fermi-Dirac statistics, which help physicists to predict how matter will behave under particular conditions. Accomplishments like this led Professor (and Senator) Orso Mario Corbino, head of the physics department of the

University of Rome, to propose to the science faculty that it offer Fermi the university's newly endowed chair in theoretical physics.

For Enrico and Laura, fascism was still a distant nusiance rather than a constant worry. It touched their lives most directly in 1929. Searching for symbols that would proclaim Italy's greatness, Mussolini conceived the idea of a Royal Academy to which the most prominent scholars in various disciplines would be named. He knew what would most attract those scholars. Royal Academy salaries were one-and-one-half times what Enrico got through the endowed chair at the University of Rome. The fascists intended to get something from the scholars, too. Accepting membership implied endorsement of Mussolini's regime. However, it was not the same as being asked to put one's hand to some detestable or immoral task. If it would supplement his teaching salary and let him alone to do his work and raise his family, Enrico would do it. He donned the fancy uniform Mussolini decreed for academy members, drove to the Farnesina Palace, specially restored for the Academy, accepted his award, and then drove himself home and continued his work.

Laura's life was shaped more by her sex and her class than by fascist dictatorship. She dropped out of the University of Rome as soon as it became apparent she was to marry. Education was to help one get a job, but married women of Laura's class didn't work outside the home. They didn't do much physical labor inside the home, either. Laura seems to have had a live-in maid for her apartment from an early point in her married life. When her children were born, she hired a nursemaid as well. Part of Laura's work was to channel some of her family's holdings to support the new Fermi family. It was her money that paid for the Fermis' apartment in a cooperative building. She was also supposed to help her husband, and he did dictate to her a book intended as a physics text for precollege students, but this was their only collaboration, as she complained she couldn't follow his thinking. Her second-most important job was to be the family consumer, but even though society assigned her sex that role, the education given girls of her class had not prepared her for it. She relied on her mother to help her purchase the furniture for their Roman apartment, and later she relied on the maid to identify cuts of meat at the butcher's shop; she herself couldn't tell a shoulder from a rump. Laura's most important job was to be a mother. She and Enrico had two children. Their daughter Nella was born on January 31, 1931, and their son Giulio came on February 16, 1936.

While Laura was learning to become a wife and mother, Enrico and his colleagues were experimenting with radioactivity. Physicists knew that some elements radiated atomic particles spontaneously (radium, for example). Two French physicists, Frederic Joiliot and Irene Curie Joliot (the daughter of Pierre and Marie Curie, physicists who pioneered the study of radiation) duplicated nature, bombarding aluminum with alpha particles to detach subatomic particles called positrons from the aluminum. Enrico took this a step further. He used neutrons to do the bombarding. When he finished bombarding one element, uranium, he found that what remained no longer had the same atomic number as uranium. He thought it might be a wholly new element, one that didn't exist in nature. At that time, though, no one could trap enough of the "new element" to determine if it really was new. They would have to wait for more experiments and for a theoretical framework for understanding what they were seeing.

Meanwhile, Enrico and his colleagues wanted to see what happened when one sent the bombarding neutrons through various mediums to the target element. They placed target elements on wooden tables, behind lead shields, in hollowed-out wax balls, and under water in Professor Corbino's goldfish pool in order to see how the neutrons traveled through the various media. They concluded that bombardment worked best when the neutrons traveled through a hydrogen-rich medium that served to slow them down. Despite her protests that she could not understand her husband, Laura did follow these experiments. She and another woman, Ginestra Amaldi, coauthored *Alchima del Tempo Nostro* (Alchemy [an allusion to the medieval efforts to turn ordinary substances into gold] of our time), which was published in 1936.

As Mussolini tightened his grip on power, fascist constraints on individuals became more onerous. People even more well known than Enrico Fermi found that their reputations provided them insufficient protection. In 1929, the same year Enrico accepted appointment to the Royal Academy, the famous conductor Arturo Toscanini resigned his position at Milan's La Scala opera house in protest against being required to include fascist music in his programs. He said the music was bad. Cynics said that Toscanini, whose dictatorial control of his orchestras was legendary, refused to bow to a fellow dictator. Confrontations between Toscanini and the authorities grew more serious. In 1931, Toscanini was invited to be guest conductor for a performance in Bologna. When he refused to include fascist music, despite the fact that Mussolini's son-in-law was expected to attend, the Bolognese fascists roughed him up on the way to the performance. Toscanini was already well known in the United States, having debuted there in 1908. He began to spend more time as a guest conductor there. In 1937, he accepted a position as conductor of the National Broadcasting Company (NBC) Radio Symphony Orchestra. In 1938, when he was visiting Italy, he got into trouble with the fascists again, and the government suspended his passport. When the fascists restored the passport, Toscanini left quickly and permanently.

Even more refugees fled Nazi Germany, where Adolf Hitler took power on January 30, 1933. Hitler's virulently antiradical and racist reputation was already well established. At the time Hitler assumed power, **Albert**

Einstein, a Nobel Prize–winning physicist and also a Jew and someone who was interested in political causes Hitler opposed (Zionism, world peace), was visiting the United States. Einstein announced he and his family would not return to Germany. Instead, he joined the faculty of the Institute for Advanced Studies at Princeton, New Jersey, and started the process of acquiring U.S. citizenship. (However, one didn't need to be as well educated as Einstein to recognize the Nazi threat. Another famous early refugee was the actress and nightclub performer Marlene Dietrich.)

In the first years of Nazi power, people who fled Nazi Germany included many who disagreed with the Nazis philosophically. For example, charging that it was promoting a "radical," "modern," and unacceptable aesthetic that was contributing to social decay, the Nazis harassed the Bauhaus, an institute that had since World War I been a pioneer in style in art, architecture, and the design of household and industrial objects. The Bauhaus disbanded rather than submit to Nazi aesthetics. Architects and designers affiliated with it left Germany, taking their best ideas with them and contributing them instead to U.S. architecture and design.

Similarly, the Nazis campaigned against psychoanalysis as a threat to individual morals and to social order. (When the Nazis entered Austria, the pioneer of pyschoanalysis, Sigmund Freud, and his daughter Anna, also a psychoanalyst, left for England.) Even before the Nazis came to power, psychoanalysts such as Karen Horney had left Europe and settled in the United States. From their new place, pyschoanalysts made important contributions to the study of the human mind. Horney became a pioneer in writing readable accounts of pyschoanalytic concepts for lay readers and in combining Freudian analysis with a woman-centered approach.

Nazi racism drove out other people. On September 15, 1935, the Nazis promulgated the Nuremberg Laws, defining an Aryan race and identifying it as superior and laying numerous restrictions on races they considered inferior, especially Jews. The most important legal burden here is that people who didn't meet the Aryan standard were barred from practicing a profession or from teaching. Militarism drove out a third wave of people. When Hitler launched a second world war by attacking Poland, and then attacking Poland's allies in western Europe, people as diverse as Dutch painter Piet Mondrian and Hungarian composer Béla Bartók fled to New York City to pursue their callings.

The Fermis' refugee story had its origins in a complicated power struggle between rival fascists Mussolini and Hitler. In 1934, when he had been in power only one year, Hitler advanced his troops to the German-Austrian border, evidently planning to bring Austria under his rule. Mussolini advanced *his* troops to the Italo-Austrian border, signaling to Hitler what awaited him if he came any closer to Italy. Hitler backed down. He developed an alternative plan. In October 1935, Mussolini began his own expansionist program with a war on Ethiopia, an independent African kingdom Italy had long wanted for a colony. It took him until June 1936, but he finally conquered the kingdom. Hitler praised Mussolini and hinted at the possibility of an alliance between the two fascist powers. Flattered, Mussolini drew closer to Hitler—only to be swallowed. After signing the "Pact of Steel" creating the German-Italian Axis, Hitler resumed his campaign for Austria, and in 1937, the Anschluss, or union of Germany and Austria, took place without struggle. Mussolini couldn't complain about what his own ally was doing.

Hitler began to pressure Mussolini to bring Italian fascism more into conformity with that of Nazi Germany, particularly in the area of anti-Semitism. In 1938, Mussolini introduced the Nuremberg Laws into Italy. It is at this point that it became important to Laura that she was a Jew. It hadn't been important to her before. During her adolescence, she passed through a religious crisis she described as the kind "which most girls cannot avoid passing, at least in Catholic Italy"; she never commented on whether her non-Catholic background contributed to it.[1] She and Enrico married in a civil service because neither was religious. She described her family as nonobservant Jews, and Enrico was a scientist who doubted the existence of God. She accepted the Catholicism prevailing in Italy's public school system. She was not bothered when Nella learned to pray to the Child Jesus, and she was as upset as any devout Christian when it seemed Nella was learning to equate the Child Jesus with Mussolini and with King Victor Emmanuel III and to believe that all three heard her prayers equally. Now, though, Laura, Nella, and Giulio were classified as Jews and subject to the restrictive laws.

Enrico began considering ways to get the family out of Italy. This would not be easy. The fascist government might not permit a professor of his stature to leave permanently. And everyone who left Italy faced the same laws, which were designed to keep Italian money in the country. No one could take out more than $50, so the four Fermis and their nursemaid would have to start life in a new country with $250. There was also the problem of where to go. Hitler's subjugation of Czechoslovakia in early 1938 indicated that nowhere in Europe was safe. The Fermis had spent the summer of 1934 in Argentina and Brazil, where Enrico lectured to packed audiences, but they do not seem to have considered moving to South America. They had been at the University of Michigan in Ann Arbor during the summer of 1930, but migrating to the United States posed problems. The United States had a quota system that judged each nation of the world as to whether its people were racially akin to old-stock Americans or not and awarded immigrant visas accordingly. Only about 5,000 Italians per year were permitted to immigrate to the United States. There was a loophole in the law. Teachers of higher education who would be working in the United States, and their families, could enter without waiting for one of the scarce visas to become available. The Fermis sent four letters to colleagues in the

United States, through four different post offices in Italy, so the government wouldn't begin to wonder what they were up to. They were afraid the government might open the letters, so one had to read between the lines to realize they were checking to see if Enrico could find a job in the United States. From the four letters Enrico got five job offers.

Then came an event that made escape a bit easier. On November 10, 1938, a long-distance telephone call from Stockholm informed the Fermis that Enrico had won the Nobel Prize for Physics. The pieces of an escape plan fell into place. The fascists were so proud an Italian had won a Nobel Prize that the government did not bar Fermi from traveling to accept it. They even accepted his explanation that he would go from Stockholm to New York, where he would teach for a semester at Columbia University. If the Fermis went straight from Sweden to the United States, they could keep the prize money as a nest egg to start a new life.

Now all the Fermis needed was permission to get into the United States. Because Enrico qualified for the consideration due teachers of higher education, they did not need to wait for one of the 5,000 visas granted annually to become available, but they did have to meet other requirements. For example, Laura, Nella, and Giulio were family members, but could they also bring their nursemaid? The maid explained that she was engaged to be married to someone who would be remaining in Italy. She was given a visa for a short stay, until the Fermis hired American servants. (As it turned out, she broke her engagement to continue to work for the Fermis in the United States.) Similarly, everyone had to pass an arithmetic test, during which the administrator, apparently unaware of Enrico's Nobel Prize, checked to see if he could add 15 + 27 in his head. Finally, everyone had to pass a medical test. The American physician examining them found that Nella had an uncorrected vision problem and was going to deny her a visa on grounds of poor health until the fact that her father was a Nobel Prize winner came up: Apparently Nobel Prize–winning parents had better ability to care for minor health problems.

The Nobel award ceremony was in Stockholm on December 10, 1938 (the anniversary of the birth of Alfred Nobel). It provided the Fermis with further evidence of how dangerous the situation was becoming. The fascists were dissatisfied with Enrico's performance at the prize ceremony, complaining that he shook hands with King Gustave V of Sweden instead of giving the king the fascist salute. From Stockholm, the Fermis went to England, where, on Christmas Eve, they boarded the S.S. *Franconia*. They arrived in New York on January 2, 1939. Enrico indeed taught at Columbia—but for more than six months. He never again lived or worked in Italy.

For Laura, exile was a step down. She had a maid and a nanny in Italy. Now her nursemaid became her general maid, and she had to help the maid. They both had to go shopping. The maid judged the quality of the produce and meat cuts and Laura read the can labels and calculated whether the price was right. They both had to cook. Laura read the directions and converted American measurements to the metric system, and the maid added the ingredients together and stirred. Laura took more charge of the children. Every day she walked Giulio to Columbia University to play in the open space at the center of campus, even though the wind rushing off the Hudson River made it difficult to navigate up Riverside Drive and around the corner at West 116th Street. She put Nella in Horace Mann School. Just as she had accepted the educational system in Italy, Laura was calm in the face of the American educational system. She was not worried at all that Nella couldn't answer some of the questions during her intelligence test. The tester had told Nella about a little boy who went into the woods, played with a small, furry, black-and-white animal, and then had to come home, wash thoroughly, and change his smelly clothes, then asked Nella to name the animal. Of course, she couldn't, Laura said—there aren't any skunks in Italy.

On January 16, 1939, two weeks after their own arrival in the United States, the Fermis were at the Hudson River dock of the Swedish passenger line to meet another physicist, the Dane Niels Bohr. Bohr brought with him the conclusion to Fermi's puzzling experiment of 1934, in which bombarding uranium with neutrons produced something else. German male chemists Otto Hahn and Fritz Strassman and Austrian female physicist Lise Meitner, all employed by the Kaiser Wilhelm Institute for Chemistry in Berlin, had tried the same experiment. In the midst of the experiment, Meitner had to leave. She was a Jew, and after the Anschluss with Austria, the Nuremberg Laws applied to her. She left for Denmark to live with her nephew, Otto Frisch. Hahn and Strassman continued their work. They succeeded in trapping enough postbombardment material for chemical analysis. What they found was neither a new element nor uranium but barium. How did the uranium turn into barium? Hahn and Strassman reported their results to Meitner, who discussed them with Frisch and with Bohr. They concluded they were witnessing an example of Albert Einstein's equation $e = mc^2$. The uranium atoms were being split apart. As they broke, they released the energy that had been used to hold them together. Frisch dubbed the process of splitting atoms "fission." Enrico considered Bohr's news so important that he broke his usual rule about not bringing home his work. He explained to Laura how Bohr and Meitner had solved the mystery of his "new element" of 1934.

Enrico did not tell Laura everything. Bohr speculated that if one could get enough uranium, and pull it apart just right, one would be able to release tremendous amounts of energy, enough to push a ship through the water, enough to power an electric generator—enough for a bomb of untold destructive power. Bohr thought the Nazis already knew this. Why else would they have forbidden the further export of uranium from Czech mines?

Enrico and Bohr began to present the idea of fission and to describe the experiments that documented it to groups of scientists. This brought them into contact with a network of refugee scientists who had escaped after Hitler took power in Germany, after the Anschluss, or after Hitler dismantled Czechoslovakia, which he did in 1938. Their first stop was Columbia University. Among the people they spoke to was Hungarian-born physicist Leo Szilard. They then went to Princeton, New Jersey, where they spoke with Albert Einstein. On January 26, the two reached Washington, D.C., where they addressed a meeting of astronomers and physicists who were exploring the possibility that it was the "fusion" of atoms—the release of energy as four hydrogen atoms combined to form a heavier helium atom— that made the stars shine. Among the people in this group were Hungarian-born physicist Edward Teller, German-born physicist Hans Bethe, and Hungarian-born mathematician John Von Neumann. The people whom Hitler considered political radicals and members of inferior races were coming together in a remarkable scientific collaboration.

It was Szilard who thought the scientists should alert the politicians. He drafted a two-page letter to U.S. President Franklin D. Roosevelt outlining the situation. Thinking the letter might carry more weight if it came from someone Roosevelt had heard of, Szilard asked Einstein to sign it. Einstein signed the letter on August 2, 1939. He gave it to a mutual acquaintance, economist Alexander Sachs, to deliver to Roosevelt personally. Before Sachs could arrange an appointment, war broke out. Hitler invaded Poland on September 1, 1939. This development meant Roosevelt was busier than ever, but it may have also made him more attentive when Sachs arranged an interview. Roosevelt understood the implications of what Sachs was saying but took little action because the United States wasn't at war with Germany. All he could do was appoint an Advisory Committee on Uranium and give it a budget of $6,000.

During 1940 and 1941 the Advisory Committee on Uranium gathered information from the experiments of various scientists. Enrico resumed the experiments he had begun in 1934. Then he had one source of neutrons, which he aimed at the uranium being bombarded. Now he tried to get the neutrons released from the uranium to bombard other uranium atoms, in other words, to set up a chain reaction. He was fortunate in that he made the acquaintance of Herbert Anderson, a physics graduate student who had helped build Columbia's cyclotron, a device used to study atoms and subatomic particles. Anderson arranged for Enrico to use that cyclotron to do experiments in setting up chain reactions. Laura knew Anderson as Enrico's personal assimilation expert, explaining U.S. university education and the English language. It is not clear whether she knew much else about Enrico's work. Enrico seldom talked about work at home even when it was not secret, and increasingly, it was secret.

Laura was left trying to figure out how to run an American household and how to raise American children. In these endeavors, she, too, had a mentor, Professor Harold Urey, a Columbia chemist. Urey steered the Fermis toward Leonia, New Jersey, where they purchased a house in a neighborhood where other professors lived. Urey also tried to initiate Laura into the mysteries of lawn care, which she found puzzling. Urey said one had to eradicate every trace of crabgrass, but what was crabgrass?

The Japanese attack on Pearl Harbor, on December 7, 1941, drew the United States into war not only with Japan but with Japan's allies, Germany and Italy. Because Roosevelt was aware that Hitler might be trying to develop an atomic bomb, he entered into a secret arms race to be the first with the new weapon. Ironically, his combat forces in this arms race included many scientists from the countries with which the United States was now at war. The Fermis, for example, were enemy aliens and had not been in the United States long enough to qualify for citizenship. The U.S. government did not bend any of its rules to accommodate the enemy aliens in the Manhattan Project, as the race to develop an atom bomb was called. Enrico had to obey the same curfew laws and travel restrictions as other enemy aliens. He had to be home by eight o'clock at night when he was in town, and if he traveled, even if it was for a secret project, he had to let authorities know where he was going. However, the U.S. government did let Fermi, and others like him, work on the project.

Security, and probably politics, did prevent Enrico from formally heading up any part of the atomic project. Instead, Arthur H. Compton, an American Nobel physics laureate on the faculty of the University of Chicago, was assigned to supervise the work of developing a chain reaction. The Fermis moved to Chicago in 1942. Laura knew that Enrico knew a secret that couldn't be shared. Shortly after the Fermis arrived in Chicago, Arthur Compton and his wife Betty had a party for the scientists working on the project and their spouses. The main activity of the party was the screening of a movie called *Next of Kin*, a dramatic account of the tragedy that ensued when someone was careless with military secrets. Taking this as a hint, Laura confined herself to her household and her husbands' colleagues' families and never asked what went on at the lab. On December 2, 1942, the Fermis hosted a party for the lab people. Laura was puzzled to hear them congratulate Enrico as they came in. She did not know that earlier that afternoon Enrico had started the first nuclear chain reaction to be controlled by human beings.

Enrico's work became even more secret during 1943 and the first two thirds of 1944. He traveled incessantly, secretly, and with a bodyguard. Laura didn't know where he was going, especially since one of the places was referred to only as Site Y. In August 1944, J. Robert Oppenheimer, an American physicist, came to talk to her about moving the family to Site Y. At that point, it was hot in Chicago and Enrico was about to depart on another of his mysterious trips. Laura decided that she would take Nella and Giulio to Site Y and wait for Enrico to join her there. It was perhaps when she got the railroad tickets that she found out she was going to a place outside Lamy, New Mexico, the nearest station.

Site Y turned out to be a compound near Los Alamos, New Mexico. It was part military installation, with a general, Leslie H. Groves, in command, and part scientific laboratory, of which Oppenheimer was in charge. It also had the aspect of a refugee camp. Laura met many other European exiles there. She resumed a friendship with Emilio Segre and struck up one with Bruno Rossi, physicists the Fermis had known in Italy. Hungarians Edward Teller and John Von Neumann, the German Hans Bethe, the Polish-born mathematician Stan Ulam, and a Chinese female physicist named Chien-Shiung Wu were also there.[2] Although the Union of Soviet Socialist Republics was not officially informed of the project, émigrés could work on it. Russian chemist George Kistiakowsky (who fled the Communist Party in the 1920s) came to Los Alamos in 1944. Even Niels Bohr was there, under a cloak of secrecy even more enveloping than usual, at least until the scientists went skiing, and he stood out, swooping elegantly down the slopes and going from a high speed to a dead stop, just as he learned to do in his native Scandinavia.

The fun days on the ski slopes were a welcome break from the everyday difficulties of life at Los Alamos. Until January 1943, the place where the laboratory was located had been a boys' school. The terrain was ill suited to accommodate a secret city of people used to middle-class comforts. There was so little water that when the laboratory arranged a party for the people who lived in the area around Los Alamos, the party almost had to be canceled because there was not enough water to boil for tea, let alone to do the dishes. There were only a few real houses, which had been built for the boys' school, and these were reserved for the leadership. Everyone else crowded into apartments. Through her floor Laura could hear her neighbors whooping with laughter as Niels Bohr told them jokes. The apartments had few conveniences, and Los Alamos technicians had to repair household devices in their free moments, as one could not bring in a repair person from outside. Laura, who had gone from a house to a three-bedroom apartment, still wanted to get household help. But that was rationed, and since she wasn't pregnant, didn't have a chronic medical problem, and didn't have any children younger than five years, she was eligible only for two half-days of household help per week, and that was only because she held a job.

This was Laura's first job outside the home. Los Alamos's managers encouraged wives to work to stave off some of the problems of confinement to their secret city. For women whose husbands were constantly at work and whose children were generally at school, work helped to fill the empty hours, and it brought in a little more income. Laura, although an intelligent woman, had left school to marry and so didn't have the college degree that qualified her for professional work. Nor did she have the clerical experience that prepared her for the pink-collar jobs women usually filled. She got a low-level clerical job working six mornings a week for a Los Alamos physician. Her experience with him was an interesting commentary on the degree of secrecy at Los Alamos and on how individuals reacted to it by self-censorship. Laura remembered that the doctor saw a steady stream of petty problems magnified into major ones by people under heavy stress. She was shocked when one young man died twenty-four days after receiving a jolt of radiation 200,000 times higher than the normal daily exposure for workers in that field. However, she did not, apparently, put together the stress, the radiation death, and the references to radiation poisoning to figure out what her husband was doing.

All she knew was he disappeared briefly in July 1945. She knew there was a test of some sort on the night of July 15, because a woman physicist left behind at Los Alamos said she and some friends were going camping in the hills around Albuquerque in the hopes of watching the test. In the early morning hours of July 16, a sleepless patient at the secret city's hospital had been looking out the windows and had seen a strange light at the test site. In the evening of July 16, Enrico returned home dead tired and went right to bed and to sleep. The next day, he said he had not felt it was safe to drive himself home and so had asked a friend to take the wheel. Laura thought that was odd; Enrico was usually an extremely independent person.

The secrecy was shattered on the morning of August 7. Laura was working in her kitchen when she heard another scientist's wife pounding up the stairs. As soon as she reached the landing, she shouted, "Our stuff was dropped on Japan."[3] Laura switched on her radio in time to hear the official announcement being read not just to Los Alamos but to the world. The United States had on the morning of August 6 dropped an atomic bomb over the city of Hiroshima. At that time, the only way to convey a sense of the importance of this to the public was to compare it to an explosive with which they had some familiarity. The new bomb was the equivalent of 20,000 tons of TNT. At the dawn of the nuclear era, Laura's feelings were of an old-fashioned sort. She was proud of her husband and of herself for supporting him in his work, and she thought the other wives felt the same.[4]

The Fermis left Los Alamos on New Year's Eve of 1945. A new job awaited Enrico in Chicago. He was part of a project to establish Institutes of Basic Research at the University of Chicago, whereby industry might directly support pure science and call on scientists for information. Enrico, though, worked at this position for less than a decade. He died of stomach cancer on November 28, 1954.

In the year of Enrico's death, Laura began her own career as an English-language writer by publishing her memoir, *Atoms in the Family*. For several years after he husband's death, Laura wrote on topics he had researched, publishing *Atoms for the World* in 1957 and *The Story of Atomic Energy*, a volume for young readers, in 1961. Also in 1961, she published two biographies, *Mussolini* and *Galileo and the Scientific Revolution*, the latter with Gilberto Bernadini. *Illustrious Immigrants* was her last book. She died in Chicago, Illinois, on December 26, 1977.

Through the title of her book, Laura Fermi supplied a phrase that has created an enduring image in the American debate over immigration—and a controversial one. On the one hand, the illustrious immigrant is an inspiring and comforting image, a person of promise, unfairly persecuted at home, who finds refuge in the United States and in turn adds luster to American culture. There were such people before Laura Fermi coined the phrase; **Carl Schurz**, who fled the reaction to the revolutions of 1848 and became secretary of the interior under Rutherford B. Hayes, counts as one. The refugees that fled fascism were prominent in U.S. life for generations, an example being Henry Kissinger, who left Germany as an adolescent and grew up to become secretary of state. The Cold War allowed that tradition to continue. The financier **George Soros**, Andrew Grove, founder of Intel, a microchip manufacturing company, and Madeline Albright, the young Czech refugee who, like Kissinger, became secretary of state, are examples of refugees who found in the United States more opportunity to use their talents.

The "illustrious immigrant," though, is also a sober reminder. Laura Fermi's immigrants got to be immigrants *because* they were illustrious. It is not clear how many people never had a chance to make their reputations before their careers were cut off by their own governments. Is it possible to develop a fair-minded, evenhanded immigration policy that works for the not-so-illustrious but the equally human?

NOTES

1. Laura Fermi, *Atoms in the Family* (Chicago: University of Chicago Press, 1954), p. 52.
2. "Chien-Shiung Wu, 84, Dies; Top Experimental Physicist," *New York Times*, February 18, 1997, Section B, p. 7.
3. Fermi, *Atoms in the Family*, p. 237.
4. Ibid., p. 240.

BIBLIOGRAPHY

Laura Fermi received an obituary in the *Bulletin of the Atomic Scientists* 34:2–3 (May 1978). Her writings that are relevant to the subject at hand include *Atoms in the Family* (Chicago: University of Chicago Press, 1954) and *Illustrious Immi-*

grants: The Intellectual Migration from Europe, 1930–1941 (Chicago: University of Chicago Press, 1968). Other books and articles on the subject include Mitchell G. Ash and Alfons Soellner, eds., *Forced Migration and Scientific Change* (Washington, D.C.: German Historical Institute and Cambridge University Press, 1996); Donald Peterson Kent, *The Refugee Intellectual: The Americanization of the Immigrants of 1933–1941* (New York: Columbia University Press, 1953); David S. Wyman, *Paper Walls: America and the Refugee Crisis, 1938–1941* (Amherst: University of Massachusetts Press, 1968); Gary David Mitchell, "The Impact of U.S. Immigration Policy on the Economic 'Quality' of German and Austrian Immigrants in the 1930s," *International Migration Review* 26:3 (Fall 1992), pp. 940–967; and a special issue of *Perspectives in American History*, "The Intellectual Migration," edited by Bernard Bailyn and David Donald. Many individuals mentioned in the entry and in Fermi's monograph had their own biographies. Among the biographies of physicists, one might note Roger Highfield and Paul Carter, *The Private Lives of Albert Einstein* (New York: St. Martin's Press, 1994); Ruth Lewin Sime, *Lise Meitner: A Life in Physics*, California Studies in the History of Science No. 13 (Berkeley and Los Angeles: University of California Press, a Centennial Book, 1996), and Stanley A. Blumberg, *Edward Teller: A Giant of the Golden Age of Physics* (New York: Scribner's, 1990). Although it is not about refugees in particular, the videotape *The Day after Trinity: J. Robert Oppenheimer and the Atomic Bomb* is very helpful in that it captures on tape the voices of Hans Bethe and Stan and Françoise Ulam. For other Italian exiles, see Joseph Horowitz, *Understanding Toscanini: How He Became an American Culture God and Helped Create a New Audience for Old Music* (New York: Alfred A. Knopf, 1987); and Gaetano Salvemini, *Italian Fascist Activities in the United States*, ed. Philip Cannistraro (New York: Center for Migration Studies, 1977). Regarding pyschoanalysts, one useful biography is Jack L. Rubin, *Karen Horney: Gentle Rebel of Psychoanalysis* (New York: Dial Press, 1978). Regarding artists, see Martica Sawin, *Surrealism in Exile and the Beginning of the New York School* (Cambridge, MA: MIT Press, 1995). Information on exile artists is also conveyed via exhibitions. Stephanie Baron has curated two exhibits of art by interwar refugees. One, "Degenerate Art," exhibited in 1991, attempted to replicate a 1937 show in which the Nazis exhibited art works of which they disapproved in order to highlight what they thought was wrong with them. The other, "Exiles and Emigres," exhibited in 1996, is more general. At this point, autobiographies of refugees who found a home in American intellectual life still appear in press; an example is Hans A. Schmitt, *Lucky Victim: An Ordinary Life in Extraordinary Times* (Baton Rouge: Louisiana State University Press, 1989). Some information can be had only from news media: Chien-Shiung Wu's obituary appeared in the *New York Times* on February 18, 1997, and material on Andrew Grove appeared in *Time* (December 29, 1997–January 5, 1998), pp. 48–72.

PATRICK ANTHONY MCCARRAN
(1876–1954)

Cold War Immigration

"McCarthyism" sums up a part of the early 1950s. It takes its name from Joseph R. McCarthy, who was first elected to the U.S. Senate in 1946. There were already signs, such as the investigation of communism in Hollywood, that people feared that the Communist Party, directed by officials in the Soviet Union, had subversive influence in U.S. life. McCarthy took that fear to new levels, charging that high U.S. authorities had been lax in preventing communist infiltration of the executive branch of the federal government. He became a leader in speaking out against such communist subversion, and when he was given charge of a Senate committee, he investigated communism ruthlessly, without regard for the rights of the accused or for people's reputations. For a while, it seemed that the government spent much of its time trying to counter a communist menace.

Before there was McCarthy, there was Patrick Anthony McCarran. McCarthy and McCarran had a few biographical details in common. They both projected images of informal camaraderie: It was Pat McCarran and Joe McCarthy. They were both Roman Catholics. They were both of Irish extraction. They both hailed from outside the Northeast and Mid-Atlantic states that dominated politics; McCarthy was from Wisconsin and Mc-

Carran from Nevada. They both fell in with the majority party in their states; the Republicans, for McCarthy, and the Democrats, for McCarran. They were both members of the U.S. Senate. They were both identified with the post–World War II anticommunist crusade.

However, there were some important differences. McCarran was older than McCarthy and had been in the Senate longer. His career helps to illuminate the connection between pre– and post–World War II policies in foreign affairs and in immigration. The Republicans were not completely united around McCarthy's anticommunism, but anticommunism did provide an issue that up-and-coming Republicans such as McCarthy (and Richard M. Nixon) could use to advance their careers. By contrast, McCarran's anticommunism revealed how fragile the supposedly invincible Democratic coalition really was. As a young senator, McCarthy had only so many ways to affect public policy. He made the most of the opportunities handed him to conduct investigations. As a senior senator, McCarran was an example of the paradoxes of the American political system. He maintained his office because he served his native Nevada well, but as he maintained it, he advanced in seniority and thus got his pick of committee assignments in which he could shape not only Nevada's fate but the nation's—and the immigrants'.

McCarran's father, also Patrick McCarran, was born in Ireland about 1832 and stowed away on a ship during the famine year of 1848. In the United States, he joined the army's cavalry, fought the Paiute Indians, and then settled in Nevada to become a homesteader and a sheep rancher. He married Margaret Shea, who had come from County Cork as a domestic servant. On August 8, 1876, this couple had their only child. He was educated in the local schools, graduating from Reno High School in 1897 as class valedictorian. He began putting himself through the University of Nevada with a job as a janitor but had to quit in his senior year when his father suffered a disabling illness.

It is a measure of his energy and ability that McCarran found other ways to achieve his goals. He made an advantageous marriage, in 1903, to Martha Harriet Weeks. Her family were also ranchers, from Elko, Nevada. They were Episcopalians and McCarran's bride had been a schoolteacher, not a domestic servant, prior to her marriage. They eventually had five children: a son, Samuel, and daughters Mary, Margaret, Norine, and Patricia. McCarran also studied law on his own. He was admitted to the bar in 1905 and practiced law for the next thirty years.

The only area in which his ambitions were thwarted was in politics. He secured a seat in the Nevada state legislature in 1902. Between 1907 and 1909 he was the district attorney general for Nye City. Between 1913 and 1918 he was on the Nevada Supreme Court; during 1917 and 1918 he was the chief justice. What he really wanted to be, though, was a senator. He made his first effort in 1916, when he challenged Democrat Key Pittman for the party nomination. It's not clear if he thought he had a chance because Pittman himself had been in the Senate only since 1912 or if he was so ambitious as to be reckless. All he got, though, was an enemy. Pittman defeated him for the nomination easily. Thereafter, they needled each other as long as they were both in politics. In 1924, they were both in Nevada's delegation to the Democratic National Convention. The convention deadlocked over the choice between William McAdoo and **Alfred E. Smith**. Pittman, the delegation leader, was irritated with McAdoo and Smith for insisting on staying in the race but more irritated with McCarran, who was undermining Pittman's attempts to broker a deal whereby both men forswore the nomination. McCarran countered Pittman's claims of neutrality by publishing results of Nevada's delegates' straw poll, which showed Pittman really favored McAdoo. When McCarran ran for the Senate again, in 1926, Pittman didn't make a move to help his fellow Democrat, and McCarran was defeated.

McCarran's big opportunity came in 1932, when the Great Depression led to a wholesale rejection of Republicans and the election of Democrats of whatever kind. This is an important point. The more McCarran saw of Franklin D. Roosevelt's New Deal, the less he liked it. Soon, he had distanced himself from Roosevelt and thus could not rely on administrative support for future political campaigns. Key Pittman was still one of Nevada's two senators and still in control of the state Democratic Party. Pittman and McCarran had another quarrel when Pittman thought McCarran tried to undermine Pittman's ultimately successful 1934 reelection bid. With no regular party support, McCarran had to develop his own organization.

To ensure his continuity in office and in influence, McCarran tended to his constituents assiduously. Early on, he identified aviation as a new industry that it would be in isolated Nevada's interest to cultivate, and he worked hard for it. (He was rewarded by having the Las Vegas international airport named in his honor.) When it benefited his constituents, McCarran could favor immigration. On March 3, 1949, he introduced Senate Bill 1165, which assisted Nevada's sheep-ranching industry by permitting skilled shepherds to enter the United States outside of the quota restrictions.[1] The bill became law on June 30, 1950. McCarran's work for Nevada ensured his reelection for the rest of his life. Eventually, his longevity in the Senate brought him seniority, which meant he could take his pick of prestigious committees that wrote laws not just for Nevada but for the United States. In 1943, after ten years in the Senate, he became chair of the Senate Judiciary Committee and also head of the Appropriations Subcommittee, which introduced to the Senate funding bills for the Commerce, State, and Justice Departments.

In the Senate, the lines between Democrats and Republicans were crosscut by other lines. There was a loose coalition of "conservatives," that is, people who were divided into Democrats and Republicans and also divided in terms of regional or economic interest but who were united by the sense that the New Deal was a dangerous innovation. The New Deal transferred power from the legislature to the executive branch of the federal government. It threatened the balance between federal and state power. It advocated the redistribution of wealth, which challenged capitalist notions that the individual, not the government, should take the lead in society and also challenged traditional moral views that people should earn their own way (and should be permitted to keep what they earned). For Nevada's senators, the New Deal shift in foreign policy was an important point. Seniority had given Key Pittman the post of chair of the Senate Foreign Relations Committee. This was a powerful position from which to urge the country to isolate itself from the growth of communism, the rise of fascism, the expansion of the Empire of Japan, and the possibility of another war. McCarran never supported Pittman publicly, but he shared Pittman's sentiments. By the time World War II came, Pittman was dead. (He passed away on November 10, 1940, five days after his reelection to the Senate). McCarran supported the war patriotically, then resumed his isolationist policies.

Yet McCarran reverted to isolationism in new circumstances. During World War II, the United States and the Union of Soviet Socialist Republics allied to defeat the Axis alliance of Nazi Germany and fascist Italy, but the alliance was always tentative, dependent on Franklin Roosevelt's personal contacts. After World War II, the United States and the Soviet Union entered into a Cold War that lasted until the 1991 Soviet collapse. Roosevelt's former secretary of agriculture and Iowa politician Henry A. Wallace argued that the Cold War need not exist and that the United States should aim for normal relations with the Soviet Union. He was in the minority, but he was part of a spectrum. George F. Kennan, who was no communist sympathizer, argued for cultivating diplomatic relations with the Soviets, too. He argued that the Soviets had no system for transferring leadership from one generation to the next; when the present leadership died out (he gave it fifteen years), the Soviet Union might collapse. Until then, the United States had to remain active in world affairs, using diplomacy, economic sanctions, and perhaps sometimes military means to "contain" Soviet expansionist tendencies within historic borders. (Hence Kennan's theory is called "containment.") When longtime isolationist Senator Arthur Vandenburg of Michigan began advocating greater involvement in world affairs, it would seem that the United States had abandoned its historic isolationism. Actually, people such as Pat McCarran remained "isolationist," albeit in another sense, trying to isolate the United States from succumbing to international communism.

The Cold War was a new kind of war. It had battlegrounds, such as Korea and Vietnam. The United States and the Soviet Union were also rivals in a battle that took place in laboratories and atomic weapons testing grounds. Most important for McCarran was the possibility that individual members of the Communist Party active in the United States could deliver the country to the Soviets.

McCarran first raised this possibility during debates over postwar Europe. Wars always create some refugees, as civilians flee advancing troops. During World War II, the Nazis deliberately uprooted over 20 million civilians. Some were sent directly to extermination camps such as Auschwitz, specifically built to kill people. Others were put to work as slave labor in agriculture and industry under lethal conditions, denied adequate food, clothing, shelter, or medical care, and worked under the supervision of guards who beat and tortured them. They died at their slave labor camps, or as they wore out, they were transported to the death camps. Altogether, 12 million captives (including nearly 6 million Jews) died before the Allies defeated the Nazis and put an end to their system. The Allies then went to work breaking up the concentration camps and getting the newly freed inmates in sufficient health to return home. However, over a million survivors of this vast uprooting could not return to their homes. In the case of Jews, Nazis had often leveled their towns after transferring or deporting them, and there was no home to return to. In other cases, the advancing Soviets had replaced the retreating Nazis. In the part of Germany and Austria occupied by American troops, the United States Army transferred the displaced persons (DPs) from their concentration camps and slave labor quarters to the best accommodations they could find, which were often the barracks the Nazis had lived in while they were guarding their prisoners. They provided as much as they could and appealed to the American public for more food and for clothing. The DPs were able to augment the food supply by growing vegetables in patches of ground between their barracks. The DPs scrounged their camps for furniture and for fabric so that as families reassembled they could curtain off the corners of their barracks into family areas, although they still had to eat at the common mess and take their recreation in public areas, as they didn't have the facilities for kitchens or for play space. The DPs also scrounged for work, supporting themselves by keeping their camps as clean as they could, providing each other with petty services, and helping the American authorities. World War II ended in Europe on May 8, 1945. However, for several years thereafter, some DPs remained in their camps, freed from Nazi tyranny and restored to health but without homes or jobs.

Harry Truman wanted to move at least some people from Germany and Austria, and also people displaced by the war in Italy, to the United States. Some DPs could be integrated into European society but not all. Italy had historically been an immigrant-sending country; its economy was even weaker than usual right after World War II. Germany was getting a new wave of refugees, *Volksdeutsch*, ethnic Germans who had lived in the Soviet

Union, Poland, and Czechoslovakia but who were being expelled as a result of Nazi occupation of those countries. The DPs could not all find jobs in the German or Austrian economy, and there was still a certain amount of ethnic prejudice and anti-Semitism. Some DPs might prefer to go to other countries, such as Israel, which became an independent state in May 1948. Truman did not want to force anyone to return to Soviet-dominated areas who did not want to go, and after three years, it was pretty clear these people did not want to. Encouraging migration to the United States would relieve the kind of unemployment and economic depression that made Europeans vote for the Communist Party. It would also, Truman thought, be handled in a way that was safe to the United States, taking, for example, people who had relatives who could help them find work and homes and assist them in adjusting to the United States, or confiding them to the care of agencies, such as the Hebrew Immigrant Aid Society, that would perform the same functions.

Truman managed to get some of what he wanted in the Displaced Persons Act of June 25, 1948. Truman had wanted to admit the DPs outside of existing quota laws. Congress worded the Displaced Persons Act to permit 205,000 people to enter the United States over a two-year period. Their visas were charged against future quotas. Italy had a quota of about 5,000 people annually. If 205,000 immigrants went from Italy to the United States between 1948 and 1950, Italy would use up the next forty-one years of quotas and would not be able to send another immigrant until 1992 (205,000 divided by 5,000 is 41, the number of years of quotas). Thus, the law took care of an emergency without increasing immigration in the long run.

In Europe, DPs now had something new to fill their time. They had to gather documents that would allow them to get passports and visas. Documentation was no easy task, as many had lost their homes and had all their personal possessions taken from them when they entered concentration camps. DPs did not have to conform to the quota system but did have to fulfill all the requirements regarding immigration that the United States had imposed since the 1880s. They had to swear they weren't anarchists or polygamists. They had to take literacy tests. They had to take medical tests that checked them for loathsome and contagious diseases. (This was a serious barrier, as the concentration and DP camps were conducive to tuberculosis.) If they had American relatives, they had to contact them and convince them to be sponsors. They also had to do the paperwork for the agency that transported them from the DP camp to the port at Bremerhaven in northern Germany and chaperoned them on the steamship that carried them to an American port, usually New York City, but sometimes Boston or New Orleans.

McCarran never supported the DP program. Even if all it did was permit countries to use future quotas in this short, two-year period, it was still going to alter the ethnic and racial composition of the United States. Ireland, which had no DPs, could not take advantage of the program. Also, he feared that in the rush of immigrants communist spies and saboteurs might pose as refugees, be admitted to the United States, and carry out subversive activities. Truman argued that the danger of spies and saboteurs was minimal. This led to a confrontation between the executive and legislative branch, and between wings of the Democratic Party, on the issue of control of subversives.

People concerned about civil liberties were already suspicious of the executive branch's record. Even before World War II started, the Alien Registration Act of June 28, 1940, required immigrants over fourteen years of age who had not become citizens of the United States to register and be fingerprinted and permitted deportation of people who had been members of radical political organizations. In 1942, Roosevelt sanctioned the relocation of Japanese immigrants and their American-born children from their California homes to camps in the interior, where they were held, without trial, until 1944. German and Italian immigrants who were not citizens were required to register as enemy aliens and to obey a separate code of laws. Throughout the war, Congress had given the executive branch power to restrict immigration in the name of national defense.

Truman authorized each department of the executive branch to conduct investigations into the loyalty of department employees and to fire those deemed security risks. The loyalty reviews may have removed security risks but at a cost to innocent people. It attacked individuals who were not members of the Communist Party but who had personal information (such as homosexuality) they wished to keep private. Fearing the communists would blackmail such people and thus force them to become spies, the authorities deemed the people security risks and fired them.

A series of events in 1950 suggested the executive branch had not been thorough enough in its search for communist spies. In December 1948, while the first groups of U.S.-bound DPs were boarding U.S. Army transport ships, the House Un-American Activities Committee (HUAC) was watching *Time* magazine editor Whittaker Chambers produce evidence that he claimed proved that State Department official Alger Hiss was a Soviet spy. Chambers had himself been a member of the Communist Party. He left it in fear of his life when he began to see how ruthless Stalin was about ensuring loyalty. To protect himself from retribution from his former colleagues, he had saved microfilmed copies of documents his spy ring had passed to the Soviets. To protect the documents from thieves, he had hidden them in a hollowed-out pumpkin in a patch in his farm in Maryland. Called to testify before HUAC, Chambers mentioned that Hiss had been part of the spy ring. When Hiss denied it, Chambers waded out into his pumpkin patch, uncorked the pumpkin, and pulled out what he said was the incriminating microfilm. Hiss sued Chambers for libel. He ended up being convicted of perjury—specifically of lying under oath about his communist affiliations—on January 21, 1950. Hiss served his time in the federal penitentiary and then went about his life, maintaining until his death that he was innocent. Only after the Soviet Union collapsed did historians get hold of documents in Soviet archives indicating that Hiss was indeed a spy.

Shortly after a jury convicted Hiss of perjury, the Federal Bureau of Investigation (FBI) began to arrest individuals connected with a ring of atomic spies. Their story started on February 5, 1950, when British authorities announced that Klaus Fuchs, a German-born British citizen, had confessed to passing to the Soviets reports on the work being conducted at Los Alamos, where scientists were supposedly building an atomic bomb in total secrecy. Fuchs gave the name of his courier, an army sergeant named David Greenglass who had been stationed at Los Alamos. Greenglass in turn named the other people in the ring, including his brother-in-law Julius Rosenberg and his sister Ethel. In this case, it was the release of secret U.S. files released a generation later that indicated Julius Rosenberg transferred secret documents between U.S. and Soviet agents and that the agents at the time thought Ethel supported her husband's work by typing notes. The Rosenbergs themselves were not confronted with the evidence at their trial because authorities thought that making their files public would reveal too much about their counterespionage techniques. Instead, the Rosenbergs were executed in 1953 without being able to see the evidence against themselves.

On February 9, 1950, right after the FBI began arresting Fuchs's associates, McCarthy delivered an address to the Wheeling, West Virginia, Women's Republican Club. McCarthy called into question the executive branch's and the Democrats' commitment to eradicating communism by charging that there were still communists working in the U.S. State Department. Anticommunism and Republicans were like a magnet and iron filings. Republicans came together on the issue that they were better at being anticommunist than the Democrats were. The same issue had the opposite effect on the Democrats. Truman argued that he had been sufficiently vigilant against communists and that McCarthy's charges were a red herring. McCarran agreed with McCarthy and weighed in with his opinion through his sponsorship of a new internal security bill that made it clear what the United States was up against:

There exists a world Communist movement which, in its origins, its development, and its present practice, is a world-wide revolutionary movement whose purpose it is, by treachery, deceit, infiltration into other groups (governmental and otherwise), espionage, sabotage, terrorism, and any other means deemed necessary, to establish a Communist totalitarian dictatorship in the countries throughout the world through the medium of a world-wide Communist organization."[2]

Because "[t]he direction and control of the world Communist movement is vested in and exercised by the Communist dictatorship of a foreign country," it was necessary to pay special attention to the possibility that communists would sneak in among legitimate immigrants. To that end, McCarran's bill specifically prohibited immigrants who were members of communist parties. In case communists changed their name, another paragraph denied admission to aliens who adhered to any doctrines common among communists or who belonged to any organizations that adhered to these doctrines. The law empowered attorneys general to deport aliens without hearings as to the justice of their cause. Denying immigrants hearings covered situations similar to that in the Rosenberg trial, in which authorities had access to confidential documents but could not declassify and publish them. Attorneys general could not deport immigrants to countries where they faced lethal persecution, but they could exercise a great deal of discretion in determining a deportation destination. New procedures were established to carry out the new supervision of the domestic and immigrant populations.

McCarran's bill went through the Senate and House and to President Truman. Truman vetoed it and published his reasons. He objected to the bill on practical grounds, claiming that new procedures would hamper the ones already in place for identifying subversives. He also objected to it as presenting complications in foreign relations. While the United States was not a totalitarian country, it did have relations with countries that were (specifically fascist Spain and communist, but nonaligned, Yugoslavia), and it could not pass antitotalitarian legislation so thorough as to require termination of diplomatic relations with countries that, while admittedly imperfect, weren't Stalinist. Finally, Truman questioned the judgment of those sponsoring this legislation; the United States, he wrote, didn't need "hysterical" legislation.[3] Nevertheless, McCarran's bill passed the Senate and the House over Truman's veto and became law on September 29, 1950. Conflict lines were drawn: between president and Congress, between one wing of the Democrats and the other, between those who thought of foreign affairs as a place where the United States should exercise leadership and those who thought the United States should isolate and protect itself.

The same year, McCarran, through a Senate Judiciary Subcommittee, proposed a new immigration law. The new law would bring the previous laws together in one code eliminating obsolete laws, reinforcing ones that were still useful, and addressing new issues. It took over a year to draft the proposed Immigration and Nationality Act, which meant that the bill was introduced at a critical time. In 1952, while McCarran was overseeing the drafting of the immigration bill, the United States was in the midst of campaigns to elect a president, one third of its Senate, and its entire House of Representatives. Truman was eligible to run for the presidency again, but after doing poorly in early primaries, he bowed out. Adlai Stevenson was the Democratic nominee but was thoroughly identified with the Truman, rather than the McCarran, wing of the party. This might be the year the Democrats fell apart, creating a vacuum into which the Republicans could step. McCarran's immigration law, then, could be a factor in attracting or repelling voters.

McCarran's law was comprehensive enough to contain something for everyone. For those concerned about the complexity of government, all immigration laws were now brought together in one place. For those who thought the laws antiquated in the face of modern tendencies to travel and to go on foreign vacations, there was a long list of nonimmigrant categories (such as tourist or student) and procedures for transferring between categories (so that a nonimmigrant could become a permanent resident). For those who worried about labor shortages, the bill introduced a new procedure for selecting immigrants on the basis of the skills they would bring to the United States. For those worried about labor competition, the bill generally skirted conflict with the bracero program (which admitted Mexican workers on a temporary basis) but in other cases had qualifications that prohibited labor migration. For those who worried about communists, the law increased the list of reasons for excluding or deporting aliens. For those who worried about civil rights, it outlined the procedures to safeguard those subject to deportation. For those concerned about discrimination, it eliminated sexual discrimination in immigration and racial discrimination in naturalization, and it ended the prohibitions on immigration from East Asia. For those who thought racial differences were important, it kept the quotas on European immigrants, assigned quotas to countries now permitted to send Asian immigrants, and limited colonial people's ability to enter the United States on the quotas of the countries that colonized them (e.g., people from the Belgian Congo couldn't enter as Belgians).

Yet instead of satisfying everyone, McCarran's bill raised an outcry. Circumstances called tremendous attention to the portions of the bill bearing on race and ethnicity. World War II had been fueled by Nazi racism. The mass movement for civil rights was still a few years away, but there were already signs (Jackie Robinson's baseball career, Truman's desegregation of the U.S. armed forces) that ending racism was an important issue in the United States. The argument Truman made about the relationship between the treatment of immigrants and the ability to conduct foreign policy was still valid. There were also some DPs still in Europe; escapees from the Iron Curtain were replacing survivors of Nazi concentration camps. Guardians of civil liberties were even more concerned about the threat McCarran's bill posed than they had been about the Truman administration's actions, and with good reason. Later, McCarran's legislation would be used to justify excluding people from the United States on the grounds that they had written unfavorably about the U.S. government and favorably about communism, even though to the people involved, such writing seemed to be simply an exercise of constitutionally protected freedom of the press.[4]

Liberal Democrats fell over each other to suggest alternatives. On March 25, 1952, Truman proposed the United States revive its Displaced Persons legislation and permit 300,000 refugees to enter the country over the next three years.[5] On April 2, **Emmanuel Celler**, a House Democrat from Brooklyn, introduced a bill worded along Truman's lines.[6] In the Senate, Minnesota Democrat Hubert H. Humphrey and New York Democrat Herbert Lehman also proposed legislation. If one believed the *New York Times*, no one supported McCarran's bill. The *Times* editorialized against it and reported that none of the foreign-language press in New York favored it.[7] The American Federation of Labor and railroad heir W. A. Harriman were on the same side, the one urging acceptance of Truman's proposal for 300,000 DPs and the other urging a veto of the McCarran law.[8] The Jewish Labor Council and the National Council of Churches agreed in opposing McCarran. The Catholics split, with the National Catholic Welfare Council supporting it and the Catholic Association for International Peace opposing it.[9] The Polish-American Congress opposed it. A New York Italian politician named Fortunato Pope warned the Italians were going to vote for Stevenson because of it.[10] A nasty fight broke out when the intensely partisan Truman accused the Republicans of supporting racist legislation. Actually Republican candidate Dwight D. Eisenhower urged repeal of racist legislation.[11]

However, McCarran was an experienced politician who knew how to get legislation passed. On this occasion, he worked with another conservative Democrat, **Francis Walter** of Pennsylvania, who, as chair of the House Judiciary Committee Subcommittee on Immigration, introduced the bill in the House. The Senate tacked on twenty-one amendments but, on May 23, 1952, passed the bill. In the House, New York Republican Jacob Javits (an example that the Republicans had the same ideological split as the Democrats) tried to force a roll call vote and get the bill returned to committee, but the bill passed there, too, on June 11.

Truman vetoed the bill on June 25. It took him so long not because he had to make up his mind but because he drafted a lengthy veto message. Part of the message was addressed over the heads of Congress, to people watching from overseas. Truman assured Asians that he would like to sign legislation permitting them to immigrate: "But now this most desirable provision comes before me embedded in a mass of legislation which would perpetuate injustices of long standing against many other nations of the world"—specifically, the quotas against European countries.[12] The rest of the message was addressed directly to its supporters. As with the Internal Security Act, Truman complained that the procedures being introduced would complicate, not facilitate, achievement of intended goals. More important, he pointed out that the real problem was the quota system. "It repudiates our basic religious concepts, our belief in the brotherhood of man, and in the words of St. Paul that 'there is neither Jew nor Greek, there is neither bond nor free, . . . for ye are all one in Christ Jesus.'"[13] It flew in the face of the egalitarianism inscribed in the Declaration of Independence. It negated the compassion proclaimed by the Emma Lazarus poem on the base of the Statue of Liberty.

McCarran responded that Truman's veto was "one of the most un-American acts I have witnessed in my career."[14] Back in the Senate, he rallied his colleagues: "In God's name, in the name of the American people, in the name of America's future, let us override this veto." The Senate passed the bill by the two-thirds majority necessary to counter the presidential veto, as did the House. The bill became law on June 27, 1952, two days after Truman's veto. Obliged to enforce it, Truman began to make arrangements to admit Asians according to the new quotas. He also used his position to make one last attack on McCarran. On September 4, 1952, he appointed a committee to study immigration and naturalization and to report to him. On January 1, 1953 (they had to hurry; Eisenhower had been elected president in November 1952), the committee returned a report titled *Whom We Shall Welcome*. This was not a question, "Whom shall we welcome?" It was a declaration of fact, drawn from a statement by George Washington, on December 2, 1783: "The bosom of America is open to receive not only the Opulent and Respectable Stranger, but the oppressed and persecuted of all Nations and Religions; whom we shall welcome to a participation of all our rights and previlege [*sic*], if by decency and propriety of conduct they appear to merit the enjoyment."[15] It was obvious that the battle over immigration would go on.

However, the extreme anticommunists had little time left to lead it. While McCarran was passing legislation, his colleagues Richard Nixon and Joe McCarthy were getting most of the public attention by investigating communism in various executive branch offices. Eisenhower accepted Nixon as his running mate: Nixon came from the populous state of California; he was identified with the new people in Congress and with the new concerns. But Eisenhower was always cool toward McCarthy. And McCarthy himself was becoming a liability. One of McCarthy's aides, David Schine, was drafted into the U.S. Army. McCarthy tried to get an exemption for him, but the army turned it down. McCarthy then decided someone in the army must want to hamper his ongoing anticommunist investigations. Who was it and what was the purpose? In 1954, McCarthy began to investigate the possibility of communist infiltration of the army, a sensational enough charge that the hearings were carried on television, a medium that did not put McCarthy in his best light. The army also had good lawyers and, of course, distinguished veterans of World War II to testify on its behalf; it turned back McCarthy's investigation. Then, McCarthy's colleagues in the

Senate appointed a committee to consider censuring the senator for his behavior.

McCarthy's army hearings took place during a congressional election year. While he agreed with McCarthy's opinions, McCarran was hoping to use them to improve conservative Democratic changes in the upcoming elections. He made peace with the other Democrats in the state, including Vail Pittman, the brother of the late Key Pittman, McCarran's perpetual rival. On September 27, McCarran was in Washington, testifying before an ad hoc Senate committee as to why McCarthy should not be censured. On September 28, he was at the Civic Center of Hawthorne, Nevada, speaking at a political event. He finished his speech, descended the platform, and was walking up a side aisle when he collapsed from a heart attack and died.

McCarthy was condemned for conduct unbecoming a senator. He died in 1957. By then, he had given his name to an era. But McCarran had given that era its immigration laws.

NOTES

1. *Congressional Index, Eighty-first Congress, 1949–1950* (Chicago, Washington, D.C., and New York: Commerce Clearing House, 1948), p. 855.

2. Henry Steele Commager, *Documents of American History*, 8th ed. (New York: Appleton-Century-Crofts, 1968), 2:555.

3. Ibid., 2:558–562.

4. C. J. Grossman, "The McCarran-Walter Act: War Against Margaret Randall and the First Amendment," *Crime and Social Justice* 27–28 (1987), pp. 220–233, and Trevor Parry-Giles, "Stemming the Red Tide: Free Speech and Immigration Policy in the Case of Margaret Randall," *Western Journal of Speech Communication* 52:2 (1988), pp. 167–183. Margaret Randall was a U.S. journalist who voluntarily surrendered her U.S. citizenship in 1966, then requested a tourist visa in 1986. Acting on the authority of the 1952 Immigration and Nationality Act, the Immigration and Naturalization Service denied her a visa.

5. *New York Times*, March 25, 1952, p. 1, col. 2.

6. *New York Times*, April 2, 1952, p. 12, col. 8.

7. *New York Times*, May 29, 1952, p. 29, col. 6; and June 18, 1952, p. 11, col. 5.

8. *New York Times*, May 23, 1952, p. 10, col. 7; and June 26, 1952, p. 16, col. 4.

9. *New York Times*, March 22, 1952, p. 10, col. 6; June 16, 1952, p. 5, col. 4; June 25, 1952, p. 16, col. 4; and August 3, 1952, p. 4, col. 2.

10. *New York Times*, June 2, 1952, p. 5, col. 5; and October 29, 1952, p. 24, col. 6.

11. *New York Times*, October 17, 1952, p. 19, col. 1.

12. Commager, *Documents of American History*, 2: 581–582.

13. Ibid., 2:583. There is a small logical error in using this to support Truman's position. Paul was not arguing for tolerance. The full passage claims that it was

common acceptance of Christ as Messiah that made Jews, Greek, slaves, and free people equal. More interesting is that the original quote, Galatians III:28, also includes a phrase about there being neither male nor female. The omission may have been deliberate. In 1944, the Republicans introduced the Equal Rights Amendment into their party platform, and it remained there until 1980. The Democrats did not support the amendment because they were afraid it would render unconstitutional the body of legislation they had passed to protect women workers from exploitation; for them there had to be a difference between male and female.

14. *New York Times*, June 26, 1952, p. 14, col. 5.

15. *Whom We Shall Welcome: Report of the President's Commission on Immigration and Naturalization* (Washington, D.C.: Government Printing Office, 1953), frontispiece.

BIBLIOGRAPHY

The most accessible of McCarran's papers are at the Nevada State Archives in Carson City, Nevada. McCarran has a biographer, Jerome E. Edwards, who has published several works, including *Pat McCarran: Political Boss of Nevada*, Nevada Studies in History and Political Science No. 17 (Reno: University of Nevada Press, 1982). The *Nevada Historical Society Quarterly* has devoted much space to this son of the state. His daughter, Sister Margaret Patricia McCarran, published a two-part memoir in 1968 and 1969; Jerome E. Edwards published "Nevada Power Broker: Pat McCarran and His Political Machine," in volume 27:3 (1984), pp. 182–198; and Christopher Gerard published "On the Road to Viet Nam: 'The Loss of China Syndrome,' Pat McCarran and J. Edgar Hoover," in volume 37:4 (1994), pp. 247–262. Monographs that include reference to McCarran but deal more generally with McCarthyism include William F. Buckley, Jr., and L. Brent Bozell, *McCarthy and His Enemies: The Record and Its Meaning* (Chicago: H. Regnery Co., 1954); Robert Griffith, *The Politics of Fear: Joseph R. McCarthy and the Senate* (Lexington: University of Kentucky Press for the Organization of American Historians, 1970); and Yelong Han, "An Untold Story: Americal Policy toward Chinese Students in the United States, 1949–1955," *Journal of American–East Asian Relations* II:1 (1993), pp. 77–99. For the conservative Democratic context, see James T. Patterson, *Congressional Conservatives and the New Deal: The Growth of the Conservative Coalition in Congress, 1933–1939* (Lexington: University of Kentucky for the Organization of American Historians, 1967). For the Nevada context, see Russell Elliott, with the assistance of William D. Rowley, *History of Nevada*, 2nd ed., rev. (Lincoln: University of Nebraska Press, 1987); and Fred L. Israel, *Nevada's Key Pittman* (Lincoln: University of Nebraska Press, 1963).

OSCAR HANDLIN
(1915–)

The Uprooted and Other Images of Immigration

Oscar Handlin's life is a story within a story wrapped around yet other stories. It includes a debate over scholarly findings, academic politics, the relationship between one's personal experience and one's research, and what one's studies mean to other people *versus* what they mean to one's self. Of these topics, the last is the most important here. Handlin's most frequently cited contribution to the immigration debate is the phrase "the uprooted." However, his most enduring may be his explanation of what immigration reveals not just about immigrants but about people born in the United States, and not just about Americans but about human beings.

Handlin was the son of immigrants. He told interviewers that his parents were Ukrainian Jews. His mother, Ida Yanowitz, arrived in the early twentieth century and worked in New York City's garment trade. His father, Joseph Handlin, migrated in 1913 or 1914, after attending a commercial college in Russia and serving in the czarist army in the Russo-Japanese War. He intended to return to Europe, but World War I prevented him from traveling. Instead, he married, and on September 29, 1915, had a son, the first of three children. Thereafter, the Handlins moved frequently, as Joseph tried his luck in a series of small businesses: a grocery, a real estate office, a steam laundry. Oscar realized he wanted to be a historian at age eight.

Oscar Handlin, courtesy of the Harvard University Archives.

He graduated from Brooklyn College in 1934, when he was not yet nineteen. He entered Harvard intending to study medieval history, but the medievalist retired. He thought he would like to work with Arthur M. Schlesinger, Sr., and so switched to U.S. history.

Handlin started his academic career at a particular point in the history of college teaching. When he came to graduate school in the 1930s, the United States was in the midst of a Depression that did not bode well for the future of college education. College was difficult to afford in a depression, and, without students, there was no need for new teachers. Even worse, in such a market, those who had jobs or wanted them acted to limit the pool of candidates by discriminating arbitrarily. Most white women were confined to women's schools, African Americans of both sexes were confined to black schools, and colleges and universities maintained limits on the numbers of Jews they trained or hired. Events after World War II improved professors' job prospects. To smooth the transition from war to peace, Congress passed a law, called the G.I. Bill, that made available to veterans low-interest loans they could use to attend college. However, even though there was a demand for Handlin's services, he still had to work to build a career in a new environment. If higher education ever had been an "ivory tower" in which professors researched their topics and taught their students in isolation from contemporary world events, it was no longer so after World War II. Postwar anticommunists, determined to eradicate even the possibility of subversive thought and activities, investigated college campuses and harassed the personnel. The student movement of the 1960s questioned the basis of traditional academics. In short, since the Depression there have been many events that could derail an academic career or could convince a professor to take up some other line of work.

Instead, Handlin spent his life as a professional historian. His dissertation won the J. H. Dunning Prize of the American Historical Association, awarded annually for the best dissertation on U.S. history. It was published in *Boston's Immigrants*. By historians' standards, it was a bestseller, reprinted in paperback and assigned to generations of college students as an introduction to immigrant, ethnic, and urban history. It also helped Handlin in his academic career. Handlin taught at Brooklyn College from 1936 to 1938. He returned to Harvard as an instructor in the fall semester of 1939 and rose through the ranks of the faculty. At the time of his retirement in 1986, he held the Carl M. Loeb University chair.

Students might think of their professors mostly as their teachers, and Handlin did teach. His work with Harvard's graduate students is particularly well documented. He trained a generation of such students to become professors themselves. Some of them did their research in the fields of immigration and ethnicity. Thomas N. Brown became a noted scholar of Irish America, Moses Rischin studied Jewish immigrants, Edwin Fenton studied Italians and labor unions, Barbara Miller Solomon researched the Immigration Restriction League for her dissertation, and Stephan A. Thernstrom worked with Handlin on *The Harvard Encyclopedia of American Ethnic Groups*. However, not all of Handlin's students studied immigration. Bernard Bailyn concentrated on colonial and revolutionary America. Robert Cross studied liberal American Catholicism, not the tradition-minded culture that Handlin noted in *Boston's Immigrants*. Nathan Irvin Huggins studied African Americans and eventually directed Harvard's black studies program. Roger Lane studied the development of urban police forces and urban crime. Arthur Mann became the biographer of New York mayor **Fiorello La Guardia**. David J. Rothman studied institutions such as prisons and asylums. Anne Firor Scott pioneered the field of southern women's history. Samuel Bass Warner wrote and taught urban history.[1]

Handlin had married Mary Flug on September 18, 1937. They teamed up to provide his graduate students with an example of how to combine personal and professional life. She accompanied him when he taught graduate seminars. Oscar's own tendency was to wait quietly to see if the students came up with something interesting. When the students fell silent and then got so anxious they got tongue-tied, Mary Handlin broke in with a question or observation. The Handlins invited students to their home and kept in touch with them during their careers. (After Mary Handlin died, Oscar remarried: to Lillian Bombach on June 17, 1977).

Professors do many other tasks for their institutions besides work with students. Handlin administered several programs for Harvard University. He was the director of the Center for the Study of Liberty in America from 1958 to 1966, director of the Charles Warren Center for the Study of American History from 1965 to 1972, and director of the University Library from 1979 to 1984.

Similarly, historians do other things to advance history besides teach it in the classroom. Handlin's main contribution outside the classroom came in publishing. He worked closely with one publisher, Little, Brown and Company of Boston, editing its Library of American Biography series. The series printed short (always one volume, usually under 300 pages) biographies designed for assignment as collateral reading in college classrooms or as material students could use for their own papers. The subjects were drawn from a variety of fields, including colonial explorer John Smith, abolitionist Frederick Douglas, inventor Thomas A. Edison, entrepreneur **Andrew Carnegie**, labor leader **Samuel Gompers**, and the reform-minded Eleanor Roosevelt. Most figures, however, came from politics. In fact, the Library of American Biography included few subjects who were there mainly as representatives of the immigrant or ethnic experience. The book about an ethnic American that Handlin contributed to the series was titled not *Al Smith, Ethnic Politician*, but *Al Smith and His America*. His second book for the series was on Abraham Lincoln. In fact, another publisher, Harlan Davidson, established another series, the American Biographical History series, in order to highlight women and members of ethnic or racial minorities. Its biography of **Fiorello La Guardia**, a politician who, like Al Smith, came from an ethnic background, was not titled *Fiorello La Guardia and His America*, but *Fiorello La Guardia: Ethnicity and Reform*.[2]

In short, Handlin was himself a kind of ethnic success story, someone who came from outside of academe and rose to the top of the field. However, he did more for the debate over immigration than to prove that the children of immigrants could rise to the learned professions. His early research had a career of its own and made its own contributions to the immigration debate.

Earlier on the day that Handlin visited Professor Schlesinger's office to discuss his doctoral dissertation, Schlesinger received a letter from another student who said he no longer wanted to work on his planned topic. Schlesinger showed Handlin the letter and described the topic as "a racial history of Boston." "There was no or very little linkage between my experience and the experience of a family of Irish peasants. I didn't know anything when I started."[3]

The time period covered in Handlin's research was 1790 to 1880. Thus, the two largest groups were the native-born Yankees and the Irish immigrants. Had **Madison Grant**, who was still alive when Handlin began researching his "racial history," written on the topic, he would have explored the Yankee and Irish gene pools, identified the character traits these pools produced, and predicted which gene pool would succeed in Boston. Handlin, however, followed a line of inquiry laid out by **Franz Boas**, who discounted the idea that genes bred character and focused instead on the historical forces that led different groups to develop different cultures. In the case Handlin studied, different groups had different political and economic experiences. Boston's Yankees had a heritage of a successful revolution against the British and lived in a city where they had to develop certain skills to survive. The Irish had a heritage of oppression under the British and had lived in rural areas where they developed skills, but none that helped them to survive in the city. Different groups interpreted their experiences through different ideological lenses: Handlin paid particular attention to the way Catholicism shaped the Irish world view.

Finally, the environment of Boston brought the groups together under particular circumstances. Boston was not yet a large city, and immigrants and natives had to compete for living space and for jobs. Interaction between the two produced something like a Venn diagram composed of one Irish and one Yankee circle. A few Yankees and Irish realized common concerns and formed an overlapping zone of tolerance. For some people in each group, contact with the other group was corrosive and bitter, and Yankees and Irish reacted by getting as far away from each other as possible, raising the possibility that as other and more varied immigrants entered the city, Boston would become a series of nearly separate circles.

Handlin supported this narrative with an array of primary sources gathered in Boston, London, and Dublin, and at places where Catholic records were stored, Notre Dame University and the Vatican. He also amassed a huge bibliography of secondary sources to help him with research into smaller immigrant groups (Germans and Italians) and with the history of Boston and of Catholicism. This was the dissertation for which Handlin won the Dunning Prize.

Handlin coined the phrase *The Uprooted* for his second major book. This was a different sort of book than *Boston's Immigrants*. Its scholarly apparatus was less apparent; it had no footnotes. The theories Handlin used to interpret his facts were less apparent, too. Handlin tried to conceal all the supporting structures behind a compelling narrative, and in that he succeeded very well. The chapter outline of *The Uprooted* has been used over and over again in books about U.S. immigration in general and about particular groups of immigrants, and has also been used as an outline for courses on immigration. Chapter one described the world from which the immigrants came and the forces in that world that made them leave. Chapter two covered the methods of travel across Europe to the port city and over the ocean in steerage to the U.S. ports. Chapter three took up the most important issue, that of earning a living in the new land. In chapters four through ten, Handlin discussed different aspects of the migrants' lives: religion, neighborhood, social institutions, politics, raising a family, assimilation. Chapter eleven broadened the scope of the book from the immigrant family to national politics and discussed the passage of restrictive legislation in the 1920s. Chapter twelve summed up Handlin's perspective on the immigrant experience.

The main theme of *The Uprooted* was "alienation," a word that had many meanings. Alienation described the relation that developed between the immigrants and their work. In Europe, however tiny the family land plot was, it was *theirs*. Members of the family worked on it together, with each family member having traditional roles and duties and each entitled to a living. In the United States, immigrants worked for others on farms, in homes as servants, and in forges, mines, railroad camps, construction sites, and above all, factories. They sold their labor to these others. Their pay was determined not by what they needed to live on but by the amount of competition for the job (and the more immigrants, the more competition, and the less pay).

A second meaning of alienation was more cultural. In Europe, families oversaw production from egg to chicken dinner, from seeds of grain to loaves of bread. In the United States, over and over again they made one part of some object, sewing sleeves for coats, stamping out lids for jars. Thus they were alienated from their work. It was different from them, and the finished product displayed none of their artistic ability and none of their personality.

A third meaning of alienation broadened the cultural definition from the world of work to the larger world. Every effort immigrants made to re-create their old world culture ended in creating a new urban, ethnic community. Immigrants settled near each other, but instead of peasant villages, they lived in urban ghettos. They practiced their traditional faith but in a different way. In Europe, the government or the upper class supported religion, and ministers provided mostly spiritual services; only a few people needed charity. In the United States, the poor supported religious institutions and called on those institutions for a wider range of services, including education. The immigrants entertained themselves and in the process contributed to vaudeville and created the ethnic press. They watched helplessly as their children became utterly different.

The Uprooted appeared in 1951. Critics reviewed it favorably, and it won the 1952 Pulitzer Prize for history. However, it is in the nature of scholarship that nothing remains well received for long. Over the next generation, scholars reacted to Handlin. They used different evidence and started with different assumptions. Eventually, they reached entirely different conclusions.

In the 1950s, scholarship focused on assimilation. Handlin's evidence suggested that assimilation was caused by a process of attrition. Immigrants did not assimilate, but they did die. The children who were already half grown at the time of migration assimilated partially. The American-born (like Handlin himself) were "the more fortunate ones," whose lives did not reflect the trauma of emigration.[4] In 1955, **Will Herberg,** then the Graduate Professor of Judaic Studies and Social Philosophy at Drew University, suggested another path by which assimilation occurred: intermarriage. In his *Protestant-Catholic-Jew*, Herbert described how the first generation either came to the United States already married or chose spouses from among the same ethnic group. Subsequent generations were somewhat more adventurous in that they chose spouses whose ancestors came from other countries. However, people looking for marriage partners did not cross religious barriers. The result was the triple melting pot alluded to in the title of Herberg's books, with German Lutherans and Scots Presbyterians melting into a common Protestantism, Irish and Italians into a common Catholicism, and Sephardim and Ashkenazim into a common Judaism.

Even at the time, there was some evidence that Handlin's concept of immigrants as "the uprooted" did not capture the whole immigrant story. In 1924, Harvard published a monograph by Princeton economist Robert F. Foerster, studying the Italian migration in the late nineteenth and early twentieth centuries.[5] Foerster established that migration was part of Italian life. Many families derived their income from two sources. Their own farming provided them with subsistence, as they ate what they grew. Travel to work on other farms, or to do unskilled labor on construction projects in Europe and North Africa, provided the family with cash income to pay rents, taxes, and bills. What Americans considered a grand drama of up-rooting was the next step in the established pattern. The migrants went further and further afield in search of ways to support the part of the family that remained at home. It was after World War I, when fascism restricted migration out of Italy and quotas limited migration into the United States, that families had to establish new ways of making ends meet and either cease to migrate or to migrate permanently. Immigrants were not alienated by migration, they incorporated migration into a traditional way of life.

By the 1960s, the evidence had mounted. Scholars who worked with one particular group, southern Italian migrants to the United States, amassed an array of evidence that these immigrants did not fit *The Uprooted* model. Rudolph Vecoli, for example, studied southern Italians who relocated to Chicago. He pointed out that Chicago actually had a counterpart in the immigrants' earlier experience. The southern Italians had lived in small towns—not rural villages—in Italy. They were already alienated from the upper classes, the political leaders, and the Catholic hierarchy in Italy and so did not experience the kind of trauma Handlin described in *The Up-rooted*.[6] Virginia Yans-McLaughlin described how, when confronted with a new work experience, southern Italians reshaped their "flexible tradi-tion." Women who were supposed to focus on housework and child care brought their children with them for short-term jobs as agricultural labor-ers, maintaining their separate sphere of activities while meeting the new need for cash income.[7] John Briggs demonstrated that the men were equally flexible, bringing the community institutions they had known in Italy to new cities in the United States.[8] Dino Cinel pointed out that migration itself was a pattern established in Europe; over the nineteenth century, northern Italians had alternated work at home with travel in search of wage labor to raise cash.[9] Other scholars verified for migrants from other countries the tendency to draw on the migrants' European cultures to cope with the American environment. When John Bodnar produced a new synthesis of immigration history in the urban United States, he changed the metaphor in the title from *The Uprooted* to *The Transplanted*.[10]

The reevaluation of Handlin's work is normal for scholarship and would have happened no matter when Handlin wrote. However, his research also had another career, one that it could have had only in the 1960s and 1970s. It became the starting point for broader discussion about what schools should teach when they taught history.

The studies of immigration that contradicted Handlin's work in *The Up-rooted* were supported by new source materials that were collected in a new way. Most of the documents Handlin used he found in archives that were connected by the entity that generated them. For example, the Boston Athenaeum collected newspapers printed by Boston publishers, and the Na-tional Archives and Records Administration collected records that the U.S. government created. Handlin tried to use a mixture of documents, but

much of his material came from governments, newspapers, and other leaders of society. Beginning in the mid-1960s, efforts to preserve immigration
records focused on documents immigrants themselves generated and on
collecting these documents into specialized archives. In 1964, Rudolph Vecoli, who compared Handlin's immigrants with his own studies of Chicago
Italians, founded the Immigration History Research Center at the University of Minnesota. This archive held documents created by immigrants,
such as ethnic newspapers and the records of organizations such as the
Sons of Italy. Silvano M. Tomasi and Lydio F. Tomasi organized the Center
for Migration Studies on Staten Island that same year. Although its library
holdings concentrate on contemporary human international migration, it
maintains an archive of material pertinent to immigrant and ethnic history,
such as documents from parishes and immigrant aid agencies that assisted
people traveling through the Port of New York. The Immigration History
Society was founded in 1965, and the Balch Institute, another archive of
ethnic materials, was established in 1971.

These new ways of preserving history were part of a new way of eval-
uating the events in history that replaced Handlin's emphasis on the degree
of assimilation with an emphasis on the degree to which immigrants did
not assimilate. New historians identified two reasons why immigrants did
not assimilate. One reason was that the natives did not let them assimilate.
Instead, native stereotypes laid a foundation for prejudice and discrimination. One publisher, San Francisco's Straight Arrow Books, published a
whole series called "Ethnic Prejudice in America," with separate volumes
reproducing cartoons, articles, and passages from books demonstrating
U.S. opposition to Italians, Jews, and other ethnic groups. A second reason
immigrants did not assimilate was that they did not need to. Their culture
was fine the way it was. In *The Rise of the Unmeltable Ethnics*, author
Michael Novak argued that it was a blessing that the melting pot did not
really work, because immigrants provided traits the United States needed.
Immigrants were hardworking, family-oriented, community-minded people
whose culture was an alternative to that promulgated by consumerism and
mass media. In short, with their emphasis on the work ethic, their opposition to loose morals, and their tolerance of the hardships that came
their way, immigrants were the real Americans.[11]

Changing the emphasis from assimilation to the perseverance of ethnic
ways happened at the same time as another change in higher education,
the emergence of "studies" programs. Rather than major in a particular
discipline, such as mathematics or music, students examined the same topic
from a variety of angels. Ethnicity proved especially compatible with this
approach. For example, students majoring in Italian-American studies
might examine Italian-American life in six different classes, with an anthropologist, historian, literary specialist, political scientist, psychologist,

and a sociologist providing different methods of research. This approach even changed Harvard's curriculum; the school developed an African-American studies program.

In an interview published in 1977, Handlin complained about the "boosterish" quality of ethnic studies programs.[12] During the 1970s, he, along with Stephan Thernstrom and Ann Orlov, was working on *The Harvard Encyclopedia of American Ethnic Groups*, which was published in 1980. He himself had only one signed article in this huge compilation, and his was on "Yankees." Handlin himself did not return to the theme for which he was most famous, the idea of immigrants as "uprooted." Upon retirement from teaching, Handlin launched a series of books surveying the entirety of U.S. history: *Liberty and Power* (1986), *Liberty and Expansion* (1989), *Liberty and Peril* (1992), and *Liberty and Equality* (1995). It might be symbolic of Handlin's approach to the subject with which he was most identified that when *Reviews in American History* published its critique of *The Harvard Encyclopedia of American Ethnic Groups*, it did so immediately after another book review by Oscar Handlin—on a book about *The Federalist Papers* and the U.S. Constitution.[13]

In short, the concept of immigrants as uprooted, the idea most associated with Handlin, had only a brief life span. Like other concepts in scholarship, it clarified everyone's thinking for only a little while. Soon, evidence piled up to suggest it was not as helpful a notion as it had once been, and scholars worked to develop new concepts.

There are more enduring aspects of Handlin's work on immigration and ethnicity. One is the way Handlin used immigration to illuminate an important aspect of the human condition. Handlin denied there was any close connection between his own background and his choice of immigration as a subject for research—he wasn't an ethnic historian celebrating his roots. However, he did admit to links between his own experience and those described in *The Uprooted*. He described sitting in the Boston Public Library, his book propped up against a windowsill, making it easier to look out and see the city. He was collecting data on a world from long ago and far away. His sources detailed how people lived in Europe before migrating to the United States. It seemed from his reading that in the winter the peasants' world shrank to the size of their houses. They were farmers, but there was little outdoor work. They could not go out in the cold with their insufficiently insulated clothing; they could not get far anyway on their unpaved roads during the few hours of daylight. All the life that usually spread out over the farmyard and field gathered together in the house, the people with the animals. "How could I know what happened in the long dead night of the peasant winter," Handlin asked, "who had never laid eyes on the drooping trees and looming crosses of the churchyard?" He tried, until once, the effort to imagine what it was like shut in with the beasts against the cold night evoked the memory of a shivering boy hastening up the pitch-dark stairwell of the tenement on Columbia Street under the bridge. At each landing the grip of fear; then the burst of light at the kitchen door and the relief, having once again come past the dread mystery for which the name was death and the certainty suppressed that he was destined again and again to make the passage until that future day when the sun's rays on the high skylight above would dissolve the dark. Some gift of feeling then linked memory to words.[14]

This is an important link, but how can one be sure Handlin wasn't just projecting his childhood fear of the dark onto other people? Handlin could use other experiences to check his gut feelings against immigrant reality. He had older relatives besides his immigrant mother and father in the United States, and on holidays, they would all get together, repeating the stories about family members. They had such fixed opinions about each other that they gossiped about people in terms of whether they were living up to their reputations or whether they were doing something unexpected. Handlin realized his relatives did not think of themselves as freestanding individuals. Rather, they thought of themselves as deriving their personalities in the context of the family network and family history. "When I reflected upon the relationships within the family, which gave each member a knowledge of the others, and therefore of the self, I understood why so many notes for *Boston's Immigrants* went unused," but finally found their place in Handlin's descriptions of relations among members of immigrant families in *The Uprooted*.[15]

The most important link between Handlin's personal experience and his writing was that while he was researching *The Uprooted*, his father lay dying in a hospital. Handlin drove from Massachusetts to New York to visit him, "knowing again there would be nothing to say, knowing too the demand for meaning in that wasting frame."[16] Keeping his father company, Handlin discerned a meaning in the older man's life. He used this discovery for "Promises," the twelfth and final chapter of *The Uprooted*. Instead of a dying father with his son at his bedside, he created another father-son couple. They were both workers, who came home after a hot day's labor to find the weather was changing and the air was cool. They sat on their chairs, catching the breeze. The father wanted to talk to his son. He wanted to ask if immigration was really worth it. "Though a rest may come, end all these struggles, what shall I have gained thereby?" However, he did not dare ask, fearing his son would not understand. He was correct; his son did not understand why his father valued the world he had left. "No, the blow that tossed you out, that forever snapped the ancient ties, that blow was an act of liberation."[17]

In philosophy, alienation such as what Handlin's father-son dialogue revealed is part of a larger school of thought called existentialism. Existentialism focuses on each human being as an individual, independent creation. Being free, humans have choices. They can choose to go with the group, conform, take someone else's word for it, and hand over their freedom. However, existentialists argued that handing over one's freedom is the morally wrong choice, not because God punishes those who hand over their freedom but because sooner or later, the consequences of letting someone else make all the decisions come back to haunt the one who handed over decision-making power. A sense of insecurity and uncertainty is a sign that one is truly independent, autonomous—and free. Handlin's focus on migration was a dramatic way of highlighting what was true of all human beings. Everyone is in some sense uprooted.

There was a distinctive kind of U.S. uprootedness, however. In the original preface to *The Uprooted*, Handlin elaborated on the theme of alienation:

Emigration took these people out of traditional, accustomed environments and replanted them in strange ground, among strangers, where strange manners prevailed. The customary modes of behavior were no longer adequate, for the problems of life were new and different. With old ties snapped, men faced the enormous compulsion of working out new relationships, new meanings to their lives, often under harsh and hostile circumstances.[18]

Upon reading this passage from *The Uprooted*, a passage from another, older work of U.S. history comes to mind:

But here I cannot but stay and make a pause, and stand half amazed at this poor people's present condition; and so I think will the reader too, when he will consider the same. Being thus passed the vast ocean, and a sea of troubles before in their preparation (as may be remembered by that which went before), they had now no friends to welcome them, nor inns to entertain or refresh their weather-beaten bodies, no houses or much less towns to repair to, to seek for succor.[19]

The quote comes from William Bradford's *History of Plimouth* [Plymouth] *Plantation*. It describes Pilgrims straggling ashore on Cape Cod in 1620. Pilgrims were what Handlin in chapter five of *The Uprooted* called "outsiders," members of dissenting faiths. The Pilgrim story has some of the same elements that reappear in the story of nineteenth-century immigrants. Pilgrims started in one world and were shaped to succeed in that world. They survived a difficult trip across the ocean, and they entered a new world for which they were ill-prepared. They tried to bring the old world to the new, but ultimately they had to change: their economic system, their social structure, their ideology. From this perspective, American history consists of a series of stories by which people formed in one environment bring their culture to another place and lose it. Covered wagons cross the Great Plains and the people who started across the prairie with values developed in the East forged new values in the West. Blacks with an outlook shaped by Southern racism and sharecropping developed a new outlook shaped by Northern racism and black urban culture.

Once we become accustomed to the theme of how the American experience challenges traditional values, we can see the confrontations that took place in more subtle ways, with pen and paper. When **Thomas Jefferson** wrote that "all men are created equal," he overturned a whole body of thought, dramatized in class structures and in slavery, that said all men were not equal. When in 1954 Chief Justice Earl Warren wrote, "We conclude that in the field of public education the doctrine of "separate but equal' has no place," he overthrew a whole history of segregation that said that it did.[20] Over and over again, U.S. history is about departing from tradition, not only when one passed from place to place, but also as one passed through time.

Handlin then, saw uprootedness as a motif throughout U.S. history, perhaps throughout human history. It is ironic that it is generally applied only to U.S. immigration history.

NOTES

1. This list of Handlin's students is abbreviated from Richard L. Bushman, Neil Harris, David Rothman, Barbara Miller Solomon, and Stephan Thernstrom, eds., *Uprooted Americans: Essays to Honor Oscar Handlin* (Boston: Little, Brown, 1979).

2. Ronald H. Bayor, *Fiorello La Guardia: Ethnicity and Reform*, American Biographical History Series (Arlington Heights, IL: Harlan Davison, 1993).

3. Bruce M. Stave, *The Making of Urban History: Historiography through Oral History* (Beverly Hills, CA: Sage Publications, 1977), p. 147.

4. Oscar Handlin, *The Uprooted*, 2nd ed., enlarged (Boston: Little, Brown, 1973), p. 217.

5. Robert F. Foerster, *The Italian Emigration of Our Times*, Harvard Economic Studies No. 20 (Cambridge, MA: Harvard University Press, 1924).

6. Rudolph J. Vecoli, "*Contadini* in Chicago: A Critique of *The Uprooted*," *Journal of American History* 61:3 (December 1964), pp. 404–417.

7. Virginia Yans-McLaughlin, "A Flexible Tradition: Southern Italian Immigrants Confront a New Work Experience," *Journal of Social History* 7 (1974), pp. 429–459.

8. John W. Briggs, *An Italian Passage: Immigrants to Three American Cities, 1890–1930* (New Haven, CT: Yale University Press, 1978).

9. Dino Cinel, *From Italy to San Francisco: The Immigration Experience* (Stanford, CA: Stanford University Press, 1982).

10. John Bodnar, *The Transplanted: A History of Immigrants in Urban America* (Bloomington: Indiana University Press, 1985).

11. Michael Novak, *The Rise of the Unmeltable Ethnic*, 2nd ed., with a new introduction by the author (New Brunswick, NJ: Transaction Publishing, 1996). The book was originally published in New York by Macmillan in 1972.

12. Stave, *The Making of Urban History*, p. 155.

13. *Reviews in American History* 9:4 (1981); see pages 424–427 for Handlin's review and pages 428–433 for the review of *The Harvard Encyclopedia of American Ethnic Groups*.

14. Handlin, *The Uprooted*, p. 315.

15. Ibid., p. 321.

16. Ibid., p. 322.

17. Ibid., p. 270.

18. Ibid., p. 5.

19. *Bradford's History of Plimouth Plantation. From the Original Manuscript. With a Report of the Proceedings Incident to the Return of the Manuscript to Massachusetts* (Boston: Wright and Potter Printing Co., 1899), pp. 94–95.

20. Henry Steele Commager, ed., *Documents of American History*, 8th ed. (New York: Appleton-Century-Crofts, 1968), 2:608.

BIBLIOGRAPHY

Oscar Handlin's scholarly papers are divided between Brooklyn College Library and Harvard College Archives. Handlin has an extensive bibliography, and some works have been revised, enlarged, and published in multiple editions. A case in point is *Boston's Immigrants, 1790–1880: A Study in Acculturation*, which was originally published as No. 50 of the Harvard Historian Studies in Cambridge, Massachusetts, by the Belknap Press of Harvard University Press in 1941. A revised and enlarged edition was published by the same press in 1959; I used an edition published in New York by Athenaeum in 1975. Similarly, *The Uprooted* was published as an Atlantic Monthly Press Book by Little, Brown in 1951. A second, enlarged, edition appeared from the same press in 1973. Although its conclusion, a passage wondering whether a Catholic could get elected president, became dated when **John F. Kennedy** broke that barrier in 1960, *Al Smith and His America* has been republished. First published in Boston by Little, Brown in 1958 as part of the Library of American Biography, it was republished in Boston by Northeastern University Press in 1987 with a new foreword by the author. Other books on various aspects of immigration include *Adventures in Freedom: Three Hundred Years of Jewish Life in America* (New York: McGraw-Hill, 1954); *The American People in the Twentieth Century* (Boston: Beacon Press, 1963); *Children of the Uprooted* (New York; G. Braziller, 1966); *Immigration as a Factor in American History* (Englewood Cliffs, NJ: Prentice-Hall, 1959); *The Newcomers: Negroes and Puerto Ricans in a Changing Metropolis* (Cambridge, MA: Harvard University Press, 1959); and *Race and Nationality in American Life* (Garden City, NY: Doubleday, 1957). Among Handlin's writings on the larger issue of teaching history are *The American College and American Culture: Socialization as a Function of Higher Education*, with Mary F. Handlin (New York: McGraw-Hill, 1970); *Truth in History* (Cambridge, MA: Belknap Press of Harvard University Press, 1979); and *The Distortion of America* (Boston: Little, Brown, 1981, 2nd ed., New Brunswick, NJ: Transaction Publishers, 1996). Handlin's bibliography of articles and book reviews is so extensive that rather than reproduce all of it here, the student is referred to the bibliography in Richard L. Bushman, Neil Harris, David Rothman, Barbara

Miller Solomon, and Stephan Thernstrom, eds., *Uprooted Americans: Essays to Honor Oscar Handlin* (Boston: Little, Brown, 1979). Handlin continued to write after 1979, but his major work on immigration after that date was as consulting editor of *The Harvard Encyclopedia of American Ethnic Groups* (Cambridge, MA: Belknap Press of Harvard University Press, 1980). Biographical information is available in *Who's Who in America*, in *Uprooted Americans*, and in two works by Bruce M. Stave, "A Conversation with Oscar Handlin," *Journal of Urban History* 3:1 (1977), pp. 199–230; and *The Making of Urban History: Historiography through Oral History* (Beverly Hills, CA: Sage Publications, 1977), pp. 145–156. Individual scholars who discuss Handlin's most seminal work, *The Uprooted*, are Plummer Alston Jones, Jr., "The Odyssey of the Immigrants in American History: From the Changed to the Changer: A Bibliographic Essay," *Immigrants and Minorities* 7:3 (1988), pp. 314–323; Henry B. Leonard, "American Immigration: A Historiographical Essay," *Ethnic Forum* 7:2 (1988), pp. 9–23; Ueda Reed, "Immigration and the Moral Criticism of American History: The Vision of Oscar Handlin," *Canadian Review of American Studies* 21:2 (1990), pp. 183–201; and David J. Rothman, "*The Uprooted* Thirty Years Later," *Reviews in American History* 10:3 (1982), pp. 311–319. A roundtable of sorts is Gary Gerstle, "Liberty, Coercion, and the Making of Americans," *Journal of American History* (September 1997), pp. 524–588, with comment by David A. Hollinger and Donna R. Gabaccia.

EDWARD M. KENNEDY
(1932–)

Immigration as a Solution to Other Problems

Edward M. (Ted) Kennedy, longtime senator from Massachusetts, emerged as a prominent shaper of the debate over immigration in the 1960s and remained in the field until the 1990s. He compiled a list of varied accomplishments, abolishing discriminatory national quotas, calling attention to refugees, and redrafting laws to increase the opportunities for individuals to qualify for immigration visas. Was there an underlying principle tying together this list of achievements? Taken individually, it looks like the answer might be no. Each law with which Kennedy was associated was passed to meet some specific situation, not to create a consistent policy regarding immigration. Nor are they tied together by Kennedy's political ambitions, because at one time he was a prominent senator during the Vietnam conflict and at another time he was running for the Democratic nomination to the presidency. However, if one looks at the immigration laws as part of a larger picture, one will see a common unifying threat, a common contribution to the debate on immigration. For Kennedy, immigration itself was seldom a problem. It was a tool to be used to solve problems.

Ted Kennedy's story starts with that of his ancestors and siblings. His forbears were Roman Catholics from Ireland. Both grandfathers entered

Edward M. Kennedy at a reception in the early 1980s, flanked by the Reverend Lydio F. Tomasi (*left*) and the Reverend Silvano M. Tomasi (*right*). Center for Migration Studies, photograph by Rocco Galatioto.

local politics. His paternal grandfather was an unelected leader who guided his constituents from his position as owner of a neighborhood saloon. His maternal grandfather served as mayor of Boston and congressional representative. His father, Joseph, made a fortune in the stock market. His mother reared nine children. Of them, the oldest, Joseph Junior, was being groomed for a career in national politics when World War II intervened. He died in aerial combat during the war. The second-oldest child, also a boy, **John Fitzgerald Kennedy**, also served in the war and was wounded but survived. After the war was over, he entered politics. He won a seat in Congress in 1946, advanced to the Senate in 1952, and was elected to the presidency in 1960.

Ted was born on February 22, 1932, fifteen years after John. He had gone to the same undergraduate school, Harvard, but hadn't done as well, having been disciplined for having someone else take a Spanish examination for him; unlike his brother, he received his law degree not from Harvard but from the University of Virginia. Like his brother, he had served in the military but was too young for World War II and had served during the Korean War instead, without being wounded, or even involved, in combat. In civilian life, he worked chiefly on his brother John's campaigns.

Once in the presidency, John had plans for Ted. He appointed his next oldest brother, Robert Francis (Bobby), to the cabinet as attorney general, a key position in terms of advancing presidential policy. He wanted to help his last and youngest brother, Ted, to win the position of U.S. senator from Massachusetts, which he himself had vacated in order to take the presidency, giving him an ally in the legislative branch. However, Ted was only twenty-nine years old, and the U.S. Constitution specified that senators must be thirty years of age. Besides, the person who had the power to appoint an interim senator, Massachusetts governor Foster Furcolo, was a political rival of the Kennedys and had his own candidate for the office. Furcolo appointed the interim senator, but an election was due in 1962. On February 22, 1962, Ted Kennedy turned thirty. On March 14, he announced his candidacy for the Senate. Even people who disdained Ted concluded the Kennedy name would see him through. Ted did win the Democratic primary and the Senate seat, taking his place in January 1963. Among his first committee assignments was a seat on the Judiciary Committee, which reviewed bills on a variety of subjects and decided whether to pass them to the Senate floor. Because the Immigration and Naturalization Service is part of the Department of Justice, immigration bills were within the Judiciary Committee's purview.

Ted was thus in a position to offer his presidential brother support on the latter's legislative initiatives. One of these was immigration. In *A Nation of Immigrants*, John Kennedy had complained that the 1952 Immigration and Nationality Act, sponsored by Senator **Patrick McCarran** and Representative **Francis Walter**, hampered U.S. global leadership. The United

States wanted allies around the world but then did not accept the nationals of some of these allies for immigration. It claimed to practice a more ethical form of government than did its communist opponents, and then it practiced an immoral form of discrimination. As president, John asked Bobby to prepare a legislative proposal. Bobby turned the task over to Adam Walinsky, an aide in the Justice Department. On July 23, 1963, John sent Walinsky's draft to Congress. **Philip Hart** (Democrat–Michigan) introduced it into the Senate the next day. **Emmanuel Celler** (Democrat–New York) introduced it into the House soon thereafter.

Then on November 22, 1963, Lee Harvey Oswald assassinated John Kennedy.

Vice President Lyndon Baines Johnson succeeded Kennedy. In 1964, he won the presidency in his own right, and his party, the Democrats, won large majorities in both houses of Congress. Among the Democrats, liberals of the Kennedy-Johnson type held a commanding position. Liberal Democrats were liberal in that, like Franklin D. Roosevelt, they favored a strong federal government. They were also liberal in that they wanted to use federal power to mitigate disadvantages caused by race or poverty. Immigration reform was a proposal to their liking.

Johnson organized his administration around the theme of continuing Kennedy's legacy. Kennedy's own family also had an interest in continuing his legacy, although for them that legacy had an additional component, that of continuing the family's role in national politics. Ted Kennedy achieved that end by supporting Johnson's efforts to pass John Kennedy's legislation. He used his maiden speech in the Senate to speak in favor of the administration's civil rights bill and to assure Congress that it was indeed what his brother would have wanted. He also offered to be the floor manager for the Hart-Celler immigration bill. Johnson agreed, though it was an unusual task to assign to a senator of only two years' experience.

In getting Hart-Celler through Congress, Ted Kennedy showed how effective a senator he could be. His chief accomplishment was keeping his committee together. Keeping committee peace was complicated by the presence of Bobby Kennedy. Bobby had resigned his position as attorney general in 1964, when Johnson announced he wouldn't ask anyone in his cabinet to be his vice presidential running mate. He then ran successfully for the Senate from New York. Bobby was a more intense person than Ted, impatient with what he thought of as old-line obstructionists hampering the liberal coalition. Among those old-line obstructionists he counted the chair of the Judiciary Committee, Senator James Eastland of Mississippi. Eastland was a Democrat but a conservative one. He did not want to change the 1952 law, because as far as he was concerned, that law did two things well: It protected the United States from the immigration of active communists, and it preserved a particular mix of ethnic groups in the population. However, Eastland did not make trouble for Kennedy. Why is not clear. The possibilities are that Eastland liked Kennedy; that Johnson, a former Democratic senator from another southern state (Texas), asked Eastland to cooperate; that Eastland realized the momentum lay with the liberal Democrats; and that Kennedy, who was the baby of his family and had learned to deal with older people, managed his relationship with the senior senator well. Whatever the reason, Eastland did Kennedy a great favor. Eastland's role as chair of the Senate Judiciary Committee also made him chair of the Subcommittee on Immigration and Nationality. He named Kennedy acting chair in 1964, allowing Kennedy to conduct the hearings on the Hart-Celler bill. The hearings ran from February 10 to August 3, with time off from mid-March through the end of May for consideration of the Voting Rights Act.

Kennedy recalled the various objections those testifying at the hearings raised. The most pressing was the "ethnic and racial pattern."[1] Even two senators on Kennedy's committee, Everett Dirksen (Republican–Illinois) and Sam Ervin (Democrat–North Carolina) opposed upsetting the racial balance.[2] The Daughters of the American Revolution, the National Association of Evangelicals, the Liberty Lobby, and the American Committee on Immigration Politics went on record to oppose the bill, at least partly because of the type of people who might be admitted under changed legislation.

Other groups supported changing immigration law but only after weighing several considerations. The American Legion and the American Coalition of Patriotic Societies realized that important persons favored change and so concentrated on modifying the bill rather than trying to defeat it. The American Federation of Labor–Congress of Industrial Organizations (AFL-CIO) did not want a law that increased job competition. However, many AFL-CIO members were also descendants of recent immigrants. The AFL-CIO decided to support more open immigration.

Support came from three groups of people. Some organizations represented people from countries that historically had been given low quotas and had been forbidden to send migrants: The American Committee on Italian Migration and the Japanese American Citizens League favored ending discriminatory quotas. Some organizations, such as the National Catholic Welfare Conference Bureau of Immigration and the National Council of Jewish Women, represented slightly different constituencies. Discriminatory national quotas that reduced total migration from southern and eastern Europe had the side effect of excluding Catholics and Jews. Religious groups, though, also took the position that discrimination on the basis of national origins was morally wrong. Finally, people such as Robert Kennedy pointed out that being morally right had pragmatic uses. The United States could not afford to appear discriminatory when it was trying to lead the free world in opposition to communism.

Kennedy made sure that opponents and proponents of the bill had their day before the Senate Judiciary Committee's Subcommittee on Immigration and Nationality. He then got the resulting bill approved by the subcommittee, the Judiciary Committee, and the Senate. When the House approved a different version of the bill, a reconciliation committee brought the two versions into harmony, and then Kennedy helped to make sure the reconciled version got through the Senate. On October 3, 1965, President Johnson sat at a desk at the base of the Statue of Liberty in New York Harbor and signed the Hart-Celler bill into law.

Johnson's signature did not end debate over the bill, for it contained some important innovations. The biggest change in the new law was the way it treated the Western Hemisphere. For the first time, there was an annual limit, of 120,000, on the number of citizens that could migrate to the United States from countries in the Western Hemisphere. The Johnson administration originally took the position that limiting hemispheric migration violated the historic relationship the United States had with other countries in the Americas. However, a majority of Congress was so tradition minded regarding racial limits that it was willing to break with diplomatic tradition in order to secure limits on potential migrants with Spanish, native Indian, and black ancestry. The administration acquiesced in order to get other elements of the bill that it wanted. Also, in 1964, in anticipation of the immigration legislation, the Johnson administration had ended nearly forty years of bracero migration, in which Mexicans crossed the border temporarily to do transient agricultural labor. Altogether, the law changed the basis of Western Hemispheric migration, without, however, changing the social, political, or economic situations that fueled the earlier migration. People of the Western Hemisphere, especially Mexicans, continued to migrate, albeit now any who came over the limit were entering illegally.

A second problem stemmed from the emphasis on family reunification. Since the 1920s, the law had permitted the migration of wives and minor children of male U.S. citizens outside the limits, in 1952, the law was rewritten to eliminate discrimination against female U.S. citizens; and in 1965, the law was amended to include parents. Also the total number of immigrants admitted under the limits was increased, and that threatened to increase the number of extralimit migrants. For example, the 1920s law admitted 150,000 immigrants under the national quota laws. If they were all male, and they all eventually brought just their wives, that would be a total of 300,000 immigrants. The new law admitted 290,000 immigrants under its various categories. If each became a citizen and sponsored both parents and a spouse, that would be 1,160,000 immigrants. And that doesn't even begin to count the children.

A third problem was also related to the emphasis on family reunification. The new law established a seven-level preference system. Five of those levels gave preference to people with relatives already in the United States. First preference went to the spouses and minor children of U.S. legal residents (immigrants who had not become citizens) and went on to other relatives, including siblings of U.S. citizens. The new law also established a maximum of 170,000 immigrants from outside the Western Hemisphere and 20,000 from any one country. Readers who realize that 170,000 divided by 20,000 equals 8.5, and that there are more than 8.5 countries outside the Western Hemisphere, can see trouble on the horizon. People with relatives in the United States not only used up all the visas for their own countries but a small number of countries used up all the visas for the world. The countries that could not send immigrants posed a diplomatic problem for the United States.

Despite the possibilities for increases in the number of immigrants, Ted Kennedy was soon criticizing the 1965 law because it didn't admit enough immigrants. Specifically, it overlooked one particular category of immigrants, refugees. When Kennedy first entered the Senate, there was no general legislation concerning refugees, because no one thought of refugees as an ongoing stream of immigrants. Refugees were created by unexpected events, such as wars. Some were cared for by special legislation, such as the 1948 Displaced Persons Act. In other cases, presidents exercised parole power; Dwight D. Eisenhower admitted Hungarians fleeing the Soviets after the crushing of the 1956 rebellion, and John F. Kennedy admitted Cubans fleeing Castro. The 1965 law did include provisions for refugees. It defined a refugee in a way consistent with U.S. foreign policy, as a person fleeing communism or unrest in the Middle East, where there was constant conflict between Israel and its Arab neighbors. The law also placed refugees third in its general preference categories, so that refugees could come only after families had been reunited and people with rare work skills had been admitted.

A combination of circumstances led to Ted Kennedy's interest in refugees. During the 1960s, the United States had a liberal Democratic president and a host of liberal Democratic representatives and senators. The representatives and senators demanded some power in Congress vis-à-vis the older and usually more conservative representatives and senators that chaired the important committees. The senior members answered this call for power by creating subcommittees and appointing the junior members to chair them. Senator Eastland assigned Senator Kennedy to chair the Senate Judiciary Committee Subcommittee on Refugees and Escapees from Communism. Apparently, Eastland thought the committee assignment would allow Kennedy to make a name for himself while doing nothing of substance. The senior senator should perhaps have remembered that Joseph R. McCarthy had turned the minor Government Operations Committee into a powerful agency that promoted his own interests. Kennedy, too, made something of the Subcommittee on Refugees, as he had it renamed.

A second issue was the Vietnam conflict. Kennedy missed the Senate's early involvement in Vietnam. On June 19, 1964, he, Senator Birch Bayh (Democrat–Indiana), and Mrs. Bayh hurried out of the final roll call vote on the Civil Rights Act to catch an airplane for Westfield, Massachusetts, to attend a party convention in West Springfield. In the foggy night, the pilot of the tiny plane lost radio contact with the tower at Barnes Airport in Westfield, flew too low on the final descent toward the runway, tripped over the treetops, and crashed. The pilot and a Kennedy aide died instantly. Senator Bayh rescued himself, his wife, and Kennedy. However, Kennedy punctured a lung, broke two ribs, and cracked three vertebrae, putting him in New England Baptist Hospital for months.

On August 7, 1964, while Kennedy was still recovering, Congress passed the Gulf of Tonkin Resolution, permitting President Johnson wide latitude in determining how to assist South Vietnam in resisting communists who held North Vietnam. One of Kennedy's biographers, James MacGregor Burns, argued that had Kennedy been at his Senate desk, he would have voted for the Gulf of Tonkin Resolution, for the liberal Democrats were also Cold Warriors.[3]

Shortly after the immigration act was signed, Dale de Haan, a staff member on the Subcommittee for Refugees, called Kennedy's attention to a new issue. The International Red Cross reported that fighting in South Vietnam was forcing people to flee their homes. This sounded like a proper topic for the Subcommittee on Refugees to investigate. Kennedy asked the State Department to plan a trip to Vietnam for himself, his administrative assistant David Burke, Senator Joseph Tydings (Democrat–Maryland), who was also a member of the Subcommittee on Refugees, and two other Senate friends, John Tunney of California and John Culver of Iowa. In October 1965 they arrived in the South Vietnamese capital of Saigon, where U.S. officials briefed them on conditions in the country. They toured military camps and visited one refugee camp.

Kennedy had mixed reaction to his trip. On the one hand, he saw nothing that led him to question Johnson's policy. He agreed with Johnson on the need to contain communism, specifically on the necessity of halting its advance in Vietnam and on using military means to do so. On the other hand, "While in Vietnam I saw for myself the indifference of the Saigon Government to the plight of their own. Government officials assured me the refugee situation was well in hand—yet I inspected one camp of over six hundred people without a toilet."[4] He suspected that authorities had spruced up the camps just before he came and feared that they ceased their work the moment he left. Even more problematic, there was nothing in U.S. law to assist the refugees. The South Vietnamese refugees Kennedy saw weren't exactly fleeing communism but fleeing South Vietnamese armies who were fighting communism. Kennedy began calling for changing the law he had just passed in order to enable better care for such refugees.

Three considerations kept Kennedy from more pointed criticism. First, he did not want to break rank with President Johnson. Ideologically, both Kennedy and Johnson were Cold Warriors who wanted to free the world of communism. Personally, Johnson claimed to be carrying out what Kennedy's brother John had started. Second, Ted did not want to get in the way of his brother Bobby. Robert Kennedy was older. He was more opposed to the war. He was not the most flamboyant antiwar personality of 1965, but that was because he, too, was stayed by the idea that Johnson represented the liberal Democratic Cold Warriors and also John Kennedy's legacy. However, if any Kennedy was going to break publicly with Johnson, it would be Bobby. Third, Edward Kennedy had only the one visit to South Vietnam to support his suspicions that something was wrong. This last he could remedy. He chaired the Subcommittee on Refugees. He could hold hearings.

And hold them he did. During 1965, people involved directly in the situation in Vietnam testified before the Subcommittee on Refugees. In the summer of 1966, Kennedy proposed additional hearings. He began to formulate the notion that military victory needed to be supplemented with social reform. The South Vietnamese would not be safe from communism until their own government, and the U.S. government that supported it, attended to the needs of the people of the countryside.

The publicity Kennedy gave the South Vietnamese refugee situation alerted Johnson to the growing opposition in the Congress to his course of action in Vietnam. Johnson responded by creating a special assistant to the secretary of state for Refugee and Migration Affairs. Kennedy increased his pressure. During 1967, he called for more hospitals for the civilian casualties in South Vietnam. In August of that year, a panel of six U.S. physicians issued a report critical of the way the South Vietnamese government handled refugees. Aid to International Development (AID) a U.S. State Department agency, countered with a report producing evidence that South Vietnam was managing the refugee situation well. Kennedy announced that conflicting reports were reason enough to hold new hearings on "Civilian Casualty, Social Welfare and Refugee Problems in South Vietnam." He held the hearings from October 9 to October 16, just before a massive antiwar demonstration held at the Pentagon in Arlington, Virginia, outside Washington, D.C., on October 21. In December 1967, he made a second fact-finding trip to South Vietnam. This time, he did not ask the State Department to arrange his itinerary. When he arrived in Saigon, he declined the initial briefing from U.S. officials. He spent two days in Saigon, then left for a week in the countryside, during which he visited military bases and refugee camps. When he returned to Saigon, authorities tried once more to give him the official briefing. Kennedy said that their report didn't describe the situation he saw in the countryside. They accused him of misplaced priorities. Refugees were a regrettable, but inevitable, consequence of U.S. efforts to prevent communist incursion into the South Vietnamese countryside. Kennedy returned to the United States in early 1968 and gave several speeches trying to puncture optimism about Vietnam. Even if the military was defeating communism, it was harming the people of South Vietnam and destroying their social fabric. When the U.S. Army vanquished its enemies and returned to the United States, how long would the victory last if only the ruined society of South Vietnam was left to uphold it?

The February Tet Offensive, in which communist South Vietnamese forces called Viet Cong launched simultaneous coordinated attacks on multiple targets across South Vietnam, stole Kennedy's thunder. The Tet victories, though temporary, revealed to the U.S. public that not only was the war creating a lot of heartrending damage, but it didn't even seem to be a successful effort. Discussion of refugees was set aside in favor of intense debate over what was going wrong in Vietnam and who was responsible. Being president, Johnson attracted much of the blame, so much so that shortly thereafter Eugene McCarthy (Democrat–Minnesota) came in second, right behind the incumbent president, in the Democrat primary in New Hampshire. Johnson changed his strategy. He tried to take politics out of U.S. efforts in Vietnam by announcing that he would not be a candidate to succeed himself in 1968.

Johnson's refusal to run for president opened the way to a race among many Democrats, including Robert F. Kennedy. From March until June, Ted was busy helping another brother run for the presidency. Bobby had been thinking about running for some time, but he entered the race suddenly. There was much to organize in order to prepare for the Democratic primaries. Bobby lost in Oregon but then did well in California, a state with numerous delegates to the Democratic convention and, more important, numerous electoral votes in the election.

On June 5, the night of the California primary, Sirhan Sirhan assassinated Robert F. Kennedy.

As the last surviving male of his generation (which was a generation before women entered politics in large numbers), Ted Kennedy was the only remaining hope for carrying on the family legacy. On July 18, 1969, his ability to carry on that tradition was severely compromised. That day Kennedy attended a party for some of Bobby Kennedy's office staff, held at Chappaquiddick, a small island east of the larger one of Martha's Vineyard. That evening, Kennedy was driving with one of the party guests, a young woman named Mary Jo Kopechne, when the car went off the road and into Massachusetts Bay. Kennedy escaped from the car, but Kopechne drowned. Kennedy did not report the accident until the next morning, a violation of the law to which he later pled guilty and for which he received a suspended jail sentence. The incident was resurrected whenever it was suggested that Kennedy might run for president. However, Chappaquiddick continued to be important because Kennedy continued to be mentioned for the presidency.

Richard M. Nixon's election in 1968 led Kennedy from general politics back to refugee issues. Nixon promised to settle the Vietnam conflict in such a way as to preserve U.S. world leadership. While he searched for a way to do so, the displacement of refugees continued. Nixon negotiated a withdrawal of troops from South Vietnam, which took place on January 28, 1973. On April 30, 1975, communist forces defeated the South Vietnamese army and extended their control to all of Vietnam. For the remainder of the 1970s, the situation in Indochina was unstable, partly because of the refugees that left Vietnam for refugee camps in other Southeast Asian countries and partly because the Vietnam conflict contributed to a brief border war between Vietnam and the People's Republic of China and a longer civil war between communist and anticommunist factions in Cambodia.

The Subcommittee on Refugees, still chaired by Kennedy, held hearings on the situation in Indochina every year from 1969 to 1975, inclusive. In 1976, Kennedy explicitly forswore running for president; his son had just had a leg amputated to prevent the spread of bone cancer, and Kennedy didn't want to expose the family to the stress of a presidential campaign. He remained in Congress, which passed a steady stream of legislation admitting and caring for Indochinese refugees. The Indochina Migration and Refugee Assistance Act of May 23, 1975, created a resettlement program for those who left Cambodia and Vietnam. On June 21, 1976, Laotians became eligible for the program. An October 28, 1977, law permitted refugees admitted under the 1975 act to adjust their status to that of permanent residents, a step toward citizenship, and extended the time period for which the refugees were entitled to special assistance. A law passed on December 22, 1987, addressed the issue of children born to members of the U.S. armed forces stationed in Vietnam and consorting with natives there. The children were permitted to come to the United States, together with their mothers and siblings, outside of national ceilings and with the benefits given to refugees. On November 21, 1989, Congress passed its last bit of immigration legislation to protect refugees from the Vietnam conflict, a law permitting former Soviet and Indochinese nationals who had been admitted into the United States on presidential parole to become permanent residents.

Meanwhile, Kennedy began to call for reform of the 1965 immigration law as it concerned refugees.[5] In 1968, the United States signed the United Nations Protocol Relating to the Status of Refugees, agreeing to abide by its standards. The United Nations had a different definition of *refugee* than the United States did. The UN definition was that refugees were people fleeing persecution at the hands of any government, not just a communist government or unrest in the Middle East. In 1969, Kennedy and Representative Michael Feighan (Democrat–Ohio) introduced a bill substituting the UN definition for the U.S. definition in its law. At that point, Nixon was in office and the Vietnam War was an important issue; the bill died without action being taken. After Nixon withdrew U.S. troops from Vietnam, Representative Peter Rodino (Democrat–New Jersey) introduced legislation to admit refugees without regard to the 20,000-visas-per-country limit. However, at that point, Watergate took precedence. Then, after the fall of Saigon, there was a flood of refugees, and Congress concentrated on laws tailored to their specific needs rather than to general laws. In 1976, Jimmy Carter was elected president. In October 1978, the Carter administration sent proposed refugee legislation, similar to that favored by Kennedy, to Congress. In February 1979, Kennedy and Representative Elizabeth Holtzman (Democrat–New York) formally introduced the bill to their respective houses of Congress. Action on general legislation for refugees was finally under way.[6] The Refugee Act became law on March 17, 1980. It changed the basic definition of a refugee to conform to the definition the United States agreed to when it signed the UN protocol on the subject. It placed the admission of refugees in a separate category, apart from the national and worldwide limits. Instead, the president and the Congress were to agree annually on a total number of refugees for that fiscal year (which meant from October 1 of one calendar year to September 30 of the next). The law established a program for working with family sponsors and not-for-profit agencies in resettling refugees in the United States. There were also provisions for readjusting the status of refugees and of asylees, refugees being those who fled a country with the announced intention of coming to the United States and asylees being those who came to the United States and then asked to be kept permanently and not sent home because they feared persecution. Finally, there were provisions for emergencies.

During this period, Kennedy determined that Jimmy Carter's leadership of the Democratic Party and the nation was inadequate, and decided to challenge Carter for the presidency in 1980. Once the Refugee Act was passed, he hit the campaign trail. However, he was not attracting as much support as he had hoped. The Kopechne drowning at Chappaquiddick still raised questions about his moral character. He underrated the support for the sitting president in the Democratic Party and in the general public, and his campaign was seen as a disrespectful attempt to outmaneuver fellow Democrats. Finally, a new star was rising in the West, Ronald Reagan, whose rhetoric pictured liberal reformers like Kennedy as people with outdated ideas and conservatism as a bold new alternative. Kennedy withdrew from the race and did not run for the presidency again.

Instead, he remained active in the field of refugee legislation. Shortly after the passage of the Refugee Act, the Cuban government announced that all people who wished to leave for the United States could try to go. At once, the United States was swamped with newcomers. When it tried to determine if individuals were admissible under U.S. law, the people asked to be admitted as refugees. There were rumors that some applicants were in fact criminals who were ineligible for admission. However, until the facts were known, each individual had to have a court appearance, and until the appearances could be scheduled, the applicants had to be kept in the United States. On May 8, Kennedy cut short his presidential campaign and returned to Washington to hold hearings on the subject.[7] In November of that year, an earthquake demolished part of southern Italy and left many people without homes or jobs. Kennedy urged Carter to admit some Italians as refugees from natural disaster.[8]

Kennedy also remained active in the field of immigration legislation. During the early 1980s, one of the provisions of the 1965 law began to cause problems. The relevant provision was the one that gave preference to family reunification, which made it difficult for people who didn't have relatives in the United States to get immigration visas. When the Irish economy began to weaken, the Irish people resorted to a traditional coping pattern. Families divided, with some members seeking to migrate in search of work, the wages from which they sent home to sustain the rest of the family. However, the Irish had difficulty migrating, because the country didn't have much recent migration to the United States, and thus individuals had no living relatives there to enable them to get family-preference visas.

The idea that the United States wouldn't help out Ireland in its economic difficulty by permitting its people to migrate had implications for diplomatic relations between the two countries. More pressing, Irish Americans began to lobby for their coethnics, claiming that the United States was in effect discriminating against those who weren't lucky enough to have relatives who migrated about the time the law changed, thus paving the way for later migration. These people were Kennedy's coethnics, and some of them were his constituents. Kennedy supported the efforts of a young congressional representative, Brian Donnelly (Democrat–Connecticut), to develop legislation that would permit these people to migrate.

The most straightforward way would have been legislation setting aside visas for people who had no relatives in the United States, but since it would be extremely difficult to prove the absence of relatives, this would be a time-consuming and expensive law. The second most straightforward way would have been to create some sort of Irish relief bill, but that would raise the specter of discriminating in favor of the Irish and would ignore the problems of people in similar circumstances but in other countries. The result was a pilot program included in the Immigration Reform and Control Act of November 6, 1986. The law set aside 5,000 visas for 1987 and another 5,000 for 1988 for persons from countries adversely affected by the 1965 law. Individuals applied for the visas, which were then distributed by a special system that gave preference to people who came from countries with low recent immigration, to people with skills or education that would enable them to get a job in the United States, and to people who spoke English. The pilot program became a permanent part of the law in the

Immigration Act of November 29, 1990, on which Kennedy worked with his Senate colleague **Alan K. Simpson**. The law set aside 55,000 visas annually outside preferences for family reunification, economics, and refugees.

Kennedy has had a long and diverse record, but how consistent has it been? For Dan Stein of the immigration-restriction lobby Federation for American Immigration Reform (FAIR), the only consistency has been Kennedy's inconsistency, with each addition to the law creating a different problem until Kennedy became "The Godfather of the Immigration Mess."[9] Kennedy had denied over and over again during the 1965 hearings that the immigration bill would increase the number of migrants, yet migration increased. Kennedy then pushed immigration still higher by adding other laws, yet he never supported the administration of the laws. The border patrol had too little money and too few officers to adequately police the borders, and there were too few Immigration and Naturalization Service staff members to process the huge backlog of immigrants awaiting clearance.

Stein's 1994 analysis was based on the notion that immigration was a problem to be solved. Kennedy's record might look more consistent if one looked at immigration itself differently. Immigration itself was never a problem for Kennedy. Instead, it could be used to solve other problems. Some of them, admittedly, were personal problems; the 1965 law, his work with refugees, and his work with the Irish brought Kennedy votes. For ambitious or endangered people around the world, immigration brought them greater opportunities or greater safety. However, immigration laws solved problems for the nation, too. The 1965 law (like the 1964 Civil Rights Act) worked to reduce racial discrimination. The 1980 refugee law coordinated one aspect of immigration policy with foreign policy. For the United States, then involved in a Cold War against the Soviet Union and a (related) hot war in Vietnam, the 1965 immigration act was a powerful statement of U.S. values, and the 1980 law offered at least some help to innocent victims of U.S. intervention abroad. Although Kennedy was most concerned with general policy in 1965, with Southeast Asian refugees in the 1970s, and with the unemployed Irish in the 1980s, his immigration legislation did indeed have a certain consistency.

NOTES

1. Edward M. Kennedy, "The Immigration Act of 1965," *Annals of the American Academy of Political and Social Science* 367 (September 1966), pp. 137–149.

2. Burton Hersh, *The Education of Edward Kennedy: A Family Biography* (New York: William Morrow, 1972), pp. 221–225.

3. James MacGregor Burns, *Edward Kennedy and the Camelot Legacy* (New York: W. W. Norton, 1976), p. 133.

4. *Look* (February 8, 1966), pp. 21–23.

5. Edward M. Kennedy, "Foreword," *San Diego Law Review* 14:1 (December 1976), pp. 1–5. This is an introduction to a special issue of the journal concerning immigration law.

6. Deborah E. Anker and Michael H. Posner, "The Forty Year Crisis: A Legislative History of the Refugee Act of 1980," *San Diego Law Review* 19:1 (1981), pp. 9–89.

7. *New York Times*, May 9, 1980, p. 14, col. 3.

8. *New York Times*, December 30, 1980, p. 14, col. 2.

9. Dan Stein, "Godfather of the Immigration Mess," *National Review* (November 7, 1994), p. 48.

BIBLIOGRAPHY

Member of a fabled family and a controversial person in his own right, Ted Kennedy has inspired numerous biographies. The ones that were especially useful here were James MacGregor Burns, *Edward Kennedy and the Camelot Legacy* (New York: W. W. Norton, 1976); Burton Hersh, *The Education of Edward Kennedy: A Family Biography* (New York: William Morrow, 1972), and *The Shadow President: Ted Kennedy in Opposition* (New York: Steerforth, 1997); William H. Honan, *Ted Kennedy: Profile of a Survivor* (New York: Quadrangle Books/A New York Times Company, 1972); Theo Lippman, Jr., *Senator Ted Kennedy* (New York: W. W. Norton, 1976). For material on the 1965 Immigration and Nationality Act, see Edward M. Kennedy, "The Immigration Act of 1965," *Annals of the American Academy of Political and Social Science* 367 (September 1966), pp. 137–149. The *San Diego Law Review* carried two pieces on refugee legislation, Edward M. Kennedy, "Foreword," to a special issue on immigration law, 14:1 (December 1976), pp. 1–5, and Deborah E. Anker and Michael H. Posner, "The Forty Year Crisis: A Legislative History of the Refugee Act of 1980," 19:1 (1981), pp. 9–89. For context on U.S. migration since World War II, see David M. Reimers, *Still the Golden Door: The Third World Comes to America*, 2nd ed. (New York: Columbia University Press, 1992). For context on refugees, see Gil Loescher and John A. Scanlan, *Calculated Kindness: Refugees and America's Half-Open Door, 1945–Present* (New York: Free Press, 1986). Regarding Ted Kennedy's work on Irish immigration, see "A Deserved Honor for Kennedy," *Irish Voice* 7:39 (September 28, 1993), p. 10. Regarding his work on general immigration, see "Irish Eyes Are Smiling; Immigration Bill: Who Needs It?" *Legal Times* (April 4, 1988), p. 14.

CESAR CHAVEZ
(1927–1993)

Migrant Farmworkers

Cesar Chavez lived a life crosscut by different identities. He was himself a U.S. citizen by birth. He identified himself with migrants, specifically with migrant laborers. Others identified him with immigrants, especially with Spanish-speaking immigrants. Chavez himself took some time to come to terms with others' characterizations of him. When he brought together his own identity as a migrant laborer and his identity as an ethnic American, he made new contributions to the immigration debate. He found a new solution to the question of labor competition, highlighted the issues of illegal immigration, and himself served as a constant reminder that U.S. citizenship extends to people of many colors and language groups.

Chavez's grandparents and parents were indeed immigrants. His paternal grandfather, also Cesar Chavez, escaped from debt peonage and potential conscription into the army in the 1880s by leaving the Hacienda del Carmen in Chihuahua, Mexico, under cover of night, and walking across the border into El Paso, Texas. By 1888, grandfather Cesar had enough money to send for his wife and children, including a two-year-old son named Librado. The family staked a claim to a farm in Yuma, Arizona, and all worked hard to make it productive. Librado followed in his father's footsteps. He married a woman named Juana, herself a Mexican immigrant

Cesar Chavez speaking at a PADRES (Hispanic Roman Catholic priests' organization) meeting in the mid-1980s. Center for Migration Studies.

who had crossed the border at age six months. He opened a grocery in Yuma and bought some land around it but stayed near his parents' home so that he could help with the farm. He and Juana had five children. Their second child and first son, whom they named for grandfather Cesar, was born on March 31, 1927.

Cesar became a migrant because of the Great Depression, which started with the crash of the New York Stock Exchange on October 29, 1929, and reached his family in February 1934. The depression stretched his father to the breaking point. Librado had extended credit to the families that shopped at his grocery, and thus he had no cash on hand to repay the money he borrowed to buy the land around his store. He lost the store and had to move his family back to the parental farm.

Despite having been born in the United States, Cesar was confused when a teacher told him he was an American. He considered himself a Mexican. He spoke Spanish at home and his uncles taught him to read it; he remembered how difficult it was when he started school and had to speak English. Other people considered people like Cesar to be other than American, too. In 1936, the federal government began work on the Imperial Dam at the north end of the Gila Valley. Although there were plenty of unemployed American citizens around to work on the dam, it was English-speaking Americans who migrated from the Southeast to the desert who got the jobs.

In 1937, the deadline came for Librado to pay back taxes on the property he had been forced to sell. Librado managed to hold out a bit longer by traveling to California to find work. He found a job as a laborer at an agribusiness, a commercial farm, in Oxnard, a little town north of Los Angeles, and called for his family to join him. Two male cousins helped to drive Juana and the five children from Arizona to California in the Chavez Studebaker. As the overloaded car crossed the desert toward California, the border patrol stopped them. During the Great Depression, jobs were scarce in the United States but even scarcer in Mexico, and the border patrol was sure they had caught a carload of Mexicans sneaking into the United States to steal jobs. It was difficult to convince them otherwise, because only the school-age children spoke English.

The border patrol finally decided to let them go, and the Chavezes drove on to Oxnard, which turned out to be a disappointment. The work was irregular, with exhausting schedules during the rush seasons and nothing at all in the slack seasons. The housing was atrocious. The Chavezes lived in a shack that had been poorly constructed to begin with and hadn't improved with age. It was set down in a small yard in an overcrowded neighborhood devoid of most amenities. The unpaved streets were dusty in dry weather and muddy in wet. Water for drinking, cooking, and washing was scarce. The communal outhouses were pathways for contagious diseases. There was electricity, which the Chavezes hadn't had in Yuma, but it wasn't an unqualified improvement. There were no light bulbs, so the sockets were useful only for teasing one's siblings: Cesar coaxed his younger brother into putting his finger into the socket to feel it tickle and then gave him an electric shock.[1]

In 1939, the family's migrant condition became permanent. For nonpayment of taxes, the state of Arizona seized the farm Librado's father had homesteaded. The Chavezes took up a weary cycle of existence. During the growing season, they anxiously made the rounds of agribusinesses, seeking temporary work. When they found it, they did exhausting labor for long hours under unhealthy and unsafe conditions for low pay, then started on another tense journey toward another temporary job. During the slack season, they made a base in a depressing San Jose barrio, or neighborhood, called Sal Si Puedes.

Commentators later alleged the barrio got its name from the residents urging each other to "get out if you can" and go on to a better life, but Chavez denied that etymology.[2] People in Sal Si Puedes were so beaten down they didn't even realize that the Great Depression had made their lives worse. Nor did World War II make their lives better. Studies of World War II indicate that because it put so many men and women into the military, the war created a labor shortage. Into that labor vacuum came people who had previously had only marginal or poorly paid jobs, such as African Americans and white women. One might think migrant farmworkers would become more valuable and highly paid, too. Instead, beginning on April 29, 1943, the United States made a series of agreements with Mexico. Collectively, this is called the bracero program (for the Mexican word for someone who works with their arms, that is, does manual labor). The program permitted labor contractors to organize labor gangs in Mexico, transport them to the United States, and hire them out to American agribusiness in need of labor. Therefore, American migrant farmworkers made no collective advances. World War II is one of the ingredients in the modern African-American civil rights movement. It plays no similar role in the modern migrant farmworker movement.

Under these circumstances, young men just bumped along. In 1944, at seventeen, Chavez started a two-year hitch with the U.S. Navy. Although he later was deeply involved in the nonviolence movement, and attributed it to the early influence of his mother, no one saw the navy as contrary to Juana Chavez's teaching. After his hitch was over, Chavez returned to his parents and to seasonal farm labor. On October 22, 1948, he married Helena Febela of Delano, California, whom he had met when they were both fifteen years old, when she worked at a local malt shop and he was in town for the grape harvest. They eventually had eight children.

Chavez did realize there was a problem but had only one way to analyze it. "We thought the only way we could get out of the circle of poverty was to work our way up and send our kids to college. That's the trap most poor people get themselves into. It's easier for a person to just escape, to get out of poverty, than to change the situation."[3]

It wasn't that easy to get out of poverty either. Chavez's limited education and work skills prevented him from getting better jobs. The seasonal nature of migrant farm labor prohibited him from putting in enough hours to earn and to save money. Fortunately for Chavez, he filled his idle time with volunteer work. Volunteerism eventually brought him into contact with his opportunity for advancement.

The Archdiocese of Los Angeles sent the Reverend Donald McDonnell to Sal Si Puedes to minister to the Mexican-American Catholics there. At first, Father McDonnell did the things Chavez expected a priest to do, and Chavez helped him with repairs around the broken-down shack that served as a church. Then, an elderly Mexican immigrant woman died, and her adult daughter came to the priest distraught because she didn't have enough money for a funeral. Chavez thought the community should take up a collection and ask Catholic Charities for a contribution, but Father McDonnell pulled out a copy of the health and welfare code and found that it was legal for a family to bury a body without an undertaker. Chavez was aghast, but the cost of the funeral did immediately drop to the price of the grave. Everything else the parishioners could do themselves and for free: transport the body from the hospital to the late woman's home, prepare it for burial, build a coffin. It was Chavez's introduction to the importance of the community doing as much of the work as it could, with as little money as possible. Father McDonnell supplemented Chavez's hands-on introduction to community work with a course of reading in Catholic social teaching from Saint Francis of Assisi to modern papal encyclicals.

In that reading, Chavez noticed a reference to Gandhi and on his own initiative read Louis Fisher's biography of Mohandas K. Ghandi. In many ways Gandhi was a very different person from Chavez. Gandhi was a Hindu, born in India in the nineteenth century, and his achievement was to mobilize masses of people in India and unite various political leaders to press for the British to liberate India. What was interesting to Chavez was the strategy Gandhi used to accomplish his goals, especially the emphasis on nonviolent opposition to the evil of imperialism. Chavez became interested in nonviolence, on two levels. He noticed it was a politically sound strategy, for it cast the nonviolent into the role of David standing up to Goliath. It also fit in well with his home training, his religious education, and his own ideas.

In 1952, Chavez came to the attention of Fred Ross. Like Chavez, Ross had been affected by the Great Depression. Ross graduated from the University of Southern California prepared to teach secondary school but could not find a job. He took a position with the New Deal's Farm Security Administration and started to learn about community work. In 1947, **Saul**

Alinsky, legendary Chicago community organizer and head of the Industrial Areas Foundation, hired Ross to work for the foundation's Community Services Organization (CSO), which was dedicated to teaching communities how to develop their own social strength. Alinsky assigned Ross to work with Mexican Americans in Los Angeles and its surrounding area, which included San Jose. When he met Chavez, Ross asked him to host a meeting. Chavez did it partly out of irritation. He could see Ross was an Anglo and didn't trust his protestations of interest in Mexican Americans. So he invited a few of the nastier characters he knew and made sure there was beer on hand, figuring that after Ross made his pitch, he could be run out of town. Instead, Chavez became so interested in what Ross was saying and so convinced of Ross's sincerity that he sent his own friends away and became involved in community organizing. A few months after he started volunteering with Fred Ross's voter registration drive, he was laid off at the lumber mill where he was then working. Unable to find paid work, he went on unemployment but now acted as a full-time volunteer. Ross persuaded Alinsky to hire Chavez, and Chavez continued on the CSO payroll from 1952 to 1962, doing various projects in different Californian Mexican-American barrios. He worked his way up to the position of executive director, and his sister Rita and brother Ricardo also worked for CSO.

In 1958, the CSO sent Chavez to Oxnard, the first place in California his family had lived. He came thinking that he could organize the people around the issue of railroad tracks that cut across the streets at street level. Friends of his had been killed by trains speeding across streets. When he held meetings intended to sound out community concerns, though, he found the locals had a more pressing issue. Although there was plenty of labor in the area, agribusinesses had convinced the federal government there was a labor shortage, and the federal government had permitted the agribusinesses to get labor from contractors who hired gangs of braceros. The agribusinesses then took advantage of the braceros, calling for more than they needed so that they could justify paying pittances, housing workers in substandard shelters, and sending them back to Mexico at the least complaint. Vis-à-vis white, English-speaking Americans, Chavez called himself a Mexican, but he did not see himself as having common cause with the Mexican braceros. He never thought of the braceros as scabs. He placed his emphasis on the collusion between agribusiness and government that permitted the former to skip the local labor pool and to hire workers who were more easily exploited. He agreed to spearhead a campaign to oust the braceros.

Chavez learned much during the Oxnard campaign. He made friends among the locals, then sent them to the job placement offices to apply for work, knowing they'd be turned down. After he had collected enough evidence to force authorities to take action, he began to orchestrate public demonstrations to call attention to the lack of work for area residents. It was the Mexican Americans of Oxnard who gave these demonstrations the touches Chavez later adopted. Marchers brought a banner depicting Our Lady of Guadaloupe, a popular devotional figure for Mexicans. They turned the protest march into a kind of pilgrimage. Although the issue remained a labor issue, the marchers were inspired by their sense of solidarity as a faith community.

The most important thing Chavez learned, though, was that the farmworkers needed a labor union. The demonstrations ousted the braceros, but only for so long as Chavez was there to organize the community. After he left, there was no contractual agreement between local laborers and agribusiness. The agribusinesses brought the braceros back in, and there was no structure, no organization, and no leader to mount a new protest. There needed to be a permanent labor organization, not a general community service program.

Chavez began to press the CSO to go into labor organizing. CSO leaders resisted, preferring the broader base of community organizing. Chavez discussed with his wife his sense that only labor organizing would do something permanent for the farmworkers. If the CSO wouldn't support labor organizing, he would have to do it alone, without the CSO salary, and that meant Mrs. Chavez had to assume a double burden. She had to become the family's main source of income, and she also had to run the household and find ways to stretch their money. She agreed to give it a try. In 1962, Chavez resigned from the CSO. The Chavezes moved to Delano, California, where Helen had family. They had given up on getting out of poverty through winning better and better jobs for themselves. They had cast their lot with staying with farmwork and seeking to make it a better job.

This may have been a case of the man meeting the hour. When Cesar Chavez was a boy, his father joined many upstart labor unions, but the unions had never been able to make collective bargaining prevail under the conditions in agribusiness. Other veterans of CSO work among California's Mexican-American farmworkers were thinking along the same lines as Chavez was, among them **Dolores Fernández Huerta**, a native Californian of Spanish and Indian descent, with tremendous personal drive. Although Huerta had been married at nineteen and had a number of children in a very short time, she also managed to get through college and to obtain the credentials to teach. In 1959, the American Federation of Labor–Congress of Industrial Organizations (AFL-CIO), the largest confederation of U.S. labor unions, began funding an Agricultural Workers Organizing Committee (AWOC), and Huerta was one of the organizers. Another was Larry Itilong, a Filipino American. On September 8, 1965, Itilong led a group of Filipino-American farmworkers laboring in the grape vineyards around Delano out on strike in protest against braceros who, on paper at least, received higher wages than the Filipinos did.

The AWOC solicited Chavez to organize for them, but he preferred to work on his own, as he had a vision he thought was broader than that of the AFL-CIO. The AFL-CIO was known for its "bread-and-butter" unionism. Although the union did contribute to candidates for political office, it did not field any candidates of its own and did not attempt to broaden the union effort into a political one. It confined itself to trying to get workers a fair share of the wealth their labor created. It bargained with employers for higher wages, shorter work hours, more time off, and better fringe benefits. Chavez thought such bread and butter unionism fell into the trap of allowing individuals to escape poverty while doing nothing to change the basic social situation. The Farm Workers Association—he didn't even want to call it a union—was going to be different. It was going to be a real community activity. And it was, at least in the sense of commanding a great deal of community involvement. Because Chavez turned down the AFL-CIO's offer to fund him, he had no salary and no office budget. Instead, the Chavez family made sacrifices. He, Helen, and the children wore old clothes and cut down on food. The Farm Workers Association drew what it needed from the community, getting volunteers to help with the office work and with organizing. Chavez gathered around him a cadre of people with their own sense of self sacrifice for the common good, including his wife Helen, who kept the family together, and Dolores Fernández Huerta, who became cofounder of the movement. His cousin, Manuel Chavez, designed the new organization's emblem: a black Aztec eagle surrounded by a white circle on a red flag.

When Chavez heard Itilong had taken his embryonic union out on strike against the Delano grape growers, he had a meeting of the Farm Workers Association. He pressed the membership to take the same step: "The strike was begun by the Filipinos, but it is not exclusively for them. Tonight we must decide if we are to join our fellow workers in this great labor struggle."[4] When it came time to take the strike vote, the hand count looked unanimous. They were no longer Filipinos or Mexicans but farmworkers.

The Delano grape strike can be analyzed in many ways. From the point of view of national politics and reform movements, it brought Chavez into the firmament of heroes. The strike started just about the time that the black power movement began to question the contributions of white civil rights activists. It attracted support from white, middle-class, college-educated people, many of them sharing Chavez's sense of the importance of religious faith. They came to help picket, to run the office, and to serve the strikers through donations and assistance. Their presence generated more publicity for the strike than the strikers could do alone. The strikers also used techniques that were used in other protest movements of the era. Chavez had already seen how the Mexican Americans of Oxnard had turned a protest march into a pilgrimage. But when in 1966 he expanded this idea and called for a march from Delano to Sacramento to put the farmworkers' case before Governor Pat Brown, people were reminded of Martin Luther King, Jr.'s, march from Selma to Montgomery, Alabama. (Governor Brown, though, did not play the same role as Governor Wallace; he left town entirely, to spend Easter with his family at Frank Sinatra's home in Palm Springs.) The religious fervor that accompanied Chavez's movement was also reminiscent of the spirit in which King worked, and the Catholics had many more visible symbols of their religion. Strikers turned the back of Chavez's station wagon into a little shrine to Our Lady of Guadaloupe for the convenience of those who wanted to pray. The laity led recitations of the rosary. Clergy also volunteered and said mass at the strike site. Finally, Chavez's commitment to nonviolence echoed that of King, and his use of fasts to encourage the movement to nonviolence echoed Gandhi. Altogether, Chavez emerged as a fresh start, a new kind of reform that could rally educated and politically active white liberals.

From the point of view of labor history, Chavez revived the sense that labor could be the fulcrum for organizing wider reforms. The principal piece of evidence for this interpretation is Chavez's use of boycotts. One can imagine a scenario in which consumers would become angry with striking farmworkers. Because the migrant farmworkers were on strike, food was not getting to market. If the farmworkers ever did resume work, it was likely to be under conditions that would lead to an increase in supermarket prices. By appealing to consumers' sympathy for the struggling workers, Chavez created a united front of strikers and consumers against agribusiness. Now, there were few purchasers for the parent companies' products, which might encourage the companies to deal with the union.

From the narrower point of view of the history of labor unions, Chavez was an example of how more inclusive labor movements transformed themselves into bread-and-butter unionism, with union leaders more interested in higher wages, shorter hours, more holidays, and better benefits rather than in systemic change. Early in the strike Walter Reuther of the United Auto Workers visited the Delano strikers and then went back to his union to convince it to offer financial support. The support drew Chavez closer to traditional unionism. In 1966, the Farm Workers Association changed its name to the National Farm Workers Union, finally using the noun that Chavez had avoided. It then consolidated with the AWOC. Eventually, this organization took the name United Farm Workers (UFW). The newly consolidated farmworker group then joined the AFL-CIO. In order to increase membership and to make the new union the agent for collective bargaining by farmworkers, the AFL-CIO created the United Farm Workers Organizing Committee (UFWOC) and made Chavez its director. Some of Chavez's supporters argued that by joining the AFL-CIO the farmworkers were giving up their unique vision of what a labor union could be. Chavez emphasized the gains in support.

The one union that opposed Chavez, though, undermined the general support. The International Brotherhood of Teamsters did have a good reason to oppose the efforts to organize farmworkers. Teamsters organized the truck drivers that hauled what the farmworkers produced. Teamster union leaders could imagine a scenario in which striking farmworkers left truck drivers without any work. Hence, the Teamsters reasoned that if anyone organized the farmworkers, it should be the Teamsters. However, nearly everyone in the farmworkers' movement charged the Teamsters with wanting to organize the farmworkers *only* to protect the truck drivers, ignoring the particular needs of farmworkers. Chavez fought his strike on two fronts, preventing the Teamsters from getting the right to organize farmworkers while simultaneously winning it for himself.

Most important, the strike brought out a new dimension in the history of immigration. The same year that the grape strike started, the federal government ended the bracero program that had precipitated it. Agribusiness could no longer turn to contractors to round up cheap labor. However, they could take advantage of immigrants who crossed the border illegally. The first such incident occurred among melon workers at the Mexican-Texas border. When Chavez was organizing the grape workers, the melon workers signed on with the United Farm Workers. In 1966, they went on strike, trying to raise their wages up over $1 an hour. The agribusinesses recruited workers in Mexico to replace the strikers. On October 24, 1966, labor organizers and strikers stationed themselves at the bridge between Ciudad Aleman in Tamaulipas and Roma in Texas. They laid down on the bridge to halt traffic, and three of them closed and locked the gate on the bridge. Police from both Mexico and the United States came to arrest them. Chavez considered the police to be in collusion with agribusiness to undermine the strike by providing scab workers. As far as the Mexican workers themselves were concerned, he thought they would act in solidarity with other workers, and he was right. On May 13, 1967, the Confederación de Trabajadores Mexicanos and Chavez's organization conducted a joint operation. Mexican labor leaders mounted a picket line on their side of the border to discourage Mexicans from crossing to take jobs that would break the strike. If the would-be workers made it past that picket line, the American labor union workers had another picket line across the Rio Grande.

The Giumarra Corporation, one of the Delano grape growers, also tried to bring in illegal immigrant labor to break the grape workers' strike. Chavez complained to the Immigration and Naturalization Service (INS). INS officials responded that they had personnel sufficient only to monitor immigrants crossing the Rio Grande and could not check on their employment once they were in the United States. In that case, the most Chavez could do was organize a protest when in 1968 Attorney General Ramsey Clark, to whom the head of the INS reported, came to speak in San Francisco.

In 1970, the grape strike ended, with Chavez forces victorious. The boycotts were costing the parent companies of the grape growers far too much. On July 29, 1970, the grape growers and the union—leaders and rank and file—convened in Reuther Hall, a building at Forty Acres, the union's headquarters. The growers signed an agreement to pay out $1.92 per worker per hour. Of that sum, $1.80 went to the worker for wages, $.10 went to the union's health and welfare fund, and $.02 went to fund union service centers. The strikers returned to work—and not a moment too soon. Chavez estimated a majority of them had lost their houses and cars due to inability to keep up with the payments during the strike.[5]

During the 1970s, Chavez continued to help organize different sectors of agribusiness, moving from grape workers to lettuce workers. He kept up the rivalry with the Teamsters, and for all it sounds like a wasteful competition between unions, the competition did the workers some good, for the UFW spurred the Teamsters to improve the representation it offered.[6] Chavez also continued to counter the threat of agribusiness exploiting illegal immigrants to save themselves money and to break strikes.

When the Delano strike ended, author John Gregory Dunne considered it a hollow victory. Citing Saul Alinsky, Dunne argued that mechanization would eventually render farmworkers obsolete.[7] Actually, agribusiness turned to mechanization only when it was economically profitable to do so, meaning only when human labor cost more than machines. Throughout the 1970s and 1980s, labor remained cheaper than machines. The economic situation in Mexico worsened. It was harder to find jobs there, and the cost of living escalated. More Mexicans took the risks of crossing the border into the United States. An underground bracero program developed whereby contractors promised to escort illegal immigrants safely past the border patrol and the desert, charging dearly for their services and not always delivering. Because they usually got their fee before they had given the immigrants any help at all, the escorts had no hesitation about abandoning them when the border patrol turned up or the going got rough in the desert. If the illegal immigrants got to the workplace, they found the same conditions Chavez had faced in his youth: periods of unemployment alternating with periods during which children who would have been thrown out of a factory or a fast-food restaurant did exhausting work for long hours under unhealthy conditions for little pay. The one difference was that if these people tried to form a union, their employers could report them as illegal immigrants and have them deported.

Chavez attacked the problems illegal immigration posed for union organizers on two fronts. He lobbied Washington for protection. His idea of protection took the form of fines and other sanctions to be levied against employers who knowingly hired illegal immigrants. After all, he reasoned, the workers could not really steal union jobs; it was the employers who were giving them away. The only punishment he advocated for illegal immigrants was for those who scabbed, accepting work at an agribusiness against which a union was conducting a strike. Chavez also worked closely with Mexican union leaders to convince Mexican workers not to scab.

This, though, was not enough. During the early 1970s, the UFW faced opposition to its policy on two fronts. Agribusiness had learned from the grape strike that it was important to have consumers on one's side. They tried to pry apart the UFW and the consumers by pointing out at every opportunity that higher wages for farmworkers would translate into higher prices at supermarkets. They complained that because consumers wanted low prices, growers were forced to pay low wages, and the only people who would work for low wages were immigrants. Agribusiness benefited from the peculiar situation of agriculture in federal labor law. Most unions were organized under the regulations of the 1935 National Labor Relations Act and the body of labor law that had grown up after it. Agriculture had been specifically exempted from that legislation. In some ways, that exemption was a help, because Chavez was not obliged to obey the codes governing boycotts embodied in those laws. In the case of preventing agribusiness from hiring illegal workers, though, exclusion from the labor laws was a disadvantage.

The second source of opposition was the Hispanic community, which was far larger than the southwestern Mexican-American farmworkers Chavez had grown up with. Under the leadership of Hispanic scholars, politicians, and activists, Hispanics developed a Hispanic identity rather than a working-class, let alone a farmworker, identity. This led them to sympathize with the many Hispanics denied the privilege of immigration rather than with the few Hispanics in agriculture hurt by job competition and scabbing. Hispanic leaders accused Chavez of opposing the interests of his own ethnic group.

The most serious incident occurred in Chavez's hometown of Yuma. In September 1974, the UFW led citrus-fruit pickers out on strike. The citrus growers recruited south of the border and persuaded Mexicans to risk illegal entry into the United States with promises of work. The UFW complained to the INS about the illegal immigration, hoping to get rid of the scabs. Instead, on September 16, the FBI arrested 25 Mexican-born union members, although none of them were in the country illegally, charging them with disturbing the peace in the course of the strike. Failing to get satisfaction from federal authorities, the UFW took matters into its own hands. Finding that many of the scabs were getting into the United States by crossing the line between the Mexican state of Sonora and the Organ Pipe National Park in Arizona, UFW members posted themselves there to turn back the scabs. Even attorneys who did not support the strikers said there was nothing illegal about the union's border patrol, but it was a direct challenge to federal authorities, who retaliated by harassing union members. Some union members turned out to be Mexican citizens with "green cards," or permits to work in the United States. Thus, the Mexican government got involved, the U.S. government grew more impatient with the UFW, and Hispanic activists became more angry that Chavez favored the union over *la raza* (the people).

Chavez argued that only with the union would the people stand a chance of a better life. He continued his strategy of advocating government support of farmworker unions. With the U.S. government, Chavez was moderately successful. The 1986 Immigration Reform and Control Act incorporated some proposals he favored. The law provided for employer sanctions for those knowingly hiring illegal immigrants. It also had provisions for an amnesty for undocumented immigrants already in the United States, which took away the threat of deportation that employers had been able to use to exploit illegals. However, the law created new problems. It had a provision reviving the bracero concept of permitting additional Mexican workers to enter the United States in the event of certified labor shortages, and Chavez knew from experience how easy it was for a grower to get government authorities to certify a labor shortage. The sanctions against illegal immigrants threatened a backlash, with employers refusing to hire anyone who appeared to be Mexican, even American-born Hispanics like Chavez.

With the Mexican government, Chavez was more successful, at least in the 1980s. On April 23, 1990, he signed an agreement with Mexican president Salinas de Gortari to the effect that Mexican citizens who were residents of the United States and members of the UFW (or members of families of UFW members) could qualify for Mexican social security benefits. Chavez also worked to make the Mexican postal system more secure so that Mexicans could mail remittances home to their families with greater confidence the money would actually get there. Chavez continued to work closely with Mexican labor unions to prevent scabbing and to spread the idea of the benefits of unionization.

Many of these gains were thrown into jeopardy by the North American Free Trade Agreement (NAFTA), which became a topic of discussion in the late 1980s and a fact in 1993. NAFTA permitted a greater flow of goods between Mexico, the United States, and Canada. Specifically, it permitted a greater flow of Mexican agricultural products to reach the United States. Unless Mexican labor leaders organized the farmworkers in their own country, it would not matter what Chavez did for farmworkers in America; buyers would just purchase cheaper Mexican products for American supermarkets and American consumers.

Chavez's analysis of the relationship between migration and labor made him a Mexican American in a unique sense of the phrase. He was, most simply, an American of Mexican descent, one of the few to become accepted as a popular American hero. From his Mexican-American experience, he drew a lesson that is important for all workers of whatever ethnic background. He knew firsthand that not everyone who crosses the border and gets a job in the United States automatically moves to a better life; ethnic and racial discrimination and the universal tendency to deny workers their due must be fought in the United States as well as elsewhere. His experience as a union organizer taught him that the problem of fairness to labor was bigger than just that of immigrants coming to compete for American jobs. It reached across national boundaries to include labor elsewhere. The fact that American buyers could import Mexican produce for American supermarkets meant that Mexican workers could stay home in Mexico and still compete for American jobs. Finally, justice was not something farmworkers—or perhaps any laborers—could win entirely by their own efforts. Immigrants didn't steal jobs so much as employers gave them away, with the tacit consent of consumers who preferred bargain prices to social justice. Thus, Chavez became a Mexican American in the sense of one who identified with workers on both the Mexican and the American sides of the border and worked with governments on both sides of the border.

Chavez did not live to see the full impact of NAFTA. In April 1993, Chavez was in San Luis, Arizona, to testify in a court case involving the union. There he died unexpectedly, most likely of complications resulting from a six-day fast he had just broken, during the night of April 22–23.

NOTES

1. Jacques E. Levy, *Cesar Chavez: Autobiography of La Causa* (New York: W. W. Norton, 1975), p. 37.

2. Ibid., p. 51.

3. Ibid., p. 89.

4. Ibid., p. 185.

5. Richard Griswold Del Castillo and Richard A. Garcia, *César Chávez: A Triumph of Spirit*, Oklahoma Western Biographies Series (Norman: University of Oklahoma Press, 1995), p. 94.

6. Burnham Holmes, *Cesar Chavez: Farm Worker Activist*, with an introduction by James P. Shenton; American Troublemakers Series (Austin, TX: Raintree Steck-Vaughn Publishers, 1994).

7. John Gregory Dunne, *Delano*, rev. and updated (New York: Farrar, Straus and Giroux, 1971), p. 170.

BIBLIOGRAPHY

The papers of the United Farm Workers are on deposit at Michigan's Wayne State University, which maintains an extensive labor archive. A spate of monographs appeared in the wake of Chavez's organizing activities in the late 1960s and early 1970s. These include John Gregory Dunne, *Delano*, rev. and updated (New York: Farrar, Straus and Giroux, 1971); a photographic essay by Paul Fusco and George D. Horowitz, *La Causa: The California Grape Strike* (New York: Collier Books, 1970); and Peter Matthiessen, *Sal Si Puedes: Cesar Chavez and the New American Revolution* (New York: Delta, 1969). Two written from the perspective of Catholic social teaching and Christian nonviolence are Mark Day, O.F.M., *Forty Acres: Cesar Chavez and the Farm Workers* (New York: Praeger Publishers, 1971); and Jean Maddern Pitrone, *Chavez: Man of the Migrants: A Plea for Social Justice*

(Staten Island, NY: Alba House, 1971). Books written somewhat after that period include Ronald B. Taylor, *Chavez and the Farm Workers* (Boston: Beacon Press, 1975); and Jacques E. Levy, *Cesar Chavez: Autobiography of La Causa* (New York: W. W. Norton, 1975). More biographies and monographs appeared after Chavez's death, including Richard Griswold Del Castillo and Richard A. Garcia, *César Chávez: A Triumph of Spirit*, Oklahoma Western Biographies Series (Norman: University of Oklahoma Press, 1995); and Susan Ferriss and Ricardo Sandoval, *The Fight in the Fields: Cesar Chavez and the Farmworkers Movement*, ed. Diana Hembree, with a foreword by Gary Soto (Orlando, FL: Harcourt Brace Jovanovich [Paradigm Productions], 1997); the latter is the companion to a documentary videotape. Chavez has also inspired numerous biographies aimed at young adults, some of them quite full of information. Among these are Burnham Holmes, *Cesar Chavez: Farm Worker Activist*, with an introduction by James P. Shenton, American Troublemakers Series (Austin, TX: Raintree Steck-Vaughn Publishers, 1994); Consuelo Rodrigues, *Cesar Chavez*, Hispanics of Achievement (New York: Chelsea House, 1991); and James Terzian and Kathryn Cramer, *Mighty Hard Road: The Story of Cesar Chavez* (Garden City, NY: Doubleday [Signal Books], 1970). Dana Catharine de Ruiz and Richard Larios, *La Causa: The Migrant Farmworkers' Story*, Stories of America Series (Austin, TX: Raintree Steck-Vaughn Publishers, 1993), takes a broader view of the process of organizing migrant farm laborers.

ALAN K. SIMPSON
(1931–)

"There Can Be No Perfect Immigrant Reform Bill"

"Folksy and witty, Alan Simpson was once lauded as the Senate's Will Rogers," *Newsweek* columnist Eleanor Clift observed. Then he changed. Simpson himself identified at least one reason for that change. Maneuvering two major reforms of immigration law from bill to signed legislation in a four-year period was like "giving dry birth to a porcupine."[1] His work on immigration law revealed Simpson as a more complex man than his colleagues had first thought. In turn, Simpson helped to make Americans realize that immigration law was inherently more complex than a focus on any one argument for or against immigration.

Simpson was not one to be easily frustrated by political processes. His family long provided political leadership to Wyoming. One great-grandfather, Finn Burnett, advised a Shoshone chief. Another, John Simpson, founded the first store and post office in the vicinity of Jackson, Wyoming. His father, Milward Lee Simpson, was governor of the state from 1955 to 1959 and senator from 1962 to 1967. His older brother Peter was in the state legislature from 1980 to 1984 and an unsuccessful candidate for governor in 1986.

Alan Kooi Simpson (the middle name was the maiden name of his mother, Lorna) was born on September 2, 1931, and grew up in Cody,

---

Alan K. Simpson (*left*), Romano Mazzoli (*center*), and Congressional Representative William F. Smith (*right*) ca. 1987. Center for Migration Studies.

Wyoming. He attended the public schools, graduating from Cody High School in 1949 and the University of Wyoming in 1954. Upon graduation, he married Ann Scholl, who had already started a career in real estate. He spent from 1954 to 1956 in the United States Army with the Fifth Infantry Division and Second Armored Division, part of the occupation forces of post–World War II Germany. He graduated from the University of Wyoming's Law School in 1958 and opened a law practice that he maintained until 1978. Besides practicing law, he moved ahead in ever-widening political circles. In 1959 he was appointed assistant attorney general for Wyoming and later city attorney for Cody. In 1964, despite Lyndon Johnson's Democratic coattails, the young Republican won election to the state legislature. By 1975, he was the majority floor leader, by 1977, the speaker pro tempore of the House. The next year Wyoming senator Clifford P. Hansen retired, and Simpson defeated other Republicans in the primary and then his Democratic opponent in order to succeed Hansen. He won reelection in 1984 and 1990. Senate Republicans elected him whip in 1985.

Wyoming became a state in 1869, when the Republicans dominated national politics. The early Simpsons allied with that party, and Alan maintained that allegiance. As new issues came up, he helped to formulate Republican policy on them. An example is his work on land-use laws while in the Wyoming state legislature. Since **Theodore Roosevelt**, the Republicans have had a reputation for seeing the environment as part of the whole of human society. It was important for humans to preserve the natural environment, but that could be done only by considering social needs, economic demands, and what was politically possible. Simpson continued that tradition while in the state legislature. During the 1960s and early 1970s, colleagues, entrepreneurs, and conservationists respected Simpson's work on Wyoming land-use laws.

A different example of how Simpson helped to form contemporary Republican policy was abortion. During his high school days, Simpson knew schoolmates who endured illegal abortions in Wyoming or who spent a great deal of money to go to the state of Washington, where abortion was legal.[2] By the time Simpson became a lawyer, abortion was an important issue in other states, although it does not seem to have been significant for his work in Wyoming. In 1973, the Supreme Court made a decision, *Roe v. Wade*, binding on all fifty states. *Roe v. Wade* ruled that during the first three months of a woman's pregnancy, an abortion was a matter between her and her physician. Simpson agreed with *Roe v. Wade* and carried that opinion with him into national politics.

The Republicans offered mixed guidance regarding immigration. An immigration policy with a minimum of rules and regulations was consistent with some Republicans' idea that government ought to govern as lightly as possible. For business-oriented Republicans, high immigration was desirable because it created a steady stream of labor, improving the employers' chances of hiring people they wanted and keeping wages low. On the other hand, there were some ways in which immigration might be bad for business. It might cost money to take care of the immigrants in the U.S. population, in which case taxes went up. Immigrants might bring subversive, anticapitalist ideas into the United States. There were also some Republicans who put other considerations ahead of business and argued that too many people of different racial backgrounds and different cultures were entering the United States; the Republican tradition included advocacy of the restrictive national quotas of the 1920s. Simpson had to decide what elements of the Republican past he wished to use to develop new immigration laws.

By the time Simpson entered the federal legislature, the 1965 law had come under heavy criticism. One argument backers of the 1965 law used to convince colleagues to vote for it was that the law itself had no effect on immigration rates, because there were few reasons for people to leave their homelands and to seek their fortunes in the United States. They were unrealistically optimistic. In 1969, the United States commenced a period of budget deficits, annually spending more than it took in via taxes. To cover these deficits, the U.S. government borrowed money. Having such a powerful competitor for loans exerted inflationary pressure on U.S. interest rates. Given that U.S. banks lent to the world, inflation soon affected the global economy. In the early 1970s, Richard Nixon altered U.S. Cold War policy, achieving agreements with the Union of Soviet Socialist Republics (USSR) and the People's Republic of China (PRC). When it was no longer necessary to build a grand alliance of many nations opposed to communism, Nixon ceased to attend to certain allies and to provide economic support. Nixon's neglect caused developing nations' economies to slow down even further. At the same time, the new Cold War policy meant that the United States concentrated on relations with the two other major atomic powers, the USSR and PRC, and delegated to medium-sized nations the work of neutralizing local radicals. Countries such as Argentina and Chile entered periods of repression. Finally, the new Cold War policy meant the United States had to withdraw from Vietnam, because its presence there was threatening to the PRC, which in turn meant that by 1975 communist forces in Vietnam dominated the entire country and refugees tried to escape to safer places. Altogether, after 1965, economic decline and political disaster meant that many more people now wanted to migrate to the United States.

The 1965 law may not have created the conditions for migration, but once people wanted to migrate, it did create the conditions that let them into the United States. Since the 1920s, U.S. law permitted legal residents of the United States to sponsor their spouses and their offspring for migration without regard to whether such migration raised total migration above the annual limit. The 1965 law expanded the family reunification program.

In theory, if the United States admitted X number of immigrants in one year, five years later, when those immigrants were sworn in as citizens, the United States would admit not only X, the total number permitted by law, but X^1, a number equal to X and representing the spouses of the new citizens admitted five years earlier, and Y, a number of unknown quantity representing the new citizens' offspring. Family reunification outside of the annual limits drove up the total number. The 1965 law also permitted U.S. citizens to sponsor more distant relatives. These relatives also had to comply with the annual ceiling requirements, so their admission did not swell annual totals above those ceilings. But once admitted and once sworn in as citizens, they brought their spouses and children, thus adding to the extralimit admissions. Soon potential immigrants were complaining it was impossible to get an immigration visa unless one already had a close family member—usually a post-1965 immigrant—already in the United States.

Further issues arose over illegal immigration. In 1964, the United States terminated its bracero agreement with Mexico, intending to replace the ad hoc agreements with laws. The 1965 law introduced the first legal limits on migration from the Western Hemisphere. Some people already had established the pattern of living in Mexico but traveling through the United States in search of seasonal labor. These people had to weigh the fact that what they had been used to doing was now illegal against the fact that this was the only way they had to make a living. As the economies of Spanish-speaking Western Hemisphere countries worsened, more people chose to break U.S. law.

In 1978, Congress mandated the appointment of a sixteen-member Select Commission on Immigration and Refugee Policy (SCIRP) to gather facts and to make recommendations regarding U.S. immigration policy. When he first arrived in Congress in January 1979, Simpson received appointment to the Senate Judiciary Committee, its subcommittee on immigration and to SCIRP. Originally, President Jimmy Carter appointed Reubin D. Askew, a Florida attorney and politician, to chair the committee. The Rev. Theodore Hesburgh, C.S.C., then president of Notre Dame University and long active in federal-level public service, replaced Askew. President Carter appointed three other citizen-members, drawn from the different ethnic groups affected by immigration law, from the legal profession, and from labor. Four cabinet members whose portfolios were affected by immigration also served ex officia: the secretary of state, the attorney general, the secretary of labor, and the secretary of health, education and welfare. The Speaker of the House appointed four members. Robert McClory (Republican–Illinois) was the ranking, or senior, member of the minority, or Republican, party on the House Judiciary Committee. McClory helped to represent Republican interests and also the interests of a state that received numerous immigrants. The three other representatives were Hamilton Fish, Jr., (Republican–New York), Elizabeth Holtzman (Democrat–New York), and Peter W. Rodino, Jr. (Democrat–New Jersey). All had been on the House's immigration subcommittee, and Holtzman was the House sponsor of an important refugee bill. The president pro tem of the Senate also appointed four people. **Edward M. Kennedy** (Democrat–Massachusetts) had been in the Senate since 1962 and had already been influential in immigration legislation. Charles McC. Mathias, Jr. (Republican–Maryland), had been in the Senate since 1969, and Dennis DeConcini (Democrat–Arizona) since 1977. When Zero Population Growth prepared a flyer to introduce the SCIRP to its members, all it could think of to put next to a photograph of Alan Simpson was "new member of Senate in 1979, a state representative in Wyoming from 1964 to 1978."

While the SCIRP held hearings, studied data, and formulated proposals, the executive branch of the U.S. government changed hands. In 1980, Ronald Reagan was elected president. Reagan was reelected in 1984 and continued to hold office until 1989. Not only was Reagan a Republican, but although born in Illinois, he was a longtime resident of California and had served as governor of that state. His vice president, George H. W. Bush, had roots in Connecticut (which state his father served as senator) and a vacation home in Kennebunkport, Maine, but resided in Texas. Western Republicans were doing well. The Republicans held a majority in the Senate, so that instead of being a young senator in the minority party, Simpson found himself warming Senator Edward M. Kennedy's former chair as the head of the subcommittee on immigration. In 1981, Simpson took responsibility for turning SCIRP findings into legislation.

During 1982 and 1983, Simpson looked for the narrowest possible issue on which to focus, to get the widest possible congressional support for action. He settled on the issue of undocumented immigrants. Even that issue had possibilities for conflict as one might be able to tell from the varied names for them; they were also called illegal immigrants. Undocumented immigrants were those who had not been admitted to the United States as immigrants. About half of them were admitted in some other capacity, as tourists or students. The half that really grabbed the public imagination, though, were those that intended to enter the United States with no visa of any kind, such as people crossing the border under cover of darkness or stowing away on ships. Punishing these people for illegal entry was not a straightforward matter. First, the United States hadn't enforced such laws for years and might not even have enough personnel in the Border Patrol and Coast Guard to do it properly. Second, in cases involving undocumented immigrants who worked, the immigrants weren't the only culprits. The people who hired them broke even more laws. They failed to provide Social Security, unemployment, worker's compensation, or even, in some cases, the minimum wages, maximum hours, and right to unionize guaranteed in U.S. law. Third, the public image of the undocumented alien was of Spanish-speaking people. The Hispanic Caucus in Congress raised the question of whether employers would refuse to hire any Hispanics for fear of hiring undocumented ones.

Sticking to the narrow agreement that something ought to be done "about" (not necessarily "for" or "against") undocumented aliens, Simpson proposed a three-point plan. The Carter administration that had formed the SCIRP had also drafted a proposed immigration bill. The bill proposed granting amnesty, or freedom from prosecution, for undocumented aliens already in the United States by a specific date, the date to be determined when the law was passed. Undocumented immigrants coming after that date were subject to penalties, usually deportation. To prevent undocumented aliens from getting jobs and to prevent employers from taking advantage of their workers, employers were forbidden to knowingly hire undocumented workers. To prevent the employers from discriminating against foreign-looking people, Simpson proposed a national, forgery-proof worker's identification card, which all Americans, citizens by birth or by choice, presented when seeking employment.

Simpson spoke in support of wiping the slate clean for past undocumented workers and then starting a more stringent policy. As he explained to the Senate:

Illegal immigration continues to depress wages and working conditions for American workers, especially low-income, low-skilled Americans who are most likely to face direct competition. Illegal immigrants continue to remain a fearful, exploitable subclass in American society, and I believe that widespread flouting of our Nation's immigration laws still leads to a disrespect for our laws and institutions in general.[3]

Simpson realized he was asking for compromise and that some of his colleagues desperately wanted to go home to their constituents able to claim they had adhered to their original positions. Simpson warned such colleagues that steadfastness could also be interpreted as stubbornness. "This will be the test: Is U.S. politics increasingly controlled by narrow and wholly selfish special interests rather than being representative of the broad public will?"

The narrowest possible basis for agreement turned out to be too broad. The proposal for a national identification card bought into the debate on immigration a new voice, that of civil libertarians. They wanted the government to be as small and unobtrusive as humanly possible. Forgery-proof right-to-work cards issued by the federal government did not fit with their vision. Ethnic political leaders dismissed the idea that the national identification cards would prevent hiring discrimination.

Nonetheless, Simpson got the bill through the Senate in 1982. The bill's cosponsor, **Romano Mazzoli** (Republican–Kentucky) was unable to get it through the House. In January 1983, the Congress elected in November 1982 sat. Simpson got the immigration bill through the Senate again, but

Mazzoli still couldn't get it through the House. House Speaker Thomas ("Tip") O'Neill managed to avoid giving any reason for the delay until October, then said he didn't think President Reagan would sign the bill. Simpson was the one who convinced O'Neill that the bill had administrative support. O'Neill then scheduled the bill for debate, but for 1984. By the time debate started, House members wanted to go home and start their biennial campaigns.

When the new Congress sat in 1985, Simpson picked up an important House ally in Representative Peter Rodino (Republican–New Jersey). Rodino did not support the Simpson-Mazzoli bill because one version eliminated the fifth level of family reunification preferences, the one permitting U.S. citizens to sponsor siblings. Simpson himself thought the elimination of the sibling preference reasonable. One could easily see the economic and emotional ties between immigrants and their spouses, children, and aging parents, but brothers and sisters were another matter. Also, eliminating the sibling preference was a crucial step in breaking the chains of family migration that filled the ranks of those admitted under the quotas and added to the numbers admitted outside quotas. However, Simpson compromised and restored the sibling preference. In return, he made a solid ally with the ability to advance the legislation through the House.

Simpson also compromised on another matter. He dropped his request that the federal government issue forgery-proof identification cards to people eligible to work in the United States. He accepted a proposal that employers determine legal status using documents governments already issued. Issuing national worker-identification cards might have been a straightforward way to solve the problem, but if it didn't seem so straightforward to others, Simpson was willing to try to see their viewpoint and to modify his own.

Most important, Simpson provided philosophical support for his modifications. He reminded the Senate, "There can be no perfect immigration reform bill."[4] He worked to balance competing special interests in the hope that everyone would agree the final result was in the national interest. And he and Mazzoli got the bill through the House, through the Senate, across President Reagan's desk, and into law as the Immigration Reform and Control Act (IRCA) of 1986. Simpson's colleagues told the press, "Everyone loves the guy."[5] Simpson basked in public approval as a competent, effective senator with a down-to-earth brand of humor and a willingness to work with his colleagues toward a common good. Storm clouds, though, were already gathering.

One of the checks and balances in the Constitution is that presidential nominations to the Supreme Court are subject to Senate approval. Reagan had campaigned on the argument that the Supreme Court was too "liberal" and promised to appoint justices who were more "conservative," especially on the issue of abortion. Charging that Reagan was politicizing the Supreme Court, Democrats on the Senate Judiciary Committee politicized the approval process as well. The stage was set for a series of confrontations between liberal Democrats and conservative Republicans. Simpson was ranked as one of the most conservative Republicans around when it came to economic issues but not abortion.[6]

In 1987 Chief Justice Warren Burger retired. Reagan nominated Associate Justice William Rehnquist for a promotion. Although Rehnquist was already on the Court, Judiciary Committee Democrats made him spend a long time in nomination hearings in order to air their ideological differences with Reagan. After the Senate confirmed Rehnquist for the Chief Justice position, Reagan nominated Antonin Scalia to replace Rehnquist as Associate. As liberal opposition to Scalia hardened, Simpson let his colleagues know he had had enough ideological fighting: "Three sitting members, though, of this United States Senate, right now, voted against the sweeping Civil Rights Act of 1964. Do we keep score on them? Do we let them know we will never forgive? They changed, they listened, they adopted, they adapted, and they learned. Don't others get the leeway in this particular arena?"[7]

Simpson did not confine his criticism to liberal Democrats. The National Organization for Women (NOW) was dedicated to allowing women the widest possible leeway in deciding for or against abortions for themselves. Molly Yard and Eleanor Smeal, president and president emeritus, respectively, of NOW, complained that the Supreme Court was being loaded with people who did not support their viewpoint. Simpson, whose position on abortion was similar to theirs, told them not to push their own interests to the exclusion of other considerations.[8]

Besides the carping over Supreme Court nominations, there were other causes for criticism. For example, people who had favored the 1965 law began to see disadvantages in that law and to argue that new laws should remedy their situation. IRCA created a program that made available 5,000 visas a year for two years to people who could not get visas under the regular national ceilings because those visas had already gone to people who could meet family reunification requirements. The program had been inspired by the Irish, who felt as though they were at a special disadvantage under the new system. (Irish immigration had been at a low point for the generation before the passage of the 1965 reforms; when it picked up again in the 1980s, the Irish were unable to get visas because they were squeezed out by other potential immigrants favored by various family reunification programs.) Representative Brian Donnelly, backed by Senator Edward M. Kennedy, had developed a pilot program that they now wanted to continue past its two-year trial period.[9]

Similarly, people who previously used braceros complained that after 1965 it was difficult to find workers. Accordingly, IRCA had a special program for legalizing undocumented aliens who were Special Agricultural

Workers (SAWs). Three million people applied for legalization. Even people who didn't complain much about immigrants complained about fraud in the SAW legalization program.

Employers checking documents had a number of problems with IRCA. Native Americans did not carry documents that the law specified they needed to prove they were eligible for jobs.[10] Along with illegal immigrants there sprung up an illegal business forging documents. Employers didn't have to verify the documents, merely to prove that they had seen them, and so had no real incentive to turn down job applicants whose documents weren't too obviously forged. IRCA did nothing about the political and economic conditions that compelled Hispanics and Asians to migrate, and events after IRCA's passage seemed conducive to more immigrants. In 1989, the Berlin Wall fell and former Soviet satellites slipped from their orbits. With freer governments, migration from eastern Europe increased. In 1991, the Soviet Union collapsed. Migration became a strategy for coping with the new Russia's social and economic insecurity.

In 1988, Simpson girded himself to revisit the field of immigration. He made another significant alliance. He worked with Senator Ted Kennedy. Kennedy was allied with the opposite ideological camp, he was a member of the opposite party, and he came from the opposite part of the country. However, he and Simpson shared a similar approach to politics. Simpson praised Kennedy's trustworthiness. When Kennedy said he would support a colleague, he indeed extended support. When it was time to negotiate, he listed the issues on which he couldn't compromise and cooperatively conceded the rest. For his part, Kennedy acknowledged, "We do not always vote together, but we have learned to work well together, especially in this area of . . . immigration matters."[11]

Simpson and Kennedy got a bill through the Senate in 1988, but the House delayed consideration until the bill died for lack of action. In 1989, Kennedy and Simpson again got a proposal through the Senate, only to have the House again delay. House members who had constituents who wanted the law passed were hamstrung by other members who had constituents who did not want the law passed. The House's window of opportunity came in November 1990. The 1990 elections were over—and with them the danger of being voted out of office by dissatisfied constituents. The 1992 elections were still too far away to worry about. The House hurriedly passed the bill, and it became law on November 29, 1990.

The bill Simpson and Kennedy sponsored increased the total number of immigrants to 700,000 per year for the years 1992–1994. In 1994, the level decreased to 675,000. The 675,000 slots were divided in a new way: 480,000 people were to be admitted in order to reunite them with their families, 140,000 were to be admitted on the basis of their contributions to the economy, and 55,000 were to be admitted on a point basis.

It was hardest to alter the distribution of the family reunification visas.

Simpson still wanted to reduce the number of people admitted as siblings of U.S. citizens, but Asians, especially, found chain migration useful for rescuing family members from persecution and poverty. The bill was able to divide the 140,000 visas given on the basis of economic contribution into different categories, including a new one for immigrants who invested $1 million in the U.S. economy and created ten jobs. The remaining 55,000 visas were available through application. Each application was awarded points according to the candidate's education level and job skills. The visas went to the candidates receiving the highest scores.

Like IRCA, the 1990 law was a compromise, addressing the most pressing questions while leaving enough unsolved issues to guarantee future legislation. The problem with that approach was that each time the subject of immigration came up, the lines were more firmly drawn, it took more effort to achieve compromise, and Simpson himself had to give more and more to see any results at all. The 1990 law had been set to operate for five years. Thus, immigration came up again in 1995, at which point, new developments complicated discussion of the subject. As part of its efforts to balance the budget, the government was seeking to cut spending and was taking a hard look at spending for welfare benefits. It was possible to trim the budget by denying benefits to legal immigrants, but it might not save enough to justify the economic and political cost of doing so. To this discussion was appended discussion on other questions related to immigrant use of public services, particularly those used by illegal immigrants. Aso, 1996 was an election year. The Democratic nominee, Bill Clinton, had been elected president in 1992, but the Republicans thought he could be ousted from office as he had ousted George Bush.

When consideration of a new immigration bill began, Simpson hoped to make the discussion as comprehensive as possible, so the bill included sections on both legal and illegal immigration, but the two issues had to be divided into two separate bills before the rest of the Senate would agree to proceed. Because Simpson had thought the majority of people were concerned about immigrant competition with natives for jobs, the original proposal for curbing illegal immigration included a revamping of the procedure whereby employers established whether job applicants were eligible to work in the United States. It turned out that there was also a widespread perception among employers that it was unfair to expect business to act as police and to check into job applicant eligibility. The proposal got nowhere until Simpson agreed to remove language that would make it difficult for employers to offer positions to job candidates abroad without violating legislation regarding illegal immigration.[12]

The bill reached a vote in the House first, where it was accepted only after significant modification. The majority of representatives voted to permit individual states to deny access to public schools to the children of illegal immigrants. The House agreed business should not be asked to assume the work of the police; instead of mandatory changes in the employee verification program, they voted only for a voluntary pilot program. On the other hand, the House did not want to give entrepreneurs an endless supply of inexpensive labor; it rejected an amendment to grant temporary work visas to a maximum of 250,000 foreign farmworkers.[13]

When the bill went to the Senate floor, Simpson's colleague on the 1990 law, Ted Kennedy, announced he would vote against it because of its welfare provisions: It would have denied legal immigrants access to Medicaid and to college grants and loans.[14] Senator Spencer Abraham from Michigan, Simpson's Republican colleague, also opposed the bill, mostly on the grounds that it would limit family reunification.[15] Senate Majority Leader Robert Dole, who was hoping to secure the Republican presidential nomination for himself, complained the Democrats were trying to force votes on the bill just to embarrass the Republicans, and he pulled the bill from the floor.[16] When Dole rereleased the bill, the senators modified it, eliminating Simpson's plan to reduce overall immigration by suspending some categories of relatives that could be sponsored by legal residents.[17] Simpson accepted the loss and stayed out of the intraparty fight that followed. House Republicans wanted to deny the children of illegal immigrants access to public schools. Dole was willing to go along with the House Republicans, but another Senate Republican leader, Henry Hyde of Illinois, opposed both Senate and House Republicans.[18] The Republicans eventually agreed not to follow the House on the school issue and to leave most questions of immigrants and welfare to the welfare reform law. New immigration legislation was approved and signed on September 30, 1996.[19] At first, it seemed the August 22 law reforming welfare would be as significant as that reforming immigration; it reinforced the standing law to the effect that illegal immigrants were ineligible for most benefits, it made immigrants ineligible for some of them, and it imposed a time limit on refugees' eligibility.[20] However, legal immigrants' access to particular welfare benefits, such as food stamps, was restored early in 1997.

This was Simpson's last immigration law. Events were already eroding his power in the Senate and changing the political environment in which he had done his best work. Almost immediately upon getting the 1990 law through Congress, Simpson had returned to the work of the Supreme Court. Thurgood Marshall retired from the Supreme Court in 1991. President Bush, who in 1988 had been elected to succeed Reagan, nominated Clarence Thomas to succeed Marshall. As a member of the Judiciary Committee, Simpson had to be on hand for the hearings. As in the Rehnquist and Scalia hearings, there were some ideological differences between the conservative Thomas and liberals in the Senate. This, time, though, it wasn't the confrontation between liberals and conservatives that shaped the hearings. National Public Radio reporter Nina Totenberg broke the story that one of Thomas's former coworkers, a lawyer and law professor named Anita Hill, had given the Judiciary Committee material that she said proved that in his office Thomas created a highly sexualized climate that demeaned women. The Judiciary Committee called on Hill to testify, then approved Thomas's nomination despite her testimony.

Simpson came in for criticism because he claimed he had evidence that Hill wasn't a credible witness but then failed to produce it. Simpson's reputation as a genial senator willing to cooperate to get legislation passed dissipated. Newspaper columnists offered amateur psychoanalyses, remarking pointedly on the use of humor as a mask for anger.[21] The press stopped praising Simpson's wit and began to comment on how often he denounced the media. Profiles and character sketches of Simpson written years after the event were careful to include his more famous criticisms: how when in 1986 the press condemned Reagan for his participation in the Iran-Contra affair, Simpson complained that the press was trying to "stick it" to Reagan in the "gazoo"; or how when in 1991 television reporter Peter Arnett criticized President Bush's conduct of Desert Storm, Simpson made unsubstantiated charges that Arnett's Vietnamese brother-in-law had worked for the Viet Cong.

Simpson was also hurt by the changing political climate within the Republican Party. Throughout the 1980s, Simpson was not quite a Reagan Republican. Reagan did little to restrict abortions but supported restriction vocally; Simpson thought abortion was for the woman involved to decide. Reagan raised the Veteran's Administration to cabinet status. Simpson faulted veterans for looking out for their own interests at the expense of other groups. In the Wyoming legislature, Simpson had worked with different groups to forge land-use laws. Reagan Republicans backed the entrepreneurs who wanted to use natural resources and ridiculed environmentalists as Luddites who thought that plants and animals were the equals of human beings.

The situation worsened as Bush succeeded Reagan and then, in 1992, Bill Clinton succeeded Bush. Off-year elections usually favor the party that doesn't control the presidency, so it wasn't unusual that when the Democrat Clinton was elected president, the Republicans would pick up a few seats in Congress in the next biennial election. However, in 1994 Republicans gained enough seats to get a majority in the House. These were not Simpson's Republicans, though. Although he and they claimed to be conservatives, they defined conservatism differently. Simpson's conservatism was of a kind traditional to the Republican Party nationally in that it tended to favor the capitalist system and traditional to the Republican in the West in that it tended to favor small government and wide scope for individual action. Younger conservatives were also conservative in the moral realm, especially about abortion. Simpson's younger colleagues also disagreed with Simpson's leadership style and methods. Trent Lott, a young Mississippi Republican, ran against Simpson for the post of Senate whip and won. For his part, Simpson explained his differences with the young conservative Republicans to an interviewer in 1996, after he announced he would not stand for reelection that fall. The new Republicans, Simpson said, did not understand how to "compromise an issue without compromising yourself."[22]

When Simpson retired from the Senate, he left a substantial record of immigration law, but the debate over immigration remained very much alive. In 1987, Simpson sponsored a law that granted amnesty to illegal immigrants; the 1996 law tossed out that precedent and required illegals seeking to legalize to go home and reimmigrate (a requirement subsequently modified). His predecessors drafted laws that emphasized racial hegemony or family reunification; he divided his legislative priorities among families, jobs, refugees, and answering the claims of various groups that the new immigration laws placed them at a disadvantage. Altogether, Simpson's was a record of compromise.

Perhaps Simpson developed his record because he had to. His successor, Trent Lott, came into office as Senate Majority Leader allied with the more unbending Republicans and then, like Simpson, developed a reputation for crafting legislative deals. However, Simpson's rhetoric elevated compromise from a strategy to a principle. Politics is an exercise in humility, in the most profound sense of that phrase. To engage in politics is to admit that one's colleagues are different but equal people with viewpoints and priorities that are just as valid as one's own and that must be respected. Among equals, a compromise in which no one gets everything but everyone gets something is an honorable way of collaborating. It wasn't only immigration that admitted of no perfect bill.

NOTES

1. Eleanor Clift, "Taking the Low Road," *Newsweek* (October 28, 1991), p. 30.

2. Claudia Dreifus, "Exit Reasonable Right," *New York Times Magazine* (June 2, 1996), pp. 24–27.

3. *Congressional Digest* 62 (August–September 1983), pp. 214, 216, 218.

4. *Congressional Digest* 65 (March 1986), pp. 86, 88, 90, 92.

5. Douglas A. Harbrecht, "Nice Guys Do Finish First—Just Ask Al Simpson," *Business Week* (November 9, 1987), p. 94.

6. "Employers May Pay If They Hire Illegals," *Business Week* (June 21, 1982), p. 38.

7. "In the Pit," *National Review* (April 10, 1987), p. 80.

8. John Newhouse, "Taking It Personally," New Yorker (March 16, 1992), p. 56ff.

9. "A Deserved Honor for Kennedy," *Irish Voice* 7:39 (September 18, 1993), p. 10.

10. The evidence is purely anecdotal. In 1987, the author had to prove citizen-

ship to be hired for a new job. "May I see your Social Security card, please?" The employment officer set it aside to photocopy for the record. "Now I need a second piece of evidence. May I see your passport?" I had never been outside the United States. "Your driver's license?" Didn't have that, either; this was the era when it was uncommon for students to have cars. "A voter's registration card?" I had discarded the one issued in my old address and hadn't received one for the new address. I was on the verge of being deported to my native Massachusetts. This really *is* a free country.

11. Deborah Levy, "Irish Eyes Are Smiling; Immigration Bill: Who Needs It?" *Legal Times* (April 4, 1988), p. 14.

12. *New York Times*, March 8, 1996, sec. A, p. 20, col. 1.

13. *New York Times*, March 24, 1996, sec. I, p. 47, col. 3.

14. Edward M. Kennedy, "Statement by Sen. Kennedy on the Adoption of the Immigration Act," Congressional Press Release, March 21, 1996. This was provided through the kindness of Senator Edward M. Kennedy's office.

15. "Angst v. Optimism," *The Economist* (May 11, 1996), p. 30.

16. *New York Times*, April 16, 1996, sec. A, p. 1, col. 1.

17. *New York Times*, May 5, 1996, sec. I, p. 42, col. 3.

18. *New York Times*, June 20, 1996, sec. A, p. 16, col. 1; June 20, 1996, sec. I, p. 8, col. 1.

19. *New York Times*, September 24, 1996, sec. A, p. 1, col. 6; October 1, 1996, sec. A, p. 1, col. 6.

20. Joyce C. Vialet and Larry M. Eig, "Alien Eligibility for Benefits under the New Welfare and Immigration Laws," *Migration World* 25:3 (1997), pp. 32–34.

21. Clift, "Taking the Low Road," p. 30.

22. Dreifus, "Exit Reasonable Right," p. 25.

BIBLIOGRAPHY

Simpson has published a specialized memoir focusing on one aspect of his public career, *Right in the Old Gazoo: A Lifetime of Scrapping with the Press* (New York: William Morrow, 1997). As a contemporary public figure, he is well served by directories such as *Who's Who* and *Current Biography* and by the periodical press. The most useful source for quotes from Simpson regarding immigration law are transcripts of Senate speeches that appeared in the *Congressional Digest* 62 (August–September 1983), pp. 214, 216, 218; 65 (March 1986), pp. 86, 88, 90, 92; and 68 (1989), pp. 240, 242, 244. For articles about Simpson, see "Angst v. Optimism," *The Economist* (May 11, 1996), p. 30; Eleanor Clift, "Taking the Low Road," *Newsweek* (October 28, 1991), p. 30; Claudia Dreifus, "Exit Reasonable Right," *New York Times Magazine* (June 2, 1996), pp. 24–27; Douglas A. Harbrecht, "Nice Guys Do Finish First—Just Ask Al Simpson," *Business Week* (November 9, 1987), p. 94; and John Newhouse, "Taking It Personally," *New Yorker* (March 16, 1992), p. 56ff. For analysis of the process of immigration legislation, see Rosanna Peroni, "IRCA Antidiscrimination Provisions: What Went Wrong?" *International Migration Review* 26:3 (Fall 1992), pp. 732–753.

JOHN TANTON
(1934–)

Of Grass and Grassroots

The play on words in the title is deliberate. John Tanton first became interested in immigration questions through a lifelong interest in the natural environment. When he determined that immigration was a significant danger to American natural resources, he also found that there were no mechanisms in the political system for getting his views across and for affecting legislation. Hence, he turned to a grassroots effort combining mass appeal, leadership by a few dedicated individuals, and attempts to influence officials at the highest levels of the federal government.

Tanton's ancestors were immigrants. His father was born in Canada, served in the Canadian Expeditionary Forces in World War I, and graduated from the University of Toronto. He left Canada after the Great Depression, which started with the 1929 crash of the New York Stock Exchange, began to spread around the world, affecting employment, wages, and prices globally. He immigrated to Detroit. Tanton's mother was of Germany ancestry but born and raised in rural Michigan. She had come to Detroit to study for her nursing diploma. Tanton valued a number of aspects of his family life. His parents were moderately religious; his mother had been raised in the Lutheran faith, and the family attended the Evangelical United Brethren Church. His parents encouraged reading. During

John H. Tanton, M.D., photograph courtesy of Dr. Tanton.

his adult life, Tanton thought his own sense of responsibility to the common good came from his family training.

Best of all, his parents gave him a rural upbringing. John was born on February 23, 1934, in Detroit, the first of three children. When he turned eleven, his family relocated to the part of Michigan where his mother had been raised. They took over a failing farm from a maternal uncle and made it succeed, mostly by having every member of the family participate in the hard work. John liked the land, and so when he won a scholarship to Michigan State University, he enrolled in the School of Agriculture with the intention of becoming an agronomist.

However, John had two paternal uncles who were physicians. When he did extremely well in college, he decided that he could learn what was necessary to become a physician, too, and switched to a chemistry major. He received his Bachelor of Arts in 1956, his medical degree in 1960, and a degree in his medical specialty, ophthalmology, in 1964. In 1966, he was admitted to the American Board of Ophthalmology, the last step toward becoming a well-qualified physician.

Meanwhile, Tanton had started a family. He met Mary Lou Brown at a get-together planned by his fraternity and her sorority; the first thing they found they had in common was boredom at these events. They married in 1958. They had two daughters, Laura in 1961, and Jane in 1965. In 1964, the Tantons decided to relocate to Petoskey, a small town in northern Michigan. They wanted to live in a rural area. This particular area also offered advantages for young Dr. Tanton's career. He wanted to work with a group of physicians and found such a group at the Burns Clinic, where a number of different specialists combined their talent and training to provide comprehensive medical care. The ophthalmologist on the Burns Clinic staff was getting older and didn't want to perform surgery anymore. Tanton soon achieved economic security in two senses of the word. While never fabulously wealthy, he had enough for his family. Also, he was safe from possible boycotts and other forms of economic retaliation against him for any unpopular opinions he might hold. Thus, he was able to engage in volunteer work, even controversial volunteer work.

Tanton's early volunteer efforts stemmed from two different interests, in medicine and in conservation. Historians such as Linda Gordon have documented the long interest American women have had in birth control. About the time Tanton entered medicine, birth control options for women expanded to include contraceptive pills. John and Mary Lou Tanton helped to open a Planned Parenthood Clinic for northern Michigan. Tanton was also involved in conservation activities. By the early 1970s, the two types of volunteer efforts were beginning to come together in his mind:

When the first Earth Week occurred in April 1970, I spent a whole week on the road. In the course of a week I gave thirty talks on population growth as part of the conservation problem. It had long been my inclination, when talking about problems, not just to complain about them but to suggest ways in which they might be addressed. So I felt that in my talks I had to examine where population growth came from. I concluded that there were, for instance, women who were having children they didn't want to have—unwanted children. Maybe that problem could be addressed, as we had tried to do through Planned Parenthood. That would be a help. And then there were women who already had large families and who perhaps still wanted more children, but who could be convinced that two, or three, or four was enough, rather than five or six. So that was another group. Then I began to notice the question of immigration as part of population growth, so I did some studies and found that in the late 1960s, immigration counted for 10–15% of U.S. population growth. I began to wonder about that as a possible category to be looked at to reduce the rate of population growth.[1]

Tanton found support for his linkage of population increase and environmental degradation in books such as Paul Ehrlich's *The Population Bomb*. In 1968, Tanton joined Zero Population Growth (ZPG), an organization created to take practical action to stem population increase and thus to ward off the possibility that there might be more human beings than the environment could support. In 1973, he was elected to a seat on the national board of ZPG, and from 1975 to 1977, he served as national president of the organization. However, when Tanton raised the issue of ZPG's stemming population increase by working to reduce immigration, he found a fundamental difference between himself and other members of ZPG. For most members of ZPG, *where* people were was irrelevant; the main issue was to maintain a level of population that the planet Earth could support. They were interested in reducing birthrates, and with the U.S. birthrate under control, they expanded their horizons to controlling birthrates in other countries. Tanton argued that just because the U.S. birthrate was down didn't mean U.S. population growth was under control; immigration also caused population growth, and thus immigration had to be reduced to fully stabilize the U.S. population.

In his conservation activities, Tanton was reaching a similar impasse. While in medical school, he joined the Michigan Natural Areas Council, a conservation group. The Michigan Natural Areas Council introduced him to politics; one of its projects was preventing the construction of a road that threatened the environment in the north shore of Michigan's Upper Peninsula, along Lake Superior. When Tanton moved to Petoskey, he organized a project to reclaim the Bear River for conservation-minded community use. In 1964, as part of the larger Great Society program, the federal government enacted the Wilderness Preservation Act. To take advantage of federal funds and other provisions of that law, the state government formed a new Michigan Wilderness and Natural Areas Council. Aware of Tanton's experience in conservation, the governor appointed him to the council. In 1969, Tanton organized a population committee for the Mackinac Chapter of the national Sierra Club. In 1970, he organized the Petoskey Regional Group of the Sierra Club. The Sierra Club's leadership, though, divided over whether to urge immigration restriction as part of a general program of environmental protection. Some club members thought that immigration restriction was too far afield from the Sierra Club's main interests in environmental preservation. (Immigration continued to be a controversial issue for the Sierra Club. In 1998, club members who wished to expand club conservation efforts to include immigration restriction convinced the club's board to organize a referendum. In a general vote, members defeated the proposal in favor of maintaining the Sierra Club's tradition of not having a policy on immigration.)

Tanton argued that controlling immigration was a legitimate part of conservation. By 1977, he had concluded that he would have to organize a new group that focused on his analysis of the situation and would work to save the U.S. environment by restricting immigration.

Tanton already had considerable experience with organization and administration. During college, he joined a fraternity, Delta Upsilon. He learned how to set agendas, run meetings, and take minutes. He developed an appreciation for organizational history and got the records of his chapter of Delta Upsilon in order, compiling a list of all past members. He made Delta Upsilon financially sound by placing a portion of each member's initiation fee into an endowment fund. During medical school, he joined a combination honor-and-service society called Galens, where he gained further experience in organizational work. Shortly after moving to Petoskey, he helped to establish a Planned Parenthood Clinic and to compile a directory of social services for the needy. His work in conservation led him to increasingly prominent leadership roles. He was the lead plaintiff in *Tanton* v. *Department of Natural Resources Board* (1972), a suit designed to stop the relevant state agency from granting a permit to a developer who wanted to dam a trout stream called the Monroe Creek. He helped to organize the Little Traverse Group, which purchased land and set it aside for preservation and which filed additional lawsuits in an effort to protect the environment. Between 1977 and 1979, Tanton put his previous experience to work in developing his new organization.

Tanton called his organization the Federation for American Immigration Reform (FAIR). The name had several advantages. Its initials spelled out FAIR, which signaled Tanton's conviction that the 1965 legislation that governed immigration at the time was unfair and should be replaced. The full title conveyed concisely what FAIR was about: It wanted to change U.S. immigration law. There was only one semantic problem. A "federation" is an organization composed of groups that in turn have their own independent existence, as the states in the Union combine to form the United States, with power divided between states and the United States. No independent groups combined to form FAIR. Tanton organized a board of directors to determine policy and priorities. Later, he organized a separate national board of advisers to provide a broad background for the board of directors' decisions. He hoped to attract a large number of members, but these would be individuals, not groups with their own agendas. The members would all support the main FAIR office, which was in Washington, D.C. The members weren't even encouraged to do much about immigration issues in their local areas, because FAIR was mostly interested in changing the federal law, and that could only be done in Washington. In his memoirs, Tanton didn't say why he chose the name, or why he chose the word *federation*, but he needed a word that began with *F* so that he could get the proper acronym.

Volunteer efforts are like any other business in that they need start-up capital. When Tanton realized that not all of his associates in conservation and population control agreed with him on the importance of reducing immigration, he began to watch carefully for those that did. One who seemed to agree with him was Jay Harris, a philanthropist who had been Tanton's predecessor as president of ZPG. After he had finished his own term as president of ZPG, Tanton spent about a year making plans. Then he contacted Harris. He outlined his proposal for FAIR and asked Harris to provide seed money. In 1978, Harris promised to give $25,000 for the first and second years of FAIR's existence and then gave $5,000 less each year for the next five years.[2] By then, FAIR would have been in existence for seven years, long enough to develop a group of supporters.

Even though Tanton hoped to build an organization with numerous supporters, he had to start with the leadership. To that end, he contacted Roger Conner. Conner was a lawyer whom Tanton had met in 1970, when they both worked to organize the first Earth Week celebration. Conner had then gone on to work for the West Michigan Environmental Action Council. By the late 1970s, he had reached the top of that field, and was looking for new challenges. He agreed to start FAIR's Washington headquarters.

After the leaders were in place, Tanton concentrated on increasing the number of followers. FAIR started a newsletter in 1979, but who to mail it to? Until 1983, FAIR relied on direct mail. It purchased mailing lists of names and addresses from organizations that had similar interests. It then hired a consultant to draft a letter soliciting interest in FAIR, printed up enough letters to match the number of names and addresses, and mailed the letters out. People who engaged in direct mail were satisfied if 1 percent of the people who got mail showed any interest. FAIR improved the results of its direct-mail campaign by borrowing a tactic from another organization, the Prison Fellowship led by Chuck Colson, that of putting a return envelope in the mailing. This made it easy for people to respond, and soon the direct-mail contributions were measured in the thousands of dollars.[3]

FAIR intended to lobby Congress directly, not to lead mass protests.

However, it was necessary to lobby for public support, too. Tanton thought that placing advertisements in newspapers was expensive, but it did attract attention and donors. Under Dan Stein, who succeeded Roger Connor as executive director, FAIR conducted another sort of public relations campaign. Stein regularly wrote letters to the editors of newspapers, and some of them did get printed. He was especially successful in getting letters to the editor accepted by the *Wall Street Journal,* which is worth noting, because that newspaper, in accord with its interests in reduced government regulation and in having as large and inexpensive a labor market as possible, favored a minimum of immigration restrictions.[4] Stein's numerous print appearances gave FAIR opportunities to influence not only Congress but the public, and it was easier to get Congress to do something if it seemed that much of the public, not just one lobbying group, favored it.

Tanton's interest in immigration soon broadened. The more he thought about immigration, the more he thought about issues that had little to do with the relation between immigration, population, and the environment. When he began thinking about issues such as job competition and language, he found books and articles that supported conclusions he was already reaching in his own mind. "We set FAIR up specifically to deal with *all* aspects of immigration policy, not just those dealing with population numbers."[5] Instead of identifying one reason to limit immigration that many could agree with, Tanton provided a number of reasons to join FAIR, some of which could also be perceived as reasons *not* to join FAIR.

The same year that FAIR began its work, 1979, a bill to set U.S. policy for admitting refugees was introduced into Congress. FAIR tried to limit the total number of refugees to be admitted. The law that was passed, though, permitted the president, in consultation with Congress, to exceed the annual limit. Soon FAIR got another chance to influence immigration legislation beyond the question of refugees. In 1979, President Jimmy Carter appointed his Select Commission on Immigration and Refugee Policy (SCIRP). In 1981, when SCIRP finished its work, Wyoming Republican senator **Alan K. Simpson** took up the task of getting new immigration legislation through Congress. FAIR emerged as a critic, and supporter, of the legislation.

FAIR managed to get some of what it wanted written into law. Tanton had observed that U.S. immigration law tended to be written as if it were permanent. Perhaps laws ought to have time limits or to be subject to congressional reapproval every so often. What he was asking for was what was colloquially known as a "sunset" provision, and such a clause, calling for a study of the working of the immigration law after a certain period of time, was written into the bill. FAIR also asked for a commission to study practical ways, such as ditch digging, fence building, or increasing the U.S. border patrol, to control immigration at the Mexican border, and such a commission was established by the legislation. However, FAIR soon learned that legislation needs to be enforced. The study of the working of the 1986 law did not appear on time. (The study of how to reinforce the border did appear on time. FAIR claimed it was inadequate and funded its own study.)

FAIR opposed a key element in Simpson's bill—amnesty for illegal immigrants—but finally decided it had to compromise. Tanton recalled:

We were, of course, concerned about the multiplier effect of amnesty. If you let some people in, their relatives will eventually come—one way or another. We were also concerned about the legitimacy of it. Here we had people standing in line around the world following the rules, waiting for a chance to migrate, and we were about to give special status to those who broke the rules, cut the line, came ahead. That rankled. And we were concerned about the precedent, because we knew that other countries around the world had declared amnesties and subsequently declared other amnesties. We had debates back and forth. Then there was the political realism, of course, to the whole thing. We had all these migrants here. They were probably not all going to be sent back home, so how should we deal with them? Then there was Senator Simpson's firm commitment to the idea of amnesty. We had worked well with him, so that also moderates what you might do and how hard you might want to knock heads on this one issue.[6]

Commitment to Senator Simpson was so firm that it resulted in a slight rewriting of history. The bill that raised so many questions for FAIR passed in 1986. It in turn came up for reform in 1990. FAIR found the 1990 law disturbing: It not only raised the limit of the total number of people admitted to the United States; it also permitted people to bring in certain family members without regard to limits, thus swelling the totals. Dan Stein included the 1990 law in a bill of indictment against Massachusetts Democrat **Edward M. Kennedy**, the "Godfather of the Immigration Mess."[7] However, Simpson cosponsored the bill in the Senate and supported it on the floor of the Senate and in the media.

Even while FAIR was organizing itself to lobby for immigration restriction in what became the 1986 law, Tanton was reconceptualizing the immigration debate. Work on immigration had introduced him to other reasons to oppose it than its contribution to population increase and environmental degradation. In 1979, at the same time that he did the legal paperwork for FAIR, Tanton did the paperwork for a second not-for-profit, politically active corporation, which would serve as an umbrella organization to sponsor any new projects he might come up with. He called the corporation U.S. Over the decade of the 1980s, under the umbrella of U.S., he organized two other agencies that concerned themselves with particular angles on the immigration issue.

Tanton also organized a procedure by which he brought together influential people whom he could influence to think about the most important issues in the broadest possible way. To name the organization, he borrowed from fifteenth-century English a word, *witenagemot*, for a body of councilors that advised the crown on matters of state, and called his group WITAN. He held the first WITAN meetings in 1984. Richard Lamm, an advocate of immigration reduction and at that time governor of Colorado, lent the prestige of his office to the movement by hosting two of the early meetings in his governor's mansion.[8] WITAN's history later intersected with that of another organization Tanton had founded.

This second organization was U.S. English. Tanton himself was no monolinguist. Describing his many interests in Petoskey, he commented, "I became interested in trying to refurbish the German that I had taken in college. My mother spoke German. I'm a great believer in the discipline of learning a language."[9] However, Tanton became convinced that there had to be only one language for the United States, that that language had to be English, that recent immigrants were insufficiently committed to learning it, and that legislation was necessary to enforce the use of English.

Influencing legislation regarding use of the English language was a more complicated procedure than legislation to reduce immigration. Thanks to an 1875 Supreme Court decision, it was clear that immigration counted as interstate commerce and thus as a matter for federal regulation. Did the federal government also have the sole right to legislate regarding English? Senator **Samuel Ichiye Hayakawa** of California had introduced to Congress a constitutional amendment making English the official language of the United States and requiring that it alone be used for official purposes. When Hayakawa was about to retire, his amendment had not even passed Congress, let alone been released for states to consider ratifying. Hayakawa agreed to let Tanton have his mailing lists. Tanton suggested to the FAIR board of directors that FAIR use Hayakawa's mailing list to jump-start its own efforts to lobby for legislation requiring the use of English. The FAIR board turned down the suggestion; Tanton thought it was because FAIR had enough to do. In 1983, Tanton organized a new agency, U.S. English, to lobby for this new cause.

By 1986, both WITAN and U.S. English seemed to be going well. That year, the state of California put on the fall ballot a referendum question regarding whether English ought to be the official language of the state. U.S. English promoted the referendum, and the voters favored it. The same year, Tanton scheduled a WITAN meeting for Middleburg, a town in rural Virginia near Washington, D.C. As usual, he prepared a memorandum to stimulate the WITAN participants so that they would come prepared to talk. As he later remembered it:

When I wrote this memo, I was not trying to be particularly cautious or definitive. Following my usual practice, I included everything that might remotely pertain to the topic, including some speculations that would have been better left out! . . . My memo was written for a group of people who were already initiated into immigration, population, and language issues. It was not written for people off the street who'd never heard any of these ideas before and had no background in them. It assumed a good deal of knowledge of the subject.[10]

These two separate events—U.S. English's success and WITAN's discussions for the initiated—came together in 1988. That year, U.S. English succeeded in placing referendums regarding whether English ought to be the official state language on the ballots for Arizona, Colorado, and Florida. Opponents to English as the official language for Arizona campained for a nay vote by linking the movements to make English official and to reduce immigration. They did this by publishing Tanton's 1986 preparatory memorandum for the WITAN meeting. When U.S. English executive director Linda Chavez read the memorandum Tanton had prepared for those who were "initiated" into the discussion of "immigration, population, and language issues," she pronounced it anti-immigrant and anti-Hispanic and resigned her position rather than continue to work with Tanton. That in turn created a stir that Tanton feared would lead to the defeat of the official-English referendum in Arizona. Therefore, Tanton also resigned his position with U.S. English so that the referendum question could be judged on its merits rather than by association with him. He took comfort from election-day results, which favored making English an official language.

Referendums to make English the official language of one state had no effect on the federal government. Other states whose citizens spoke various languages took another path; in New York State, public service campaigns are conducted in many languages and voting information is published in Chinese, English, and Spanish. The official-English movement did have a long-term side effect: It was a stage in altering the debate over immigration into a debate over the motives of the different participants in that debate.

Tanton began to study his pro-immigrant opponents and to develop an hypothesis regarding their motives. He identified two possible explanations for pro-immigrant action. One was political expedience. For example, during the debate over the 1986 law, FAIR's lobbyists noticed that the Hispanic congressional representatives claimed they opposed the bill on behalf of the larger Hispanic community. On the other hand, historic events such as the efforts of **Cesar Chavez** among farmworkers indicated the Hispanic community was split into various groups. FAIR commissioned a survey that revealed there was no one Hispanic position on the 1986 bill; findings helped solidify support for the bill. Another example of how immigration could be used as part of a plan to advance a political cause was the sanctuary movement of the early 1980s. People fleeing violence in Guatemala and El Salvador found it difficult to get immigration visas. They tried to apply as refugees, but the United States would not accept their applications because the United States was allied with the governments in power in

Guatemala and El Salvador and didn't want to admit their allies were at best unable to control their own countries and at worst were dictatorships violently suppressing opposition. U.S. citizens who wanted to challenge U.S. policy in Central America encouraged Guatemalans and Salvadorans to enter the United States anyway, promising to offer them sanctuary in churches, knowing it would be acutely embarrassing for the federal officials to raid houses of worship to remove impoverished refugees. Tanton thought sanctuary advocates exploited immigrants to score foreign policy points.

Tanton further hypothesized that his opponents were inspired not by the issue of immigration but by the broader questions immigration raised. He identified five areas besides immigration in which he and his opponents had substantial differences of opinion. First, Tanton thought the world had set limits and fixed boundaries. Although he was not exactly sure what the number was, there was some limited number of people the U.S. environment could support, and the country had to be sure not to exceed it. He contrasted that to the view of human capital economists who stressed human ability to solve human problems and pointed to a past record of eradicating particular diseases and reducing world hunger. Past performance, though, does not guarantee future prospects.

Second, Tanton emphasized the importance of the nation-state. He agreed that the United Nations could solve some worldwide problems, including some having to do with the environment. However, he did not think it realistic to suppose many nations, especially many new nations just emerging from colonial status into independence, would cede their authority to a higher level of government. He thought that his opponents wanted to create a one world system into which everyone would fit.

Third, Tanton believed in emphasizing the common ground among the people of a particular nation-state. "I *do* hold to the metaphor of 'the melting pot,' " he declared to interviewer Otis Graham during an oral history. "I hold that as a country we should be trying to efface, or at least to minimize, our differences and accentuate our similarities so that in the face of all the diversity we have, we can get along better with one another."[11] Tanton thought his opponents emphasized that diversity to the point where the country was "just an address for disparate groups that happen to live in North America, and who live out their separate lives with little interaction with one another."[12]

Fourth, Tanton identified language as an especially important unifier. He argued his case on practical grounds. Just as a country had one currency or one system of weights and measures, so it ought to have one language to facilitate communication between its residents. He also argued that language had tremendous symbolic importance. Around the world, would-be separatists rallied their forces around the flag of a distinct language. Discouraging different languages would make it harder to emphasize differences and easier to emphasize commonalities.

Fifth and finally, Tanton thought there was a distinct U.S. culture. He characterized his opponents as hewing to a particular sort of hyphenated Americanism. In this definition, the modifier carried all the cultural connotations. To say that one was Mexican American or Chinese American or German American was to say that one drew one's whole culture from the Mexican, Chinese, or German part of the phrase. On the contrary, Tanton argued, the American part of the phrase connoted a specific culture. It was possible not to be a hyphenated American and still to have a culture worth preserving. In fact, that was the culture Tanton was particularly interested in preserving.

Viewed this way, Tanton's opponents in the immigration debate were as threatening to public life as the immigrants themselves. Gradually, Tanton expanded his work to include a critique of the pro-immigrant forces. This brought Tanton to a new field, controversial writing. Tanton considered himself a slow starter when it came to writing. "During four years of high school I wrote only one paper, of five or six hundred words, and that was on farm tiling!"—a drainage method he knew from having seen it practiced on his family's own farm.[13] However, years of taking minutes and drafting material for meetings, plus reading Jacques Barzun's *Simple and Direct*, honed Tanton's style. In 1975, he entered an essay in a competition in which all participants wrote on the topic "Limits to Growth" and won third prize, $3,000. One of the other contestants was the editor of a journal called the *Ecologist*. He liked Tanton's essay so well that he published it as a cover article. To accompany the founding of FAIR, Tanton published *Rethinking Immigration Policy*. Over the years, he published opinion articles and letters to the editor in the *Christian Science Monitor*, the *Houston Chronicle*, and the *Wall Street Journal*. He also published at least one article, "Immigration and Criminality in the U.S.A.," in a research-oriented periodical.[14] Tanton's writing career became more central to him in 1990, when he founded the *The Social Contract*. The quarterly ran articles on immigration but also broadened its scope to discuss the underlying philosophy that led to support or rejection of particular political positions.

Tanton also produced two books in the early and mid-1990s, and they are significant for understanding the direction of the debate on immigration. In 1993, he and Wayne Lutton coauthored a book entitled *The Immigration Invasion*, published by Tanton's Social Contract Press. Even favorable reviewers regarded *The Immigration Invasion* as "a handbook, almost a work in progress in its frantic pack-rat compilation of press clippings, the assimilation and accuracy of which" left even supporters uneasy.[15] However, even critics admitted that the issues it raised deserved consideration.[16] *The Immigration Invasion* was interesting for three other

reasons. First, it was part of a spurt of books specifically on the perils of
U.S. immigration policy. It was preceded in print by a year by Virginia D.
Abernathy's *Population Politics: The Choices That Shape Our Destiny.*[17]
The year after *Immigration Invasion* came out saw the publication of Brent
A. Nelson's *America Balkanized: Immigration's Challenge to Government,*[18] Peter Brimelow's *Alien Nation: Some Common Sense about America's Immigration Disaster* and by Roy Beck's *The Case against
Immigration: The Moral, Economic, Social, and Environmental Reasons
for Reducing U.S. Immigration Back to Traditional Levels.*[19] Second, the
spurt of books moved steadily toward the mainstream: *Immigration Invasion* was self-published, but Brimelow's book was published by Random
House and Beck's by W. W. Norton, the former a commercial press that
published many items of general interest and the latter a press with a good
reputation for scholarly works on U.S. history. For commercial publishers
to produce books frankly opposing immigration indicated a faith that this
was a subject of widespread interest. Finally, the appearance of the reviews
reinforced Tanton's observation that the immigration debate had created
two camps. Reviewers generally agreed Tanton wrote about important topics. They also agreed that his subjects needed more careful research. They
divided into friends and foes regarding his conclusions.[20]

Tanton's second book of the 1990s came in 1996, when he coedited a
volume of essays from *The Social Contract* that were then published as
Immigration and the Social Contract: The Implosion of Western Societies.[21]
Compared to *Immigrant Invasion*, this anthology was a much neater and
more organized compendium of anti-immigrant arguments, with specialists
writing on issues such as labor competition. It was also much more focused
in that it looked beyond immigration to what Tanton was coming to consider the real central issue, "the implosion of Western society." The title
The Social Contract called to mind not only Tanton's quarterly but, more
important, John Locke's theory of the origin of government. In his 1691
Two Treatises on Civil Government, Locke explained that individuals, realizing their vulnerability to outside forces, banded together in a social
contract designed to protect and promote the interests of those who created
it. Tanton then brought the social contract to bear on immigration. The
world, he pointed out, was a limited place, with finite resources and a
ceiling on its capacity for growth. Ultimately, the only way for one population group to expand was at the expense of another. Equally important,
there was no global social contract. Only like-minded people, those who
wanted to protect and preserve a shared culture, joined the social contract.
It is worth noting that Tanton's two coeditors hailed from Australia. One,
Denis McCormack, was the Australian liaison for *The Social Contract*
quarterly. The other, Joseph Wayne Smith, was a college professor. It was
not just immigration to the United States that Tanton was concerned about.
It was immigration to anywhere that Western civilization had established

a foothold.[22] For their part, Tanton's opponents agreed there were profound differences between their values and his. For both sides, immigration ceased to be the focus of the debate. Whether or not one favored reducing immigration became, as Tanton himself observed when he titled his memoirs, "A Skirmish in a Wider War."

It would be difficult to deny that the most important issues of life are the questions of what one values and why. However, a debate over immigration that yields to a debate over values leaves questions about immigration still to be settled. It also leaves them less likely to be settled if all the two sides can agree on is that they have such disparate value systems that they cannot agree.

NOTES

1. "A Skirmish in a Wider War: An Oral History of John H. Tanton, Founder of FAIR, The Federation for American Immigration Reform," interview with Otis L. Graham, Jr., Captiva Island, FL, April 20–21, 1989, pp. 10–11.

2. Ibid., p. 22.

3. Ibid., p. 43.

4. For example, see "Illegal-Alien Law: Your Stance Is a Riot," *Wall Street Journal*, June 20, 1991, sec. A, p. 15, col. 2; "Deep Denial on the Immigration Issue," ibid., September 10, 1993, sec. A, p. 19, col. 1; "Immigrants and Rose-Colored Myths," ibid., August 4, 1994, sec. A, p. 13, col. 1; and "Coming to America," ibid., March 19, 1996, sec. A, p. 19, col. 1.

5. Tanton and Graham, "A Skirmish in a Wider War," p. 31.

6. Ibid., p. 41.

7. Dan Stein, "Godfather of the Immigration Mess," *National Review* (November 7, 1994), p. 48.

8. Ibid., p. 62.

9. Tanton and Graham, "A Skirmish in a Wider War," p. 23.

10. Ibid., p. 71.

11. Ibid., p. 66.

12. Ibid., p. 67.

13. Ibid., p. 2.

14. John Tanton, "Immigration and Criminality in the U.S.A.," *Journal of Social, Political and Economic Studies* 18:2 (Summer 1993), pp. 217–234.

15. Peter Brimelow, "The Immigration Invasion," *National Review* (October 24, 1994), pp. 64–67.

16. Lawrence Fuchs, "Four False Alarms and Two Beams of Light," *International Migration Review* 30 (Summer 1996), pp. 591–600.

17. Virginia D. Abernathy, *Population Politics: The Choices That Shape Our Destiny* (New York: Insight Books, 1993).

18. Brent A. Nelson, *America Balkanized: Immigration's Challenge to Government* (Monterey, VA: American Immigration Control Foundation, 1994).

19. Peter Brimelow, *Alien Nation: Some Common Sense about America's Immigration Disaster* (New York: Random House, 1995); and Roy Beck, *The Case*

against Immigration: The Moral, Economic, Social, and Environmental Reasons for Reducing U.S. Immigration Back to Traditional Levels (New York: W. W. Norton, 1995).

20. See, for example, Fuchs, "Four False Alarms"; and Eileen Mulhare, "Are Immigrants 'Invaders'? A Response to Lutton and Tanton," *International Migration Review* 30 (Spring 1996), pp. 348–350.

21. John Tanton, Denis McCormack, and Joseph Wayne Smith, eds., *Immigration and the Social Contract: The Implosion of Western Societies* (Aldershot, England, and Brookfield, VT: Avebury, 1996).

22. To further buttress the argument that the real issue is the clash of cultures, Peter Brimelow, author of *Alien Nation*, might qualify as an alien, at least in the sense of having been born in Great Britain. However, Brimelow's argument against immigration is based on the idea that after 1965, U.S. immigration law admitted mostly people from outside the traditional U.S. culture background.

BIBLIOGRAPHY

The papers of Dr. Tanton's chief vehicle for influencing the debate on immigration, the Federation for American Immigration Reform (FAIR), are at the Department of Special Collections at the Melvin Gelman Library at the George Washington University. Historian and FAIR activist Otis L. Graham, Jr., conducted an oral-history interview with Dr. Tanton during a stay at Captiva Island, FL, on April 20–21, 1989. For a quick sense of FAIR's legislative agenda, see Stephen Moore, "New Year's Resolutions," *National Review* (January 29, 1996), pp. 46–48. Tanton's own book-length publications include *Rethinking Immigration Policy* (Washington, DC: Federation for American Immigration Reform, 1979). He and Wayne Lutton coauthored *The Immigration Invasion* (Petoskey, MI: The Social Contract, 1994). He, Denis McCormack, and Joseph Wayne Smith edited *Immigration and the Social Contract: The Implosion of Western Societies* (Aldershot, England, and Brookfield, VT: Aveburg, 1996). Tanton's is the publisher of *The Social Contract*, for which he has written numerous pieces. He has published articles in other periodicals, an example being "Immigration and Criminality in the U.S.A.," *Journal of Social, Political and Economic Studies* 18:2 (Summer 1993), pp. 217–234. Items by Tanton appeared in the *Christian Science Monitor*, January 27, 1982, August 11, 1986, April 17, 1992; and in the *Houston Chronicle*, May 30, 1988. This entry mentions the titles of various books that provide support for specific portions of Tanton's argument. Mention should also be made of Juan F. Perea, *Immigrants Out! The New Nativism and the Anti-Immigrant Impulse in the United States*, Critic America Series, ed. Richard Delgado and Jean Stefancic (New York and London: New York University Press, 1997), which summarizes opposition to Tanton's positions but also provides a good example of how both sides of the debate share some of the same assumptions and some of the same debate methods.

APPENDIX: BRIEF BIOGRAPHIES

Abbott, Grace. Born Grand Island, Nebraska, November 17, 1878; died Chicago, Illinois, June 19, 1939. Daughter of a woman who was an abolitionist, suffragist, and graduate of Rockford Female Seminary (**Jane Addams**'s alma mater), Abbott herself graduated from Grand Island College and gravitated toward social reform. From 1908 to 1917 she was secretary of the Chicago-based Immigrants' Protective League. In 1914, she took leave of this job to serve as secretary of the Massachusetts Immigration Commission, during which time she prepared a report on providing better legal aid to migrants. From 1919 to 1921 she was the first and only director of the Illinois State Immigrants Commission. From 1921 to 1934 she headed the Children's Bureau of the U.S. Department of Labor, and from 1934 to her death she taught public welfare administration at the University of Chicago's School of Social Service. *Reference*: Costin, Lela B. *Two Sisters for Social Justice: A Biography of Grace and Edith Abbott*. Urbana: University of Illinois Press, 1983.

Adams, John. Born Braintree, Massachusetts, October 19, 1735; died Quincy, Massachusetts, July 4, 1826. Adams was president of the United States at the time of the passage of the Alien and Sedition Acts, the multifaceted laws affecting the possibility of war with France and partisan politics as well as immigration. *References*: Brown, Ralph A. *The Presi-*

dency of John Adams. American Presidency Series. Lawrence: University of Kansas Press, 1975. Shaw, Peter. *The Character of John Adams.* Chapel Hill: Published for the Institute of Early American History and Culture, Williamsburg, VA, by the University of North Carolina Press, 1976.

Alinsky, Saul David. Born Chicago, Illinois, January 30, 1909; died Carmel, California, June 12, 1972. Alinsky's contribution to the debate on immigration came through his ability to develop grassroots organizations. He began with an interest in criminology; he did participant-observer research on Al Capone's gang. He then left scholarship for social work, taking care of juvenile delinquents. In 1938, this son of Orthodox Jews began working with Irish Catholic neighborhoods "back of the yards" near Chicago's meatpacking plants. He was successful enough to attract secular and Catholic support and, during the 1940s, his Industrial Areas Foundation spread his techniques of community organizing. During the civil rights era, he organized black neighborhoods in Woodlawn, Chicago, and Rochester, New York. Late in life he organized the offspring of white immigrants and ethnics, now middle class and fearful of the changes they thought increased black residency brought to their neighborhoods. *Reference*: Horwitt, Sanford D. *Let Them Call Me Rebel: Saul Alinsky, His Life and Legacy.* New York: Knopf, 1989.

Angell, James Burrell. Born Scituate, Rhode Island, January 7, 1829; died Ann Arbor, Michigan, January 1, 1916. In 1880, as minister to imperial China, Angell was appointed to a three-member commission to negotiate a new treaty with that country. He led the way to drawing up the treaty that made it possible for Congress to then pass the 1882 Chinese Exclusion Act.

Antin, Mary. Born Polotzk, Russia, June 13, 1881; died Suffern, New York, March 15, 1949. Mr. Antin came to the United States in 1891 and brought the family in 1894, hoping to get away from a series of failed businesses and increasing anti-Semitic legislation. His second daughter, Mary, learned English rapidly, came to the attention of her teachers, and moved from magazine to book publishing. Her most famous work was *The Promised Land* (1912), an autobiographical memoir. In 1901, she had married Amadeus William Grabau, a German Lutheran and professor of natural history at Columbia University. They separated in 1919; he moved to China in 1920 and died there in 1946. She recovered her interest in her ancestral Judaism; her last published essay, "House of One Father" (which appeared in *Common Ground* in 1941), was on her native town. *References*: Antin, Mary. *From Plotzk to Boston*. With a new introduction by Pamela S. Nadell. Masterworks of Modern Jewish Writing Series. New York: M. Wiener, 1986. Antin, Mary. *The Promised Land*. Introduced and notes by Werner Sollors. New York: Penguin Books, 1997. Warner, Sam Bass, Jr. *Province of Reason*. Cambridge: Belknap Press of Harvard University Press, 1984. This is a series of biographical essays, one of which is on Antin.

Arendt, Hannah. Born Hanover, Germany, October 4, 1906; died New York City, December 6, 1975. Educated at the University of Marburg, the University of Freiburg, and the University of Heidelberg, where she received a doctorate in 1928, Arendt traveled in the circles of the leading intellectuals of her day. When Hitler came to power in 1933, Arendt, who was of Jewish descent (but not a practitioner of the faith) escaped to Paris, where she worked for Youth Aliyah, helping to send Jewish youngsters to British Palestine. In 1940, Hitler invaded France, and Arendt fled again, this time to the United States, becoming one of the "illustrious immigrants" about whom **Laura Fermi** wrote. Arendt married Bard College art historian Heinrich Bluecher and made her own academic base at the New School for Social Research in New York City. She became a noted author of books such as *The Origins of Totalitarianism* (1951), in which she combined her passions for philosophy and for current affairs. *Reference*: Parekh, Bhiku C. *Hannah Arendt and the Search for a New Political Philosophy*. Atlantic Highlands, NJ: Humanities Press, 1981.

Balch, Emily Greene. Born Jamaica Plain, Massachusetts, January 8, 1867; died Cambridge, Massachusetts, January 9, 1961. A scholar, Balch received her B.A. from Bryn Mawr and did postgraduate work at Harvard Annex (now Radcliffe), the University of Chicago, the University of Berlin, and on her own. She was on the faculty of Wellesley College from 1896 to 1918. Like many college women of the Progressive Era, she was active in a variety of reforms having to do with immigration, labor, urban planning, and social welfare. The one with which she was most thoroughly identified is world peace; Wellesley's board of trustees refused to renew her contract in World War I because of her pacifist views, and in 1946 she shared the Nobel Peace Prize with another American, John R. Mott of the YMCA. In matters of immigration, Balch's specialty was Slavic migrants. From 1904 to 1906 she divided her time between studying Slavs in their old homes in the Austro-Hungarian Empire and in their new ones in the United States. The resulting book, *Our Slavic Fellow Citizens*, remains an important source in this field. *Reference*: Randall, Mercedes Moritz. *Improper Bostonian: Emily Greene Balch, Nobel Peace Laureate, 1946*. New York: Twayne Publishers, 1964.

Barney, Nora Stanton Blatch. Born Basingstoke, England, September 30, 1883; died Connecticut, January 18, 1971. Reformers agitated for female suffrage in England and in the United States at about the same time, and Nora Barney was a physical bridge between these two groups of like-minded reformers. She also linked them to earlier suffragists: her maternal grandmother was Elizabeth Cady Stanton, the first to voice the demand for votes for women. Her mother, Harriet Stanton Blatch, migrated from the United States to England and became active in the suffrage movement there. Besides following in her female ancestors' footsteps, Barney achieved much for women in other areas. She was the first woman to whom Cornell University granted a degree in civil engineering, and she intended to be an assistant to her first husband, Lee De Forest, inventor of the radio vacuum tube. (De Forest objected, which contributed to their divorce.) In 1919 she married an engineer named Morgan Barney and then went into real estate. She maintained an interest in reforms ranging from suffrage to the proposed equal rights amendment to the development of a "people's parliament" that would truly represent the people of the world and what she argued was their deep desire for peace.

Berlin, Irving. Born with the name Israel Baline in Temun, Russia, May 11, 1888; died in New York City, New York, September 22, 1989. It is difficult to think of twentieth-century U.S. musical theater without this immigrant. Moses Baline, a Jewish cantor, brought his family from czarist Russia to New York in 1893 and died three years later. His son began working as a street singer, got an indoor job as a singing waiter in Chinatown's Pelham's Cafe, published his first lyrics to a song, "Marie from Sunny Italy," in 1907, first played and sang his own musical compositions in *Up and Down Broadway* in 1910, and had his first hit tune with "Alexander's Ragtime Band" in 1911. Soon other people, including Fred Astaire, Bing Crosby, the Marx Brothers, and Ethel Merman, were singing his tunes. He contributed to revues and operettas and wrote musical scores and lyrics for Broadway plays and for Hollywood movies. He wrote the score for one Broadway play based on stories of the American West, *Annie Get Your Gun*. He provided songs for secularized versions of Christian holidays: *In Your Easter Bonnet* and *White Christmas*, which was, until it was surpassed by Elton John's 1997 recording of the song he played at the funeral of Diana, Princess of Wales, the best-selling recording in the United States. In 1918, he penned "God Bless America." He revised the tune in 1938, and Kate Smith made it a permanent part of the U.S. patriotic repertoire. *References*: Bergreen, Lawrence. *As Thousands Cheer: The Life of Irving Berlin.* New York: Viking, 1990. Hamm, Charles. *Irving Berlin: Songs from the Melting Pot: The Formative Years, 1907–1914.* New York and Oxford: Oxford University Press, 1997.

Bingham, Theodore. Born Andover, Connecticut, May 14, 1858; died at his summer home in Chester, Nova Scotia, Canada, September 6, 1934. Bingham's contribution to shaping immigration politics came during his brief tenure (January 1, 1906, to June 27, 1909) as police commissioner of New York City. He was universally praised as honest and dedicated to reforming police and controlling crime. However, his methods upset both police and citizenry; one factor leading to his dismissal was his refusal to remove from the police headquarters Rogues' Gallery a photograph of a nineteen-year-old minor who had been arrested but had not been found guilty of any crime. In 1908, he caused a stir with a report criticizing the city's Jews for a high rate of criminal behavior. In 1909, he came in for criticism for insufficiently protecting Lieutenant **Joseph Petrosino** during the latter's investigation into Italian criminal activities, which led directly to his assassination. Altogether, Bingham's actions served to highlight the stereotype of immigrants as prone to crime.

Boas, Franz. Born Minden, Westphalia, Germany, July 9, 1858; died New York City, New York, December 21, 1942. When the commission headed by **William Paul Dillingham** needed someone to provide statistical evidence that immigrants were innately inferior to native-born Americans, it hired Boas—and his evidence did not match the hypothesis. Boas demonstrated that environment mattered at least as much as heredity and that, in terms of their growth, the children of immigrants resembled native-born Americans more than they did their own parents. Other scholars thought that culture might be static or that cultures outside Europe were primitive ones in the process of evolving toward the advanced European model. Boas, a pioneer cultural anthropologist, provided proof for a new theory of culture. By studying native tribes in Alaska and the Pacific Northwest he accumulated evidence for the theory that culture was flexible and inherently diverse: What previous people called primitive culture was really fully formed culture, suitable for a particular environment. Boas's findings implied that the restrictive immigration laws of his day rested on false premises. There were no people genetically incapable of assimilation. *Reference*: Hyatt, Marshall. *Franz Boas, Social Activist: The Dynamics of Ethnicity.* Contributions to the Study of Anthropology No. 6. New York: Greenwood Press, 1990.

Booth, Evangeline Cory. Born London, England, Christmas Day 1865; died Hartsdale, New York, July 17, 1950. Booth played a role in bringing to the United States the Salvation Army, which her father, William, founded in London the year she was born. She first came to the United States to settle a dispute between her father and his first U.S. missionary, his son Ballington. The dispute was resolved by replacing Ballington with a sister, Emma. When Emma died in a train wreck in 1904, Evangeline put aside her own work in Canada to take on the U.S. mission field. She held that post until 1934, when she was elected general of the Salvation Army, which necessitated her moving back to London. However, she had become a U.S. citizen in 1923, and, in 1939, she retired and returned there. *References*: Lavine, Sigmund A. *Evangeline Booth, Daughter of Salvation.* New York: Dodd, Mead, 1970. Wilson, Philip Whitwell. *Gen. Evangeline Booth of the Salvation Army.* New York: Charles Scribner's Sons, 1948.

Buchanan, Patrick Joseph. Born Washington, D.C., November 2, 1938. Unsuccessful candidate for the Republican nomination to the presidency in 1992 and 1996, Buchanan is identified with opposition to immigration. He has moved between various types of journalism, writing books and syndicated editorial columns on modern conservatism, editing newsletters, and participating in televised talk programs. He has also moved between journalism and Republican politics, serving the administrations of presidents Richard M. Nixon, Gerald R. Ford, and Ronald N. Reagan. *Reference*: Buchanan, Patrick J. *Right from the Beginning.* Boston: Little, Brown, 1988.

Cabrini, Frances Xavier. Born Sant' Angelo Lodigiano, Lombardy, Italy, July 15, 1850; died Chicago, Illinois, December 22, 1917. Cabrini always wanted to be a missionary, preferably to China. To further that end, she trained as an elementary schoolteacher and then entered a convent. In 1880, she founded a community of sisters of her own, the Missionaries of the Sacred Heart, and took the title by which she was known the rest of her life, Mother Cabrini. In 1889, she led the first group of sisters on their first international mission—to minister to Italian immigrants in the United States. Under her management, the Missionaries spread across the United States, Central America, South America, and Europe. They performed all kinds of work: education, health care, the care of children in orphanages, ministry to immigrant families and to people in prison. On July 7, 1946, only twenty-nine years after her death, the Catholic Church placed Cabrini in its canon of saints. On September 8, 1950, Pope Pius XII proclaimed her the patroness of immigrants. *Reference*: Sullivan, Mary Louise, M.S.C. *Mother Cabrini: "Italian Immigrant of the Century."* New York: Center for Migration Studies, 1992.

Cahan, Abraham. Born Podberezya, then in czarist Russia, July 7, 1860; died New York City, New York, August 31, 1951. The Cahans moved to Vilna when their only son was ready for school. There he developed a love for his Jewish heritage, a commitment to socialism, and a facility with language and entered the teaching profession. He also entered radical politics, which is what led him to flee Russia. He arrived in New York City on June 6, 1882. There he became most famous for founding and editing a Yiddish-language paper, the *Jewish Daily Forward*. He also wrote novels with themes of immigration and identity; the best known is probably *The Rise of David Levinsky* (1917). He also participated in socialist and union politics. In the course of his work, he forged a path of assimilation whereby Jewish immigrants from eastern Europe, formerly excluded from the societies in which they lived, brought to the new society the insights and outlook derived from their cultural and religious heritage. *References*: Cahan, Abraham. *The Education of Abraham Cahan.* Trans. Leon Stein, Abraham P. Conan, and Lynn Davison. Philadelphia: Jewish Publication Society of America, 1969. **Higham, John.** "Abraham Cahan: Novelist between Three Cultures." In *Send These to Me: Jews and Other Immigrants in Urban America.* New York: Atheneum, 1975. Higham wrote this essay as an introduction for a reprint of Cahan's most famous novel, *The Rise of David Levinsky.* Marovitz, Sanford E. *Abraham Cahan.* Twayne's United States Authors Series. New York: Twayne, 1996.

Cahensly, Peter Paul. Born Limburg an der Lahn, Rhine province of Nassau, Germany, October 28, 1838; died Marienhof, Koblenz, Rhineland, Germany, December 25, 1923. The Cahenslys were wholesale grocers, and it was through observing the shipping of foodstuffs that their heir became interested in the problems of migrants. A Catholic, Cahensly in 1871 organized the Saint Rafaelsverein, named for the archangel who is the patron saint of travelers, to aid and advocate for the immigrants during their journeys and in their new homes. The Saint Raphael movement then spread, as Catholics in other European countries organized societies with the same name through which they could help their compatriots and coreligionists abroad. In 1890, leaders of these national societies met in Lucerne, Switzerland, to draft a description of immigrant needs for the consideration of Pope Leo XIII. Cahensly presented the petition to the Holy Father. It created a controversy in the United States, with U.S. bishops complaining that the European laity was interfering with the normal workings of the Catholic hierarchy and that it was retarding assimilation. **Reference:** Colman, James Barry, O.S.B. *The Catholic Church and German Americans.* Milwaukee, WI: Bruce, 1953. While not a biography of Cahensly, this monograph contains biographical information on him and describes his role in U.S. immigration history.

Cameron, Donaldina Mackenzie. Born at a sheep station at the Molyneaux (now Clutha) River, Otago Land District, New Zealand, July 26, 1869; died Palo Alto, California, January 4, 1968. The Camerons came from Scotland to New Zealand a few years before Donaldina was born and moved to California in 1871; throughout her life Donaldina remained a British citizen. She entered Presbyterian missionary work. In 1895, she arrived at 920 Sacramento Street, site of a mission to Chinese migrant women. By 1900, she was director of the place. Her work included efforts to oppose the importation of Chinese women as indentured servants in the prostitution trade. She helped women caught up in this trade: housing and feeding them, protecting them from exploitation, training them for other work, and guiding them to suitable marriages. By the 1920s, Cameron had also developed an extensive educational and cultural program. Following Presbyterian policy, she retired in 1934 at age sixty-five. In 1952, the mission home was renamed in her honor. *References:* Martin, Mildred Crowl. *Chinatown's Angry Angel: The Story of Donaldina Cameron.* Palo Alto, CA: Pacific Books, 1977. Pascoe, Peggy. *Relations of Rescue: The Search for Female Moral Authority in the American West, 1874–1939.* New York: Oxford University Press, 1990. While not a biography of Cameron, this places her in the context of the reform for which she was most famous.

Carnegie, Andrew. Born Dunfermline, Scotland, November 25, 1835; died at his summer house of Shadowbrook, Massachusetts, August 11, 1919. The personification of the rags-to-riches, immigrant-makes-good story, Carnegie came to the United States in 1848 after his father, a linen weaver, was first impoverished and then displaced by the developing factory system. By hard work, education, luck, and ruthlessness, he worked his way up from bobbin boy in a factory to owner of a great steel firm. In January 1901 he sold his Carnegie Company to J. P. Morgan, who used it to build U.S. Steel. Thereafter, he concentrated on philanthropy. *Reference:* Livesay, Harold C. *Andrew Carnegie and the Rise of Big Business.* Library of American Biography, edited by Oscar Handlin. Boston: Little, Brown, 1975.

Cather, Willa Sibert. Born Back Creek Valley, Virginia, December 7, 1873; died New York City, New York, April 24, 1947. Cather's own family moved her to Nebraska when she was a youth. Her experiences among the diverse people on the prairies became the basis for her novels and short fiction. *O Pioneers!* (1913) explored the families who settled the Great Plains. *My Antonia* (1918) had as its main character a Bohemian immigrant girl who grew to be a farm wife. *Death Comes for the Archbishop* (1927) is a fictional account of the life and work of Jean Lamy, a French cleric who became a missionary prelate among the Hispanics and Indians of the Southwest. *Shadows on the Rock* (1931) is set among French Canadians in Quebec. *References*: Robinson, Phyllis C. *Willa, the Life of Willa Cather.* Garden City, NY: Doubleday, 1983. Sergeant, Elizabeth Shipley. *Willa Cather: A Memoir.* Athens: Ohio University Press, 1992.

Celler, Emmanuel. Born and died in Brooklyn, New York, May 6, 1888, and January 15, 1981, respectively. House sponsor of the 1965 amendments that abolished the national quota system, Celler was entirely a New York product. He was educated in city public schools and at Columbia University, where he took a J.D. in 1912. Admitted to the bar the same year, he entered politics in 1922 as a delegate to the Democratic state convention and as a representative from Brooklyn. Having been defeated in his 1972 bid in the Democratic primary, Celler relinquished his House seat on January 3, 1973, and returned to the legal profession in Brooklyn. *Reference*: Celler, Emmanuel. *You Never Leave Brooklyn: The Autobiography of Emanuel Celler.* New York: J. Day Co., 1953.

Commons, John Rogers. Born Hollansburg, Ohio, October 13, 1862; died Raleigh, North Carolina, May 11, 1945. Commons graduated from Oberlin College, also his mother's alma mater, in 1888, and went to the Johns Hopkins University at a time when the various modern social sciences—economics, sociology, political science—were becoming distinct from one another. Although he never received his terminal degree, he became identified with the field of economics. His contribution to the study of immigration is threefold. First, he preserved immense quantities of data: He prepared a report on immigration for the U.S. Industrial Commission (1902–1904); worked on the "Pittsburgh Survey," a comprehensive study funded by the Russell Sage Foundation; edited the ten volumes of *A Documentary History of American Industrial Society* (1910–1911); and edited the first two of the four volumes of *History of Labor in the United States* (1918). Second, he was both a political activist and a scholar, whose theories regarding labor law and the role of the courts in mediating economic disputes contributed both to the study of economics and to the actual working of the law in Wisconsin, where he lived from 1904 until 1932. Third, in 1907, he published *Races and Immigrants in America*. This contributed to the notion that racial characteristics were immutable, passed on through generations, and thus that assimilation was unlikely. It also contributed to the idea that some national groups had characteristics that made them desirable immigrants, whereas others did not. *Reference*: McCracken, Harlan Linnaeus. *Keynesian Economics in the Stream of Economic Thought*. Baton Rouge: Louisiana State University Press, 1961.

Dillingham, William Paul. Born Waterbury, Vermont, December 12, 1843; died Montpelier, Vermont, July 12, 1923. When the Senate established a commission to study immigration, this Republican senator from Vermont was appointed one of its three members; the other two elected him chairman of the commission. In 1907, the Dillingham Commission produced a forty-one-volume report that concluded by advocating limiting the immigration of certain nationalities. Dillingham introduced such legislation in 1913, 1920, and 1921, the latter being the first of the quota laws of that decade.

Einstein, Albert. Born Ulm, Germany, March 14, 1879; died Princeton, New Jersey, April 18, 1955. When Adolf Hitler came to power in 1933, the Einsteins happened to be visiting the United States. A Jew, a Zionist, and a pacifist, Albert announced they would not return to Nazi Germany. Instead, he became the example of how much the United States could gain through the admission of refugees. At that point, he had already won the Nobel Prize for physics (in 1921). His work in theoretical physics had given all physicists an understanding of how nuclear weaponry might be possible. He signed a letter to Franklin D. Roosevelt explaining that it was also possible the Nazis were working on such a weapon, which spurred U.S. efforts to develop nuclear weapons. *Reference*: Highfield, Roger, and Paul Carter. *The Private Lives of Albert Einstein*. New York: St. Martin's Press, 1994.

Fillmore, Millard. Born Locke, Cayuga County, New York, January 7, 1800; died Buffalo, New York, March 8, 1874. Fillmore was Zachary Taylor's vice president and succeeded to the presidency upon Taylor's death on July 9, 1850. He served until succeeded by the next elected president, Franklin Pierce, in 1853. In 1856, he tried to win the presidency in his own right, running as the candidate of the American, or Know-Nothing, Party. He came in a distant third. Thereafter, he was caught up in Civil War politics and in civic affairs in Buffalo, where he helped to organize a university, a historical society, and a hospital. While there are some biographies that focus on his presidential administration, there are none that focus on his brief association with the nativist movement. *References*: Grayson, Benson Lee. *The Unknown President: The Administration of President Millard Fillmore*. Washington, DC: University Press of America, 1981. Smith, Elbert B. *The Presidencies of Zachary Taylor and Millard Fillmore*. American Presidency Series. Lawrence: University of Kansas Press, 1988.

Fitzpatrick, John Bernard. Born Boston, Massachusetts, November 15, 1812; died there February 13, 1866. As third bishop of his native city (August 11, 1846, to his death), Fitzpatrick was **John Hughes**'s contemporary and shared with him the logistical and cultural challenges of caring for the refugees of the Irish potato famine during a period of virulent nativism. However, he came from a different background—his maternal grandfather was a patriot who served in the American Revolution, and he himself graduated from the prestigious (and public) Boston Latin School—and the policies he chose, even though there were not accepted by most American Catholics, form an interesting contrast to Hughes's. *Reference*: O'Connor, Thomas H. *Fitzpatrick's Boston, 1846–1866: John Bernard Fitzpatrick, Third Bishop of Boston*. Boston: Northeastern University Press, 1984.

Flower, George. Born Hertford, England, 1788; died Grayville, Illinois, January 15, 1862. In 1818, Flower became one of the pioneers of Albion, Illinois. For many years he was the leader of the settlement. His policies did much to make it a viable community, and his publications may have stimulated immigration into the area. His efforts to prevent the introduction of slavery into Illinois, though, eventually cost him his farm, his community, and the life of his eldest son.

Garvey, Marcus Moziah. Born Saint Anne's Bay, Jamaica, August 17, 1887; died London, England, June 10, 1940. Garvey's travels began in 1907, when he left home for Kingston, Jamaica, and then for Panama, Costa Rica, and London. He gained a sense of a widespread African diaspora and found a calling in the effort to unite far-flung black people in racial solidarity. He was a leader in forming the Universal Negro Improvement Association (UNIA) in Jamaica in 1914. In 1916, he moved to New York City to establish a branch in Harlem. There he advocated a return of blacks to Africa, which would then become a mighty nation, the equal of the European Great Powers that heretofore had colonized it. Garvey took practical steps to achieve the return to Africa, including the establishment of the Black Star Line of oceangoing passenger ships. He financed the shipping company by selling stock to black investors. The company collapsed, taking the investments with it, and in January 1922 authorities arrested Garvey and three colleagues on charges of using the federal mail to perpetrate a fraud. Garvey was convicted and sentenced to five years in a federal penitentiary in Atlanta, Georgia. President Calvin Coolidge commuted the sentence in 1927, at which point federal authorities deported Garvey to Jamaica. *Reference*: Cronon, Edmund David. *Black Moses: The Story of Marcus Garvey and the Universal Negro Improvement Association*. 2nd ed. Madison: University of Wisconsin Press, 1981.

Glazer, Nathan. Born New York City, New York, February 25, 1923. With **Daniel Patrick Moynihan** he coauthored *Beyond the Melting Pot* (1963), which put forth the thesis that ethnic groups never completely assimilated to one standard American type. Other books of his in the immigration field include: *American Judaism* (1956), *Ethnicity: Theory and Practice* (1975), *Ethnic Dilemmas*, (1969, 1982), *Clamor at the Gates: The New American Immigration* (1985), *Affirmative Discrimination: Ethnic Inequality and Public Policy* (1975, 1987), *The New Immigration: A Challenge to American Society* (1988), and *We Are All Multiculturalists Now* (1997). He also wrote numerous other books on other important topics in sociology. He received his Ph.D. in sociology from Columbia University in 1962 and was from 1968 to 1993 affiliated with Harvard University.

Goldman, Emma. Born June 27, 1869, Kovno, Lithuania; died May 14, 1940, Toronto, Canada. Radicals formed an international community, and Emma Goldman was a leading example of it. She came to the United States in 1886 to escape the limited opportunities of a lower-middle-class woman in her home. However, her early experiences in the United States, including factory work in Rochester and news of the 1886 Haymarket affair, taught her that the United States was not yet paradise. She tried to reform it in every way possible, interesting herself in anarchism, women's rights, and sexual rights for women and for homosexuals. Deported to the nascent Soviet Union in 1919, she proved as much a critic of the developing communist state as she had been of U.S. capitalism. She left Russia in 1921, and thereafter traveled to wherever it seemed her activism could make a difference. She happened to be in Toronto at the time of her death; her remains were brought to Chicago for burial. *References*: Falk, Candace. *Love, Anarchy and Emma Goldman*, 2nd ed. New Brunswick, NJ: Rutgers University Press, 1990. Goldman, Emma. *Living My Life*, 2 vols. New

York: Alfred A. Knopf, 1931. Wexler, Alice. *Emma Goldman in Exile.* Boston: Beacon Press, 1989.

Gompers, Samuel. Born London, England, January 27, 1850; died San Antonio, Texas, after taking fatally ill while on a speaking tour in Mexico, December 13, 1924. The Gomperses were working-class Jews who migrated from the Netherlands to England before Samuel's birth, then to New York City when he was thirteen, by which time Samuel had already been apprenticed to a cigarmaker. He helped to form the American Federation of Labor (AFL), which elected him its first president in 1886 and returned him to that office until his death. He not only personified the close link between labor and immigration in the United States but was in the vanguard of union response to the new immigrants of the late nineteenth and early twentieth centuries. He tended toward the exclusion of immigrants from southern and eastern Europe, unskilled workers who threatened skilled workers' job security and who were difficult to organize in the traditional craft union framework. *Reference*: Livesay, Harold C. *Samuel Gompers and Organized Labor in America.* Library of American Biography, edited by Oscar Handlin, Boston: Little, Brown, 1978.

Harnden, William Frederick. Born Reading, Massachusetts, August 23, 1812; died Boston, Massachusetts, January 14, 1845. Although Harnden was never able to parlay his ideas into a lasting fortune, he contributed to the debate on immigration through innovations in transportation and communication. Harnden and Co. began in 1839 by delivering small, valuable packages between Boston and New York. The business then expanded to other U.S. cities and to Europe. Harnden diversified his European offices to provide money exchange and inexpensive tickets from U.S. coastal cities to the interior via Boston packet boats in the Hudson River and the Erie Canal.

Hart, Philip Aloysius. Born Bryn Mawr, Pennsylvania, December 10, 1912; died Washington, D.C., December 26, 1976. First elected to the Senate from Michigan on the Democratic ticket in 1958, Hart was less than a month away from retirement from that office at the time of his death. In 1965, Hart was the Senate sponsor of the immigration reform law. *Reference*: O'Brien, Michael. *Philip Hart: The Conscience of the Senate.* East Lansing: Michigan State University Press, 1995.

Hayakawa, Samuel Ichiye. Born Vancouver, British Columbia, Canada, July 18, 1906. Hayakawa was elected to the Senate from California on the

Republican ticket in 1976. He declined to run for the office again in 1982. In and out of office, he was identified with the efforts to make English the official language of the United States.

Henie, Sonja. Born Oslo, Norway, April 8, 1912; died aboard a plane traveling from Paris to Oslo (of leukemia), October 12, 1969. The United States represented a different sort of opportunity for Henie, who was already a three-time Olympic champion in ladies' figure skating when in 1936 she turned professional in order to appear in ice-skating reviews and to make movies in Norway and in Hollywood. Her films helped to transform ice skating from a technical skill in which atheletes traced figures on ice into an art form in which performers danced on skates. Her transformation of ice skating helped to popularize both the sport and the art. She became a U.S. citizen in 1941 and toured with the United Service Organization (USO) in World War II, but remained an international celebrity. She and her third husband, Norwegian shipping magnate Neils Onstad, built the Henie-Onstad Art Center near Oslo, and it is there she is buried. *Reference*: Henie, Sonja. *Wings on My Feet*. New York: Prentice-Hall, 1940.

Herberg, Will. Born Liachovitzi, Russia, June 30, 1901; died Morristown, New Jersey, March 27, 1977. The Herberg family migrated to Brooklyn in 1904, where it had a difficult time financially and in other ways. Herberg had to overcome his father's desertion and his own suspension from New York's City College (for absenting himself from military science classes) in order to become an intellectual. He began as a Marxist, left the party when he recovered his ancestral Jewish faith, and went on to become a theologian and philosopher, a professor at Drew University (1961–1976), and religion editor of William F. Buckley's *National Review* (1961–1977), which served as a forum for developing modern conservatism. Herberg's *Protestant-Catholic-Jew* (1955) is a classic work on assimilation. He publicized statistics indicating a "triple melting pot" in which people of varying ethnic groups intermarried within their faith tradition and analyzed the notion that, having lost their ethnic connections, individuals adopted religious affiliations to re-create a sense of belonging, albeit under circumstances more closely under their control. *References*: Ausmus, Harry J. *Will Herberg: A Bio-Bibliography*. Bio-Bibliographies in Law and Political Science No. 2. Westport, CT: Greenwood Press, 1986. Ausmus, Harry J. *Will Herberg: From Right to Right*. With a foreword by Martin E. Marty. Chapel Hill: University of North Carolina Press, 1987.

Higham, John. Born in the borough of Queens in New York City, New York, October 26, 1920. His first book, *Strangers in the Land* (1955), established Higham as a leading historian of U.S. thought regarding immigration. His other books on U.S. immigration history are a collection of essays entitled *Send These to Me*, of which two significantly different editions were published, and *Ethnic Leadership in America* (1978). He also published in the field of historiography. He was from 1971 to 1989 on the history faculty of the Johns Hopkins University, from which he received his B.A. in 1941. From 1958 to 1971, he was on the history faculty of the University of Michigan, and prior to that he taught at Rutgers and at the University of California at Los Angeles.

Hine, Lewis Wickes. Born Oshkosh, Wisconsin, September 26, 1874; died Hastings-on-Hudson, New York, November 3, 1940. Hine was teaching at the Ethical Culture School in Manhattan when his school principal suggested he learn to take photographs in order to document school events. Hine soon found other uses for his camera. He photographed immigrants coming to the country through Ellis Island. He then photographed their settlement process, capturing the tenements in which they lived and the work they did. He came to the attention of the National Child Labor Committee and began photographing evidence of the extent of the problem with which they were concerned, smuggling his camera into factories and surreptitiously interviewing child workers in order to get captions for his pictures. In 1918, he went abroad to photograph the relief efforts of the American Red Cross after World War I. In 1931, he photographed the construction of the Empire State Building, in the process of which he took as many risks as the construction workers, carrying his photographic equipment up the steel skeleton of the building and perching himself on a crane to take a picture of the workers riveting together the last two beams. In 1939, shortly before his accidental death following surgery, he did a similar series of railroad workers at their jobs. *References*: Gutman, Judith Mara. *Lewis W. Hine and the American Social Conscience*. New York: Walker, 1967. Rosenblum, Nina, director. *America and Lewis Hine*. New York: Daedalus Productions, 1984. This is a videorecording.

Hope, Bob. Born Eltham, England, May 29, 1903. Poverty, discrimination, and inability to secure educational credentials limited immigrant socioeconomic mobility. Thus, many immigrants crowded into fields one can enter on talent alone: sports and entertainment. Bob Hope was the most famous example of this principle. Passing through Ellis Island as a child, he entered show business through vaudeville and then became successful in many venues: the stage, radio, motion pictures, and television. From World War II to the early years of the Vietnam War he went into the field to entertain members of the U.S. armed forces stationed abroad. *References*: Hope, Bob, and Bob Thomas. *The Road to Hollywood: My Forty-Year Love Affair with the Movies*. Garden City, NY: Doubleday, 1977. Mielke, Randall G. *Road to the Box Office: The Seven Film Comedies of Bing Crosby, Bob Hope, and Dorothy Lamour, 1940–1962*. Jefferson, NC: McFarland and Co., 1997.

Howe, Frederic Clemson. Born Meadville, Pennsylvania, November 21, 1867; died Oak Bluffs, Martha's Vineyard, Massachusetts, August 3, 1940. Howe planned to be a journalist but had the misfortune to finish school (he received a Ph.D. from Johns Hopkins University) in 1892, just before a depression cut employment. He turned to his second choice, the law, secured the necessary training, and joined a law firm in Cleveland, Ohio. From there he entered the Progressive movement and became a supporter of Woodrow Wilson. In 1914, Wilson appointed Howe Commissioner of Immigration for the Port of New York, and he dedicated himself to reforming Ellis Island to improve the care of immigrants passing through. However, his opposition to the 1915–1916 preparedness campaign and to the 1919 Red Scare led congressional representatives who disliked his positions to launch harassing investigations of his reforms. Howe resigned his commission and redirected his energy to railroad reform. He later returned to presidential politics, supporting Robert L. LaFollette and then Franklin D. Roosevelt. He worked for the New Deal in the Agricultural Adjustment Administration. *Reference*: Howe, Frederic C. *The Confessions of a Reformer*, with an introduction by James F. Richardson. Kent, OH: Kent State University Press, 1988.

Huerta, Dolores Fernández. Born Dawson, New Mexico, April 10, 1930. Born Dolores Fernández, her parents divorced when she was a toddler and she was raised among her mother's relatives in Stockton, California. She maintained contact with her father, the first in the family to work as a migrant laborer and to become a labor activist. She had a short, unsuccessful marriage that left her with two children to care for; she went back to college and secured provisional teaching credentials. She then became involved with the Community Service Organization (CSO), a self-help organization organizing Latin American communities, and also with Vincent Huerta. They married and had five children before divorcing. About the time her second marriage failed, she was becoming interested in issues affecting migrant workers. Through her CSO work, she met **Cesar Chavez** and with him founded the United Farm Workers; she bore primary responsibility for organizing supportive boycott efforts on the East Coast. She also developed a relationship with her colleague's brother, Richard Chavez, by whom she had four children. In 1988, she was badly hurt by baton-wielding police who were trying to break up a public meeting. It took her several years to recover, but she resumed her work in migrant labor activities.

Johnson, Albert. Born Springfield, Illinois, March 5, 1869; died American Lake, Washington, January 7, 1957. Johnson interrupted his career in newspaper editing for one in Congress. He was first elected representative from the state of Washington in 1912 on the Republican ticket and was reelected until the 1932 Democratic landslide. Among his duties was chair of the House Committee on Immigration and Naturalization. He was the House sponsor of the 1924 quota law.

Jones, Mary Harris. Born Cork, Ireland, May 1, 1830; died Hyattsville, Maryland, November 30, 1930. The Harrises migrated to Toronto, Canada, in 1838, where young Mary received her education. In 1859, she came to the United States. She married in 1861 and within six years had four children. In 1868 she lost her entire family to yellow fever and had to resume earning her own livelihood, which led to an interest in labor organizing. Her first major venture into organizing came in 1877, when she assisted strikers in Pittsburgh. During the 1880s, she eked out a living in order to volunteer her efforts as a labor organizer. In 1890, the United Mine Workers (UMW) gave her a paid job as an organizer. She left the UMW briefly in a quarrel over a mineworkers' strike that year but returned to it in 1911, remaining with it for the rest of her life. She had interests beyond the UMW, however. She supported the railroad workers in the 1894 Pullman strike, organized a march of mill children to the Long Island home of **Theodore Roosevelt** to embarrass him into supporting child labor laws, and publicized the tactics of mine owners, including John Rockefeller, who secured state militia support in subduing striking miners in their Colorado mines in 1913–1914. These activities made Mother Jones sound like a radical, and she did support socialism at the turn of century but turned to the Democrats in World War I. She never participated in women's movements such as the suffrage campaign. She came to embody a kind of unionism common among immigrants, in which such extremist-sounding activities as strikes helped to secure the conventional goal of guaranteeing the wages and benefits necessary to support a family in middle-class comfort. *References*: Dale Fetherling. *Mother Jones, the Miners' Angel: A Por-*

trait. Carbondale: Southern Illinois University Press, 1974. Mary Field Patron, ed., *The Autobiography of Mother Jones*, revised ed. Chicago: Charles H. Kerr, 1976.

Jordan, Barbara. Born Houston, Texas, February 21, 1936, and died there January 17, 1996. The first black woman in many fields, Jordan accomplished much. A graduate of Texas Southern University and Boston University she went into elective politics and was elected to Congress from Texas in 1972, 1976, and 1978. She also served in several appointive offices. The one that is of most significance here was her work on a special committee on immigration that recommended reducing overall immigration by issuing fewer visas and by eliminating certain categories of family relationship that qualified migrants for preference within the visa system.

Kallen, Horace Meyer. Born Berenstadt, Germany, 1882; died Palm Beach, Florida, where he was vacationing, February 17, 1974. The Kallen family migrated to Boston in 1887, and Horace received a bachelor's degree from Harvard in 1903 and a Ph.D. in 1908, and also the good opinion of such philosophers as George Santayana and William James. Kallen's contribution to the immigration debate came when he did the philosophical work that led him to accept cultural pluralism. He applied the same analysis to his Jewish heritage, redefined Jewish culture, and helped to begin the Reconstructionist movement. His opinions on other matters led him to repeated confrontations with academic administrators. He was dismissed from Princeton in 1905 for his agnosticism and from the University of Wisconsin in 1918 for his support of pacifists. He served longest, from 1919 to 1973, at the New School for Social Research. At the time of his death he was living in retirement in Oneonta, New York. *References*: Konvitz, Milton R., ed. *The Legacy of Horace M. Kallen*. Rutherford and Cranbury, NJ: Fairleigh Dickinson University Press and Associated University Press, 1987. Schmidt, Sara. *Horace M. Kallen: Prophet of American Zionism*. Brooklyn, NY: Carlson Publishing, 1995.

Kellor, Frances Alice. Born Columbus, Ohio, October 20, 1873; died New York City, New York, January 4, 1952. By age two, Kellor had lost her father. She did housework to put herself through the first two years of high school, then left school to start a newspaper career. She returned to school, received her LL.B. from Cornell, and started studying sociology at the University of Chicago. In 1905, at the invitation of middle-class labor activist Mary Dreier, Kellor made her permanent home in New York City. Her first work with immigrants came in 1908 when New York Governor

Charles Evans Hughes appointed her secretary of the New York State Immigration Commission, a position she held until 1913. In 1909, she had helped organize the New York Branch of the North American Civic League for Immigrants, which supported efforts to welcome and assimilate newcomers. When she finished her Immigration Commission work, she became director of the Civic League's legislative committee. When World War I started, her interests shifted to citizenship classes. She continued her Americanization work into the 1920s.

———————

Kennedy, John Fitzgerald. Born Brookline, Massachusetts, May 29, 1917; died Dallas, Texas, November 22, 1963. In his person, Kennedy altered the immigration debate; his presidency was long taken as a sign that Irish-American Catholics had found their place in the United States. As part of his campaign, Kennedy authored a small book on the subject, *A Nation of Immigrants*. *References*: Burner, David. *John F. Kennedy and a New Generation*. Library of American Biography, edited by Oscar Handlin. Boston: Little, Brown, 1988. Kennedy, John F. *A Nation of Immigrants*. Introduced by Robert F. Kennedy, with a new preface by John P. Roche. New York: Harper and Row, 1986.

———————

La Guardia, Fiorello Henry. Born in the borough of Manhattan, New York City, New York, December 11, 1888; died in the Bronx, New York, September 20, 1947. As mayor of New York from 1933 to 1945, La Guardia personified the changing of the guard from the Irish who had dominated city politics since the 1880s to the newer ethnic groups. His own father was Italian and his mother a Jew from Trieste, part of the Austro-Hungarian Empire at the time. La Guardia upheld Republican reform during the 1920s, when that party was dominated by those who believed in a laissez-faire approach to government. During the Great Depression, he worked with Franklin D. Roosevelt, a Democrat but a fellow New Yorker (from up the Hudson River) in using New Deal funds to restore New York's economy. *Reference*: Bayor, Ronald H. *Fiorello La Guardia: Ethnicity and Reform*. American Biographical History Series, edited by Alan M. Kraut and Jon L. Wakelyn. Arlington Heights, IL: Harlan Davidson, 1993.

———————

Larsen, Peter Laurentius. Born Christiansand, Norway, August 10, 1833; died Decorah, Iowa, March 1, 1915. From a post as teacher of German, French, and Hebrew at a university in Christiana (now Oslo), the young

Lutheran minister joined the Norwegian migration. He reentered the teaching profession, serving at Concordia Seminary, a Lutheran school in Saint Louis, and helping to found Luther College, a Norwegian Lutheran institute.

Lazarus, Emma. Born New York City, New York, January 22, 1849; died there November 19, 1887. Born into an old New York family of Sephardic Jews, Lazarus was first influenced by the Transcendentalists. After the 1882 assassination of Czar Alexander II and the anti-Semitic decrees that followed, she became more interested in worldwide Judaism. At about the same time, New York publisher Joseph Pulitzer was raising funds to place the Statue of Liberty in New York Harbor. Emma Lazarus wrote a sonnet that she contributed to the fund-raising effort. At the time, the sonnet represented a new interpretation of the statue. When the French government presented it to the U.S. government, the statue was seen as Liberty, a female goddess, enlightening the world—something going out from the United States. Lazarus's poem, "The New Colossus," with its last line "I lift my lamp beside the golden door!" pictured the Statue of Liberty as welcoming people into the country. It has become the most familiar interpretation of the Statue of Liberty, and a small plaque with the full poem is included in the statue's museum. *References*: Vogel Dan. *Emma Lazarus*. Boston: Twayne, 1980. Young, Bette Roth. *Emma Lazarus in Her World: Life and Letters*. With a foreword by Francine Klagsbrun. Philadelphia, PA: Jewish Publication Society, 1995.

Lee, Ann. Born Manchester, England, February 29, 1736; died Niskeyuna, now Watervliet, New York, September 8, 1784. Lee's early life was miserable. She was born to a poor family, denied opportunity for literacy, employed as a mill hand, pushed into an unwanted marriage, and had four children who died in infancy. Convinced that God had taken her children in punishment for her sins, specifically lust, Lee retreated within herself, going without food or sleep. Only an intense religious experience brought her back to the world, and then she embarked on a new life. In 1758 she had joined a religious group popularly known as the Shakers; she became its leader. On May 19, 1774, she sailed to the American colonies, where she made many converts and established communities in which they lived. The Shakers organized commune farms in New England, the Mid-Atlantic, and the Midwest. Their distinctive architecture and furniture design, and their equally distinctive communities of celibate men and women, have become as much a part of the social and religious landscape as the native-born Mormon and Christian Scientist faiths. *References*: Campion, Nardi

Reeder. *Mother Ann Lee: Morning Star of the Shakers*. Hanover, NH: University Press of New England, 1990. Hume, Jean M., ed. *Mother's First-Born Daughters: Early Shaker Writings on Women and Religion*. Religion in North America. Bloomington: University of Indiana, 1993.

Long, Breckinridge. Born Saint Louis, Missouri, May 16, 1881; died at Montpelier Manor, his country home, Laurel, Maryland, January 26, 1958. During World War II, Long was a special assistant secretary of state handling emergency war matters. These included the Visa Section of the State Department, which put him in the position of denying visas to those who needed them to escape the Nazi's Final Solution. That he did not do much to assist these desperate people is clear; why is a mystery. Some have pointed to Long's personal opinions, citing ant-Semitism, antiradicalism, and acceptance of the existence of an international Jewish conspiracy. Others have faulted the environment and the lack of attention to refugee issues generally. Still others have pointed to his personal experience with fascism. From 1933 to 1936 he was ambassador extraordinary and minister plenipotentiary to fascist Italy, where he observed fascist interest in military conquest but not much racism. *Reference*: Israel, Fred L., ed. *The War Diary of Breckinridge Long: Selections from the Years 1939–1944*. Lincoln: University of Nebraska Press, 1966.

Marshall, Louis. Born Syracuse, New York, December 14, 1856; died Zurich, Switzerland, September 11, 1929. Marshall's earliest contribution to the immigration debate was through his work as a lawyer. He successfully argued *Tutun* v. *United States* and *Luria* v. *United States*, which established, respectively, that naturalization is a judicial, not a merely administrative, action and that naturalized citizens have equal rights with native-born ones. His first work in Jewish affairs came in 1902, when he chaired a committee investigating a riot that took place during the New York City funeral procession of Rabbi Jacob Joseph. Thereafter, he served a number of Jewish organizations. He interested himself in Zionism and was attending a conference on the subject at the time of his death. *Reference*: Rosenstock, Morton. *Louis Marshall: Defender of Jewish Rights*. Detroit: Wayne State University Press, 1965.

Mazzoli, Romano Louis. Born Louisville, Kentucky, November 2, 1932. Educated at Notre Dame (B.Sc. 1954) and the University of Louisville (J.D. 1960), Mazzoli entered politics as a delegate to the Democratic National

Convention in 1968. He served as a state senator in Kentucky from 1968 to 1970. He was first elected to the House of Representatives on the Democratic ticket in 1970 and announced his retirement before it was time for him to run for reelection in 1994. He was the first House sponsor of the bill that eventually became the 1986 Immigration Reform and Control Act.

Morse, Samuel Finley Breese. Born Charlestown, Massachusetts, April 27, 1791; died New York City, New York, April 2, 1872. Morse trained as a portrait painter and helped to found the National Academy of Design. It was in order to see the fine art that he spent the years from 1829 to 1932 in Europe. While in Rome he developed an intense antipathy to the papacy. When he returned to the United States he fueled antivism by publishing anti-Catholic material and by running for office. At the same time, he was becoming interested in using electricity for long-distance communication. He developed the first working telegraph and the system of dots and dashes known as Morse code. It is for this last accomplishment that most people remember him. A memorial statue placed at the East 72nd Street entrance to New York's Central Park in 1871 was commissioned by the nation's telegraphers and shows Morse with his invention. *Reference*: Mabee, Carleton. *The American Leonardo: A Life of Samuel F. B. Morse*. With an introduction by Allan Nevins. New York: Alfred A. Knopf, 1943.

Moynihan, Daniel Patrick. Born Tulsa, Oklahoma, March 16, 1927. Moynihan's family relocated to New York City before their son entered school; in 1976, he was first elected to represent that state in the Senate. However, his main contribution to the immigration debate has been literary. In 1963, he and Harvard sociologist **Nathan Glazer** coauthored *Beyond the Melting Pot*, a study of New York City politics that concluded that (1) ethnic groups had never quite lost their particular identities, but (2) political leaders could use these ethnic identities to build coalitions. *Reference*: Schoen, Douglas. *Pat: A Biography of Daniel Patrick Moynihan*. New York: Harper and Row, 1979.

Nast, Thomas. Born Landau, Germany, September 27, 1840; died Guayaquil, Ecuador, where **Theodore Roosevelt** had sent him as U.S. consul, December 7, 1902. The images of urban ethnic machine politics Americans carry in their heads come from the work of this immigrant cartoonist. Nast came to New York City with his family in 1846, showed a talent for drawing, and accordingly studied to be an illustrator. From 1861 to 1886 *Harper's* regularly published his work. He originated the Democratic donkey, the Republican elephant, Santa Claus, and a series of scathing pictorial attacks on William M. ("Boss") Tweed. He also gave vent to his opinion that Catholicism threatened the public schools by drawing a group of alligators swimming menacingly toward schoolchildren huddled on the shore; turning the cartoon sideways revealed the "alligators" as bishops in their vestments and miters. *Reference*: Keller, Morton. *The Art and Politics of Thomas Nast*. New York: Oxford University Press, 1968.

Negri, Pola. Born Apolonia Chalupec in Lipno, Poland, New Year's Eve, 1899; died San Antonio, Texas, August 1, 1987. When the movies were first invented, so few people knew anything about them that the few people who did came together in an international community of film professionals. Negri had intended to become a ballerina but had to give it up when she contracted tuberculosis. She then went into acting, made her first film in Warsaw in 1914, moved to Berlin to perform on stage and screen there in 1918, and came to Hollywood in 1922. She had complementary on and off screen personalities, portraying a vamp in the movies and romancing Charlie Chaplin, Rudolph Valentino, and nobility from several European countries in real life. The advent of sound ended the international film community: Negri's heavy accent made her less marketable in U.S. movies. Ironically, Berlin was no longer a good venue either. When Negri returned there in 1935, Nazi authorities, suspicious that she might be part Jewish, tried to prevent her from performing. Although Hitler himself overruled his troops, Negri went to Paris. In 1941, after the Nazis defeated France, Negri returned to the United States. Instead of accepting her accent as a handicap, she developed a different persona and appeared in a comedy (*Hi Diddle Diddle*, 1943) and a Disney movie (*The Moonsprings*, 1964). *Reference*: Negri, Pola. *Memoirs of a Star*. New York: Doubleday, 1970.

Nettleton, Alfred Bayard. Born Berlin township, Delaware County, Ohio, November 14, 1838; died Chicago, Illinois, August 10, 1911. President Benjamin Harrison appointed him assistant secretary of the treasury in July 1890. As part of that job, he was director of the United States Immigration Bureau, in which capacity he oversaw the 1891 opening of the immigration station on Ellis Island.

Park, Robert Ezra. Born Harveyville, Luzerne County, Pennsylvania, February 14, 1864; died Chicago, Illinois, February 7, 1944. Recipient of a Ph.D. from the University of Heidelberg (1904), author, active in reform, onetime writing assistant to **Booker T. Washington**, Park was from 1913 to his death affiliated with the Sociology Department of the University of Chicago. He was an early student of immigrant society and published two books on the topic: *Old World Traits Transplanted* (with Herbert Miller, 1921), and *The Immigrant Press and Its Control* (1922). *References*: Matthews, Fred H. *Quest for an American Sociology: Robert E. Park and the Chicago School*. Montreal: McGill-Queens University Press, 1977. Raushenbush, Winifred. *Robert E. Park: Biography of a Sociologist*. With a foreword and an epilogue by Everett G. Hughes. Durham, NC: Duke University Press, 1979.

Peerson, Cleng. Born Hesthammerfarm, Tysvaer parish, Norway, 1783; died Bosque County, Texas, December 16, 1865. Peerson first began promoting Norwegian migration to the United States in 1821, when he helped a band of Norwegian Quakers look for a new home in New York. In 1925, he settled another group of Norwegians at a community he was organizing near Rochester in the same state. In 1834, he led a party of these settlers to the Fox River in Illinois, the first of many Norwegian settlements he helped to create in the Old Northwest and in Texas.

Penn, William. Born London, October 14, 1644; died at his home in England, July 30, 1718. Penn began the tradition of diversity among U.S. immigrants. The son of Admiral Sir William Penn, as a young man he became a member of the Society of Friends (Quakers), then a much-maligned sect. In 1670, his father died and young Penn inherited his estate, which included an outstanding loan to King Charles II. In 1681, the king repaid the loan with land he claimed in the New World and insisted Penn call the territory Pennsylvania in his father's memory. Penn recruited settlers across national and religious boundaries, attracting Germans as well as English, and many of the sects that developed in post-Reformation Europe. *References*: Peare, Catherine Owens. *William Penn: A Biography*. Philadelphia, PA: Lippincott, 1956. Soderlund, Jean R., ed. *William Penn and the Founding of Pennsylvania, 1680–1684: A Documentary History*. Philadelphia: University of Pennsylvania Press and Historical Society of Pennsylvania, 1983.

Post, Louis Freeland. Born on a farm between Danville and Vienna, New Jersey, November 15, 1849; died Washington, D.C., January 10, 1928. During **Woodrow Wilson**'s administration, Post was assistant secretary of labor; he used his office to investigate and reverse deportations ordered by **A. Mitchell Palmer** as part of his crusade against immigrant radicalism and then defended himself against impeachment proceedings brought against him by Mitchell-minded partisans. It was a dramatic episode for which Post was fitted by his lifelong interest in reform movements and his career as a lawyer. *Reference*: Newcomb, Arthur W. *Louis F. Post: A Big Democrat with a Little d*. Pamphlets in American History. Chicago: Saul Bros., n.d.

Powderly, Terence Vincent. Born Carbondale, Pennsylvania, January 22, 1849; died Washington, D.C., June 24, 1924. Most famous for his leadership of his Knights of Labor from 1879 to 1893, Powderly campaigned for William McKinley, and McKinley rewarded him in March 1897 with the position of commissioner-general of immigration. It was he who first issued the order excluding potential immigrants suffering from contagious eye diseases, and also he who suggested migrants be cleared for admission in their home countries, so that people wouldn't have to cross the ocean only to be denied entry into the United States. **Theodore Roosevelt** removed him from office in 1902, accusing him of attempting to exert political influence on the commissioner of immigration stationed in New York. *Reference*: Falzone, Vincent J. *Terence Vincent Powderly: Middle Class Reformer*. Washington, D.C.: University Press of America, 1978.

Rand, Ayn. Born Leningrad (now Saint Petersburg), February 1, 1905; died New York City, March 6, 1982. Between the time Rand was born and the time she graduated from the University of Leningrad in 1924, she had lived under a czar, the liberal coalition, and Lenin, and had determined the Soviet Union was too repressive for her. Upon her graduation, an aunt in Chicago asked her to come for a visit and she came to stay. She used her comparison of the Soviet Union and the United States to create a philosophy she called Objectivism. She popularized her thought in several novels, including *We the Living* (1936), *The Fountainhead* (1943), and *Atlas Shrugged* (1957). She reached fewer people, but in a more systematic way, via the Branden Institute in New York City. Her work is being continued at The Ayn Rand Institute in Los Angeles. *References*: Branden, Barbara. *The Passion of Ayn Rand*. Garden City, NY: Doubleday, 1986. Peikoff, Leonard. *Objectivism: The Philosophy of Ayn Rand*. New York: E. P. Dutton, 1991. Riesel, Mimi. *The Ayn Rand Companion*. Westport, CT: Greenwood Press, 1984.

Reed, David Aiken. Born Pittsburgh, Pennsylvania, December 21, 1880; died while vacationing in Sarasota, Florida, February 10, 1953. Reed followed his well-connected father into the legal profession and into politics.

In 1922, he challenged an incumbent Republican senator for the Republican nomination in the Senate race and was elected, partly on the basis of the support he enjoyed from the Mellons, Pittsburgh's first family of finance. Reed sponsored immigration quota laws in the Senate in the 1920s. In 1929, President Herbert Hoover, who had not been in office when the laws were passed, tried to block the legislation's operation, but Reed outmaneuvered him. An opponent of Franklin D. Roosevelt and of every aspect of the New Deal, Reed was unseated by his Democratic opponent in a 1934 Pennsylvania Senate race.

Reiersen, Johan Reinert. Born Vestre Moland, Norway, April 17, 1810; died Prairieville, Texas, September 6, 1864. As an editor in Norway, he praised his country's emigrants and their choice of the United States as a destination. He himself first saw the United States in 1843, and his investigative travels resulted in an 1844 book, *Pathfinder for Norwegian Emigrants to the United North American States and Texas*. In 1845, he established the first Norwegian community in the state of Texas, at Brownsville, and two years later he established a second, at Prairieville. From Texas, he edited the Norwegian journal *Norway and America*.

Rolvaag, Ole Edvart. Born on the island of Donna, Helgeland, Norway, April 22, 1876; died Northfield, Minnesota, November 5, 1931. Rolvaag started to follow the family trade of fishing, then, at age twenty, migrated to the United States. After three years as a farmhand, he entered Saint Olaf College, where he was first a student and then a professor of Norwegian. He is most famous for two novels of Norwegian life on the prairies, which he wrote in Norwegian and which were translated into English and published together as *Giants in the Earth* in 1927. *References*: Haugen, Einar. *Ole Edvart Rolvaag*. Boston: Twayne Publishers, 1983. Reigstad, Paul. *Rolvaag: His Life and Art*. Lincoln: University of Nebraska Press, 1972.

Rosenthal, Herman. Born Friedrichsstadt, Courland, in imperial Russia, October 6, 1843; died New York City, New York, January 27, 1917. Rosenthal immigrated to the United States in 1881 to found agricultural colonies for Jews fleeing persecution fostered by Russian czars. However, his linguistic skills drew him to work in other settings. In 1894, he was appointed chief of the discharging department at Ellis Island. In 1898, he resigned that post to become the chief of the Slavonic Division of the New York Public Library. He contributed to periodicals in English and German, edited one in Hebrew, and was chief of the Slavonic division project that produced *The Jewish Encyclopedia*. He also translated between various languages.

Ross, Edward Alsworth. Born Virden, Illinois, December 12, 1866; died Madison, Wisconsin, July 22, 1951. Ross earned his Ph.D. in political science at the Johns Hopkins University in 1891, but he soon developed an interest in the emerging discipline of sociology and did his scholarly work in that field. From the Progressive period to the New Deal, he combined scholarship with political advocacy, studying the sources of social stability, popularizing his findings in books and lectures, and working to see that public policy reflected the conclusions he drew from his research. Among those conclusions were the importance of equitable distribution of wealth, especially to farmers and laborers—and immigration restriction. Ross's interest in restriction began during the Progressive period when he picked up the racist ideas of the day. It was part of a package of Progressive opinions that cost him his first job; he was dismissed from his tenured post at Stanford University when his advocacy of railroad regulation, tax reform, silver coinage, and immigration restriction ran afoul of those of the university's sole source of financial support, the widow Jane Lathrop Stanford. Thereafter, Ross added academic freedom to the list of reforms he advocated. He also showed great interest in the social development of foreign peoples, including an interest in the Bolshevik Revolution that was dangerous given the antiradical temper of the time, but he did not change his opinion that what he considered inferior races should not be allowed to come to the United States. *Reference*: Weinberg, Julius. *Edward Alsworth Ross and the Sociology of Progressivism*. Madison: State Historical Society of Wisconsin, 1972.

Rossiter, William Sidney. Born Westfield, Massachusetts, September 9, 1861; died Concord, New Hampshire, January 13, 1929. A printer and publisher by profession, Rossiter became interested in statistics when he was made the liaison between the Bureau of the Census and the Government Printing Office that published its reports. He was the first to try to calculate the proportion of various ethnic groups within the total U.S. population by sampling the ethnic surnames in the raw data. Although the method didn't account for those who aglicized their names, thus obscuring their ethnic origins, his method became the basis for the determining of the numbers in the quota system used from 1921 to 1965.

Rubinstein, Helena. Born Krakow, Poland, on Christmas Day 1870; died New York City on April 1, 1965. A free market can be oppressive: many people had to become immigrants because market forces were cutting jobs in their homelands and creating them in other places. A lucky few can use a free market as an opportunity; Rubinstein fell into that category. She developed business skills helping her father in his egg business, went to Australia to try her luck at an uncle's sheep farm in Coleraine, and then went on to Melbourne, where she opened a beauty shop with a dozen jars of face cream brought from Europe. She had come upon a metaphorical gold mine. White women migrating from Europe disdained suntans and freckles as the marks of women who toiled outdoors, but even hats could not prevent the effects of the Australian sun. Making $100,000 in only two years, she moved to London to start a major beauty business, the Helena Rubinstein Company. In 1915 she, her husband, a U.S. journalist named Edward Titus, and their two sons moved to New York in an attempt to avoid World War I. She went on to become an innovator in beauty goods and services, to travel in the circles of artists and diplomats (her second husband was Prince Artchil Gourielli Tchkonia of the Republic of Georgia, then in the Soviet Union), and to give generously to charities for Catholics and Jews in Boston, New York, and Israel. *Reference*: Rubinstein, Helena. *My Life for Beauty*. New York: Simon and Schuster, 1966.

Rynning, Ole. Born Ringsaker, Norway, April 4, 1809; died Beaver Creek, Illinois, August 1838. While running a private school he owned, Rynning became interested in Norwegian economic problems and in immigration as a way to help affected individuals. In 1837, he led a party of pioneers to a new settlement at Beaver Creek, Illinois. He had time to publish one book of advice, *A True Account of America for the Information and Help of Peasant and Commoner*, before he was stricken by an epidemic that swept through his settlement.

Salmon, Thomas William. Born Lansingburg, New York, January 6, 1876; died in a fall from his yacht after suffering a stroke, offshore of the U.S. Atlantic coast, August 13, 1927. His first contribution was in the field of medical science, when he helped to establish the path of contagion for a diphtheria epidemic that swept the Willard, New York, state hospital for mental patients. He entered the United States Public Health Service in 1903 and was assigned to the immigration service in 1904. He worked to devise ways to identify people hoping to immigrate who did not meet mental health criteria and also on treating mental health problems within U.S. immigrant communities. *Reference*: Bond, Earl D., with the collaboration of Paul O. Komora. *Thomas W. Salmon, Psychiatrist*. New York: W. W. Norton, 1950.

Scalabrini, Giovanni Battista. Born Fino Mornasco, Como, Italy, July 8, 1839; died Piacenza, Emilia-Romagna, Italy, June 1, 1905. Scalabrini was from 1876 to his death bishop of a sprawling rural diocese and became acquainted with the issue of immigration and with the problems of immigrants during his pastoral visits. He organized the Società San Raffaele for the protection of Italian immigrants. He founded an institute of priests and brothers, now known as the Society of Saint Charles-Scalabrinians, to provide Catholic migrants with clergy of their own cultural and linguistic background. He also worked with institutes of female religious who were active in the care of migrants, most notably **Frances Xavier Cabrini** and the Missionaries of the Sacred Heart, Clelia Merloni and the Apostles of the Scared Heart, and siblings Giuseppe and Assunta Marchetti, with whom he is considered cofounder of the Missionary Sisters of Saint Charles-Scalabrinians. Scalabrini also influenced thinking on migration through his writings, which show his sense of the role of immigration in the developing world economy and the problem of governments that permitted easy migration but also left migrants vulnerable to exploitation. *Reference*: Caliaro, Marco, and Mario Francesconi. *John Baptist Scalabrini: Apostle to Emigrants*. New York: Center for Migration Studies, 1977.

Schurz, Carl. Born Liblar, near Cologne, Germany, March 2, 1829; died New York City, New York, May 14, 1906. Schurz embodied the notion that an American is defined not by birth but by commitment to certain values. As a nineteen-year-old college student he was already trying to remake his homeland into a democratic republic. When one of his professors was sentenced to life imprisonment for his political activities, Schurz arranged an escape for them both. He arrived in the United states in 1852. He was then involved in the politics of the nascent Republican Party. He also held appointed office: He was Abraham Lincoln's first minister to Spain (he resigned the position to return to the United States to promote abolition and to do military service as a brigadier general of volunteers) and also Rutherford B. Hayes's secretary of the interior. *Reference*: Trefousse, Hans. *Carl Schurz: A Biography*. Knoxville: University of Tennessee Press, 1982.

Segale, Blandina, S. C. Born Cicagna, province of Liguria, Italy, January 23, 1850; died Cincinnati, Ohio, February 23, 1941. Rose Segale embodied the notions that the frontier was not just cowboys and Indians and that whites on the frontier were not all alike. Her family arrived in New Orleans when she was four years old and moved on to Cincinnati, where Rose saw her first Sister of Charity. She entered the convent in 1866. Thereafter, she went by her religious name, Blandina. In 1872 the Sisters of Charity sent her to their mission in Trinidad, Colorado. She also worked in Santa Fe and Albuquerque. She established institutions such as schools, hospitals, and orphanages, working with people of all denominations, races, and ethnic backgrounds. Where police and the courts were weak, she helped to prevent lynching and to divert suspected criminals, such as Billy the Kid, from illegal activities. Her memoir of this period remains exciting reading. The Sisters of Charity recalled her to Cincinnati in 1894, where she found a new calling. She and her blood sister, Sister Justina Segale, S. C., worked among the growing Italian population of Cincinnati. They opened the Santa Maria Institute, which they named a "settlement" to signal their intention to emulate some of the work of **Jane Addams**, and they provided many services for new immigrants. This second career ended in 1933, when she retired to the Sisters of Charity motherhouse. *Reference*: Segale, Blandina, S. C. *At the End of the Santa Fe Trail*. Cincinnati: Sisters of Charity of Cincinnati, 1996.

Seward, William Henry. Born Florida, Orange County, New York, May 16, 1801; died Auburn, New York, October 10, 1872. Most famous for purchasing Alaska and also well known for declaring that there is a higher law than the Constitution and thus leading antislavery efforts to scuttle the Compromise of 1850, Seward's primary contributions to the debate over immigration were to provide an alternative to nativism and to show the road not taken. During his term as governor of New York, Seward declared himself in favor of sharing tax revenues with Catholic parochial schools. New Yorkers overwhelmingly rejected his proposal, but Seward later reaped the rewards of his position. In New York, he allied with such figures as Archbishop **John Joseph Hughes**. Nationally, he allied with Abraham Lincoln, who appreciated his antinativist politics sufficiently to appoint him secretary of state. He continued in that position during Andrew Johnson's administration, during which he arranged the purchase of Alaska from czarist Russia. *Reference*: Taylor, John M. *William Henry Seward: Lincoln's Right Hand Man*. New York: HarperCollins, 1991.

Shipman, Andrew Jackson. Born Springvale, Virginia, October 15, 1857; died New York City, New York, October 17, 1915. Shipman converted to Catholicism during his studies at Georgetown University, from which he graduated in 1878. In 1880, he took a job as superintendent of W. P. Rend and Co. coal mines in Hocking, Ohio, where he became interested in the Slavic immigrants who worked there. He had long been interested in the history, languages, and religions of central Europe. He combined these two interests to become a champion of a minority within American Catholicism: eastern European and Levantine Catholics who were loyal to the Roman pope but whose church language and ritual were closer to Orthodox practices.

Simkhovitch, Mary Kingsbury. Born Chestnut Hill, Massachusetts, September 8, 1867; died New York City, New York, November 15, 1951. Being a member of an old New England family, Mary Kingsbury had the opportunity to follow her mother to an all-female institution of higher education. She found such a prospect confining, however, and instead went to Boston University, where she received her B.A. in 1890. Her extracurricular activities drew her into housing reform, and then into postgraduate education, which in turn introduced her to her future husband, Vladimir Simkhovitch, a Russian-born Columbia University economics professor. In 1902, after extensive experience in settlement house work and living, she founded the Greenwich House Settlement in Greenwich Village, New York, then a large Italian area. She brought to her new neighbors her interest in culture and in Progressive reform. *Reference*: Simkhovitch, Mary Kingsbury. *Neighborhood: My Story of Greenwich House*. New York: Norton, 1938.

Sinclair, Upton Beall, Jr. Born Baltimore, Maryland, September 20, 1878; died Bound Brook, New Jersey, November 25, 1968. With the publication of *The Jungle* in February 1906, Sinclair painted an indelible work picture in which Lithuanian workers in Chicago packing plants put human faces on the exploitation migrants and workers suffered at the hands of individual capitalists and impersonal market forces. Descended from an old Southern family, Sinclair came by his interest in immigrant workers through his commitment to socialism. He joined the Socialist Party in 1902, worked with another author, Jack London, to form the Intercollegiate Socialist Society in 1905, and ran as Socialist Party candidate for Congress from New Jersey in 1906. He left the party briefly in 1917, over its opposition to the world war, and permanently in 1934, when he ran for governor of California, unsuccessfully, on the Democratic ticket. He was a productive author who dealt with social issues in genres ranging from muckraking journalism to the novel. One of his novels, *Dragon's Teeth* (1942), won a Pulitzer Prize. *Reference*: Yoder, Jon A. *Upton Sinclair*. New York: Ungar, 1975.

Smith, Alfred Emmanuel. Born and died in the borough of Manhattan, New York City, New York, December 30, 1873, and October 4, 1944, respectively. The personification of the ethnic in politics, Smith was the first person of Irish Catholic background to run for president of the United States. His background was actually more diverse than this. His maternal grandfather was Irish Catholic, his maternal grandmother was an Irish Protestant convert to Catholicism, his paternal grandfather was Italian, and his paternal grandmother was German. His politics brought together ethnic and native Progressives. He surrounded himself with people who were closely identified with particular ethnic groups, such as Charles F. Murphy, of Irish extraction, and Belle Moskowitz, whose parents were Jewish German immigrants. He also worked with reformers such as Robert Wagner (also of German descent) and Frances Perkins. His successful campaign to head the Democratic ticket in 1928 confirmed the importance of the urban ethnic voting bloc within the party. *References*: Handlin, Oscar. *Al Smith and His America*. Library of American Biography, edited by Oscar Handlin. Boston: Little, Brown, 1958. O'Connor, Richard. *The First Hurrah: A Biography of Alfred E. Smith*. New York: Putnam, 1970.

Soros, George. Born Budapest, Hungary, August 12, 1930. In 1944, the Soros family escaped from Nazi-occupied Hungary and went to England, where George received his education. He relocated to New York City in 1956, where he made a fortune in finance. Through his Open Society Institute, he then used his money for various politically controversial philanthropies. He began by assisting eastern European nations after the 1989 collapse of the Soviet empire left them free from political and military domination but vulnerable to exploitation in the emerging global economy. When the U.S. federal government began to rewrite social welfare legislation so as to limit benefits to new immigrants, refugees, and resident aliens, he organized the Emma Lazarus Fund to advocate naturalization and to protect the interests of immigrants and naturalized Americans. *References*: Slater, Robert. *Soros: The Life, Times and Trading Secrets of the World's Greatest Investor*. Burr Ridge, IL: Irwin Professional Publishing, 1996. Soros, George. *Soros on Soros: Staying Ahead of the Curve*. New York: Wiley, 1995.

Strong, Josiah. Born Naperville, Illinois, January 19, 1847; died New York City, New York, April 28, 1916. A example of the paradoxes of progressivism, Strong was a Congregational cleric who helped to pioneer the Social Gospel movement. He also founded the League for Social Service, helped to establish the Federal Council of Churches, and came up with the idea for the "safety first" campaign that valued human welfare above cost or convenience. He also wrote books, *The New Era* in 1893 and, most important for the immigration debate, *Our Country* in 1885. The latter provided a blueprint for an ideal society, listing the characteristics such a society would have and how the United States could achieve it. Immigration restriction was one of the suggestions made in the name of this progressive goal.

Szold, Henrietta. Born Baltimore, Maryland, December 21, 1860; died Jerusalem, then in British Palestine, February 13, 1945. Szold first entered immigration work in November 1889. Baltimore's Jewish community had formed the Isaac Bar Levison Hebrew Literary Society to reach out to Jewish refugees fleeing czarist anti-Semitic decrees, and she made sure its programs included Americanization classes. However, she became most famous for working with migrants to Palestine. She became interested in Zionism in 1893, visited Palestine in 1903, and helped form Hadassah to assist Jews in that region in 1912. Beginning in 1918, she divided her time between Palestine and the United States. When Hitler came to power, she arranged to have German-Jewish youths come to Palestine to complete their education, which probably saved them from the Nazis' Final Solution. *References*: Dash, Joan. *Summoned to Jerusalem: The Life of Henrietta Szold.* New York: Harper and Row, 1979. Gidal, Tim. *Henrietta Szold: A Documentation in Photos and Text.* New York: Gefen Publishing House, 1996. Krantz, Hazel. *Daughter of My People: Henrietta Szold and Hadassah.* Northvale, NJ: Jason Aronson, 1995.

Tilton, Edward Lippincott. Born New York City, New York, October 19, 1861; died Scarsdale, New York, January 5, 1933. Tilton was the architect who in December 1897, with his partner William A. Boring, won the competition to design the second immigration station at Ellis Island after the first, a wooden building, was destroyed by fire. Their plan won a gold medal at the Paris Exposition of 1900, the same year the building opened for use.

Turner, Henry McNeal. Born near Abbeville, South Carolina, February 1, 1834; died Windsor, Ontario, Canada, May 8, 1915. Though born free, able to secure some education, and able to follow a professional career in the ministry that culminated in consecration as a bishop of the African Methodist Episcopal Church, Turner often felt the effects of U.S. racism himself and was a leader for enslaved and recently freed blacks. He was an early advocate of the idea that blacks should gather in Africa and build a nation there. He thrice visited Africa to assess what Christians were doing there and what missionaries and migrants might contribute. Disillusioned by racism, he said he did not want to die on U.S. soil and had just arrived in Canada for a church conference when he suffered a fatal stroke. *Reference*: Angell, Stephen Ward. *Bishop Henry McNeal Turner and African-American Religion in the South*. Knoxville: University of Tennessee Press, 1992.

Wald, Lillian D. Born Cincinnati, Ohio, March 10, 1867; died Westport, Connecticut, September 1, 1940. Determined to avoid the usual young, middle-class woman's life of housekeeping, study, and sociability, Wald enrolled in New York Hospital's training school for nurses. In March 1893, she had her first experience nursing a patient living in a tenement house and thereafter decided to develop the fields of home and public health nursing. That year, she and a companion opened what in 1895 became the Henry Street Settlement. Henry Street became a center of innovative nursing and public health programs, broadened its programs to include the endeavors common at other settlement houses, and propelled Wald into politics. In 1933, when the massive social work necessary after the depression required more strength than she had, Wald retired as head worker of one of New York's most important sites for community service. *References*: Coss, Clare. *Lillian D. Wald, Progressive Activist*. New York: Feminist Press at the City University of New York, 1989. Daniels, Doris Groshen. *Always a Sister: The Feminism of Lillian D. Wald*. New York: Feminist Press at the City University of New York, 1989. Siegel, Beatrice. *Lillian Wald of Henry Street*. New York: Macmillan, 1983.

Walker, Francis Amasa. Born Boston, Massachusetts, July 2, 1840; died in Springfield, Massachusetts, January 5, 1897. Most famous as the education administrator who brought the Massachusetts Institute of Technology into the Progressive Era, Walker made his contribution to the immigration debate through his academic specialities, economics and statistics. A graduate of Amherst in 1860, he studied law, served in the Civil War, taught Greek and Latin, and wrote editorials for the *Springfield Daily Republican* before entering civil service in 1869. He oversaw the taking of the 1870 federal census. It was in working with census figures that Walker noticed the declining birthrate of natives vis-à-vis that of immigrants, the data that became the basis for the "race suicide" concerns of the late nineteenth and early twentieth centuries.

Walter, Francis Eugene. Born Easton, Pennsylvania, May 26, 1894; died Washington, D.C., May 31, 1963. First elected to the House of Representatives on the Democratic ticket in the landslide of 1932, Walter held on to his seat until his death. In 1952, he was the House sponsor of major immigration legislation. Thereafter, he was so attentive to preserving that law as written that his death was one reason the next immigration reform didn't happen until 1965. *Reference: Memorial Service Held in the House of Representatives and Senate of the United States, Together with Remarks Presented on Eulogy of Francis Eugene Walter, late a Representative from Pennsylvania.* Washington, DC: U.S. Government Printing Office, 1963.

Wiesel, Elie. Born Sighet, Romania, September 30, 1928. An adolescent when the Nazis began transporting Romanian Jews to slave labor and death camps, Wiesel was among those liberated from Buchenwald in 1945. In 1960, he produced a memoir of his experience, *Night*. Over the years, he has combined teaching, writing, and service in various organizations devoted to documenting the Final Solution, commemorating its victims, and caring for its survivors. He has also worked in other areas of Jewish history and on the underlying sources of human conflict. He received the Nobel Peace Prize in 1987. *References*: Stern, Ellen Norman. *Elie Wiesel, Witness for Life.* New York: Ktav Publishing House, 1982. Wiesel, Elie. *All Rivers Run to the Sea.* Translated by Jon Rothschild. New York: Knopf, 1995.

Wilson, Pete. Born in Lake Forest, Illinois, August 23, 1933, but achieved his greatest fame in California. He was a member of the California legislature from 1966 to 1971, the mayor of San Diego from 1971 to 1983, and one of California's U.S. senators from 1983 to 1991. In 1991, he became governor of the state. Wilson has opposed immigration, especially into California. In the absence of federal laws to restrict it, he supports state laws to deny illegal immigrants access to public schools or to welfare benefits paid for by state tax dollars.

Wilson, Thomas Woodrow, known in adult life simply as Woodrow, born Staunton, Virginia, December 28, 1856; died Washington, D.C., February 3, 1924. Prior to entering politics, Wilson was a scholar. Some of his writings indicate he thought the "new immigrants" of the end of the nineteenth century did not measure up to the high standards set by earlier immigrants such as his own Scots ancestors. However, when he had the power of the presidency, he used it to block restrictionists; the literacy law of 1917 had to be passed over his veto. Many factors came together in that veto: the need to keep support for World War I, the urban ethnic vote for Wilson's Democratic Party, and Wilson's own highly moralistic personality. *References*: Blum, John Morton. *Woodrow Wilson and the Politics of Morality.*

Library of American Biography, edited by Oscar Handlin. Boston: Little, Brown, 1956. Clements, Kendrick A. *The Presidency of Woodrow Wilson.* American Presidency Series. Lawrence: University of Kansas, 1992. Link, Arthur S. *Woodrow Wilson and the Progressive Era, 1900–1917.* New American Nation Series, edited by Henry Steele Commager and Richard B. Morris. New York: Harper and Row, Publishers, 1954.

Zangwill, Israel. Born London, England, February 14, 1864; died Midhurst, Sussex, England, August 1, 1926. Zangwill made his contributions to the debate on U.S. immigration from England, where his family had gone to escape Czar Nicholas I's decree conscripting Jewish youths into the Russian army. He grew up to become a writer in several genres. He helped to launch the Jewish Publication Society of America by publishing through it his novel *The Children of the Ghetto* (1892). His most famous work was a play, *The Melting Pot* (1908), which has provided a major metaphor for U.S. immigration. Zangwill was also interested in Zionism. In 1904 he founded the Jewish Territorial Organization to assist Jews forced to flee the anti-Semitism of the Russian Empire. *Reference*: Udelson, Joseph H. *Dreamer of the Ghetto: The Life and Works of Israel Zangwill.* Judaic Studies Series. Tuscaloosa: University of Alabama Press, 1990.

SELECTED BIBLIOGRAPHY

There are many monographs giving overviews of immigration. The classic is Oscar Handlin, *The Uprooted*, 2nd ed., enlarg. (Boston: Little, Brown and Company [An Atlantic Monthly Press Book], 1973). Useful recent books include Thomas Archdeacon, *Becoming American: An Ethnic History* (New York: Free Press, 1983); Elliott Robert Barkan, *And Still They Come: Immigrants and American Society, 1920 to the 1990s*, American History Series (Wheeling, IL: Harlan Davidson, 1996); John Bodnar, *The Transplanted: A History of Immigrants in Urban America* (Bloomington: Indiana University Press, 1985); Leonard Dinnerstein and David Reimers, *Ethnic Americans: A History of Immigration*, 3rd ed. (New York: Harper, 1988); Donna Gabaccia, *From the Other Side: Women, Gender, and Immigrant Life in the U.S., 1820–1990* (Bloomington and Indianapolis: Indiana University Press, 1994); James Stuart Olson, *The Ethnic Dimension in American History*, 2nd ed. (New York: St. Martin's Press, 1994); David M. Reimers, *Still the Golden Door: The Third World Comes to America*, 2nd ed. (New York: Columbia University Press, 1992); Philip Taylor, *The Distant Magnet: European Emigration to the USA* (New York: Harper, 1971); and Reed Ueda, *Postwar Immigrant America: A Social History* (New York: St. Martin's Press [Bedford Books], 1994). One scholar who wrote much on the U.S. response to immigrants is John Higham. See his *Strangers in the Land: Patterns of American Nativism, 1860–1925*, 2nd ed. (New Brunswick, NJ: Rutgers, the State University, 1963; reprint New York: Atheneum, 1969). Higham also has two editions of *Send These to Me*, the first subtitled *Jews and Other Immigrants in Urban America* (New York: Atheneum, 1975), and the second subtitled *Immigrants in Urban America* (Baltimore: Johns Hopkins University Press, 1984); they have slightly different essays.

Besides the biographies of individuals listed beneath the specific entries, there are also useful collective biographies. Standard references include *Who's Who in America* (New Providence, NJ: Marquis Who's Who, 1996); *Dictionary of American Biography* (New York: Charles Scribner's Sons, 1946–1996); Edward T. James, Janet Wilson James, and Paul S. Boyer, eds., *Notable American Women*, 3 vols. (Cambridge, MA: Belknap Press of Harvard University Press, 1971); Barbara Sicherman, Carol Hurd Green, Ilene Kantrov, and Harriette Walker, eds., *Notable American Women, the Modern Period: A Biographical Dictionary* (Cambridge, MA: Belknap Press of Harvard University Press, 1980); and the Biographical Dictionaries of Minority Women series (New York and London: Garland Publishing, 1994). *Biographical Directory of the United States Congress, 1774–1989* (Washington, D.C.: Government Printing Office, 1989), and *Who's Who in American Politics*, 15th ed., 2 vols. (New Providence, NJ: R. R. Bowker, 1995), are harder to find but very useful. There are numerous specialized biographical dictionaries, including Joan Comay, *Who's Who in Jewish History after the Period of the Old Testament*, new edition revised by Lavinia Conn-Sherbok (London and New York: Routledge, 1995); Judy Barrett Litoff and Judith McDonnell, eds., *European Immigrant Women in the United States: A Biographical Dictionary* (New York and London: Garland Publishing [Biographical Dictionaries of Minority Women], 1994); William McGuire and Leslie Wheeler, *American Social Leaders* (Santa Barbara, CA: ABC-CLIO, 1993); and Diane Telgen and Jim Kamp, eds., *Notable Hispanic American Women* (Detroit, MI: Gale Research Inc., 1993). Both Gale Research and Greenwood Press publish handy one-volume references for specific ethnic groups. For example, Gale publishes *Notable Asian Americans* (Helen Zia and Susan B. Gall, eds.; New York: Gale Research, 1995), which is oriented toward contemporary personalities. Greenwood offers *Dictionary of Asian American History* (Hyung-Chan Kim, ed.; Westport, CT: Greenwood Press, 1986), which presents essay-length overviews on various subjects, complete with notes, bibliography, a chronology, and census data. There are also series that specialize in presenting short, one-volume biographies for the general reader. While not every subject in these series is relevant to the debate over immigration, the series are still useful to know about. Oscar Handlin has edited the Library of American Biography Series for Little, Brown of Boston since the 1950s. A more recently organized series is the American Biographical History Series, edited by Alan M. Kraut and Jon L. Wakelyn for Harlan Davidson of Arlington Heights, Illinois.

INDEX

About the Author

MARY ELIZABETH BROWN is assistant professor in the Social Science Division of Marymount Manhattan College and also assists with special projects at the Center for Migration Studies. She has done research on the intersection of U.S. immigration and religious history and is the author of such books as *Churches, Communities and Children: Italian Immigrants in the Archdiocese of New York, 1880–1945* (1995).